Death by Design

Science, Technology, and Engineering in Nazi Germany

Edited by

ERIC KATZ

New Jersey Institute of Technology

PEARSON
Longman

New York   San Francisco   Boston
London   Toronto   Sydney   Tokyo   Singapore   Madrid
Mexico City   Munich   Paris   Cape Town   Hong Kong   Montreal

Senior Acquisitions Editor: Janet Lanphier
Executive Marketing Manager: Sue Westmoreland
Production Manager: Denise Philip
Project Coordination, Text Design, and Electronic Page Makeup:
   Stratford Publishing Services.
Cover Design Manager: John Callahan
Cover Designer: Kay Petronio
Cover Photos: Main rail entrance of Auschwitz-Birkenau, 1945. YIVO Institute
   for Jewish Research, courtesy of United States Holocaust Memorial Photo
   Archives. Diagram of the incineration system, with a double quadri-muffle
   furnace, for crematorium IV in Birkenau. © Jean-Claude Pressac.
Manufacturing Buyer: Lucy Hebard
Printer and Binder: R. R. Donnelley & Sons
Cover Printer: Phoenix Color Corporation

For permission to use copyrighted material, grateful acknowledgment is made to
the copyright holders on p. 311–312, which are hereby made part of this copyright
page.

Library of Congress Cataloging-in-Publication Data

Katz, Eric 1952–
   Death by design : science, technology, and engineering in Nazi Germany /
edited by Eric Katz. — 1st ed/
      p. cm.
   Includes bibliographical references.
   ISBN 0-321-27634-5
   1. Technology — Germany — History — 20th century.   2. Holocaust,
Jewish (1939–1945) — Germany.   3. Nazis — Germany.   I. Katz, Eric.

   T26.G3D33 2006
   940.53'185—dc22   2005030060

Please visit us at **http://www.ablongman.com**

ISBN 0-321-27634-5

1 2 3 4 5 6 7 8 9 10—DOC—08 07 06 05

For Lillian and Murray

and

for the families:

Like
Breitman
Solai
Barbash
Davis
Zeller
Stein
Katz

all who perished and all who survived

Contents

Part I

Details of the Killing Operations

Part II

Technology, Management Policy, and Politics: General Issues

Part III

The Role of Architectural Design in Nazi Germany

Part IV

Medicine and Biology in Nazi Germany

Part V

Engineering, Technology, and Business

Part VI

Concluding Ethical Considerations

List of Abbreviations

The following list contains abbreviations that appear mostly in the main text. Individual chapters may have additional lists of abbreviations used in their sources and footnotes.

14f13 Name given to the medical policy of euthanasia by which Germans with mental and physical disabilities were killed by medical professionals in Nazi Germany

A-4 Aggregate-4 (the V-2 rocket)

AG Aktien Gesellschaft (joint stock company)

BI Bauinspektion (building inspection)

DAF Deutsche Arbeitsfront (German Workers Front; the organization of German workers that replaced the independent labor unions after the Nazi ascension to rule)

DAW Deutsche Ausrüstungswerke GmbH (German Equipment Works)

Degesch German Corporation for Pest Control, a subsidiary of I.G. Farben

Dehomag The German subsidiary of IBM

DEST Deutsche Erd-und Steinwerke GmbH (German Earth and Stone Works; a business corporation created and run by the SS)

GBI The Office of the Inspector General of Building in the Reich Capital Berlin

GmbH A corporation with limited liabilities

HAHB or SS-HHB Hauptamt Haushalt und Bauten (the SS Main Office of Budget and Building)

IG Interessengemeinschaft (a loose-knit corporate entity with independent divisions; often used to refer to I.G. Farben)

IKL Office of the Inspector of the Concentration Camps

KDK Kampfbund für deutsche Kultur (Combat League for German Culture; also referred to as Kampfbund)

KGL Kriegsgefangenenlager (prisoner-of-war concentration camp)

KL Konzentrationslager (concentration camp)

NSDAP National Socialist German Workers Party, official name of the Nazi Party

POW Prisoner of war

RFSS Reichsführer SS (Head of the SS, Heinrich Himmler)

RKF Reichskommissar for the Reinforcement of Germandom

RM Reichsmark, the unit of German money (1 RM equals approximately US $5 [2005])

RSHA Reich Security Main Office

SA Sturmabteilung (Nazi Storm Troopers, the paramilitary wing of the Nazi Party)

SDG Sanitätsdienstgrade (Sanitation brigades)

SPD Social Democratic Party

SS Schutzstaffel (the elite Nazi organization; literal meaning: defense squadron)

SS-HHB or HAHB Hauptamt Haushalt und Bauten (the SS Main Office of Budgets and Building)

SS-WVHA or WVHA Wirtschaftsverwaltungshauptamt (SS Business Administration Main Office)

V-2 Long-distance rocket

VW Volkswagenwerke, the German car company

ZBL Zentralbauleitung (Central Construction Directorate/Office)

—— ⌵ ——
Preface

In our days many men have lived in this cruel manner [as in the concentration camps], crushed against the bottom, but each for a relatively short period; so that we can perhaps ask ourselves if it is necessary or good to retain any memory of this exceptional human state. To this question we feel that we have to reply in the affirmative. We are in fact convinced that no human experience is without meaning or unworthy of analysis, and that fundamental values, even if they are not positive, can be deduced from this particular world which we are describing. We would also like to consider that the [Nazi concentration camp] was pre-eminently a gigantic biological and social experiment.

—*Primo Levi*, Survival in Auschwitz

This is a book about the role of science and technology in the development and operation of the Nazi death camps, focusing specifically on those aspects of science and technology that are practical and action-oriented: engineering, architectural design, medicine, and organizational management. The impetus for considering this subject lies in the words quoted above from a survivor of the Auschwitz-Birkenau concentration camp, Primo Levi (1919–1987), an Italian Jew and a chemist by training and profession. All human experiences, even the most evil, should be examined and analyzed in order to discover and to understand their fundamental values. This is especially true for the domains of science and technology, which have produced some of the greatest achievements of human civilization—but also, it seems clear, some of the worst atrocities in human experience.

This collection of essays is based on a relatively simple idea: the various labor and extermination camps of the Third Reich—places such as Auschwitz-Birkenau, Buchenwald, Treblinka, and Majdanek—were designed and built to be locations for efficient mass-produced death. The Holocaust did not "just happen" like a natural disaster such as an earthquake or hurricane. The operation of the death camps as one part of the Nazis' so-called "final solution" to the Jewish "problem" was thought out in advance. Engineers, architects, various physical scientists, medical professionals, and businessmen all participated in the planning and operation of the concentration and extermination camps that were the foundation of the Final Solution. If we are to understand the meaning and values of these camps, we must examine in detail the work that highly trained, intelligent professionals performed in their design and operation.

The existence of the Nazi death camps—their design, creation, and operation—also raises larger philosophical, sociological, and political questions about the relationship between totalitarian regimes and the development of science and technology. To what extent is the development of science and technology "owned" by the political and social forces that dominate a country or a civilization? Can science and technology be a pure search for new knowledge and instruments for the betterment of human life, or must these fields be corrupted by politics and social values? Considering these questions through the historical case study of the Holocaust is extremely important for the education of engineers, architects, physicians, corporate managers, and other professionals—virtually any student in a scientific or technological field. This collection of readings thus brings to the foreground a perspective that is generally neglected in studying the history of the Holocaust: that science and technology—engineering, architectural design, medical practice, and organizational management—were indispensable components of the Nazi project for the destruction of European Jewry. In the Germany of the Third Reich, science and technology advanced the goals of Hitler and the Nazi regime.

The readings in this collection introduce the roles of practical science and technology in Nazi Germany and are meant for students of the Holocaust and students in various technological fields, such as engineering, architecture, industrial and business management, and medicine. As an anthology of essays, this book enables a reader (or instructor) to read (or to assign) the chapters in any particular order based on the desires and goals of the reader or instructor. But the editor has organized the essays to present the material as a guide to increasing understanding regarding the technological, social, and philosophical issues. The essays begin with the details of the Nazi killing operations, and proceed through a general account of politics and technology in the Third Reich. Then follow sections in which essays on particular technological professions are emphasized: architecture, medicine, and engineering and industrial management. A concluding essay examines the philosophical and ethical issues. Thus the readings move from an analysis of the details of engineering design through a consideration of other professions to general issues such as the role of science and business in an evil political regime.

The thirteen chapters are grouped into six parts after a brief historical background introduction. The three chapters in Part I focus on the precise details of the killing operations at Auschwitz-Birkenau, the most technologically sophisticated of all the Nazi killing centers. We are given an eyewitness account of the killing procedures, as well as two detailed histories of the engineering and construction of the gas chambers and crematoria. In Part II chapters 4 and 5 provide an overview of politics and organizational management in the totalitarian Nazi regime. Chapter 4 discusses the general characteristics of technology in a totalitarian regime, providing much historical information on the development of science and technology in Nazi Germany. Chapter 5 focuses on the engineers and managers of the SS, their backgrounds, education, and ideological commitments. Part III—chapters 6, 7, and 8—shifts the emphasis to architecture and the memoirs of Albert

Speer, Hitler's personal architect and one of the most powerful figures in the Third Reich. Architectural design plays a surprisingly large role in understanding the nature of technology in Nazi Germany, and an analysis of Speer's career is extraordinarily valuable for all students planning careers as technological professionals. In Part IV, chapters 9 and 10, the focus again shifts, now to the role of medical science in the Third Reich. Nazism was based in part on the ideas of biological determinism and racial superiority, and these ideas are shown to have effects on the way that Nazi medical scientists did research on cancer (chapter 9). Moreover, the concept of medicalized killing as a means of purifying the community led to the worst excesses of the killing centers, where physicians played a prominent role in the organization of mass murder and medical experiments (chapter 10). Part V, chapters 11 and 12, focuses on issues in technological and industrial management by reviewing the connections to the Nazi regime of two major business organization: IBM and I.G. Farben. Finally, Chapter 13 concludes the volume by discussing the philosophical and ethical issues regarding the so-called neutrality or objectivity of science and technology, using information from the previous chapters to provide detailed examples for the ethical arguments.

The role of the professional elite in the establishment of the killing centers cannot be overemphasized. Industrial managers, engineers, architects, medical doctors, and other professionals were instrumental in the design, development, and operation of the extermination and slave-labor camps. Without their expert knowledge and skill, the efficient system of mass-produced death could not have been constructed and the goals of the Final Solution could not have been accomplished. If we are to take seriously the survivor Primo Levi's pleas for an analysis of the worst experiences of human life, we must examine the actions of the German professional classes that designed and built the Nazi death camps.

Eric Katz

A Brief Historical Background

Adolf Hitler, as leader of the National Socialist German Workers' Party (NSDAP or Nazi Party), became Chancellor of Germany in January 1933. The Nazi party was a fascist political organization made up of followers of an ultra right–wing, antidemocratic, and extremely nationalistic ideology, and its rise to power began the so-called Third Reich, the re-establishment of a strong authoritarian government after the chaotic democracy of the Weimar Republic, which ruled Germany from 1919 until 1933. The success of the Nazi party was in part a result of the political and social disorder of the Weimar period combined with lingering resentment on the part of the German people for their defeat in the First World War (1914–1918) and the harsh punishment inflicted on the German nation by the victorious allies (Great Britain, France, and the United States). The Versailles peace treaty of 1919 required Germany to pay large economic reparations to the allied governments, limited severely the size of the German military, and prevented the union of Germany and its close cultural neighbor, Austria. The Weimar period, during the 1920s, saw great economic disruption in German society as a result of hyperinflation and the subsequent total loss of the value of paper money. It was, moreover, a time of extreme social and cultural revolution in which new ideas about family roles, sexual politics, artistic expression, and a general re-examination of values all led to changes in individual behavior and social life.

Reacting to this cultural, political, and social environment, the Nazi party, under the leadership of Hitler, promised a return to order and the greatness of the German nation. Although the terms *socialist* and *workers* are contained in the full name of the Nazi party, the Nazis were the antithesis of the left-wing democratic socialist and communist parties of the first part of twentieth century Europe. The term *national* in the name of the party is the guiding ideal. As a fascist political organization, the Nazis believed that the productive forces of the state should be harnessed for the good of the nation as a whole, that each individual citizen ought to sacrifice his or her own personal interests for the life of the nation. The fundamental idea of Nazism was thus an extreme form of nationalism. A central tenet of the Nazi political ideology was the belief in the supremacy of the German *volk*, the German people, conceived as the vanguard of the Aryan race of human beings. But the German *volk* was tied inextricably to its land—the Nazi ideal of "blood and soil"—and it was imperative that the Germanic peoples in all the lands of Europe be united in one pan-Germanic empire.

Consequently, the Nazi ideology was inherently racist. Only true Aryans could be members of the German *volk*. All foreigners and members of other races were excluded from the glories of the German nation, and those of the Jewish race were especially suspect. The Nazis viewed Jews as a racial category, not as members of a religious group who adhere to the doctrines of Judaism. People were considered Jewish by ancestral lineage, not merely spiritual beliefs and practices. Someone in Germany could consider himself a Christian and follow the principles of a Christian religion (such as German Lutheranism), but if his parents or grandparents were Jews, he was considered Jewish by the Nazi government. The identification of those members of the Jewish race was a major consideration of Nazi domestic policy because Jews were thought to be an enemy of the German *volk*, a disease or cancer that weakened and attempted to destroy the German nation from within. Thus, as we shall see in chapters 9 and 10, the Nazis used the medical metaphor of a disease as a justification for the cleansing, purging, and healing of the German people. The medical metaphor of purifying the German race eventually led to the killing of all those members of the society who were considered unfit or undesirable—the physically handicapped, the mentally ill, and all members of suspect social and racial groups, such as Jews and Gypsies, and to a lesser extent, homosexuals and Communists.

Central to the development of the Nazi regime and the events of the Holocaust was the role of an elite corps of Nazi party members known as the SS—the *Schutzstaffeln* (defense squadrons). The SS was an elite paramilitary wing of the party, composed of the best and the brightest of the Nazi party, fanatical believers in the leadership of Hitler as the Führer ("Leader") of the German nation. The head of the SS was Heinrich Himmler, after Hitler perhaps the most powerful man in the Third Reich. Himmler was one of the earliest followers of Hitler, participating in the failed 1923 attempt to take over the German government by a violent revolution (the so-called Beer Hall *Putsch* of November 1923). In 1929 he established the SS as a special praetorian guard of the Nazi party, and after the Nazis assumed control in 1933, he greatly expanded the size and role of his corps. Eventually, the SS became the chief executive force in the Nazi regime, in charge of security (the Gestapo, or secret state police force), the concentration camp system, and its own distinct military units (the *Waffen-SS*).

The central role of the SS in the Third Reich is important for an understanding of the readings in this book for two reasons. The first is ideological: Himmler and the SS had a particular vision of the future of the Germanic and Aryan people, a New Order to be established in the lands of eastern Europe. This vision was rooted in a medieval notion of an aristocracy based on valor, personal ability, and race purity, similar to the Order of Teutonic Knights. The SS, as the elite vanguard of the German nation, would fill the role of the new aristocracy. Himmler was also intensely interested in agriculture and the control of land production. He envisioned an Aryan pastoral paradise in the countries to the east of Germany, colonized by the German *volk* led by the SS. This Aryan agricultural Eden would have to be purified of all foreign elements, especially Jews and Gypsies, who were considered parasites on the body of the nation, but also Poles and other Slavic people. These ideas were strongly advocated by Himmler and the SS corps and helped to shape both domestic and foreign policy in Germany, including the drive for an imperialistic war of conquest.

The second reason why the SS is so important is practical: as the most powerful wing of the Nazi party, the SS controlled the concentration camp system. All labor camps, detention camps, and extermination camps were operated under the command of the SS. The SS also expanded its role into the control of private industry, forming business enterprises (such as brick-making factories and stone quarries) that were able to use the slave labor from prisoners of war (mostly soldiers captured from the Soviet Union), workers from occupied countries in Europe, and Jews. The SS, in addition, "sold" the labor of the prisoners in the camp system to private industries, such as the petrochemical corporation, I.G. Farben (see Chapter 12).

Almost as soon as Hitler became Chancellor in 1933, the process of war preparation began with a massive government investment in military rearmament. The military buildup violated the Versailles treaty. Hitler pursued a policy that challenged the major European powers to stop him. By October 1933, Germany had withdrawn from the League of Nations, and by late 1934, Hitler was seeking the return of German lands that had been given to France in the 1919 peace treaty. In early 1935, the important industrial area of the Saar was given back to Germany by France after a plebiscite by the people of the region. March 1935 saw the return of conscription into the German military, also a violation of the Versailles treaty, and a year later Hitler accomplished his greatest triumph to date: the re-occupation of the Rhineland. The Rhineland region of Germany was the area on the western side of the Rhine River bordering France, Belgium, and Luxembourg. The conditions of the Versailles treaty and an additional treaty (the Pact of Locarno in 1925) had prohibited the German military from using the Rhineland—it was to remain demilitarized. A demilitarized western front was intolerable for Hitler and the German army, since it left Germany defenseless against any possible aggression from France and its allies. In March 1936, the German army entered the Rhineland and reestablished a permanent military presence. The major European powers did nothing.

The success of the Rhineland remilitarization firmly established Hitler as the Führer, an almost divine leader of the German people. Domestic opposition to his policies melted away as he continued the drive to reestablish a Germanic empire. In March 1938, Hitler annexed Austria, also in violation of the Versailles treaty, and prepared to take over parts of Czechoslovakia known as the Sudentenland, which had a majority German-speaking population. The annexation of parts of Czechoslovakia seemed to open the real possibility of a war because France and the USSR had treaties with Czechoslovakia guaranteeing its sovereignty. But in the infamous Munich Agreement of September 29, 1938, Britain and France agreed to let Germany annex the Sudentenland region, believing Hitler's promise that German expansion would then stop. A part of Czechoslovakia would be sacrificed for the sake of world peace. Neville Chamberlain, the Prime Minister of Britain, arrived home in triumph because the British people believed he had averted a catastrophic world war. "Peace in our time," he declared. War was actually only eleven months away.

Throughout late 1938 and early 1939, Germany slowly took control over more of central Europe, and in March 1939 Hitler violated the Munich Agreement by absorbing the Czechoslovakian provinces of Bohemia and Moravia into the Third Reich. Then, on August 23, 1939, Hitler signed a Nazi–Soviet Nonaggression Pact with Josef Stalin, the leader of the Soviet Union. A secret protocol in the agreement called for the division of Poland between Germany and the Soviet Union. With this pact, Hitler no longer had to worry about fighting a war on two different fronts, west and east. He could safely attack western Europe (France and Great Britain) without fearing an attack from behind, in the east, from Russia. On September 1, 1939, German forces invaded Poland, the country that may have had the largest concentration of Jews in the world—3.3 million. France and Great Britain declared war on Germany in support of the Polish people, but they were unprepared to help militarily in any significant way. Poland was overwhelmed by the superior military power of Germany and surrendered on September 28, 1939. Hitler now turned to the west, and France. World War II had begun, and it was not to end in Europe until May 1945 with the total defeat of Germany and its allies.

THE PERSECUTION OF THE JEWS

During the years leading up to and including the war, Hitler undertook a domestic policy of brutal treatment of the Jewish population in Germany and in all the regions and countries that Germany annexed or controlled. The harsh restrictions on Jewish life began almost as soon as Hitler took office in January 1933. In the spring of 1933, Hitler announced a boycott of all Jewish businesses, non-Aryan civil servants and teachers were dismissed from their positions, non-Aryans were prohibited from becoming lawyers, quotas were established to limit the number of non-Aryans in schools and universities, and Jews were prohibited from the ritual (kosher) slaughtering of animals for their food supplies. The anti-Jewish laws and regulations increased over the course of the next few years, and in September 1935, the Nuremberg laws were put into effect. In part, these laws decreed that only persons of "pure German blood" could be citizens of the Reich. The Nuremberg laws also prohibited marriage and extramarital sexual relations between Germans and Jews. These laws had the effect of determining once and for all who was a Jew within the German nation. The determination of Jewishness was now a function of "blood," of race and ancestral history. The Nuremberg laws were thus the crucial first step in the eventual destruction of the Jews of Europe, since these laws determined who was to be eliminated for the purification of the Aryan empire.

Once we understand the Nuremberg laws as the beginning of the destructive process that led to the Holocaust, we can get a concise overview of the Nazi persecution of the Jews by following the schematic framework of historian Raul Hilberg, whose three-volume history, *The Destruction of the European Jews,* is considered a classic text in the field. Hilberg distinguishes six stages in the Nazi persecution and destruction of the Jews: (1) definition or identification; (2) expropriation of property; (3) concentration of population; (4) mobile killing operations; (5) deportation; and (6) killing center operations. Let us look briefly at each stage so that we can see the overall historical context of the use of science and technology in the development of the Nazi death camps.

1. Identification, as noted, was the process put in place by the Nuremberg laws. Jewish identity was defined by decree as a function of ancestral lineage, not religious practice alone. Anyone with three or four Jewish grandparents was determined to be a Jew, as were those with one or two Jewish grandparents who practiced the Jewish religion or were married to a Jew, or both. Those with one or two Jewish grandparents, not married to a Jew, and who did not belong to a Jewish religious community, were considered to be Mischlinge (of mixed race). Mischlings were considered to be non-Aryans (and thus subject to some restrictive legislation) but were not considered to be Jews. German-born Mischlings thus escaped the destructive process of the Holocaust, but Mischlings in lands occupied or conquered by Germany during the war were considered to be Jews.

2. Once a certain section of the population was identified as Jews, the Nazi government was able to promulgate laws and regulations that limited their access to property, professions, and money. At first, special taxes were instituted on Jewish businesses, but eventually Jews were prohibited from owning and operating commercial ventures. Jewish physicians were prohibited from treating Aryan patients. Decrees were issued requiring Jews to work in special labor camps, such as Mauthausen, which began operation in May 1938. The process of expropriation culminated in a decree of December 1938 that eliminated Jews from the economic life of the German Reich— Jews were required to sell off all industrial enterprises and real estate and to surrender all their negotiable securities such as stocks and bonds.

A climactic event during this period of the Jewish persecution was the so-called "Night of Broken Glass" or Kristallnacht, November 9–10, 1938. Under orders from Joseph Goebbels, the Minister of Propaganda (and one of Hitler's closest associates), Jewish businesses and synagogues were attacked throughout Germany and Austria. Over 250 synagogues were destroyed, 7,500 stores looted, and 91 Jews killed. In addition, 30,000 Jews were sent to concentration camps.

3. The concentration of the Jewish population was effected by establishing ghettoes in major cities and requiring all Jews to live in these Jewish districts. Before the war, the concentration of the Jewish populations in major cities was more a function of the economic restrictions imposed on Jews and the laws prohibiting the mixing of Jews and Aryans than a deliberate policy, because Jews were forced to leave the countryside and small towns in order to survive. But after the conquest of Poland, the establishment of Jewish ghettoes was a specific policy designed to facilitate the destruction of the Jewish population. The most famous of these ghettoes was the Warsaw Ghetto in the capital city of Poland. At its peak, the population of the Warsaw Ghetto was approximately 500,000 people; when the Nazis began the final phase of its elimination process—leading to the Warsaw Ghetto uprising of April 1943—fewer than

60,000 Jews were left. After a month-long armed battle between Jewish resistance fighters (aided by the Polish underground) and the German army, the ghetto population was entirely liquidated.

After the Jewish population was concentrated into distinct and separate living areas, the final phases of the destruction of European Jewry could begin. Although Hitler had prophesied the total annihilation of the Jewish people in Europe in a speech in January 1939, and although high-level discussions of the plans for this destruction were continuous throughout 1940 and 1941, the actual implementation of plans to kill all European Jews did not really begin until Germany invaded the Soviet Union on June 22, 1941. The Soviet Union was home to almost three million Jews, concentrated in the western states (such as the Ukraine). The Jewish population of the Soviet Union thus lay in the direct path of the invading German armed forces and could be killed along with the Soviet Army troops. Germany now entered the killing phase of the destruction of the European Jews. This killing phase had two distinct parts: mobile killing units and centers of mass murder (the death camps.)

4. Mobile killing units, called *Einsatzgruppen* (special-duty or strike-force units), were established to accompany the invading German army into the Soviet Union. Composed of SS troops and police, the special assignment of these units was to hunt down Jews and Gypsies—and communist officials— and kill them in those Soviet territories occupied by the advancing German military. The killing was initially accomplished by the direct shooting of the victims, with the bodies thrown into pits. Mobile gassing units were also established using trucks and the carbon monoxide fumes from the engine exhaust. Perhaps the most famous of the Einsatzgruppen operations was the massacre at Babi Yar, a ravine near Kiev in the Ukraine. Over a two-day period (September 29–30, 1941), 33,000 Jews were shot and their bodies thrown into the ravine. Over one million Jews were killed by the Einsatzgruppen before the units were disbanded in early 1943. By then, the SS had developed a more sophisticated method of mass murder: deportation to the extermination camps.

5. As Germany expanded its conquests into eastern Europe, the Jews of each occupied country were deported to centralized killing centers in Poland. This policy was announced at the Wannsee conference of January 1942, where Reinhard Heydrich (the second in command of the SS, under Himmler) met with a number of bureaucrats from several German ministries. Deportation required the coordination of many facets of German society—for example, railroads and the construction industry had to work with the SS and the military to accomplish the movement of the large numbers of Jews. In Poland and the occupied territories alone there were over two million Jews still alive in 1941, despite the deaths of over half a million in the ghettoes. Jews would also have to be transported from the countries Germany had conquered in the war or that were allies or satellites—for example, France, Hungary, and Romania (to name just a few).

6. Four centers used exclusively for killing the deportees were established: Chelmno, Belzec, Sobibor, and Treblinka. Two other camps, Majdanek

and Auschwitz-Birkenau, were primarily killing centers but also served as forced-labor camps. Over the course of the war years, these camps refined the method of killing large numbers of people quickly and easily and disposing of the corpses in an efficient manner (see chapters 2 and 3). The original gas chambers used carbon monoxide gas, but at Auschwitz-Birkenau the use of the more powerful insecticide Zyklon B (prussic acid) was introduced in the spring of 1942. The death totals of the various extermination centers are remarkable: Chelmno: 320,000; Belzec: 600,000; Sobibor: 250,000; Treblinka: between 700,000 and 850,000; Majdanek: 360,000; Auschwitz-Birkenau: 1.2 million (including 100,000 prisoners that were not Jewish: Poles, Gypsies, and Soviet prisoners of war).

The Auschwitz-Birkenau killing center was the largest and the last to cease killing operations. The gas chambers and crematoria remained in use until the beginning of November 1944. The camp was liberated by the advancing Russian army in late January 1945.

A Brief Summary of the Readings

The readings in this collection derive from a number of sources: the memoirs of actual participants in the Nazi death camp system, historians of science and technology, philosophers, and social critics. The chapters are designed to give the reader both a broad overview of the scientific and technological knowledge that was used in the camps and specific details about the engineering processes, architectural designs, and the role of medicine and business management in the extermination camp system.

The first chapter is an excerpt from the memoir of Miklos Nyiszli, a Hungarian Jew and a medical doctor who survived the Auschwitz-Birkenau camp. Nyiszli's account of his survival was published originally in Hungarian in 1947 and thus provides us with one of the earliest of the survivor memoirs. The selection printed here is Nyiszli's simple description of the killing process at Birkenau, from the arrival of the railroad transports at the camp to the disposal of the ashes of the corpses in the Vistula River. In a few brief pages, Nyiszli explains each step of the killing process as it operated in the summer of 1944 and thus provides a clear understanding of the operation of the camp so that the more technical readings to follow can be set in their proper context.

The second and third chapters, Franciszek Piper's "Design and Development of the Gas Chambers and Crematoria in Auschwitz" and Jean-Claude Pressac and Robert Jan van Pelt's "Engineering Mass Murder at Auschwitz," each provide detailed accounts of the design and construction of the gas chambers and crematoria at the Auschwitz-Birkenau extermination camp. Piper's chapter reviews individually the design and construction of all five crematoria and gas chambers that operated at the camp, as well as the two provisional bunkers used as temporary gas chambers and plans for further expansion that were never completed. Pressac's chapter, which is significantly longer than Piper's, also provides a detailed narrative of the business and financial dealings that went into the design and construction of the gas chambers.

In Chapter 4, "Technology and Politics in Totalitarian Regimes: Nazi Germany," Paul R. Josephson presents an overview of Nazi technology and its relationship to the political beliefs of the Third Reich. Within totalitarian regimes, technology is often a symbol of political power, to be used in domestic and foreign policy. The Nazis used technology as a means of furthering the interests of the German *volk*: technologies that were deemed to be Jewish, such as modernist Bauhaus architectural design, were banned.

Gigantic technological projects were conceived as a means of demonstrating the superiority of Aryan culture.

Chapter 5 contains an excerpt from Michael Thad Allen's book *The Business of Genocide* and focuses on the ways in which Nazi ideology influenced the engineers and industrial managers of the SS in their operations of legitimate business enterprises and the slave-labor camps and extermination centers. Allen discusses several engineers, including Hans Kammler, the Chief of Engineering in the SS, to try to answer the question why intelligent technological professionals were able to support the evil aims of the Nazi regime. Organizational unity and ideological consensus play strong roles in dictating the actions of the Nazi technological professionals.

In Chapter 6, "Architectural Aesthetics and Political Ideology in Nazi Germany," Paul Jaskot continues the discussion by examining the role of aesthetics—primarily through the history of architecture—in the development of the Holocaust. The design and construction of architectural projects demonstrates that the political and social decisions of the Nazi hierarchy were part of the overall culture of German society. The architectural design of the labor and extermination camps was merely the culmination of a cultural process that began with Hitler's overt depiction (in his book *Mein Kampf*) of Jewish building design as being the cause of problems in the modern world. Jaskot also provides details of the SS labor camps used to produce the stone required for the massive building projects designed by Hitler and his chief architect and master builder, Albert Speer.

Chapter 7 is composed of several selections from the memoirs of Albert Speer (1905–1981), one of the most powerful men in the Third Reich, and indeed, one of the highest ranking Nazis to escape execution after the war. Speer wrote *Inside the Third Reich* during his twenty-year imprisonment. Beginning as Hitler's architect, in charge of the design and construction of massive new buildings for the Nazi regime, Speer eventually became chief Armaments Minister in charge of all industrial and military production during the war. In these selections, he considers the relationship between his training as an architect and his service to the goals of Nazism.

In Chapter 8, "Albert Speer: Ethics, Architecture, and Technology," law professor Jack L. Sammons, Jr. considers the ethical case for and against Speer's participation in the Nazi regime. Speer claims in his memoirs (and in the selection reprinted in this volume) that his moral failure consisted of the separation of his skills as a trained architect from the overall goals and consequences of Nazism. Sammons rejects this traditional rationalization of the evil effects of a technical project—in part, the claim that the technical expert cannot be concerned with extraneous ethical values—and argues that Speer betrayed the higher ideals of his craft in aligning his technical expertise with the evil aims of Nazism.

Chapter 9, an excerpt from Robert N. Proctor's book *The Nazi War on Cancer,* is the first of two chapters that deal with the role of biology and medicine in Nazi Germany. Proctor's essay discusses the way that Nazi ideas of biological determinism—the theory that the genetic characteristics of race determined all traits in individuals—influenced research and industrial policy regarding cancer. The Nazi belief in the supreme power of racial characteristics was an impediment to evaluating the environmental factors that caused cancer. The Nazi ideology of Jewish racial inferiority was also a problematic obstacle to scientific understanding. The Nazis believed that Jews actually caused cancer among the Aryan population, yet Jews themselves were less susceptible to some forms of cancer.

Chapter 10 contains several selections from Robert J. Lifton's classic study, *The Nazi Doctors.* First, Lifton presents an overview of the way that a medical metaphor—the Jews as a disease to the body of the Aryan nation— became institutionalized as a policy of medicalized killing, first of undesirable physical and mental types (the handicapped and insane) through a governmental policy of mandatory euthanasia, and eventually unparalleled killing of the entire Jewish population. In the extermination centers, medical personnel were always involved in the selection of prisoners for gassing, so the idea that the murder of Jews was a medical and social necessity was maintained throughout the operation of the camps. Finally, the Jewish prisoners were a captive population, useful for extreme forms of medical experimentation that could not be conducted with free, rational subjects. Lifton presents several in-depth studies of these horrific experiments.

In Chapter 11 are several excerpts from Edwin Black's controversial book *IBM and the Holocaust.* Black investigates the history of IBM to demonstrate its complicity in the selection, deportation, and killing of the Jews of Europe. IBM supplied Germany with sophisticated information-managing machine technologies that may have enabled the German government to identify all Jews living in Germany and the occupied lands of the Reich. IBM helped its German subsidiary, Dehomag, to dominate the industry throughout the European continent, even during the war. IBM machines were also used to help manage the German economy. Thus IBM, under the leadership of its chairman, Thomas Watson, profited from the Nazi project to exterminate the Jews of Europe.

Chapter 12, an excerpt from Joseph Borkin's book *The Crime and Punishment of I.G. Farben,* also focuses on a profitable business enterprise, the petrochemical giant, I.G. Farben. Borkin reviews the history of the business decisions that led to the alliance between the SS and I.G. Farben. This industrial conglomerate built a manufacturing plant on the grounds of the Auschwitz-Birkenau concentration camp (the Monowitz site) for the production of fuel and rubber. The plant used the slave labor from concentration camp prisoners at the main Auschwitz camp—indeed, Primo Levi, the Italian chemist, was employed at the Monowitz factory. Over 25,000 prisoners were worked to death at the Farben facility at Auschwitz. I.G. Farben was also involved in the manufacture and sale of Zyklon B, the insecticide that was used in the new, sophisticated gas chambers built at Auschwitz-Birkenau in 1942 and 1943.

The issue of the value-neutrality of science and technology is the primary focus of the last essay in this collection, Eric Katz's "Technological

Evil: Cultural Values in the Holocaust." This chapter considers the philosophical arguments that demonstrate that all technological artifacts are endowed with the values of the culture that produced them, and then uses the development of the Nazi concentration camps as a practical example to illustrate the theoretical arguments. As the concluding chapter in the book, this essay draws on several of the historical cases developed in earlier essays, particularly concerning the engineering design of the gas chambers at Auschwitz-Birkenau and the architectural design of the slave labor camps. This final essay serves as a fitting summary of many of the major issues raised in the collection.

CHAPTER 1

The Killing Process at Auschwitz-Birkenau

❧

The first chapter is a stark and emotionless description of the entire killing process at the most sophisticated and efficient of the Nazi death camps, Auschwitz-Birkenau. In the following chapters (especially chapters 2 and 3) we will learn how the camp and its tools for mass-produced death were designed, developed, and organized. Here, in an excerpt from the memoir of Dr. Miklos Nyiszli, we have a description of each step of the process as it operated in the summer of 1944. Nyiszli was a Hungarian Jew and a medical doctor who survived the Auschwitz-Birkenau camp because he was indispensable to the medical experiments performed by the infamous Nazi doctor Josef Mengele. Because he was a pathologist, Nyiszli was personally chosen by Mengele to be his medical assistant and coroner, performing autopsies on prisoners who died or were killed in the camp. Nyiszli was thus a member of the Sonderkommando, the special prisoner unit that carried out the technical operations of the mass murders. In a few brief pages, Nyiszli's clinical eye describes the killing, from the arrival of the railroad transports at the camp to the disposal of the ashes of the corpses in the Vistula River. Nyiszli's eyewitness account provides us with a clear understanding of the operation of the camp so that the more technical readings to follow can be set in their proper context. Nyiszli's account of his survival was published originally in Hungarian in 1947 and thus offers one of earliest of the survivor memoirs.

From *Auschwitz: A Doctor's Eyewitness Account*

Miklos Nyiszli

TRANSLATED BY TIBÈRE KREMER AND RICHARD SEAVER

The strident whistle of a train was heard coming from the direction of the unloading platform. It was still very early. I approached my window, from which I had a direct view onto the tracks, and saw a very long train. A few seconds later the doors slid open and the box cars spilled out thousands upon thousands of the chosen people of Israel. Line up and selection took scarcely half an hour. The left-hand column moved slowly away.

Orders rang out, and the sound of rapid footsteps reached my room. The sounds came from the furnace rooms of the crematorium: they were preparing to welcome the new convoy. The throb of motors began. They had just set the enormous ventilators going to fan the flames, in order to obtain the desired degree in the ovens. Fifteen ventilators were going simultaneously, one beside each oven. The incineration room was about 500 feet long: it was a bright, whitewashed room with a concrete floor and barred windows. Each of these fifteen ovens was housed in a red brick structure. Immense iron doors, well-polished and gleaming, ominously lined the length of the wall. In five or six minutes the convoy reached the gate, whose swing-doors opened inwards. Five abreast, the group entered the courtyard; it was the moment about which the outside world knew nothing, for anyone who might have known something about it, after having traveled the path of his destiny—the 300 yards separating that spot from the ramp—had never returned to tell the tale. It was one of the crematoriums which awaited those who had been selected for the left-hand column. And not, as the German lie had made the right-hand column suppose in order to allay their anxiety, a camp for the sick and children, where the infirm cared for the little ones.

They advanced with slow, weary steps. The children's eyes were heavy with sleep and they clung to their mothers' clothes. For the most part the babies were carried in their fathers' arms, or else wheeled in their carriages. The SS guards remained before the crematorium doors, where a poster announced: "Entrance is Strictly Forbidden to All Who Have No Business Here, Including SS."

The deportees were quick to notice the water faucets, used for sprinkling the grass, that were arranged about the courtyard. They began to take pots and pans from their luggage, and broke ranks, pushing and shoving in an effort to get near the faucets and fill their containers. That they were impatient was not astonishing: for the past five days they had had nothing to drink. If ever they had found a little water, it had been stagnant and had not quenched their thirst. The SS guards who received the convoys were used to the scene. They waited patiently till each had quenched his thirst and filled his container. In any case, the guards knew that as long as they had not drunk there would be no getting them back into line. Slowly they began to re-form their ranks. Then they advanced for about 100 yards along a cinder path edged with green grass to an iron ramp, from which 10 or 12 concrete steps led underground to an enormous room dominated by a large sign in German, French, Greek and Hungarian: "Baths and Disinfecting Room." The sign was reassuring, and allayed the misgivings or fears of even the most suspicious among them. They went down the stairs almost gaily.

The room into which the convoy proceeded was about 200 yards long: its walls were whitewashed and it was brightly lit. In the middle of the room, rows of columns. Around the columns, as well as along the walls, benches. Above the benches, numbered coat hangers. Numerous signs in several languages drew everyone's attention to the necessity of tying his clothes and shoes together. Especially that he not forget the number of his coat hanger, in order to avoid all useless confusion upon his return from the bath.

"That's really a German order," commented those who had long been inclined to admire the Germans.

They were right. As a matter of fact, it *was* for the sake of order that these measures had been taken, so that the thousands of pairs of good shoes sorely needed by the Third Reich would not get mixed up. The same for the clothes, so that the population of bombed cities could easily make use of them.

There were 3,000 people in the room: men, women and children. Some of the soldiers arrived and announced that everyone must be completely undressed within ten minutes. The aged, grandfathers and grandmothers; the children; wives and husbands; all were struck dumb with surprise. Modest women and girls looked at each other questioningly. Perhaps they had not exactly understood the German words. They did not have long to think about it, however, for the order resounded again, this time in a louder, more menacing tone. They were uneasy; their dignity rebelled; but, with the resignation peculiar to their race, having learned that anything went as far as they were concerned, they slowly began to undress. The aged, the paralyzed, the mad were helped by a Sonderkommando squad sent for that purpose. In ten minutes all were completely naked, their clothes hung on the pegs, their shoes attached together by the laces. As for the number of each clothes hanger, it had been carefully noted.

Making his way through the crowd, an SS opened the swing-doors of the large oaken gate at the end of the room. The crowd flowed through it into another, equally well-lighted room. This second room was the same size as the first, but neither benches nor pegs were to be seen. In the center of the rooms, at thirty-yard intervals, columns rose from the concrete floor to the ceiling. They were not supporting columns, but square sheet-iron pipes, the sides of which contained numerous perforations, like a wire lattice.

Everyone was inside. A hoarse command rang out: "SS and Sonderkommando leave the room." They obeyed and counted off. The doors swung shut and from without the lights were switched off.

At that very instant the sound of a car was heard: a deluxe model, furnished by the International Red Cross. An SS officer and a SDG (*Sanitätsdienstgefreiter:* Deputy Health Service Officer) stepped out of the car. The Deputy Health Officer held four green sheet-iron canisters. He advanced across the grass, where, every thirty yards, short concrete pipes jutted up from the ground. Having donned his gas mask, he lifted the lid of the pipe, which was also made of concrete. He opened one of the cans and poured the contents—a mauve granulated material—into the opening. The granulated substance fell in a lump to the bottom. The gas it produced escaped through the perforations, and within a few seconds filled the room in which the deportees were stacked. Within five minutes everybody was dead.

For every convoy it was the same story. Red Cross cars brought the gas from the outside. There was never a stock of it in the crematorium. The precaution was scandalous, but still more scandalous was the fact that the gas was brought in a car bearing the insignia of the International Red Cross.

In order to be certain of their business the two gas-butchers waited another five minutes. Then they lighted cigarettes and drove off in their car. They had just killed 3,000 innocents.

Twenty minutes later the electric ventilators were set going in order to evacuate the gas. The doors opened, the trucks arrived, and a Sonderkommando squad loaded the clothing and the shoes separately. They were going to disinfect them. This time it was a case of real disinfection. Later they would transport them by rail to various parts of the country.

The ventilators, patented "Exhator" system, quickly evacuated the gas from the room, but in the crannies between the dead and the cracks of the doors small pockets of it always remained. Even two hours later it caused a suffocating cough. For that reason the Sonderkommando group which first moved into the room was equipped with gas masks. Once again the room was powerfully lighted, revealing a horrible spectacle.

The bodies were not lying here and there throughout the room, but piled in a mass to the ceiling. The reason for this was that the gas first inundated the lower layers of air and rose but slowly towards the ceiling. This forced the victims to trample one another in a frantic effort to escape the gas. Yet a few feet higher up the gas reached them. What a struggle for life there must have been! Nevertheless it was merely a matter of two or three minutes' respite. If they had been able to think about what they were doing, they would have realized they were trampling their own children, their wives, their relatives. But they couldn't think. Their gestures were no more than the reflexes of the instinct of self-preservation. I noticed that the bodies of the women, the children, and the aged were at the bottom of the pile; at the top, the strongest. Their bodies, which were covered with scratches and bruises from the struggle which had set them against each other, were often interlaced. Blood oozed from their noses and mouths; their faces, bloated and blue, were so deformed as to be almost unrecognizable. Nevertheless some of the Sonderkommando often did recognize their kin. The encounter was not easy, and I dreaded it for myself. I had no reason to be here, and yet I had come down among the dead. I felt it my duty to my people and to the entire world to be able to give an accurate account of what I had seen if ever, by some miraculous whim of fate, I should escape.

The Sonderkommando squad, outfitted with large rubber boots, lined up around the hill of bodies and flooded it with powerful jets of water. This was necessary because the final act of those who die by drowning or by gas is an involuntary defecation. Each body was befouled, and had to be washed. Once the "bathing" of the dead was finished—a job the Sonderkommando carried out by a voluntary act of impersonalization and in a state of profound distress—the separation of the welter of bodies began. It was a difficult job. They knotted thongs around the wrists, which were clenched in a viselike grip, and with these thongs they dragged the slippery bodies to the elevators in the next room. Four good-sized elevators were functioning. They loaded twenty to twenty-five corpses to an elevator. The ring of a bell was the signal that the load was ready to ascend. The elevator stopped at the crematorium's incineration room, where large sliding doors opened automatically. The kommando who operated the trailers was ready and waiting. Again straps were fixed to the wrists of the dead, and they were dragged onto specially constructed chutes which unloaded them in front of the furnaces.

The bodies lay in close ranks: the old, the young, the children. Blood oozed from their noses and mouths, as well as from their skin—abraded by the rubbing—and mixed with the water running in the gutters set in the concrete floor.

Then a new phase of the exploitation and utilization of Jewish bodies took place. The Third Reich had already taken their clothes and shoes. Hair was also a precious material, due to the fact that it expands and contracts uniformly, no matter what the humidity of the air. Human hair was often used in delayed action bombs, where its particular qualities made it highly useful for detonating purposes. So they shaved the dead.

But that was not all. According to the slogans the Germans paraded and shouted to everyone at home and abroad, the Third Reich was not based on the "gold standard," but on the "work standard." Maybe they meant they had to work harder to get their gold than most countries did. At any rate, the dead were next sent to the "tooth-pulling" kommando, which was stationed in front of the ovens. Consisting of eight men, this kommando equipped its members with two tools, or, if you like, two instruments. In one hand a lever, and in the other a pair of pliers for extracting the teeth. The dead lay on their backs; the kommando pried open the contracted jaw with his lever; then, with his pliers, he extracted, or broke off, all gold teeth, as well as any gold bridgework and fillings. All members of the kommando were fine stomatologists and dental surgeons. When Dr. Mengele had called for candidates capable of performing the delicate work of stomatology and dental surgery, they had volunteered in good faith, firmly believing they would be allowed to exercise their profession in the camp. Exactly as I had done.

The gold teeth were collected in buckets filled with an acid which burned off all pieces of bone and flesh. Other valuables worn by the dead, such as necklaces, pearls, wedding bands and rings, were taken and dropped through a slot in the lid of a strongbox. Gold is a heavy metal, and I would judge that from 18 to 20 pounds of it were collected daily in each crematorium. It varied, to be sure, from one convoy to the next, for some convoys were comparatively wealthy, while others, from rural districts, were naturally poorer.

The Hungarian convoys arrived already stripped. But the Dutch, Czech, and Polish convoys, even after several years in the ghettos, had managed to keep and bring their jewelry, their gold and their dollars with them. In this way the Germans amassed considerable treasures.

When the last gold tooth had been removed, the bodies went to the incineration kommando. There they were laid by threes on a kind of pushcart made of sheet metal. The heavy doors of the ovens opened automatically; the pushcart moved into a furnace heated to incandescence.

The bodies were cremated in twenty minutes. Each crematorium worked with fifteen ovens, and there were four crematoriums. This meant that several thousand people could be cremated in a single day. Thus for weeks and months—even years—several thousand people passed each day through the gas chambers and from there to the incineration ovens. Nothing but a pile of ashes remained in the crematory ovens. Trucks took the ashes to the Vistula, a mile away, and dumped them into the raging waters of the river.

After so much suffering and horror there was still no peace, even for the dead.

QUESTIONS FOR DISCUSSION

1. How many different technologies (or technological artifacts or machines) were used in the gas chambers and crematoria? Review the operation of each of the different technological devices.

2. The procedure of mass killing at Auschwitz-Birkenau was highly organized to prevent disruptions by the intended victims. Review and discuss the aspects of the process that were designed to relieve victim anxiety.

3. Technology often makes killing easier in that the killer is separated from the victim by time and/or distance (as in air-raid bombing or intercontinental missiles). Discuss in what ways the mass killing procedure at Auschwitz-Birkenau made killing easier by distancing the killer from the victim; also consider the ways in which the killing was made more immediate and direct. In this regard, can the "clinical" descriptions by Nyiszli be seen as a means of professional and technical distancing?

4. Aside from the killing itself, what aspects of the killing procedure at Auschwitz-Birkenau seem to be particularly immoral or disrespectful? Does technology contribute to the immorality of the process?

CHAPTER 2

Design and Development of the Gas Chambers and Crematoria in Auschwitz

—— ❖ ——

This detailed overview of the gas chambers and crematoria complexes at the Auschwitz-Birkenau concentration camp is written by historian Franciszek Piper, head of the Department of Historical Research at the Auschwitz-Birkenau State Museum. Auschwitz-Birkenau was the largest and most infamous of the Nazi death camps, the site where the technology of mass-produced death reached the zenith of scientific and engineering development. The camp was divided into three main sections: Auschwitz I, the original camp built for prisoners of war; Auschwitz II, or Birkenau, the largest section of the camp redesigned as a mass-killing center; and Auschwitz III, or Monowitz, the site of an industrial factory operated by the chemical company I.G. Farben (see Chapter 12). Prior to the construction of the gas chambers at Auschwitz, the killing of Jews and other undesirables in Nazi Germany was accomplished by carbon monoxide gas, mainly at medical euthanasia stations or hospitals, and by the use of mobile killing units in automobiles and trucks. But the operations at Auschwitz perfected the killing technique. As Piper explains, the plans for the gas chambers and crematoria at Auschwitz began in the late summer of 1941, and their design, development, and construction continued through the spring of 1943, when a total of five complexes were in operation. There were also provisional or temporary gas chambers—the

8

so-called "little red house" and "little white house"—that were used before the more sophisticated units were completed and later, during the summer of 1944, when there was a need for increased capacity. It is estimated that 20,000 people a day were killed and their corpses incinerated at the peak of operation. Over one million people were gassed and cremated at Auschwitz-Birkenau. Such a colossal number of murdered victims required a high degree of technological and organizational planning. In this chapter, Piper presents the historical and technological details of the development of the killing operation. We will see that the details of technology, engineering, and architecture provide important insights into the intentions and policies of the Nazi regime.

Gas Chambers and Crematoria

Franciszek Piper

In the wake of SS chief Heinrich Himmler's decision in the summer of 1941 that Auschwitz was to play a part in the plan to annihilate European Jews,[1] a new method of mass killing in gas chambers was introduced. When Himmler notified camp commandant Rudolf Höss of his decision, he described the gas chambers enigmatically as "installations."[2] It was the chief of the Reich Main Security Office's Jewish Department, Adolf Eichmann, who spelled out the details of the proposed installations to Höss. In keeping with Himmler's announcement, Eichmann arrived at Auschwitz shortly thereafter.[3] He explained to Höss the workings of the static gas chambers in euthanasia stations[4] and the mobile chambers installed in automobiles.[5] He commented, however, that neither type was suitable for the mass-scale extermination that was planned for Auschwitz.

The type of gas to be used remained an open question. Owing to difficulties in transportation and utilization, carbon monoxide in cylinder containers as used in euthanasia stations was deemed unsuitable. Eichmann, whose position and official contacts offered him greater access to relevant firms and institutions, promised to locate a gas suitable for the task. Ultimately, Zyklon B (prussic acid), hitherto used for disinfection, turned out to be available locally.

The first experiments with prussic acid as a killing agent took place in late summer 1941 in the basement of block 11 (until August 1941, it had been designated as number 13). The first and best-known mass killing operation during this period was the murder of some 600 Soviet prisoners of war and about 250 sick prisoners on September 3–5.[6] A situation report covering the period from August 15 to September 15 was compiled by the prisoner underground:

> The camp has been the scene of a hideous crime when on the night of September 5–6, about 600 Soviet prisoners, including political officers of the army, were crammed into a bunker together with some 200 Poles. After the bunker had been sealed they were poisoned by gas, their bodies brought to the crematorium and incinerated.[7]

For many reasons the cellars of block 11 proved unsuitable for the task of mass gassings. A complicated maze of corridors and cells hampered the removal of bodies and the airing of the bunker, which, according to the commandant, should take two days.[8] Not only did the equipment and personnel have to be moved out while gassing was in progress, but it also proved exceedingly difficult to keep the entire proceeding secret. The block itself was located on the grounds of Auschwitz I, the main camp, near the buildings where prisoners were held. Although no one was allowed to leave the buildings during gassings, prisoners could watch the operation surreptitiously, witnessing both the marching of the victims to the site and the removal of the bodies. For these reasons the gassing procedure was relocated to the camp crematorium.

CREMATORIUM I

The so-called old crematorium in Auschwitz,[9] later designated as crematorium I, was initially designed for burning the bodies of prisoners who died a natural death or were killed or executed. The crematorium also was used to incinerate the bodies of prisoners from Birkenau and the satellite camps. Construction began in early July 1940, when a building that had served as a depot before the war was remodeled. The crematorium was put into operation in September 1940.[10] Until that time, the bodies of dead prisoners were shipped off to Gliwice and incinerated in the municipal crematorium.

The extant plan, dated September 25, 1941, shows that the crematorium building was 26.57 meters long, 14.61 m wide, and about 3 m high. It had one entrance on the northwest side and included a furnace room with three two-retort furnaces and a charnel house that was 78.2 sq m (17 m in length and 4.6 m in width).[11] The concrete roof was flat. The building had earth embankments on three sides with openings for the window of the coke plant (through which coke was thrown inside). There were two windows in the furnace room that were probably used to lower the temperature inside the building. An external chimney was connected to the furnaces by underground flues. The entrance to the building was camouflaged by a concrete-slab wall several meters high that enclosed a courtyard. Two massive gates, made of wooden beams, led to the courtyard. In front of the entrance were meticulously kept flowerbeds. The crematorium was screened from view from the camp by a one-story building that housed the SS hospital. The east and north sides were screened by the barracks of the political department and camp workshops. According to official German figures, the "capacity" of the expanded crematorium was 340 bodies in 24 hours.[12] Crematorium I operated until July 1942, with an interlude at the turn of 1941–42 for the construction of a third furnace.

With the launching of new large crematoria in Birkenau (March–June 1943), incineration of bodies in the old crematorium was discontinued, and the bodies of prisoners who died in the main camp and the satellite camps were shipped to Birkenau for cremation. The prisoner personnel who serviced crematorium I were also transferred to Birkenau on July 19, 1943.[13] After that time, the crematorium building was used to store cinerary urns and medicines. In 1944, it was converted into an air-raid shelter for SS personnel from the nearby hospital.[14]

Following the experimental gassing of the Soviet prisoners of war and sick prisoners in block 11, the room that had served as the mortuary was converted to a gas chamber.[15] The conversion included sealing the doors that led to the washing room and the furnace room, and boring openings in the ceiling through which Zyklon B was to be poured.[16] Later, a ventilator was installed to air the premises, which facilitated the removal of the bodies.[17]

Filip Müller, a member of the *Sonderkommando,* the prisoners who serviced the crematoria, testified that the chamber could hold over 700 people. Former camp commandant Höss and former prisoners testified that even more prisoners could be crammed inside.[18]

The victims consigned to gassing in crematorium I usually were brought into the camp in late evening or early morning by train or in cars that pulled up at the entrance. In the former case, the victims disembarked at a loading ramp that adjoined the camp and were marched to their destination.

In his memoirs, Höss described the first gassing of a transport of Soviet prisoners of war in the chamber.

I have a clearer recollection of the gassing of 900 Russians that took place shortly afterwards in the old crematorium, since the use of block 11 for this purpose caused too much trouble. While the transport was detraining, holes were pierced in the earth and concrete ceiling of the mortuary.

The Russians were ordered to undress in an anteroom; they then quietly entered the mortuary, for they had been told they were to be deloused. The whole transport exactly filled the mortuary to capacity. The doors were then sealed and the gas shaken down through the holes in the roof. I do not know how long this killing took. For a little while a humming sound could be heard. When the powder was thrown in, there were cries of "Gas!" then a great bellowing, and the trapped prisoners hurled themselves against both doors. But the doors held. They were opened several hours later, so that the place might be aired.[19]

After that, the chamber was used to gas several hundred Soviet POWs at a time,[20] as well as numerous transports of Jews who were killed wholesale, including entire families regardless of sex or age.[21] One camp functionary, Pery Broad, who witnessed the mass murders, recalled that

a sad procession walked along the streets of the camp. It had started at the railway siding . . . branching out from the main railway line, which led to the camp. . . . Suspecting nothing the column marched in, five persons abreast, and came to a halt in the yard. They numbered from 400 to 500 people. The SS man, somewhat nervous, waited for the last man to enter the yard. At that moment he quickly shut the gate and bolted it. Grabner and Hossler were standing on the roof of the crematorium. Grabner spoke to the Jews who awaited their fate, suspecting nothing: "You will now bathe and undergo disinfection; we don't want any epidemics in the camp. Then you will go to your barracks and get some hot soup. You will be assigned to jobs according to your professional qualifications. Now undress and put your clothes in front of you on the ground." The first lines entered the mortuary through the anteroom. . . . As soon as the last person had entered, the SS guards disappeared without much ado. Suddenly the door was closed; it had been gas-proofed with rubber and reinforced with iron fittings. Those inside heard the heavy bolts being secured. A deadly, paralyzing terror gripped the victims. They started to beat on the door, hammering it with their fists in helpless rage and despair.[22]

The gas chamber attached to crematorium I operated until fall 1942. The last victims were several hundred prisoners of the Sonderkommando in Birkenau who were employed in the killing operations. They were gassed in early December 1942.[23] Their murder was but one of a series of mass murders of Sonderkommando prisoners, doomed as witnesses and executors of Nazi crimes. One of the handful of Sonderkommando prisoners who survived the successive hecatombs, Müller, serviced crematorium I from May 1942 to July 1943. He concluded on the basis of personal observation that several tens of thousands of Jews from Upper

Silesia, Slovakia, France, Holland, Yugoslavia, and the ghettos of Theresienstadt, Ciechanow, and Grodno perished there.[24]

BUNKERS—PROVISIONAL GAS CHAMBERS

In the first months of 1942,[25] the gassing operation was extended to nearby Birkenau owing to the small capacity of the gas chamber and ovens in Auschwitz and the difficulties in camouflaging the proceedings. The move signaled the implementation of the Nazi plan to exterminate European Jews and coincided with the arrival of the first Jewish transports. Construction of the new camp had been under way since October 1941.

Initially the victims were gassed in one gas chamber. By mid-1942,[26] the mass murders took place in two provisional gas chambers that were installed in the cottages of two peasants, Harmata and Wichaj, who had been evicted earlier.

The building in which the first gas chamber was installed, called bunker 1 by the SS men, had been earmarked for that purpose the previous year, when Eichmann first visited Auschwitz. It was an unplastered brick building with a tile roof (which explains its nickname, the "little red house"). It measured 15 m long and 6.3 m wide.[27] As part of the remodeling, its windows were bricked up. Only small openings remained, which could be closed with flaps sealed at the edges with felt. The number of inner rooms was reduced from four to two. Each had only one door with a sign "Zur Desinfektion" (To Disinfection). The doors were made of wooden beams and sealed at the edges with felt. There were no peepholes. The doors could be shut by tightening two bolts that doubled as door handles. The interior walls of the two rooms were painted white, and the floors were strewn with sawdust. The building was surrounded by fruit trees. Nearby stood a barn and two barracks that were constructed during the conversion work.[28]

Bunker 2 was brought into operation several months later. It was housed in a brick building that was thatched and plastered (and therefore nicknamed by the prisoners the "little white house"). It was bigger than the first building, measuring 17.07 m by 8.34 m.[29] Like the first building, its windows were bricked up, with only small openings covered with wooden flaps. It had four rooms of different sizes, each with its own entrance and exit. The doors were the same as the doors in bunker 1. As part of the conversion work the wooden ceiling was replaced with concrete.

The new gas chambers were the sites of systematic and unceasing murder of Jews who were brought in mass transports from various German-occupied European countries. On the loading ramp, in the process called "selections," some of the men and women were picked for work in the camp. But the majority of the prisoners, including all the elderly, the children, and many women, were consigned for immediate extermination.

According to Shlomo Dragon, who serviced the bunker from December 1942 to the spring of 1943, signs were posted on the gas chamber doors. On the outside of the entrance, which was visible when the door was closed, a sign read "Hochspannung—Lebensgefahr" (High Tension—Lethal Danger). It served as a precaution against accidentally opening the chamber filled with dead bodies and gas. On the interior side, which was visible when the door was open (the side the victims saw as they entered) was the sign "Zum Baden" (To the Baths). On the exit door, behind which lay the rail tracks and pits for burning dead bodies, was affixed the sign "Zur Desinfektion."[30]

Bunkers 1 and 2 were surrounded on all sides by woods. Three barracks that served as dressing rooms were nearby. Mass graves, screened from view by hedges, were located several dozen to several hundred meters from both gas chambers. They were later replaced by incinerating pits. Small trolleys or flat-bed trucks that rolled on narrow-gauge tracks transported the corpses from the gas chambers to the pits.[31]

Train transports that carried the victims were unloaded at the ramp of the freight railway station situated 2.5 km from the bunkers. When transports arrived at night, the victims were hauled in trucks to the killing site. During the day, trucks were only used to transport victims who were unable to walk the distance on their own. The able-bodied were marched past the barracks of the Birkenau camp then under construction and across the meadows, where building sector 3 was later erected. The SS men who escorted the victims sometimes engaged them in innocent conversation aimed at putting the victims off guard. The marching column was accompanied by a car with the emblem of the Red Cross. The car carried the poison gas under SS guard. It also carried an SS doctor with medicines and an oxygen bottle for use in an emergency, such as the accidental poisoning of SS men taking part in the gassing.

Upon arrival, the victims were told that before taking up residence in the camp they had to go to the bath and undergo delousing. They were also told to remember the spot where they left their effects. They were told to undress, either in the barracks or outside behind hedges. From there, under a rain of blows and attack dogs, they were chased into the gas chamber. Those who could not be accommodated were shot, or in instances where there were a large number of people, they were held naked in the barracks until the gas chamber was emptied.

Once the chamber was full (according to Höss, bunker 1 could hold 800 people[32] and bunker 2 about 1,200[33]), the gas-proof doors were screwed shut and the trained SS disinfectors wearing gas masks discharged the contents of Zyklon B cans into each bunker room through vents in the side walls. All the victims were dead within several minutes.

One of the SS doctors who oversaw the gassing procedure, Johann Kremer, testified after the war that after the gas had been poured in, "Shouting and screaming of the victims could be heard through that opening and it was clear that they fought for their lives (*Lebenskampf*). These shouts lasted a short while. I should think it was several minutes, though I cannot give a precise estimate."[34] In addition to extending emergency medical assistance to the disinfectors, the SS doctors were there to ascertain that the victims were dead.

The gas chamber was opened a half hour after the gas was administered to ensure there were no survivors. When the pace of incoming transports slowed, the bodies of victims who were gassed at night or late in the evening remained in the bunkers under SS guard until morning. Only then were the doors opened, the premises aired, and the Sonderkommando prisoners brought in to remove the bodies.

The Sonderkommando prisoners worked in several teams. Those servicing the gas chamber wore gas masks. Their task was to remove the bodies to the yard, where gold teeth were extracted, jewelry recovered, and women's hair cut. Another team loaded the corpses onto the narrow-gauge trolleys and transported them to deep pits, where they were placed in layers and covered with chlorinated lime and soil. Since the entire area was floodlit, the work could be carried out day and night. Each time the bunkers were emptied, Sonderkommando prisoners whitewashed the walls and washed the floors.[35]

During Himmler's second inspection visit to Auschwitz on July 17, 1942, he witnessed the entire procedure of liquidation of one transport—from unloading the train cars to gassing (in bunker 2) and removing the bodies.[36] It cannot be ruled out that his observations resulted in the decision to cremate the bodies instead of burying them. In fact, shortly after Himmler's visit, Standartenführer Paul Blobel of Eichmann's office arrived at Auschwitz with orders to exhume all the buried bodies, burn them, and scatter the ashes to prevent the possible reconstruction of the number of victims.

Consequently, as early as September 1942, unearthing of the mass graves at Birkenau commenced. The bodies that had been buried because the main Auschwitz crematorium could not accommodate them at the time were cremated. The fires were stoked with oil refuse and methanol. At the same time, the bodies of the more recently gassed victims were also being incinerated. First they were burned on timber pyres with 2,000 bodies each. Later they were burned in pits along with the bodies that had been buried there earlier. Alternate layers of bodies and timber were placed in a pit 30 m long, 7 m wide, and 3 m deep. The four corners were doused with flammable liquid. One of the SS men would then throw a burning comb or a rag soaked in oil on the pyre to set it on fire. Body fat that drained off in special cavities was used to stoke the fire. By late November 1942, all the mass graves, containing over 100,000 corpses, had been emptied.[37]

In the spring of 1943, with the launching of new gas chambers and crematoria, the two bunkers were shut down. Shortly thereafter, bunker 1 and the nearby barracks were dismantled. The incineration pits were filled in with earth and leveled. The same work was performed on the pits and barracks of bunker 2, but the bunker itself was left intact. It was brought into operation again in May 1944 during the extermination of Hungarian Jews.[38] At that time several incineration pits were reexcavated and new barracks for undressing were constructed.

The bunker was operative until the fall of 1944. It was dismantled when the gassing was discontinued that November. The ashes from the incineration pits were removed, and the entire terrain was leveled.[39]

CREMATORIA II, III, IV, AND V—CONSTRUCTION AND OPERATION

Himmler inspected Auschwitz on March 1, 1941, and ordered that a POW camp be built. Acting on his orders, Department II of the Main Budget and Construction Office drew up a preliminary plan[40] for the construction of a camp nearby at Birkenau for 125,000 prisoners.[41]

Among other projects, the plan provided for the construction of a crematorium capable of incinerating 1,440 bodies in 24 hours. It was projected to consist of five three-retort ovens for burning bodies, one oven for burning refuse, and one underground mortuary.[42] The site was to be in the main camp at Auschwitz.

In consideration of the ongoing preparations for the extermination of Jews, it was decided to adapt the installation for mass killing by constructing a gas chamber next to it, in an underground facility also designated as a mortuary. The second room was to serve as a "dressing room."[43] Both were to be ventilated mechanically.

An order placed with the firm Topf and Sons of Erfurt on October 22, 1941, stressed the urgency of the entire undertaking, demanding fast delivery: two weeks for technical drawings of the foundations and three months for parts of the ovens (fireclay elements, metal castings, pipes, ventilators).[44] However, before the construction work began, Heinz Kammler, chief of group C of the SS Economic-Administrative Main Office and one of the closest associates of Himmler, arrived at Auschwitz on February 27, 1942, and ordered that the five-oven crematorium projected for Auschwitz be constructed at Birkenau.[45]

The oldest preserved technical drawings of the crematorium that was built at Birkenau are dated January 15, 1942. They were made by SS-Unterscharführer Ulmer of Zentralbauleitung (the Central Construction Administration), checked by SS-Untersturmführer Walter Dejaco of the same office, and approved by the office head, SS-Sturmbannführer Karl Bischoff (drawing nos. 936, 937, 938).[46] More detailed drawings and plans followed in short order.

With the completion of the first stage of planning on July 1, 1942, the Zentralbauleitung offered two construction firms, Huta Hoch- und Tiefbau AG and Schlesische Industriehaus Lenz und CO AG in Kattowitz, which had been cooperating with the camp for some time, to undertake the construction of the crematorium building (number II).[47] Ovens and other equipment were to be installed by Topf and Sons. On July 13, 1942, Huta responded to the proposal by submitting its offer along with a cost estimate totaling 133,756.65 marks.[48] Lenz, however, replied that owing to manpower shortages it could not undertake the project. Under these conditions, the Zentralbauleitung instructed Huta to undertake the construction of the crematorium forthwith in line with the submitted offer.[49]

Shortly thereafter, orders were placed with Huta for the construction of three more crematoria, designated on technical plans by the numbers III, IV, and V. Again the ovens and other equipment were to be installed by Topf and Sons. In September 1942, the Zentralbauleitung placed an order with the same firm for five ovens and three installations of mechanical draft for crematorium III, and in October for ventilation for the "dressing room" and the gas chamber. In both cases Topf and Sons confirmed receipt of the orders, thanked the SS authorities for commissioning them to do the work, and expressed satisfaction at the degree of cooperation hitherto.[50]

In addition to plans and technical drawings, Topf and Sons supplied many items to Birkenau: fireclay and metal parts for 12 crematoria ovens (ten three-retorts and two eight-retorts), two ovens for refuse burning, engines, ventilators for chimney drafts, engines and ventilators for gas chambers and "dressing rooms," two electrical elevators for removing corpses from the gas chamber to the oven room, and a number of stretchers for sliding bodies into the retorts.[51] The letter from the Zentralbauleitung, dated February 26, 1943, indicates that the firm also was to supply ten gas testers (*Gasprüfer*) for crematorium II. No specific information about this equipment is available.

Despite the hectic pace of work, which went on day and night, the approved deadlines for launching the crematoria failed to be met.[52] The camp administration did not take delivery of the crematoria and gas chambers until the spring and summer of 1943: crematorium IV on

March 22, crematorium II on March 31, crematorium V on April 4, and crematorium III on June 25 (or 26).[53]

A letter from the Zentralbauleitung to group C of June 28, 1943,[54] indicates that the capacity for a 24-hour period was estimated at 340 bodies for crematorium I; 1,440 each for crematoria II and III; and 768 each for crematoria IV and V. Thus the five crematoria could incinerate 4,765 bodies each day. This estimate coincided with the guidelines established in 1941 concerning the capacity of a five-retort crematorium for prisoners of war, according to which two bodies could be incinerated in one retort within 30 minutes. The next month, however, crematorium I was shut down, reducing the capacity to 4,415.

In their efforts to increase the burning capacity of the ovens, the camp authorities recommended that the incineration time be reduced to 20 minutes and the number of bodies be increased to three, depending on the size of the body.[55] As a result, the capacity of the crematoria almost doubled, reaching about 8,000 bodies in 24 hours, according to the statement of a Sonderkommando prisoner, Feinsilber.

Situated behind the fences surrounding the Birkenau barracks, the crematoria constituted a separate complex of installations of mass extermination. Crematoria II and III had their own barbed-wire fences. Two gates led to the crematorium II compound and one gate to crematorium III. Trees and bushes planted all around functioned as a natural screen, or "greenbelt" (*Grüngürtel*), that hid them from view by unauthorized persons—above all the prisoners who lived in adjoining barracks. A common fence enclosed crematoria IV and V. The latter was also screened from view by a tall hedge concealing the bodies that were burned outside.[56]

Crematoria II and III were constructed according to nearly identical, symmetrically printed plans. They consisted of three principal parts, two of which were underground—the "dressing room," with an area of 392.45 sq m (49.49 × 7.93), and the gas chamber, 210 sq m (30 × 7). The "dressing room" was 2.3 m high, the gas chamber, 2.4 m high.[57] The third part, the furnace room, was 337.2 sq m (30 × 11.24) and was on the ground floor.

The two underground rooms, designated on camp charts as mortuaries (*Leichenkeller*), were windowless and had to be lit artificially. The ceiling, which was made of reinforced concrete and covered with grass turf, was supported by concrete posts arrayed in a straight line and linked by a bearing beam. According to the original plan, the "undressing room" was to be nearly twice as large as the gas chamber to enable the victims to undress in relatively uncramped conditions. Both the gas chamber and the "dressing room" were mechanically ventilated. The power was supplied by generators in the attic of the crematorium. The outlet of the ventilation shafts was situated above the roof of the crematorium.[58]

Wooden benches were placed along the walls of the "dressing room." Above them were numbered wooden clothes hooks. A narrow passage, about 5 m long, connected the "dressing room" with the gas chamber. The passage ended with a spacious anteroom with an entrance to the gas chamber. The entrance door, 1.92 m high and 1 m wide, was made of two layers of planks with a proofing sheet between them. The edges of the door and the door frame were padded with felt. A circular peephole, made of two glass plates 8 mm thick and air-proofed with rubber gaskets, was mounted in the door at eye level. After several incidents in which the victims trapped inside broke the glass, the peephole was covered with a semi-circular grille on the gas-chamber side. Later the hole was covered with a sheet of iron. The doors were shut by means of iron bolts, which also served as door handles, and secured with screws. The inside walls of the gas chamber were plastered and whitewashed. Electrical installations and lamps were located on both sides of the bearing beam, and perforated plates mounted on wooden blocks were installed beneath the ceiling in imitation of showers. Ventilation shafts were situated where the walls met the ceiling and the floor. The vent of the upper (intake) shaft was covered with perforated sheet iron, whereas the vent of the lower (extraction) shaft was covered with a metal grille.[59]

Zyklon B was distributed in the gas chamber through four introduction columns custom-made in the metalwork shops of the camp. They were shaped like pillars and made of two wire grids with a movable core. Cross sections of the pillars, 3 m high, formed a square, each side measuring 70 cm. Fastened to the floor, they passed through openings in the ceiling, ending outside as little chimneys closed with a concrete cover equipped with two handles. The external grid (made of wire 3 mm thick) formed interstices measuring 45 mm × 45 mm, and was fastened to cube-shaped metal scantlings (cross section 50 mm × 10 mm). Interstices of the external grid—150 mm apart from the internal grid and similarly fastened—were smaller (25 mm × 25 mm). The two grids served as a screen for the movable core that could be introduced through the opening in the ceiling. The core consisted of a tin prism measuring 150 mm × 150 mm at the cross section. The bottom of the core was flat, and the top was a cone. A wire mesh with interstices of one sq mm extended from the base of the core to the base of the cone, and was fastened to a post 25 mm away. The entire length of the core was covered with tin. When Zyklon B pellets fell onto the cone, they spread uniformly throughout the core and stopped in its lower part. After the gas evaporated, the entire core was removed from the gas chamber and the used pellets of diatomite were poured out.[60]

Photographs taken by Allied aircraft in 1944 indicate that the gas introduction columns of crematorium II were arrayed in a straight line, roughly along the longitudinal axis of the gas chamber, whereas in crematorium III they were spaced in pairs on both sides of the axis. This placement was meant to ensure rapid and uniform spread of the poison inside the chamber.

At the end of 1943, each of the gas chambers in both crematoria was divided by a wall, and the passage linking them was closed by a door identical to the entrance door. After that time, smaller transports were led into the back room.[61]

The underground part of the building contained two other rooms in addition to the undressing room and the gas chamber. One was used to store hair, spectacles, and other effects of the murdered victims. The second served as a convenient storage room for Zyklon B pellets. The shaft of the elevator that was used to transport corpses to the furnace room was equipped with doors and adjoined the anteroom. Initially the elevator consisted of a provisional platform (*Plattoaufzug*) that measured 2.76 m in length and 1.43 m in width.

Crematorium II had a second entrance to the anteroom, situated in the angle formed by the undressing room and the gas chamber. In addition to the stairway it housed a special concrete chute (*Rutsche*) through which corpses brought for cremation from the camp were lowered straight down to the elevator shaft.[62]

The furnace room occupied the largest interior space on the ground floor of the crematorium. It housed five furnaces, each with three retorts (about 2 m long, 80 cm wide, and 1 m high) that were used to push the bodies into the furnace. There were two generators of coke gas on the opposite side. The fumes were funneled to a single chimney through flues under the floor. Initially the furnaces of crematorium II were equipped with a forced-draft installation. The draft was produced by three intake ventilators situated between the furnaces and the chimney. Within a short time, however, they burned out. Similar ventilators were not installed in the remaining crematoria.[63]

To the left of the entrance to crematorium II was a room described in the plans as a dissecting room (*Sezierraum*). It was in this room that prisoner-physician Miklos Nyiszli conducted dissections of bodies of twins for SS Dr. Josef Mengele. According to Dr. Nyiszli, a similar room in crematorium III housed a melting pot to melt gold teeth.[64]

In addition, crematoria II and III were equipped with special furnaces for incinerating less-valuable articles, such as personal papers, women's purses, books, and toys, that were found in the luggage of the murdered victims. Incriminating camp documents were also incinerated there, particularly in the last stage of the camp's existence. The furnaces, designated as "garbage incinerators" (*Müllverbrennungsofen*) in the technical plans, were housed in an outbuilding that adjoined the crematorium chimney. The disinfected hair of gassed women was dried in the attic. And in the summer of 1944, Sonderkommando prisoners who serviced the crematoria resided in the attics of crematoria II and III.[65]

Crematoria IV and V were similar to the other two in that they consisted of three basic components: dressing room, gas chamber, and furnace room. But the components were arranged differently. To cut costs, both the gas chamber and the dressing room were on the ground floor instead of underground.[66] The entire structure measured 67.5 m in length and 12.87 m in width (not counting an outbuilding that served as the coke storage room). Near the crematorium entrance were lodgings of Sonderkommando prisoners and a kitchen. To the left of these structures sat three gas chambers: one with an area of 98.19 sq m (11.69 × 8.40); the second 95.34 sq m (12.35 × 7.72), and the third 43.25 sq m (11.69 × 3.70). The combined area of the three gas chambers was 236.78 sq m.[67] Sometime later, the smaller chamber was further divided into two, and gas-proof doors, nearly identical to those in the gas bunkers, were constructed.

In addition to the interior doors, the two largest gas chambers had doors that led directly outside. The doors were used to air the premises and to remove the corpses for cremation in incineration pits. Instead of windows, the exterior walls of the gas chambers had openings 30 cm wide and 40 cm high, which were covered with gas-proof flaps. The preserved original plans indicate that the first chamber had three such openings, the second two, and the remaining smallest chambers one each. Plans provided for the construction of a waste-disposal system in the two largest chambers, as well as heating furnaces to facilitate quicker evaporation of the Zyklon B gas pellets. Although signs reading "Zum Desinfektion" were posted in the chambers, neither automatic ventilators nor dummy showers were installed. The part of the crematorium building that housed the gas chamber was lower and looked like an outbuilding.[68]

A spacious dressing room, covering 245.02 sq m (19.84 × 12.35), lay to the right of the crematorium entrance. Initially, no windows were planned, but preserved photographs taken during the construction phase indicate that ultimately small openings, similar to those in the gas chamber walls, were made in the exterior walls. It cannot be ruled out that this modification was made with a view to the possibility of using the dressing room as a gas chamber in the event that there was an accumulation of transports. Behind the dressing room was an anteroom with a crematorium chimney and further down another room that housed one eight-retort furnace with four coke hearths. Fumes were evacuated through two chimneys by natural draft. Adjoining this room was the office of the crematoria chief, the sanitation office, and the coking plant.[69]

The extermination process and cremation of the corpses in crematoria II and III went as follows. After selection for death, the Jews who could walk were marched from the loading ramp to the crematorium. The weak, the invalid, and the sick were transported on trucks. In the crematorium yard, the SS men told the prisoners that they would undergo a disinfection that consisted of delousing and bathing. The victims were led down the staircase to the dressing room in the basement, where they could see the signs (in German) "To the Baths" and "To Disinfection." Similar signs were posted on a portable board in the native language of the victims.

On the way to the gas chamber some victims were issued a piece of soap and a towel. As a rule, the women and children went in first, followed by the men. Each group was led inside the chamber behind a cordon of SS men that edged toward the door as the chamber filled. With the refractory ones spurred on by blows and dogs, about 2,000 persons on average were crammed inside.

When the chamber was full or the entire transport was inside and the personnel had left (two SS noncommissioned officers always stayed until the end), the doors were shut, the bolts were slid into place, and the screws were tightened. On order of the supervising SS doctor (the job was assigned to, among others, Josef Mengele, Hans König, and Hans Thilo), the SS disinfectors (Scheinmetz, among others) opened the Zyklon B cans and poured their contents into the vents down the induction shafts inside the chamber.

Within several minutes, 20 at most, all the victims were dead. The time required for the gas to take effect depended on various factors that affected the evaporation of the gas: temperature, humidity, the congestion inside the chamber. Whenever the outside air temperature was higher than the inside temperature, the cool air was extracted by ventilators from the chamber before the gas pellets were poured inside. To speed up the evaporation of the poison gas in winter, iron baskets filled with red-hot coke were brought inside. Some unsuccessful attempts were made to heat the chamber interior with heat from the chimney flues.

Höss, who personally observed the killing in the gas chambers, described the process:

> It could be observed through the peephole in the door that those who were standing nearest to the induction vents were killed at once. It can be said that about one-third died straightaway. The remainder staggered about and began to scream and struggle for air. The screaming, however, soon changed to the death rattle and in a few minutes all lay still.[70]

About a half hour after the induction of the gas, the ventilation was turned on, the door was opened, and Sonderkommando prisoners wearing gas masks began dragging the corpses out of the chamber. In cases of great congestion, many of the dead were found half-squatting, their skin colored pink with occasional red or green spots. Some foamed at the mouth, others bled from the ears.

In the gas chamber's anteroom, the bodies were relieved of spectacles and artificial limbs, and the women's hair was cut off. Thereupon the corpses were loaded on the elevator platform and lifted to the ground floor. Some of the corpses were dragged directly to the oven area. Others were moved to the corpse storage room opposite the elevator, which also served as a site of executions by shooting. Just before incineration, Sonderkommando prisoners removed jewelry, which they tossed into a special numbered crate.

Teeth with metal fillings, crowns, and bridges made of gold or other precious metals were extracted from the mouths of the gassed victims and deposited in a crate marked "Zahnstation" (dental station). Sonderkommando prisoners who were dentists by occupation performed this task under SS supervision. The only ones whose mouths were not inspected were children. If in the course of the sporadic inspections it was established that not all gold teeth had been extracted, occasionally the Sonderkommando prisoner guilty of neglect was punished by being thrown alive into the furnace.

It took about four hours to empty the gas chamber. Initially the corpses were delivered to the furnaces on small trolleys that ran on rails, as was done in the main camp. The trolleys also served to load the corpses into the furnace retorts. This arrangement, however, did not last long. On the initiative of the *Kapo* August Bruck, special corpse stretchers, which could be rolled into the retorts, were introduced. To facilitate the loading, the corpse stretchers were lubricated with soapy water. Methods of loading the corpses varied; each team servicing the furnaces had its own technique. For example, H. Tauber's team would put two corpses into one retort two times, then add as many children's corpses as possible to the second load.

It took about 20 minutes to cremate three corpses in one retort. However, in their efforts to reduce the number of loadings, prisoners cremated four to five corpses at one time and extended the cremation time to about 25 to 30 minutes. When the time was up, the next load would be put into the retort, regardless of the degree of incineration of the preceding load. The incompletely incinerated bones fell through the grille into the ash pit, were ground with wooden mortars along with the ashes, then poured into pits near the crematorium. Next they were removed from the pits and poured into the Vistula River or nearby ponds. Sometimes they were used to prepare compost; other times they were used directly to fertilize the fields of the camp farms.

About 2,500 corpses could be cremated in 24 hours in each of crematoria II and III. This rate exceeded the crematoria capacity as calculated by Topf and Sons (1,440) by 43 percent. (Topf assumed that two corpses could be cremated in a half hour.) The excessive overloading caused breakdowns of the furnaces, ventilators, and chimneys.[71]

In the killing process at crematoria IV and V, the prisoners were also brought in cars or were marched to the crematoria, then led to the dressing room. There one of the SS men—the Kommandoführer—would stand on a bench in front of them and explain that the healthy would go to work and the sick and the women and children would remain in the barracks. But first, they would go to the bath.

After undressing, the prisoners were led through the anteroom to the gas chamber. When the chamber was full, the SS guards shut the doors, and one of them, wearing a gas mask, climbed a ladder or a chair. When the SS doctor on duty gave a sign, the SS man would pour Zyklon B pellets into the opening. In the summer of 1944, Mengele served most often as the duty doctor in crematoria IV and V, and Kommandoführer Scheinmetz, who supervised the Sonderkommando work in crematorium V, poured the pellets.

Half an hour later, on orders of the same SS doctor, the gas chamber doors were opened, and the Sonderkommando prisoners, who had been locked up in the coke plant during the gassing, went to work. Wearing gas masks, they dragged the corpses to the hallway, where the women's hair was cut. Next the corpses were transported to the dressing room and stacked in layers. The gas chambers had to be emptied as quickly as possible to make room for the next transport. When it was not possible to remove all the corpses from the dressing room before the next transport arrived, the doomed prisoners undressed outside, behind the hedge that screened crematorium V and the incineration pits from the road.

Yehuda Backon, a survivor who later became a painter in Jerusalem, arrived at Birkenau from the Theresienstadt ghetto when he was 14 years old, in 1943. He came into contact with Sonderkommando prisoners while he was at Birkenau and later testified in the Eichmann trial.

Presiding judge: Describe the drawing [made close to the time of liberation, and accepted as an exhibit by the court].

Answer: Here is crematorium number 2, the modern one. Numbers 1 and 2 were identical. Numbers 3 and 4 were somewhat less modern. Lodgings of the Sonderkommando men, forced to live there, were at the top.

Presiding judge: Inside the building?

A: In the fall of 1944 they had to live inside the crematorium, here on top, while some were put up in the gas chambers of crematoria nos. 3 and 4.

Presiding judge: In the attic?

A: In crematoria 1 and 2, and in crematoria 3 and 4, they lived right inside the gas chambers.

Presiding judge: It had windows, as shown in your drawing?

A: These were "corridors" of the prisoners. Windows were in the lower part, this was the place where the corpses were burned, and the place where they undressed. In crematoria 1 and 2, the gas chambers were underground. People descended several stairs, then had to undress. I recall that Sonderkommando men related, they wanted to tell everything, and I told them that perhaps I would be able to tell the story. So they told me everything in detail. When a transport arrived, they had to climb down. Outside were signs "Baths" and "Sauna." Then they were brought to *Entkleidungskammer* [dressing room]. To the side there were benches and clothes hooks with numbers. Sometimes men and women entered separately, and on other occasions, when time was short, they entered together. They had to undress and the SS man told them: "Remember your clothes hook number, put the clothes in one pile so that you'll get them back on the other side." People asked for water, as they were very thirsty after a long journey in sealed train cars. They were told: "Well, hurry up, coffee is waiting for you in the camp, and it's getting cold," and other such reassuring remarks, to calm them. Naked, they had to move on, on the left-hand side, to the gas chambers. In crematoria 1 and 2 there were two rooms of the gas chambers next to the Entkleidungskammer. In addition, there was another structure called *Rutschbahn* [chute] for people with artificial limbs who could not walk on their own, with a slide which brought them straight to the dressing rooms close to the gas chambers. In crematoria 1 and 2 there was a very long room divided into two, because sometimes there were not enough people, and to save the gas, they were brought only inside one part of the room.[72]

The corpses stacked up in the dressing room were removed to a narrow room, where Sonderkommando prisoners extracted dentures, crowns, bridges, etc., made of gold and precious metals; removed jewelry that had not been taken during the undressing; and brought the corpses to the cremation furnaces.

Servicing the furnaces and the cremation process in crematoria IV and V did not differ significantly from the practices followed in the two other crematoria. According to the Zentralbauleitung letter, given the normal pace of cremation (half an hour for two corpses in one retort), each crematorium could incinerate 768 corpses in 24 hours. However, Sonderkommando prisoners testified that up to 1,500 corpses were burned in 24 hours (three to five within 20 to 30 minutes).

Furnace overload caused frequent breakdowns. For example, in the initial stages of the extermination of Hungarian Jews, crematorium V had to be shut down due to a breakdown of the chimneys. As a result, some bodies were incinerated in crematorium IV. The remainder were burned at the rate of about 5,000 corpses in 24 hours in the incineration pits near the crematoria. The same number were incinerated in the pits of bunker 2, which was reactivated in the spring of 1944.

Thus in the summer of 1944, the combined capacity of all the incineration installations reached the staggering number of 20,000 victims. A few months later, in light of Germany's deteriorating situation on the war fronts, and possibly in connection with negotiations launched on Himmler's instructions, gassing of prisoners was discontinued. The last victims to undergo selection was a transport from Theresienstadt, which arrived at Auschwitz on October 30, 1944. The next transport, from Sered, which arrived on November 3, 1944, was registered in the camp in its entirety.[73]

Three weeks later, on November 25, 1944, Himmler ordered the demolition of the Auschwitz gas chambers and crematoria. The same day, work began on dismantling the installations of crematorium II at Birkenau. After the furnace, the chimneys, the roof, and all the installations in the walls of the crematorium building were taken apart, openings were made for dynamite charges to blow up the entire structure. In connection with the halt in the influx of mass transports, a quarantine camp for male prisoners (BIIa) was liquidated on November 3.[74]

Among others, 70 Sonderkommando prisoners worked to liquidate the installations of mass murder. In addition, two special women's labor squads were formed. On December 1, 1944, a special group, initially comprising 100 women prisoners, began dismantling crematorium III. On December 5, 50 more women were incorporated into the squad. At the same time, another squad of 50 women was formed. Its task was to remove the ashes from the incineration pits, fill them in, and cover them with turf.[75]

About the same time, work was completed on dismantling the remains of crematorium IV, which had been burned during a Sonderkommando revolt, and on bunker 2 and the nearby barracks that had served as dressing rooms.[76]

On January 20, 1945, an SS detachment that had been dispatched to Auschwitz shot about 200 Jewish women prisoners and ordered another group of prisoners to move crates with dynamite to crematoria II and III. Both buildings were blown up the same day. Crematorium V, the last to remain in operation, as late as January, was blown up on January 26, 1945, one day before the liberation of the camp.

There was no time to remove the ruins of the destroyed installations, so the Nazis were only partially successful in obliterating the traces of their crimes. The walls and floors and the underground dressing rooms and gas chambers of crematoria II and III remained relatively intact.

The rails built into the floor of the furnace room are clearly visible, and parts of the walls also have been preserved. Some of the furnace parts of crematorium V have been preserved. The furnaces of the other crematoria were dismantled and removed before the buildings were blown up. Assorted metal furnace parts were found on the grounds of the camp farmsteads (bunkers 1 and 2). . . .

More than one million persons were murdered in the gas chambers of Auschwitz-Birkenau. Murder on such a large scale could not have been accomplished without the installations described in this essay. Preserved camp records and witness accounts, some of which were used in this study, allow one to reconstruct with relative precision the technical aspects of the process of mass murder.[77]

QUESTIONS FOR DISCUSSION

1. Why was the initial location for the gassing of prisoners—the cellars of block 11—inappropriate for the mass killings planned by the Nazi hierarchy?
2. Why is the conversion of crematoria I at Auschwitz from an incineration building to a combination of gas chamber and incineration complex important for an understanding of the mass killings of the Holocaust?
3. Consider the differences between the killings at the provisional gas chambers—the red and white bunkers—and the killings at the new gas chambers and crematoria, numbers II, III, IV, and V, at Birkenau. Why were the new units needed by the Nazis?
4. The cremation of dead bodies is not, by itself, an evil practice. Consider what aspects of the Nazi cremation procedure made it evil.
5. Piper refers to the fact that Allied aerial photographs clearly show the gas introduction columns on the roofs of crematoria II and III. What does this make you think about the knowledge of the Allied forces about the killing operations at Auschwitz-Birkenau? Why did the Allies not bomb the death camps to prevent (or slow down) the killing?

NOTES

1. Rudolf Höss, *Commandant of Auschwitz* (London, 1961), p. 206.
2. According to Raul Hilberg, Himmler took the decision to use gas chambers in the east and in the killing centers on the advice of the chief physician of the SS, Dr. Grawitz; see Hilberg, *The Destruction of the European Jews* (Chicago, 1961), p. 562.
3. Höss, p. 206.
4. Ibid., p. 207.
5. These automobiles were sealed vans into which exhaust fumes were piped. This particular killing method was invented by Oberdienstleiter Victor Brack of the main party Chancellery of Adolf Hitler. In September 1941,

the Einsatzkommando, headed by Standartenführer Paul Blobel, used such vans in the Ukraine. From December 1941 on, similar mobile gas chambers operated in the death camp at Chelmno on Ner and in Semlina, Serbia. See Hilberg, p. 561; Gerald Reitlinger, *The Final Solution* (London, 1971), pp. 145–46; Artur Eisenbach, *The Nazi Policy of Extermination of Jews* (in Polish) (Warsaw, 1961), p. 274.

6. Danuta Czech, *Kalendarium der Ereignisse im Konzentrationslager Auschwitz-Birkenau 1939–1945* (Reinbek bei Hamburg, 1989), pp. 116–19. Among testimonies touching on this issue that were given during the trial of Höss and members of the Auschwitz personnel, particularly noteworthy are testimonies of former prisoners who on orders of the SS took part in various activities in connection with preparing rooms in block 11, selection of the sick, and removal of corpses (Marian Dybus, Wladyslaw Fejkiel, Wladyslaw Tondos, Bogdan Glinski, Marian Przeda): Archives of the Auschwitz-Birkenau State Museum (ASAM), collection Trial of Höss, vol. 4, card 156, vol. 27, card 107, vol. 4, card 176, vol. 27, cards 72–73; collection Trial of Auschwitz personnel, vol. 54, cards 211, 134. See also collection Statements, vol. 32, cards 81–86, vol. 67, card 57, accounts by Konrad Szweda and Adam Szczerbowski. See also a study by Stanislaw Klodzinski, "The First Gassing of Prisoners and POWs in the Auschwitz Camp" (in Polish), in *Przeglad Lekarski-Oswiecim* (1972), p. 80, where the author discusses and summarizes findings of a questionnaire dealing with this event, administered by him to several hundred subjects.

7. "The Auschwitz Concentration Camp in Light of the Documents of Delegatura (Representation) of the Republic of Poland in the Country" (in Polish), *Zeszyty Oswiecimskie,* special issue no. 1 (1968), pp. 13–14. Other references are on pp. 11 and 14. See also materials of the camp underground, ASAM, collection Underground materials, vol. 5b, card 363.

8. Höss, p. 209.

9. ASAM, Trial of Höss, vol. 11, card 23.

10. The date has been established by this author on the basis of an entry in the personal file of prisoner Waclaw Lipka. The entry says that from September 1940 on, the latter worked as a stoker in the crematorium.

11. Jean-Claude Pressac, *Auschwitz: Technique and Operation of the Gas Chambers* (New York, 1989), pp. 151, 159.

12. ASAM, collection Bauleitung, BW 30/42/card 2, letter from the Zentralbauleitung to Kammler, June 28, 1943. The Polish Commission for the Investigation of Nazi Crimes determined that the capacity of crematorium I was 350 corpses in 14 hours; ASAM, PH, vol. 11, card 24.

13. *Amidst a Nightmare of Crime: Notes of Prisoners of Sonderkommando Found at Auschwitz* (Oswiecim, 1973), p. 47; testimony of Jankowski-Feinsilber, ASAM, Mauthausen files, entries in employment files of prisoners Jozef Ilczuk and Waclaw Lipka.

14. Jan Sehn, *Concentration Camp Oswiecim-Brzesinka* (Warsaw, 1957), p. 152. Plan no. 4287, "Ausbau des Alten Krematorium: Luftschutzbunker für SS-Revier mit einem Operationsraum," dated September 21, 1944, ASAM, collection Bauleitung; Pressac, p. 156.

15. According to D. Czech, this occurred as early as September 1941; see *KL Auschwitz, as Seen by the SS: Höss, Broad, Kremer* (Oswiecim, 1978), p. 45, n. 45. According to former prisoner Badenitz, gassing in crematorium I commenced in September 1941; ASAM, Trial of Höss, vol. 16, card 89. According to former SS man Stark, the chamber was brought into operation in the fall of 1941.

16. The openings were made by prisoner Sulkowski; ASAM, collection Statements, vol. 74, card 74. When crematorium I was converted into an air-raid shelter, the openings were bricked up. The surviving fragments allowed the reconstruction of four openings after the war. Broad and Müller claimed that there were six such openings. See ibid., vol. 96, card 60, account by former prisoner Adam Zlobnicki; Filip Müller, *Eyewitness Auschwitz: Three Years in the Gas Chambers* (New York, 1979), p. 38; *KL Auschwitz*, p. 157 (Broad).

17. Prisoner Michal Kula was employed in installing the ventilator; ASAM, Trial of Höss, vol. 25, cards 17–18.

18. Former prisoner Koczorowski, who had access to the plans of crematorium I, testified that the gas chamber was designated as a mortuary (*Leichenhalle*) for 600 persons; ibid., vol. 4, card 32. According to Filip Müller, over 700 persons could be accommodated inside. Höss spoke about 900 Soviet POWs crammed inside, whereas former prisoner Halgas stated that groups of 1,000 people were gassed there; see Müller, p. 44; Höss, p. 164.

19. Höss, p. 164.

20. Former prisoner Kula witnessed the chasing of 300 prisoners to the crematorium; ASAM, Trial of Höss, vol. 25, cards 17–18; testimony of M. Kula, collection Statements, vol. 98, card 239. According to Halgas, at least 5,000 to 6,000 Soviet POWs were gassed in the mortuary of crematorium I; ibid., account by former prisoner Kazimier Halgas.

21. Ibid., vol. 4, card 21, testimony of former prisoner J. Krokowski.

22. *KL Auschwitz*, pp. 173–74 (Broad).

23. Czech, *Kalendarium*, p. 349, quotes the figure of 300 prisoners, whereas Jankowski-Feinsilber (*Amidst a Nightmare*, pp. 45–46) mentions 390.

24. Müller, p. 51. According to Pressac, p. 132, no more than 10,000 persons were gassed in this chamber. Broad resorts to generalities: "One transport after another disappeared in the Auschwitz crematorium every day. More and more victims kept coming in," *KL Auschwitz*, p. 175 (Broad). On the part played by crematorium I in the machinery of extermination, see also Georges Wellers, "The Existence of Gas Chambers," in *The Holocaust and the Neo-Nazi Mythomania* (New York, 1978), p. 110.

25. Insufficient source material does not allow us to determine the exact date of bringing bunker 1 into operation. According to Czech (*Kalendarium*, p. 161), it became operative in early spring 1942. This is confirmed by Höss, p. 209.

26. According to Czech, *Kalendarium*, p. 239, bunker 2 was launched on June 30, 1942; according to Höss, p. 211, it was in the summer of 1942. In any event, launching of bunker 2 took place before the inspection visit of Himmler on July 17–18, 1942.

27. Measurements on the basis of cadastral survey. We may conclude that the total area of the building was 93.5 sq m. Assuming that the walls covered approximately 10 sq m, we estimate that the area of both interior rooms was about 83 m; ASAM, negative no. 21416/7.

28. Ibid., collection Statements, vol. 70, card 51, vol. 113, cards 77–78, accounts of Franciszek Gulba and Jozefa Wisinska; Trial of Höss, vol. 11, cards 105–17, vol. 24, card 217, testimony of Shlomo Dragon; Höss, p. 211; *KL Auschwitz*, pp. 175–81 (Broad).

29. The total area of the building was 142.36 sq m. The combined area of the four interior rooms was 105 sq m. These figures were computed on the basis of the findings of the survey of the foundations, July 29, 1985; ASAM, call no. DP-Z.Bau 2044/Bw 2/5/53.

30. Ibid., Trial of Höss, vol. 11, cards 103–5, testimony of Shlomo Dragon.

31. Ibid., card 105, vol. 24, card 220, testimony of Shlomo Dragon and Wilhelm Wohlfarth; Höss, p. 210; *KL Auschwitz*, pp. 175–81 (Broad).

32. Höss, p. 208. Given the density of 10 persons per one sq m, bunker 1 could accommodate about 830 persons.

33. Following Dragon, Sehn estimated the combined capacity of the two bunkers at 2,000 persons. However, in view of the size of both buildings, this appears to be an overestimate. The capacity of 1,200 given by Höss is corroborated by, among others, an entry in Johann Kremer's diary dated October 12, 1942, concerning the gassing in bunker 2 of the entire transport from the Netherlands (of the total of 1,703 victims in this transport—Kremer quotes the figure of 1,600—1,251 were sent to the gas chamber); *KL Auschwitz*, p. 222; Höss, p. 211. Assuming the density of 10 persons per sq m, the chamber could contain 1,050 persons.

34. *KL Auschwitz*, pp. 212–13.

35. ASAM, Trial of Höss, vol. 4, card 74; vol. 11, cards 30, 103–6; vol. 17, card 142; vol. 21, cards 4–5; vol. 28, cards 45–47, testimonies of Reinhold Puchala, Shlomo Dragon, Wlodzimierz Bilan, Rudolf Höss, Arnost Rosin, as well as conclusions of the commission investigating the Nazi crimes in Auschwitz; see also ibid., Trial of the Auschwitz personnel, vol. 44, cards 240–46, vol. 55, card 240, testimonies of Erich Merbach and Marian Przad.

36. Höss, p. 21.

37. Höss wrote that this took place late in the summer of 1942. That year, similar operations of liquidation of mass graves were carried out in the killing centers at Chelmno, Treblinka, Sobibor, and Belzec. In every one of these locations, the practice of burying the bodies was replaced by cremation outdoors. See Höss, p. 211; ASAM, Trial of Höss, vol. 11, card 100, testimony of Michal Kula.

38. At that time, this chamber also was referred to as bunker 5, *KL Auschwitz*, p. 184 (Broad); Höss, p. 216; ASAM, Trial of Höss, vol. 6, card 35, testimony of Otton Wolken; vol. 4, card 73, testimony of Jozef Plaskura.

39. In 1965, Hydrokop, a chemical mining technical enterprise based in Krakow, was commissioned by the Auschwitz-Birkenau State Museum to carry out geological tests at Birkenau aimed at determining the locations of incineration pits and pyres. Specialists of Hydrokop bored 303 holes up to

3 m deep. Traces of human ashes, bones, and hair turned up in 42 sites. Documentation of all the holes and the diagrams of their distribution are preserved in the Conservation Department of the museum.

40. The exact dates of the drafting of the project and of its original version are not known. We have only an annotation to the preliminary version, dated Auschwitz, October 31, 1941 (*Erläuterungsbericht zur Vorentwurf*), ASAM, microfilm 1034, cards 1–17.

41. This figure is quoted in ibid., cards 4, 7.

42. When annotations to the preliminary project were drafted, i.e., by late October 1941, the conception of the purpose and outfitting of this crematorium had lost its relevance. The Bauleitung's letter of commission, dated October 22, 1941, which was sent to the furnace builder, Topf and Sons, indicates that not one but two underground mortuaries were planned for construction near the crematorium. See ASAM collection Bauleitung, BW 30/34, card 116.

43. In a Bauleitung letter of March 6, 1943, mortuary 2 was referred to as "undressing room" (*Auskleideraum*). In another letter, one of the underground mortuaries was designated as "gas cellar" (*Vergasungskeller*); ASAM, Trial of Höss, vol. 11, card 9; microfilm 1060, card 100. Höss, p. 215, confirms that the underground spaces at crematoria II and III served as undressing rooms and gas chambers and were outfitted with an automatic ventilation system.

44. ASAM, collection Bauleitung, BW 30/34, card 116.

45. Ibid., BW 30/25, Bischoff to Topf and Sons, March 5, 1942, BW 30/34, card 37, Bischoff to Amt C III, March 30, 1942; BW 30/34, card 35, Amt C III to Topf and Sons. In a letter to Zentralbauleitung of March 2, 1942, Oswald Pohl approved the construction in 1942 of a crematorium at Birkenau; see *Trials of War Criminals before the Nuremberg Military Tribunals,* vol. 5 (Washington, D.C., 1950), pp. 612–13, Nuremberg Document NO-4464.

46. Ibid., collection Zentralbauleitung, BW 30/4–6.

47. Ibid., call no. D.-Z.bau/6.

48. Ibid., collection Zentralbauleitung, BW 30/26, cards 1–20, the Huta firm to Zentralbauleitung, July 13, 1942. The sum of 133,741.65 marks is mentioned therein; later this figure was revised; ASAM, call no. D.-Z.bau/6, inventory no. 29754.

49. On July 29, 1942, Zentralbauleitung acknowledged in writing receipt of the offer, ibid., collection Zentralbauleitung, BW 30/26.

50. Ibid., collection Bauleitung, BW 30/34, card 114, Topf and Sons to Zentralbauleitung, September 30, 1942; BW 30/34, card 113, Topf and Sons to Zentralbauleitung, October 31, 1942. On August 20, 1942, Zentralbauleitung offered to the Köhler firm of Myslowice to submit tender for bricklaying work in the construction of chimneys to crematoria IV and V. Tenders were to be opened on August 30, 1942; BW 30/26, cards 52–53.

51. Ibid., collection Zentralbauleitung, BW 30/34, card 48, Zentralbauleitung to Topf and Sons, cable of February 26, 1943.

52. Ibid., collection Bauleitung, BW 30/34, cards 1–101, Prüfer to Zentralbauleitung, January 29, 1943, report on the results of inspection of the con-

struction of crematoria in Birkenau. Crematorium II was scheduled to be brought into operation on February 15, 1943; crematorium III, on April 17, 1943; crematorium IV, on February 28, 1943. The date of launching of crematorium V was made contingent on the weather.

53. Ibid., BW 1, file 73 (unnumbered pages), document entitled "Aufstellung der Bereits übergebenen Bauwerke die Standortverwaltung." June 25, 1943, was mentioned as the date of delivery of crematorium III, whereas in the letter from Zentralbauleitung to Kammler, dated June 28, 1943, the date was June 26; ibid., BW 30/42, card 2.

54. Ibid., BW 30/42, card 2.

55. Höss, p. 224, confirms the existence of this practice. In contrast, Tauber maintains that Sonderkommando prisoners were under orders to load no more than three corpses every half hour. If we accept Höss's contention that the cremation of one load of corpses lasted 20 minutes and every second load consisted of two corpses only, the number of corpses incinerated in crematoria II and III would reach 2,700 in each and in crematoria IV and V 1,440 in each, yielding a total of 8,280. Höss, however, wrote that 2,000 corpses each were cremated in crematoria II and III and 1,500 each in crematoria IV and V, giving the total of 7,000 corpses cremated in 24 hours. See ASAM, Trial of Höss, vol. 11, card 135, testimony of Tauber; Höss, pp. 215, 216.

56. ASAM, Trial of Höss, vol. 11, card 67; Nuremberg Document NO-4463; Zentralbauleitung to Ceasar, November 6, 1943, concerning the supply of 1,600 tree and bush seedlings for a hedge, which would screen crematoria II and III from view ("Grüngürtel als naturlicher Abschluss zum Lager"); collection Statements, vol. 113, card 5, account of former prisoner Alter Fajnzylberg alias Feinsilber; Trial of Höss, vol. 11, card 65a, an official note drafted in connection with Pohl's visit to Auschwitz on June 16, 1944. Pohl approved, among other things, the planting of a second hedge around the crematoria and camouflaging them by means of rough mats ("Die Tarnung durch Rohmatte"); see *KL Auschwitz*, documentary photographs, no. 166.

57. Measurements quoted from plan no. 933, dated January 19, 1942; ASAM, collection Bauleitung, BW 30/2. See also Trial of Höss, vol. 11, card 36, protocol.

58. The ventilation system does not figure in the undressing room plans. Its installation is indicated in the preserved correspondence dealing with construction of the crematoria; Pressac, pp. 355–78.

59. ASAM, Trial of Höss, vol. 2, card 100; vol. 11, cards 128–30; vol. 21, card 6, testimony of Michal Kula; Protocol, testimonies of H. Tauber and R. Höss; collection Statements, vol. 49, card 81, testimony of former prisoner Szwemberg, who worked in laying electric installations in the gas chambers.

60. Ibid., Trial of Höss, vol. 2, cards 99–101; vol. 11, cards 116, 130; vol. 25, card 33, testimony of former prisoner Michal Kula, employed at metalwork shop where the wire-grid shafts were manufactured; see also testimony of Shlomo Dragon and H. Tauber.

61. Ibid., vol. 11, cards 128–30, testimony of H. Tauber; collection Statements, vol. 94, card 33, testimony of Wladyslaw Girsa.

62. Ibid., Trial of Höss, vol. 11, cards 36–37; Survey protocol, vol. 11, card 128, testimony of H. Tauber.
63. Ibid., cards 32, 133; Protocol, testimony of H. Tauber.
64. Miklos Nyiszli, *Auschwitz: A Doctor's Eyewitness Account* (New York, 1960), p. 72.
65. ASAM, Trial of Höss, vol. 11, cards 34, 133; Survey protocol, testimony of H. Tauber; Nyiszli, p. 43.
66. Höss, p. 217.
67. ASAM, Trial of Höss, vol. 11, card 40; Survey protocol.
68. The description is based on accounts by two former Sonderkommando prisoners employed in crematoria IV and V, Shlomo Dragon and Alter Feinsilber, on conclusions of the Polish prosecuting bodies; and on plans, photographs, and the preserved foundations. Ibid., cards 40, 108; Survey protocol, testimony of Shlomo Dragon; collection Statements, vol. 113, cards 4–5, testimony of former prisoner Alter Fajnzylberg alias Feinsilber.
69. Ibid.
70. Höss, pp. 223, 224. ASAM, Trial of Höss, vol. 11, cards 45–46, 136–37; vol. 21, card 7. Survey protocol, testimony of H. Tauber; testimony of Höss, March 14, 1946; Nyiszli, pp. 50–51.
71. ASAM, Trial of Höss, vol. 11, cards 47, 131–39; vol. 45, card 128; Survey protocol; testimony of former prisoners H. Tauber and K. Markus. According to Tauber, 2,500 corpses were incinerated in crematoria II and III each, whereas Höss, pp. 215–16, gives a lower estimate of 2,000.
72. Trial of Eichmann, testimonies (in Hebrew), vol. 2 (Jerusalem, 1963), pp. 114–15.
73. According to H. G. Adler, gassings in Auschwitz were discontinued on November 2, 1944; Adler, *Theresienstadt 1941–1945* (Tübingen, 1955), p. 694.
74. According to the testimony of the leader of the Hungarian Zionists, Rezso Kastner, a copy of the order to demolish gas chambers and crematoria, shown to him by Himmler's associate Kurt Becher, bore the date November 25, 1944. This date is borne out by an annotation in a manuscript by an anonymous author, a prisoner and Sonderkommando, to the effect that dismantling of crematorium II commenced on November 25. In contrast, Adler, p. 694, accepts the date of November 26. See also Ota Kraus and Erich Kulka, *Die Todesfabrik* (Berlin 1957), p. 229; R. L. Braham, *The Destruction of Hungarian Jewry* (New York, 1963), pp. 919, 920; testimony given by Kastner in London on September 13, 1945, ASAM, call no. D-AuII-3/1, card 8, Quarantane-Liste; ibid., Trial of Höss, vol. 22, card 81, indictment.
75. Czech, *Kalendarium,* pp. 940, 941, 952. Until December 12, 1944, the size of the labor squad of women prisoners employed in dismantling of crematorium III remained unchanged.
76. An anonymous author wrote in notes found after the liberation of the camp: "Dismantling of the walls of crematorium IV commenced on October 14, 1944. The job is done by prisoners of Sonderkommando. Today, November 25, they began dismantling crematorium II, and crematorium III is next. Interestingly, the first to be dismantled is the ventilation motor and pipes, which are sent to other camps—some to Mauthausen, others to Gross-

Rosen. Since this is used to gas human beings on a large scale—no such mechanisms existed at all in crematoria IV and V—one is led to believe that identical sites for exterminating Jews will be established on the grounds of those camps," *Amidst a Nightmare,* pp. 120–22. The transfer of the ventilation system from Auschwitz to Mauthausen is confirmed by Hans Marsalek, although we have no information about elements of the cremation furnaces themselves. In his study of the Gross-Rosen camp, Mieczyslaw Moldawa wrote that the furnaces got bogged down at some point en route and did not reach the camp. See Marsalek, *Die Geschichte des Kozentrationslager Mauthausen: Dokumentation* (Vienna, 1974), p. 162; Moldawa, *Gross-Rosen: A Concentration Camp in Silesia* (in Polish) (Warsaw, 1979), p. 33; Andrzej Strzelecki, *Evacuation, Liquidation, and Liberation of KL Auschwitz* (in Polish) (Oswiecim, 1982), pp. 125–26, 135–36, 202.

77. One attempt undertaken by neo-Nazi apologists in the late 1980s to cast doubt on the existence of installations of mass murder is the so-called Leuchter Report. Its main argument, allegedly refuting the fact that prussic acid was used in gas chambers, is that the amounts of prussic acid compounds found on the walls of the gas chambers were negligible compared to those found in disinfection chambers. The author of this report completely ignores the facts explaining these differences: in gas chambers, the amount of prussic acid used was reduced to the minimum needed to kill the victims; the time during which different gas chambers were in use; the state in which various installations were preserved (with the exception of the gas chamber of crematorium I, used sporadically for one year, ruins of the remaining chambers were exposed to changing weather throughout the postwar period).

CHAPTER 3

Engineering Mass Murder at Auschwitz

─────────── ❡ ───────────

In this chapter historical scholar Jean-Claude Pressac and professor of architecture Robert Jan van Pelt tell the story of the invention, design, and modification of the various crematoria furnaces and gas chamber buildings that were employed in the killing operations at Auschwitz and Birkenau. Pressac originally published his findings in 1989, but after the fall of the Iron Curtain of the Soviet Union in that year, more detailed records of the design of Auschwitz-Birkenau were released. After 1991, van Pelt collaborated with Pressac to revise the history of the engineering and architectural process of the camp. It is a history filled with the details of engineering and architectural design, as well as the mundane activities of engineering firms as they cost out and receive payments for their work. The principal engineering company that built the furnaces for Auschwitz was Topf and Sons, and the engineer in charge of most of the design and construction was Kurt Prüfer. Prüfer worked with Karl Bischoff, the SS officer who oversaw all construction at the Auschwitz-Birkenau concentration camp. Because of the release of important documents that were hidden in the Soviet Union until 1990, Pressac and van Pelt are able to reconstruct virtually the daily operations of Topf and Sons and the SS as they revise and develop their plans for the camps. The engineering and architectural records present indisputable proof of the planned extermination of the Jewish people in Europe, as well as fascinating details about the technical problems the engineers faced in the creation and operation of the killing apparatus. It is clear that engineering skills were essential to the implementation of the Final Solution; to a certain extent we can conclude that the success or failure of the Holocaust rested on the capacity and functionality of the crematoria furnaces.

From "The Machinery of Mass Murder at Auschwitz"

Jean-Claude Pressac
with
Robert Jan van Pelt

THE DESIGN, CONSTRUCTION, USE, MODIFICATIONS, AND DESTRUCTION OF THE CREMATORIA AND GAS CHAMBERS OF THE AUSCHWITZ/BIRKENAU CONCENTRATION CAMPS

This essay presents the history of the instruments of extermination employed by the Germans against Jews and others at Auschwitz-Birkenau. It is based on ten years' study of the archives of the architectural and construction office of the Nazi Schutzstaffel (SS), which built the camps at Auschwitz. Two-thirds of these archives survive in Moscow. Taken by the Soviet Army in 1945, they were unavailable for study until the demise of the Soviet Union. The rest remain at Auschwitz, as part of the holdings of the Auschwitz-Birkenau State Museum....

In 1928, two engineers from Hamburg, Hans Volckmann and Karl Ludwig, applied for a patent for a new kind of incinerating furnace to be used for cremation.[1] Until then, a standard incineration furnace had a core that consisted of a crucible, or muffle, which took in the coffin, and a burner. Added to this core was an economizer, which retrieved heat from the combustion gasses to channel it through a complex heat exchanger back into the crucible. The economizer made it possible to shut off the burner at an early stage of the incineration process and continue it with the energy already absorbed into the furnace. Yet there was one problem: though the economizer saved on fuel, it was expensive to construct. The complex system of overlapping circuits sometimes took up as much as two-thirds of the total mass of the furnace. Volckmann and Ludwig aimed to slash the prevailing prices by replacing the cumbersome economizer with a cheaper system based on the introduction of compressed cold air into the crucible.

The patent did not bring the expected riches, and by the end of 1934, Volckmann and Ludwig's system had disappeared from the German market. But another company was able to capitalize on the idea. Kurt Prüfer, an engineer in the small department of crematorium construction of the reputable Erfurt firm of Topf and Sons, famous for its industrial blast furnaces, adapted Volckmann and Ludwig's idea, and in 1935, Topf installed in various German crematoria seven gas-heated furnaces without an economizer that used compressed air instead.[2]

Topf's crematorium furnaces had acquired a good reputation when, in 1937, a new market opened. In May, the SS leadership in Munich decided to build a crematorium in the concentration camp at Dachau and invited bids for a furnace. Until that year, Nazi concentration camps had used the crematoria of the nearest towns to incinerate the remains of prisoners who died in the camps. Yet at times that created inopportune publicity; also, the mortality rate in the camps sometimes exceeded the limited capacity of the civilian crematoria.

A response to the SS invitation came from Walter Müller of Allach, a firm that had a proven record with the Munich SS, as it had built the central heating system for the local SS barracks and the SS training camp at Dachau. Müller proposed to construct a single-muffle furnace without an economizer and with a compressed-air device. . . .

Müller claimed that there was a direct relation between increased use and increased economy. If the cold furnace required 175 kilograms (kg) of coke to start up a new incineration, it needed only 100 kg if it had been used the day before; a second and third incineration on the same day would not require any extra fuel, thanks to the compressed air; and those that followed would call for only small amounts of extra energy. . . .[3]

In spring 1939, the issue of the crematoria acquired new urgency. By that time, a new office in Berlin had taken control of SS construction activities in the concentration camps. This Central SS Office of Budget and Building (SS-Hauptamt Haushalt und Bauten, or SS-HHB), with the resources to finance and service the building and operation of crematoria, awarded Topf and Sons the Dachau contract because Prüfer realized that a concentration camp didn't need an indestructible civilian furnace embellished with a marble neo-Grecian pediment, as Müller had proposed. Instead, Prüfer proposed a stripped-down mobile furnace with two incinerating muffles, a fuel oil burner, a system to blow compressed air into the muffles, and forced draft. Its estimated yield was two corpses

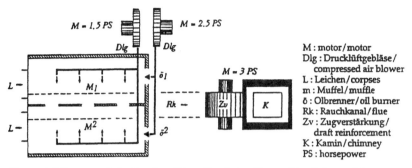

Figure 1. Diagram of the Topf and Sons fixed, double-muffle oil-heated furnace, installed at Buchenwald. Unless otherwise noted, all diagrams were prepared from drawings © Jean-Claude Pressac.

an hour.[4] The SS-HHB accepted this simple, efficient model, which at 8,750 RM (1992: $35,000) was modestly priced.[5]

The furnace was in operation at Dachau by the end of 1939, when Prüfer received an order from the Buchenwald concentration camp. Camp authorities there had first raised the need to install a crematorium in June 1938.[6] Close to Erfurt, Buchenwald now became Prüfer's preserve, the testing ground for two of his furnace models.

The first model (figure 1) was a fixed version of the mobile model at Dachau. Its base price, 7,753 RM (1992: $31,000), was cheaper than the furnace at Dachau. The discount was possible because its construction on the spot in Buchenwald made it possible to use prisoner labor, which the SS furnished at no cost to the company. The SS also provided certain materials, such as cement, lime, sand, and bricks, at no charge. Added to the base price, however, was an extra 1,250 RM (1992: $6,000) for a reinforced draft in the chimney.[7]

By the time Topf began construction of the Dachau furnace, Poland had been carved up between Germany and the Soviet Union. Germany not only recovered its pre-1919 eastern territories but also annexed additional land that before the First World War had belonged to Russian and Austrian Poland. This strip of land included the town of Oswiecim, or Auschwitz, as the Germans knew it. The town of 12,000 inhabitants was located at an important railway junction, allowing easy communication with Berlin, Warsaw, Lwow (Lemberg), and Vienna. And in its suburb of Zasole stood 22 sturdy Polish army barracks, deserted since the end of hostilities.

In early 1940, the SS decided to install in the former army base a camp for quarantining 10,000 Polish prisoners. The camp was to have its own incinerating furnace. The SS-HHB requested Topf to submit estimates for a mobile, double-muffle oil-heated furnace at Auschwitz and for one at the concentration camp of Flossenburg. In March, the

SS-HHB gave Topf the order to produce the two furnaces for 9,000 RM (1992: $36,000) each. . . .[8]

On May 10, 1940, German armed forces attacked the Low Countries and France, and gasoline, petroleum, and fuel oil were rationed in Germany. Because all the furnaces in the concentration camps had oil burners, it was likely that the crematoria would now face shortages. . . .

At the end of May, the Auschwitz Neubauleitung (New Construction Administration) communicated to Topf that the mobile furnace it had on order should use coke.[9] Prüfer decided not to tamper with the mobile model, which could not be so easily adapted, but instead to redesign the fixed, double-muffle furnace supplied earlier to Buchenwald. Both Auschwitz and Flossenburg went along with the modification, which added two external coke burners on both sides of the underground flue that linked the furnace to the smokestack.[10]

As Prüfer was remodeling the Buchenwald furnace, the Auschwitz Neubauleitung began on June 28 to adapt an old powder magazine on the former army base into a shell for the new crematorium. Wilhelm Koch and another overseer from Topf arrived at the site on July 5. They decided to rotate the furnace 90 degrees in relation to the underground flue in order to obtain the most efficient use of the available space. Twenty days later, the furnace was installed at Auschwitz.

Equipped with an electric forced-draft fan capable of removing 4,000 cubic meters (cu m) of smoke an hour and fitted with an electric blower to inject blasts of cold air into the crucibles, the furnace was 50 percent more powerful than the Dachau model of 1939.[11] Fritz Sander and Paul Erdmann, Prüfer's superiors at Topf, estimated an output of 30 to 36 bodies in 10 hours, or about 70 bodies for a 20-hour cycle.[12] The furnace required three hours of maintenance a day. Yet the furnace could not yet be tested. The Bauleitung had not completed the 10-m smokestack. Only on August 15 was everything ready, and a first cremation was carried out satisfactorily in what came to be known as Auschwitz's crematorium I.

Further incinerations followed without causing any problems, and thus the recently appointed head of the Auschwitz Neubauleitung, SS-Sergeant Schlachter, informed the SS-HHB after a month of trials that the crematorium functioned flawlessly. Schlachter had another reason to be pleased with Topf. Despite the radical change in the furnace model, which had raised the actual cost of the furnace by a little over 25 percent, the firm had decided not to renegotiate the original price.[13] Patriotically absorbing the extra cost and allowing the quality of the furnace to speak for itself, Topf paved the road for future commissions. . . .

In Auschwitz, preparations were under way for the construction of a second double-muffle furnace at the crematorium, for which Topf had quoted the same price as for the first (7,753 RM), yet which did not include a forced-draft ventilator. That was not an oversight; Prüfer assumed that the already-installed ventilator would suffice for two furnaces.[14] On November 19, 1940, Prüfer was in Auschwitz to decide on the exact site for the second furnace. He was accompanied by Schlachter's deputy, Walter Urbanczyk, who until the next October was effectively in charge of crematorium construction. They decided to build the second furnace alongside the first.[15]

Prüfer suggested that Urbanczyk call on another Topf employee, Karl Schultze, to see if concentration of two furnaces in one tight and unventilated space would create difficulties in the adjacent autopsy room and morgue. Urbanczyk followed up on the suggestion, and Schultze submitted within a few days a proposal for a limited ventilation system to extract air from the autopsy room and morgue.[16] The Neubauleitung asked Schultze to modify the 1,784 RM proposal because it did not service the furnace room.[17]

At the beginning of January 1941, the first furnace in the crematorium at Auschwitz broke down, giving new urgency to the construction of the second furnace.[18] On January 17, a railway car left Erfurt with parts to repair the damaged furnace and material for the construction of the second one. Work began on January 20 and was finished a month later.[19] Topf, however, had failed to send a modified design for the ventilation of the crematorium, and as its construction had become urgent, Schlachter turned to the firm of Friedrich Boos, which was about to install central heating in the SS guards' quarters. Having the requisite material and technology for the ventilation system, Boos constructed it between February 23 and March 1....[20]

Schultze meantime tackled the problem of ventilating the autopsy room and morgue in the crematorium building. These were still ventilated together by grilled suction sleeves dropping from two collecting pipes (one for each room). These pipes ran into an angle of the ceiling and led to a blower that was coupled to the evacuation smokestack and dispensed 6,000 cu m an hour. This system cost 1,727 RM, 54 RM less than for the first device because the pipes were not as long, owing to the modifications made by Schultze. The furnace hall (320 cu m) was ventilated separately by a vertical pipe with four grilled openings (two per furnace) leading to a number 300 blower with a .75-horsepower (hp) motor, dispersing 3,000 cu m of air an hour. This, too, was linked to the evacuation smokestack and cost 757 RM.

For the warm air, Schultze required only a coefficient of 10 cu m an hour per cu m to be deaerated. Topf justified this separate circulation to prevent the warm air from entering the morgue.[21] Schultze's concept was simple: instead of completely recasting the project, he added a second one to the first so as to meet the new specifications demanded of him.

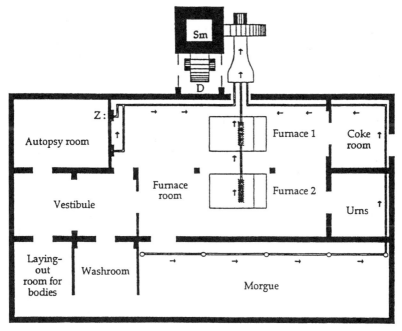

Figure 2. Organization of the air extraction system of crematorium I at Auschwitz in the third design by Karl Schultze, dated February 24, 1941. Blowoff: 8,300 cu m an hour; 3-hp motor. Z—air intake grille in the form of shutters, placed vertically.

Such reliance on previous studies would become the rule during the working out of ventilation systems for later crematoria of Birkenau. On February 15, the Neubauleitung rejected this proposal, insisting that the air suctioned in must no longer pass through a separate smokestack but must go into the smokestack evacuating smoke from the furnaces.[22]

On February 24, a third project was sketched out (figure 2)[23] The deaeration of the morgue was left unchanged, with five vertical suction devices attached to a horizontal collecting pipe, going all the way to the smokestack of the furnaces. The ventilation of the autopsy room was replaced by air intake grilles in the form of shutters. A pipe with four openings ran above the furnaces. The three collecting pipes met in the furnace room, and their effluent was swept into a number 550 blower with a 3-hp motor, dispersing 8,300 cu m of air an hour, spewing into the smokestack from the furnaces. Materials for this device would cost 1,884 RM, and its assembly 596 RM. This proposal was accepted on March 15 by Urbanczyk, who then asked Topf to manufacture and deliver it in the shortest time possible. The firm estimated it would take up to six months, or until August 15.[24]

The first visit to Auschwitz, on March 1, 1941, of SS chief Heinrich Himmler was a watershed in the history of the camp. Himmler decided to enlarge the camp to hold 30,000 prisoners and to create at nearby Birkenau a camp for 100,000 prisoners of war. Furthermore, he decided to provide IG Farben-industrie with 10,000 prisoners for building an industrial zone dedicated to the production of methanol and synthetic rubber, to increase agricultural activity within the camp zone, and to develop the camp's workshops. Himmler also announced that an armaments plant would be installed close to the camp.

The 100,000 prisoners of war were to be used as a labor force for the creation of a "colony" (*Siedlung*) at Auschwitz. In this vast scheme for the total Germanization of the city and its surroundings, Auschwitz was to be a pilot project and the seedbed for other German colonies in the east. For a year and a half, an architect from Breslau worked on the planning of this city.[25] Only the Nazi defeat at Stalingrad on January 31, 1943, put an end to his labors.

Himmler's plans did not affect ongoing activities at the Auschwitz crematorium. The second furnace proved unsatisfactory for lack of proper draft. After unsatisfactory communications with Topf,[26] Schlachter decided to address the problem himself. Increasing the height of the smokestack to 20 m got the draft going again.

Another and ultimately more pernicious problem was a situation stemming from the close presence of SS-Untersturmführer Maximilian Grabner, head of the Political Department of the camp. Grabner used a hut right behind the crematorium for his Gestapo interrogations and the morgue as his place of execution. When both furnaces were going, which happened almost every day, they released so much heat that the ventilation system, which was supposed to extract air from the morgue, actually sent hot air into it from the furnace room. The only way to prevent this was to disconnect the morgue from the ventilation system—with unwanted consequences in the hot summer air. Grabner denounced this "scandal" to the Bauleitung and asked that it equip the morgue with two ventilators, one to bring fresh air in (to aerate, *belüften*) and one to take stale air out (to deaerate, or *entlüften*) and discharge it in conformity with the earlier plans through the smokestack.[27]

The continuous incinerations had done more than just disturb Grabner's comfort. They had also cracked the smokestack. All cremation was stopped between June 23 and 28 to hoop the chimney with iron bands. . . .[28]

In Auschwitz, preparations began for the construction of the prisoner-of-war camp (*Kriegsgefangenenlager,* or KGL) that Himmler had ordered set up at Birkenau. On October 1, 1941, the chief of buildings of the SS-HHB, SS-Oberführer Hans Kammler, appointed

SS-Hauptsturmführer Karl Bischoff to head a special office to oversee construction of the camp (Sonderbauleitung für die Errichtung eines KGL). Bischoff was on the job as of that day.

Bischoff had been a member of the Luftwaffe since 1935 and had worked as a warrant officer in northern France and Belgium, setting up airfields from which attacks were launched against England. In that time he became acquainted with Kammler, who also worked for the air force. After the Battle of Britain, Bischoff was left with little to do, and Kammler, who had moved to the SS, suggested that Bischoff make a similar move. He offered him officer rank and independence as the chief architect of an enormous prisoner-of-war camp.[29]

Bischoff accepted the offer, but not before negotiating the privilege of appointing his own man as head of the crucial design section of the Bauleitung. He had in mind the Austrian architect Walter Dejaco, who had worked for a short time under Schlachter and was employed in fall 1941 at the SS-HHB. After Kammler agreed, Bischoff traveled to Auschwitz and went to work. Dejaco was to follow on October 24, but Bischoff did not await the arrival of his new chief designer.

Within one week after Bischoff took control, his office produced the first plan for a camp of 125,000 inmates. It proposed a large enclosure divided into three sectors: one for quarantining prisoners and two for lodging them. A second plan, drawn up on October 14, introduced a railway spur between the quarantine camp and the rest.[30]

As he was developing the design, Bischoff realized that his camp, which was expecting to handle 100,000 prisoners of war, could not rely on the crematorium in the main camp, which was designed to service 10,000 inmates. Hence on October 11, he telegraphed Topf to dispatch Prüfer to Auschwitz.[31] Prufer arrived ten days later, and he and Bischoff closeted themselves for the next two days.[32] The two men liked one another; both were veterans of the Great War, professional builders, energetic and hardworking, and beholden for their careers to nobody but themselves.

Prüfer convinced Bischoff to create the necessary incineration capacity at the POW facility by grouping three incinerating crucibles in a single furnace and lining the necessary number of furnaces next to each other. That would make it possible to create a large incineration capacity in one relatively compact building. The triple-muffle furnace seemed a natural evolution of Topf's double-muffle model, and the arrangement combined efficiency with economy. Prüfer did not yet dare to suggest a quadruple-muffle model.

Assuming one crucible for 8,000 prisoners, Prüfer calculated that 15 crucibles would suffice. That translated into five furnaces of three crucibles each, linked to a common smokestack. Prüfer calculated that each crucible could handle two bodies every 30 minutes and that the installation as a whole therefore would be capable of burning 60 bodies an hour, or 1,440 bodies in 24 hours. Running day and night, the new crematorium theoretically could incinerate all the inmates of the projected camp in three or four months.

The building was not to be at Birkenau but in Auschwitz's main camp, behind the existing crematorium, across from the administration buildings.[33] Prüfer sketched a plan for a crematorium measuring 55 to 60 m by 12 m (175 feet by 37 feet).[34] Its center was to be a large furnace room. Adjacent to it were to be a storage room for coke, rooms for washing and laying out corpses that had been selected for dissection, and an autopsy room, replacing the autopsy room of the existing crematorium, which would be displaced by the third furnace. A central projecting wing was to house a furnace for burning refuse, two ventilators to create a forced draft, and a double smokestack. The basement was to have two vast morgues. One morgue was to store "fresh" bodies; the other was for corpses about to be incinerated. An elevator was to connect the morgues to the furnace and autopsy rooms.[35] Prüfer and Bischoff decided that Schultze was to design the ventilation system to extract air from the furnace hall, the autopsy room, and the two morgues below.[36] In conformity with the arrangement in the existing crematorium, one of the morgues was also to receive a system to bring in fresh air.

Dejaco arrived in Auschwitz just as Prüfer was about to leave, and he was given the job of elaborating the engineer's sketches into a design. He produced two drawings: a plan of the ground floor and an elevation. In the plan, he indicated the dimensions of the morgues below: the "B. Keller" (*Belüfteterkeller,* or aerated cellar) was to measure 7 m by 30 m, and the "L. Keller" (*Leichenkeller,* or morgue) 8 m by 60 m. An architect who worked in Berlin for the SS-HHB, Werkmann, was also asked to apply himself to the problem. His crematorium improved on Prüfer's initial sketch: it was more monumental in elevation and more practical in plan. For example, Werkmann included a chute to facilitate the transport of corpses from an entrance on the ground floor to the morgues in the basement. He did not fix the length of the morgues, both of which he designated "L. Keller." In all respects more accomplished than Dejaco's design, Werkmann's proposal was accepted and signed by Kammler and sent to Auschwitz on November 20.

In Erfurt, meanwhile, Topf worked on the design of the furnaces for the new crematorium. As the size of the crucibles in the triple-muffle furnace was larger than those in the double-muffle furnaces, the firm decided to increase from two to three the number of ventilators to create a forced draft. It also decided to increase their total extractive power from 20,000 to 120,000 cu m an hour. One of the brothers who owned the firm, Ernst-Wolfgang Topf, assured the Sonderbauleitung that "the installation being built would be appropriate and well-designed."[37]

...Around this time, the older of the two proprietors of the firm, Ludwig Topf, was called up to serve the Fatherland as an ordinary soldier in a construction battalion. The firm's personnel resented this, because the bachelor Ludwig was more easygoing than his aggressive, pretentious, and harsh younger brother (who was married and therefore exempt). Prüfer asked Bischoff's support to gain Ludwig's exemption, permanently if possible. He justified the extraordinary request with the fabrication that Ludwig had been instrumental in developing the triple-muffle furnace and the new crematorium could not be completed without his supervision. Bischoff pulled some strings, and in December, Ludwig got his leave.[38] Once back in Erfurt, he managed to get out of all his military obligations. But he was now beholden to Bischoff.

Prüfer by now had acquired a reputation at the SS-HHB as a "magician" of cremation. In mid-November 1941, the head of technical operations of the SS-HHB building department, SS-Sturmbannführer Wirtz, invited Prüfer to Berlin. The topic of discussion was the installation of a "crematorium site" at Mogilev, in Russia.[39] Prüfer had just come to the conclusion that it was technically possible to increase the number of crucibles from three to four per furnace, and he suggested to Wirtz that a double furnace with four muffles would do fine as a basic element (figure 3). Two elements were to provide one unit with eight crucibles.

Compared with the Auschwitz furnace, the Mogilev version was simple. To be heated with wood, it had neither doors for closing the burner generators nor internal thermal insulation. It was also cheap. One unit with eight muffles cost only 13,800 RM (1992: $55,200), that is, 1,725 RM per crucible (compared with 2,126 RM per crucible in the three-muffle version and 5,000 per crucible in the two-muffle version already installed in Auschwitz). The SS-HHB wanted to build four units, a total of 32 crucibles, and came to an agreement with Topf on December 4. The total job was worth 55,200 RM (1992: $220,000)....[40]

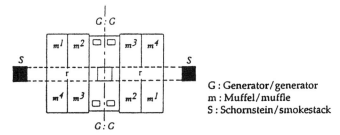

Figure 3. Diagram of the Topf quadri-muffle furnace.

Amid all the excitement of the Mogilev contract, Topf also had to look after the installation of the third furnace for crematorium I at Auschwitz. On November 20, an overseer named A. Mahr had begun laying the foundations for the furnace. He worked for three weeks[41] but could not continue because the Collmener Schamottenwerke of Colditz in Saxony had not delivered the fireclay to Topf. Mahr returned to Erfurt.

Shortly after Mahr's departure, the first lethal gassing was carried out with Zyklon B at Auschwitz in the cellars of block 11. Zyklon B, a hydrocyanic acid (prussic acid) pesticide, was made by the Degesch company of Frankfurt am Main and supplied through a wholesaler, Tesch and Stabenow of Hamburg. It was available in metal containers of four sizes (200 g, 500 g, 1 kg, and 1.5 kg), which also included an inert, porous medium and an irritant designed to alert the unprotected user to the presence of the odorless gas. Under most conditions, the pesticide was not dangerous, as the prussic acid would only vaporize at a temperature of 27 degrees Celsius.[42] Zyklon B had first been introduced at Auschwitz in July 1940, when it was used to fumigate the former Polish barracks, which were to house the camp's SS guards. It had remained a staple fumigant through 1940 and 1941.[43]

In December 1941, Zyklon B was administered for the first time not to vermin but to 250 "incurable" concentration camp inmates and 600 Soviet prisoners of war.[44] According to Höss (who was away at the time), death was immediate. Others claimed that some victims were still alive two days later and that it was necessary to introduce a second batch of poison. The killers were experimenting; they did not know yet how much Zyklon B was lethal for how many people, and they did not fully realize that hydrogen cyanide vaporizes only at 27 degrees Celsius. The basement of block 11 had not been heated. Cremation of the 850 victims also presented an unexpected problem: the intensive operation caused the second furnace to deteriorate.[45]

When the experiment was over, it had become clear that the cellars of block 11 were less than ideal as gas chambers because of lack of ventilation. Also, the distance from block 11 to the crematorium was too great—the killers did not want to move 850 corpses through the main street of the camp. The morgue of the crematorium recommended itself as a more efficient gas chamber. It had a mechanical ventilation system that could extract the poison gas, and being a one-story structure, it provided an easy means of introducing Zyklon B into the room through three square stacks to be created on the roof.[46]

The new gas chamber in the morgue at crematorium I operated probably intermittently from January 1942 until May, when it had to be shut down for construction of the third furnace. By that time it had also become clear that the crematorium did not provide the "privacy" necessary for the gassings, and shortly before Topf's men moved in to construct the new furnace, the decision was made to transfer the gassings to Birkenau.

In the winter of 1941–42, Birkenau became more and more integrated with the main camp. On December 1, the building office of the main camp and Bischoff's Sonderbauleitung KGL merged into a new organization, the Zentralbauleitung der Waffen SS und Polizei, Auschwitz O/S (Central Building Authority of the Waffen SS and the Police, Auschwitz, Upper Silesia), headed by Bischoff. From mid-January to the beginning of February 1942, this office produced eight blueprints for the new POW crematorium (called series 900), based on Werkmann's design of the preceding November.[47] Dejaco made small changes to Werkmann's design, relocating the smokestack and adding a third room in the basement for crematorium operations. This room, labeled morgue 3, was to receive the corpses for registration. The projected location of the crematorium, in the main camp, remained unchanged.[48]

At the end of January 1942, Prüfer returned to Auschwitz to plan the building of the third furnace for crematorium I and, probably in response to Bischoff's wish, to discuss the possibility of constructing a backup incineration facility in Birkenau in addition to a new crematorium. Prüfer now proposed a crematorium with two stripped-down versions of his triple-muffle furnace, without a compressed-air blower and using only a small amount of iron in their structure. Placed around a central smokestack, the furnaces were to cost 14,652 RM (1992: $58,600).[49]

But then Kammler, who had become head of the building department of the powerful successor to the SS-HHB, the SS Wirtschafts-Verwaltungs-hauptamt (SS-WVHA, or Economic-Administrative Main Office), annulled the project during his visit of February 27.[50] He suggested that it made more sense to build the new crematorium at Birkenau. Topf was not happy; yet it was prepared to forgo any further claim if the SS took care of the 1,769.36 RM (1992: $7,500) which the firm had invested in studying the aborted project.[51] The company was paid, but it would come to regret taking the money. . . .

On April 30, a railroad car arrived in Auschwitz from Erfurt loaded with 11 tons of material, which included two-thirds of the metal parts and all the compressed-air blowers for the five triple-muffle furnaces to be built in the new crematorium in Birkenau, the iron fittings needed for the third double-muffle furnace of crematorium I, and all the deaeration equipment.[52] Most of the car's contents were stockpiled. Only the iron fittings for the third double-muffle furnace were of immediate use.

At the same time, Prüfer was supervising the construction at Buchenwald of the first of two triple-muffle furnaces. He hoped that early completion would provide him with concrete data before setting up five similar furnaces in Birkenau. . . . The first Buchenwald furnace was not operational until August 23 and the second on October 3. After 12 and six weeks of operation, Prüfer revised his original estimate for Auschwitz. Extrapolating the Buchenwald data for Auschwitz, Prüfer concluded that the five furnaces of the new crematorium in Birkenau could incinerate 800 corpses in 24 hours.[53] That was sharply lower than the original figure of 1,440 mentioned a year earlier.

In May, Höss selected a little farmhouse (the "little red house") on the edge of the birch forest at Birkenau to be the new gas chamber. It was to replace the morgue in the first crematorium, which was undergoing repairs. The house, measuring 60–80 sq m, consisted of two rooms into which 500 persons could be crammed. The doors were made airtight, the windows were walled up, and small openings were installed for the insertion of Zyklon B into the rooms. No mechanical ventilation was installed to extract the gas from the two rooms. The executions were to occur in the evening; and after all the prisoners had died, the doors were to be opened and remain open for the whole night. By daybreak it would be possible to remove the bodies without danger and transport them to burial pits dug in the birch forest. Bunker 1, as the execution site was to be known, entered into service that month (May 1942). . . .

To this point, Auschwitz had played a completely marginal role in the killing of Jews. The cumulative evidence of documents in the archive of the Zentralbauleitung proves that the adaptation of the camp for genocidal purposes only started in June 1942. This conclusion contradicts Auschwitz commandant Rudolf Höss's statement, made in 1946, that Himmler had informed him that Birkenau would be used as a killing center in the summer of 1941. The evidence that we have studied suggests that Höss retrospectively confused 1941 with 1942. Himmler must have summoned Höss to Berlin at the beginning of June 1942 to inform him about the future use of the camp. One condition that justified the choice of Auschwitz applied both in 1941 and 1942: the camp's excellent rail connections. But another factor of prime importance had arisen only since the end of 1941: an extraordinary crematorium capable of incinerating 1,440 (or was it only 800?) corpses a day. It was the combination of these two circumstances that made Auschwitz attractive to Himmler.

The mass murders were to begin on July 1. That created a problem: the crematorium existed only in plan. Since May 17, a single detachment of 100 prisoners had been digging foundations, but that was all.[54] Furthermore, bunker 1 could not be used for continuous gassing, since it had no mechanical ventilation to speedily extract the gas. In addition, the camp was short of materials. Yet such considerations were mere cavils for Himmler, and he trusted that Höss would be able to find a solution.

Not far from bunker 1 was another farmhouse, whitewashed and, with a surface of 105 sq m, slightly larger than the "little red house."

Höss decided to transform it into a gas chamber following the pattern of bunker 1. The place could hold 800 persons.

Bischoff was called in to advise on the ventilation. He recalled an article by Dr. G. Peters, director of Degesch, the manufacturer of Zyklon B,[55] which described a delousing system using Zyklon B with eight little gas chambers of 10 cu m each, set up side by side. Each cell had two gas-tight doors (made of metal or wood), one serving to take in personal effects on the dirty side and the other to remove them on the clean side. There was a radiator for heating and interior circular ventilation which assured, first, the regular passage of the agent over the goods to be deloused and second, when the 60- to 90-minute treatment was over, efficient deaeration. Peters's article had already served as a source of inspiration when, in December 1941, Dejaco had proposed to install in the future reception building at Auschwitz a delousing system with 19 similar gas chambers (set up in two rows). . . .

It was easy to install a modified form of the parallel rooms with doors at both sides in the little farmhouse. Yet the radiators to provide circular aeration posed a problem. This system had to be set up by Boos, and the delivery process would be subject to long delays.[56] It was decided to drop this idea and limit the modification to the installation of four small parallel gas chambers of 50 cu m each. As the gas chambers were oriented to the prevailing wind direction (north-south in Birkenau), it was thought that natural ventilation would suffice. The method for introducing the poison gas was copied from bunker 1. One or two 500-g boxes of Zyklon B per cell would cause rapid death. The "little white house," or bunker 2, was operational by the end of June 1942.

Nature competed with man to create mass death in Auschwitz. SS doctors were confronted in May with a massive outbreak of typhoid fever as the result of untreated water. By the end of June, SS officers and employees of the camps' 17 civilian firms were forbidden to drink the camp's water. Mineral water was provided free. To make matters worse, typhus broke out. The camp doctors were surprised. They thought that prophylactic measures (quarantining, shearing of hair) and hygiene (local disinfection of hair, showers) applied to the prisoners upon arrival would prevent the introduction of the plague into the camp by eradicating the agent of the disease, lice.

The trouble came from persons who had not been subjected to the delousing treatment, the free or civilian workers, who were in everyday contact with the prisoners. By the middle of 1942, the new arrangements in the Auschwitz region (the concentration camp complex and the Siedlung) had brought in civilian companies employing a thousand civilian workers. They were lodged as circumstances permitted. While the staff and the bosses of the work sites resided in houses or apartments requisitioned from the town of Auschwitz, the bulk of the workers were quartered in wooden barracks adjacent to the camps. On July 1, the first case of typhus occurred in the workers' barracks, followed within two days by three new cases.[57]

The death rate of the prisoners soared. From May to December 1940, an estimated 220 died each month. From January to July 1941, this number tripled. From August to December 1941, it reached 1,000; by July 1942, it had passed 4,000.[58] The unsanitary situation was obviously getting out of control. The typhus had to be prevented from spreading to the surrounding region. On July 10, a partial quarantine was declared.

But if the exits from the camp were blocked, its entrances were open. Convoys of Jews had begun to arrive. On July 4, the first selection of prisoners was applied to a convoy of Slovakian Jews, and those judged unfit for work were immediately gassed. Within a week this procedure had become routine.

Visitors who received a better welcome were Himmler and Kammler, who arrived in the camp on July 17 to inspect the progress of the Siedlung and the IG Farben complex. Bischoff briefed his superiors with maps, blueprints, and scale models. The presentation was followed by a visit to the camp's various agricultural and industrial operations and Birkenau. In the afternoon, Himmler was present at the selection of a convoy of Dutch Jews and the gassing of the unfit in bunker 2. Then he went to the IG Farben work site in Monowitz. A grand reception brought the day to a close.

The next day, Himmler inspected the main camp. He saw the three double-muffle Topf furnaces and the crematorium's new smokestack under construction. After a few other excursions, Himmler ordered Höss to speed up the work, to raise the camp's population capability from 100,000 to 200,000, and to get rid of the repugnant pits full of corpses behind the bunkers. Höss also received a promotion, to the rank of lieutenant colonel in the SS.[59] Himmler never returned.

Höss had succeeded in hiding from Himmler the deplorable unsanitary conditions in the camp, and the typhus epidemic continued its ravages. Within a week after Himmler's departure, the situation became catastrophic. On July 23, the camp was placed under total quarantine. Everything had to be deloused immediately: personal effects, barracks, buildings, and workshops. Tons of Zyklon B were needed to save the camp. The only way to get large quantities rapidly was through the WVHA's intervention. Not willing to admit that they had fooled Himmler, the Auschwitz SS explained that the epidemic had broken out only after his departure. On July 22, Berlin authorized a truck to fetch two-and-a-half tons of the product. A week later, a second truck was sent on its way. Yet even that did not suffice.

Around August 20, the epidemic was still raging, but the stockpile of Zyklon B had disappeared. The Auschwitz hierarchy was loath to request more prussic acid, as it implied they had been incapable of bringing the situation under control. Then someone got the idea to justify the purchase of further quantities of Zyklon B by referring to the gassing of Jews. The higher-ups of the WVHA knew that Jews were killed with the insecticide, yet they did not know how much poison was used in the operation. In fact, only 4 kg of prussic acid was enough to kill a transport of 1,000 persons. Inflating by more than 3,000 percent the quantities needed to do the job in the gas chambers allowed the SS to siphon off more than 95 percent for delousing. The trick worked. On August 26 and September 14, massive new purchases of Zyklon B were approved for "special treatment" and "special actions," terms that referred to the liquidation of unfit Jews at Birkenau.[60]

All of this happened while the camp had no crematorium to clean up after the killers. As a result of setting up the third furnace and building the new smokestack, the crematorium had been unusable for three months, and the effects of its stoppage had been especially noticeable once the typhus epidemic began multiplying the corpses. . . . Thus 10,000 bodies that ought to have been incinerated had been buried in pits in the birch forest at Birkenau along with the bodies of the unfit Jews who had been gassed. Once started up again after completion of the new smokestack on August 8, the three double-muffle furnaces operated at their maximum capacity (200 to 250 incinerations a day). That caused new damage to the smokestack on August 13. It became clear that this first crematorium was nearing the end of its career.

Even two months earlier, as more and more Jews were being killed on arrival, completion of the new crematorium had become a matter of highest urgency. On June 18, a railway car had left Erfurt with five tons of material, comprising the missing parts of the five triple-muffle furnaces, the furnace for refuse, and the three blowers for the forced draft. The 1.5-hp motors followed on August 6.[61]

At the beginning of July, the Zentralbauleitung invited a tender for the construction of the crematorium's shell from the two firms involved in construction in Birkenau, Huta and Lenz & Company. Lenz refused on account of a shortage of personnel.[62] On July 13, Huta accepted the proposal to handle the construction of the building for 133,756.65 RM (1992: $535,000).[63] The firm agreed to begin work on Monday, August 10.

In a report filed three months later with the WVHA, the Auschwitz Zentralbauleitung indicated that it had been necessary to set about building the new crematorium immediately owing to the situation created by the "special actions."[64] This statement formally confirms the essential role played by the new crematorium in the choice of Auschwitz as the site for the annihilation of Jews. Originally envisaged as a normal instrument of sanitation for a prisoner-of-war camp, this crematorium had taken on new importance thanks to the combination of Prüfer's commercial convictions, professional passions, creative genius, and cordial ties with Bischoff.

Slowly the men in the WVHA had begun to associate the "final solution of the Jewish problem" with the capacity of the new crematorium—or crematoria, as Bischoff had begun to consider the construction of a second crematorium in Birkenau. Himmler had ordered that the camp should accommodate 200,000 inmates, and the Zentralbauleitung had completed a design for the enlarged camp at the end of July. The corollary to this increase in population was an extra crematorium. For the sake of architectural balance, Bischoff decided to erect the two buildings side by side, each the mirror image of the other. The number of incinerating crucibles was raised to 30, or one for every 6,670 prisoners. Yet perhaps even that would not be enough, as convoy after convoy poured in.

Prüfer arrived in Auschwitz on August 18 to take stock. A day later, camp authorities approved the construction of two more crematoria above and beyond the one under construction (originally intended for POWs) and the second one that had been planned to cope with the expansion of the camp. Prüfer picked up more than 80,000 RM (1992: $320,000) in new contracts.[65]

Preparatory studies cleared Prüfer's path. Bischoff had already decided on a second crematorium with 15 crucibles alongside the first. He also had considered building an incinerator alongside bunkers 1 and 2 to absorb their "production," which, according to Himmler's order, must no longer be buried but burned. With so many crematoria under consideration, Bischoff introduced a new nomenclature. The existing crematorium in Auschwitz was to be called crematorium I; crematoria II through V were to be built in Birkenau. Added to this array were four other crematoria to be built eventually in Birkenau. Crematoria II and III were to be equipped with five three-muffle furnaces, and crematoria IV and V were to have two stripped-down three-muffle furnaces each. . . .

Prüfer now considered the technical aspects of crematoria IV and V. The stripped-down triple-muffle furnace, which he had proposed for the first Birkenau crematorium earlier that year, had not been further developed. Pressed for an instant solution, Prüfer recalled the proposed Mogilev double furnaces with four muffles. As the series was already in production, the Erfurt factory could rapidly manufacture others. Bischoff approved Prüfer's idea and had blueprints drawn up on August 14.[66] They showed only the layout of the double furnace with its two smokestacks; the diagram of the morgue remained incomplete (figure 4).

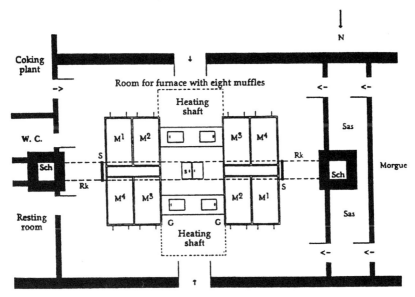

Figure 4. Diagram of the incineration system, with a double quadri-muffle furnace, for crematorium IV in Birkenau. W.C.—toilet; Sas—sluice and storage.

On the morning of August 19, Prüfer went to the Auschwitz Bauhof, the warehouse where materials were stockpiled, to see whether all the metal parts of the five triple-muffle furnaces had been received and were in good condition. He found, among the 11 tons of materials sent from Erfurt on April 16, most of the metal elements destined for the second double-muffle furnace in Mauthausen. They had remained in storage at Erfurt because of SS Lieutenant Naumann's obstinate dilatory tactics. Prüfer decided to exploit the mistake to his own advantage.

After lunch, Prüfer attended a meeting with the smokestack expert Robert Köhler at the Bauleitung chaired by SS Second Lieutenant Fritz Ertl (Bischoff had been called to Berlin). They decided to begin construction of the five furnaces for crematorium II as soon as Martin Holick, who had just started up the first triple-muffle furnace at Buchenwald, was on hand. . . .

It was clear to all participants in this meeting that crematoria IV and V were to be involved in mass murder. Ertl, in his report on the meeting, designated bunkers 1 and 2, located in the Sperrgebiet at Birkenau, as "bath installations for special action." Köhler took personal responsibility at the meeting for committing his own firm to these "special works." Prüfer did not have full power to commit his company to such a deal, so he acted on his own. Yet he knew that his superiors would back him, since Ludwig Topf owed his demobilization to the SS. . . .

Despite the availability of thousands of prisoners, the Auschwitz Zentralbauleitung was unable to carry out the construction of the Birkenau crematoria all by itself. While its members were capable of running fairly simple work sites (building wooden barracks or residential houses), they needed outside help for more technical projects. Both for preliminary studies done by civil engineers from the specialized firms they called on and for actual construction, which was directed by several work-site foremen sent there by the company in question, outside help was crucial. To manage relations, Bischoff assigned to each specific project a second lieutenant specialist called at first SS-Fachführer, then Sonderführer. The Sonderführer would deal with the civilian firm, oversee the execution of the works in progress, and see to it that the job was finished promptly.

Eleven civilian companies were involved with the construction of the new crematoria in Birkenau. . . . Each work site employed 100 to 150 persons, of whom two-thirds were prisoners and one-third civilians, all directed by overseers from the companies concerned. . . .

On the morning of September 23, the head of the WVHA, SS-Gruppenführer Oswald Pohl, suddenly appeared in Auschwitz to find out where all the tons of Zyklon B were going.[67] Pohl went first to the Zentralbauleitung, had the overall layout of the camp explained to him, and got a description of the buildings that had been completed, those under construction (including the four crematoria in Birkenau), and the ones still on the drawing board. When he asked about the Zyklon B, he was told that the product was for the simultaneous destruction of lice and Jews. Pohl had no further questions on that topic. To prevent typhoid and malaria, he recommended speeding up construction of a large water-purification plant. . . .

The approach of the Silesian winter made it more and more difficult to use bunkers 1 and 2. The temperature outside kept falling, and the prussic acid ceased to vaporize properly. At the end of October 1942, the Zentralbauleitung began to consider transfer of the gassing from bunkers 1 and 2 to a room in a crematorium. It urgently requested Topf to send all the blueprints of the projected ventilation systems.[68] Within a week, it received the overall blueprints for installing the aeration and ventilation systems in crematoria II and III and the definitive blueprint for the ventilation system of crematorium I, which had arrived in April and had never been installed.

It was decided to transform morgue 1 of crematorium II into a gas chamber. One indication that such a decision was taken is a "leak"—that is, any mention in a document (writing, blueprint, photograph) of an abnormal use of the crematoria that could not be explained except by the massive gassing of human beings—that occurred on November 27, when one of

Bischoff's assistants, Wolter, called Topf to ask for a master metalworker to install the ventilation systems in the morgues of crematorium II. His colleague Janisch, who was formally in charge of the site, canceled the request. Wolter drew up a note to inform Bischoff what had happened. In this note he designated the corpse cellar in crematorium II as "special cellar" (*Sonderkeller*).[69] That was not the only slip. Every document in a 120-item inventory of material needed for the completion of Birkenau, undertaken between December 10 and 18, was captioned "Re: Kriegsgefangenenlager Auschwitz (Durchführung der Sonderbehandlung)," or "Concerning: Prisoner-of-War Camp Auschwitz (Carrying Out of Special Treatment)," which referred to the killing operations.[70]

Another leak occurred when Dejaco set out to adapt the crematoria to their genocidal function. The ground floor, with the hall of furnaces and its service rooms, did not need modification, but the basement had to be changed to accommodate the new function. The building that was under construction provided for a chute at the center of a staircase to transfer corpses more easily from the surface to the two underground morgues, whereas victims to be gassed could walk down to the morgue that was now destined to serve as the gas chamber. The corpse chute no longer served any purpose and had to go.

On December 19, Dejaco sketched a new configuration of the basement that provided for a staircase for the victims (drawing 2003).[71] According to the captions in the blueprint, the staircase became the only access to the morgues—which implied, strictly speaking, that the dead would have to walk down the staircase. The blueprint arrived too late at work sites 30 and 30a; the concrete for the chutes had already been poured. Later, when the SS decided to add to the gas chamber a clothes room (Leichenkeller 2) with its own stairway, the part where the chute projected into the vestibule interfered with the passage of the victims. The top of the chute was demolished, and its outlet was masked by a wooden partition.

Dejaco faced greater problems than the simple one of locating stairs and chutes. By November, the SS had become accustomed to the operational procedure of bunkers 1 and 2, in which the victims undressed in the barracks-stables, were gassed in the bunkers, and their bodies dumped in pits, and it made sense to apply it to the crematoria. Yet the builders ran up against problems with layout and compatibility. For crematoria II and III, the choice of Leichenkeller 1 (ventilated) as a gas chamber was obvious. The SS also planned to use the two remaining morgues as gas chambers, wrongly imagining that the high yield anticipated for the five triple-muffle furnaces would allow a staggered operation. In this configuration, an outside undressing room was indispensable. It was to open directly onto the service stairway connecting the two halls by way of the central vestibule. Moreover, it proved necessary to improve the ventilation of Leichenkeller 2 (which was only deaerated) by adding an aeration system to bring air into the room. After the furnaces had been tested and their output better estimated, it became clear that they could not handle the "yield" of two gas chambers. Consequently, Leichenkeller 2 became an undressing room. In this configuration, deaeration no longer served any purpose (except to ventilate the body odors of the victims, which could just as easily be done by a natural air current).

Leichenkeller 1 proved in the end to be too large for a gas chamber. At the end of 1943, in order to "regularize" the operation of crematoria II and III, the camp administration divided their gas chambers in two, allowing no more than 100 sq m for the killing of 1,000 new arrivals (unfit for work) in 24 hours. . . .[72]

Crematoria IV and V had an incinerating yield much smaller than that of II and III, and so their gas chambers had to be more modest. The SS combined its need for low-capacity gas chambers (100 sq m) for "treating" small groups of victims with the idea of staggered operations, and thus on January 11, 1943 it established the definitive blueprint for the killing procedure at crematorium IV.[73]

As we have seen, this concept required the construction of an external undressing room. Yet, to save money, it was decided that in good weather the victims could undress outdoors (as they did in the summer of 1944). In the winter, the central hall doubled as undressing room and morgue. The victims came in, undressed, then walked naked into the two gas chambers. After being killed, they were dragged back into the central hall and laid there before being incinerated. The procedure did not make much sense from a functional point of view, especially when compared with the rational arrangement of the new crematorium at Dachau, in which victims could walk through the entrance into a heated clothes room to undress, then walk into a heated and deaerated gas chamber ("shower room") for killing; their bodies could then be taken to the morgue and on to the furnace hall. The gas chamber at Dachau could be placed in the center because it was fitted with a system of mechanical deaeration. Fortunately, it was never put into service.

Designing gas chambers and incineration furnaces and getting them built are two different things. Even in Auschwitz there were limits to what the SS could get done. . . .

Bischoff pulled out all the stops to finish crematorium II by January 31.[74] He informed Topf that it had to deliver the materials needed according to the original schedule, so that crematoria II and III could be finished by January 31 and crematoria IV and V by March 31. Prüfer was asked to come to Auschwitz to coordinate everything.

Prüfer's arrival was preceded by that of Heinrich Messing, who left Erfurt by train on January 4, arrived at Auschwitz at dawn the next day, and was immediately taken to crematorium II, where he worked for 10 hours setting up the forced-draft system for the chimney. Thereafter Messing worked, regularly and without resting, 11 hours a day every day of the week except Sunday (when he had to work for only eight hours). The three forced drafts for crematorium II were in place by January 26.[75] Yet the crematorium was still not complete: the compressed-air blowers, which controlled the speed of incineration, had not been installed. Messing began setting them up on January 26 and finished the job on February 7. . . .

At that point, Topf and the Zentralbauleitung were on such close terms that the latter asked Prüfer to come and spend two or three days a week supervising the work sites. Apparently Prüfer did not go along with this but instead sent Martin Holick and Arnold Seyffarth to Auschwitz in early February. Prüfer also promised to send a second master metalworker to finish the installation of the ventilation systems, but the man never arrived. Progress on the construction of the ventilation system for crematorium II had halted because of the failure of various subcontractors to honor their obligations. That led to a postponement of the installation of the aeration and deaeration systems for the gas chamber (morgue 1), originally planned for February 8. The missing parts finally arrived in Auschwitz on February 11. This three-day stoppage irritated Bischoff, and he complained to Kammler. He was particularly unhappy because Topf's last shipment did not include the motor for deaerating Leichenkeller 2.

Letters and telegrams exchanged on February 11 and 12 between the Zentralbauleitung Lei-chen-keller and Topf mention a wooden blower for Leichenkeller 11.[76] This reference confirms the use of the morgue as a gas chamber: Bischoff and Prüfer thought that the extraction of air mixed with concentrated prussic acid (20 g per cu m) required a noncorroding ventilator.

Other new elements of equipment needed for crematorium II were detectors for measuring traces of prussic acid. Prüfer's and Schultze's superiors at Topf and Sons, Sander and Erdmann, were informed of this singular request. Sander contacted several companies seeking the detectors. The Zentralbauleitung urged in a telegram of February 26 the immediate shipment of the gas detectors to Auschwitz, as the gas chamber could not be completed without them.[77]

Another point of concern was the power of the ventilation system in the gas chamber. It had been designed to provide high aeration and low deaeration, which fitted its use as a morgue. As a gas chamber, it should work the other way around. Sander and Prüfer wrote to the Zentralbauleitung on March 2:

> Re: Crematorium (II). We acknowledge receipt of your telegram stating: "Immediate shipment of 10 gas detectors as agreed. Estimate to be furnished later." Concerning this matter, we can tell you that for two weeks now we have been making inquiries of five different firms about the apparatus you want indicating the traces of prussic acid [*Anzeigegeräte für Blausäure-Reste*]. We have received negative responses from 3 firms and we are still awaiting answers from the other 2. When we receive further information on this subject, we will let you know immediately so that we can put you in touch with the firm making this apparatus. Heil Hitler!

The Bauleitung received this letter, which amounts to another leak of the existence of a lethal gas chamber in crematorium II, on March 5.

Another last-minute problem arose because of defective arrangement of the three forced drafts around the smokestack. Transfer of heat from the smokestack to the ventilation system was to increase the temperature in all the rooms serviced by the system. Prüfer had pointed out this drawback on February 19 and had suggested channeling the excess heat to morgue 1—a suggestion that clearly reveals that the morgue, which must by definition remain cool, had become a gas chamber.[78] Heating the morgue would ensure more rapid diffusion of Zyklon B. The plan was immediately accepted by the SS, and on February 22, Topf sent to Auschwitz a cast-iron blower with an extractive power of 9,000 to 10,000 cu m an hour, priced at 522 RM (1992: $2,100).[79]

A relatively minor item that had not yet been made was a metal connecting pipe, in the shape of a trident, to be placed in the loft between the ceilings of the rooms with forced draft and the blower, which fed into the smokestack used to evacuate the gas from the gas chamber. A sliding damper in the smokestack allowed control of the flow of air. Closed and with activated blower, the flow of hot air would go to the gas chamber and preheat it. Open, it would allow for the extraction of the toxic gas. The order for the connecting pipe was officially approved on March 6 at a price of 1,070 RM. It was to be manufactured within the week.

Schultze went to Auschwitz on March 1, and Prüfer joined him on March 4.[80] That day the five triple-muffle furnaces in crematorium II were tried out for the first time in the presence of Prüfer, Schultze, SS men from the Bauleitung and the Political Department, and high-ranking SS men from Berlin. For this purpose, fifty corpses of overweight men had been selected in bunker 2 and transported to crematorium II, where they were put into the furnaces. The incineration lasted, according to the rough estimate of Henryk Tauber, a stoker from the Sonderkommando, 45 minutes. The officials, who timed the incineration with watches in hand, noted that it took longer than planned. After this trial, Prüfer judged that the furnaces were not dry enough and recommended that they be heated for a week without being used.[81]

On March 10, Schultze and Messing tested the aeration and deaeration systems of the gas chamber in crematorium II. Apparently the installation was still not quite right, because Messing continued to work on it on March 11 and 13.[82] Then, on the evening of Saturday, March 13, the ventilation system was declared operational.

That same night, 1,492 women, children, and old people, selected from a convoy of 2,000 Jews from the Krakow ghetto, were killed in the new crematorium.[83] Six kilos of Zyklon B were poured into the stacks that opened into the four grillework columns implanted between the pillars that supported the ceiling.[84] Within five minutes, all the victims had succumbed. The aeration (8,000 cu m an hour) and the deaeration system (same strength) were then started up and, after 15 to 20 minutes, the atmosphere, which had been practically renewed every three to four minutes, was sufficiently pure so that members of the Sonderkommando could enter the stiflingly hot gas chamber. During this first gassing, the Sonderkommandos wore gas masks as a precaution. The bodies were untangled and dragged to the goods elevator. Hair was clipped, gold teeth pulled out, wedding rings and jewels removed. Once hoisted into the furnace hall, the bodies were dragged onto a broad moistened gutter right in front of the muffles and pushed into the furnaces. Incineration of the 1,492 "pieces" lasted for two days.

Although the gas chambers of crematorium II had been put into operation, it was not yet completed. After liquidation of the Jews from Krakow, crematorium II remained inactive until March 20, when 2,191 Greek Jews from Salonika were gassed.[85] As their bodies were being incinerated, a fire broke out on the level of the forced drafts, which had overheated. Prüfer and Schultze, hurriedly summoned to the scene, surveyed the damage on March 24. On March 25, they decided to remove the forced draft and thus abandoned the possibility of preheating the gas chamber. They also decided to replace the wooden blower for the deaeration system of the gas chamber with a metal one, as the danger of corrosion had been exaggerated.[86] Through March, Messing continued to work on the ventilation system of the undressing rooms, which was not finished until March 31. That day the undressing barrack was pulled down, and the future victims entered the undressing room by a stairway opened up at its western end.

Crematorium II was finally delivered on March 31 at a cost of 554, 500 RM (1992: $2,215,000).[87] The memorandum acknowledging receipt of the building indicated that morgue 1 was equipped with a gas-tight door, four "wire netting inserting devices" (*Drahtnetzeinschiebvorrichtung*, i.e., grillework columns for pouring Zyklon B into the gas chamber), and four "wooden lids" (*Holzblenden*). The deaeration system of morgue 2, which was of no interest once it became an undressing room, was not equipped with a motor. Hence the system was useless.

In early April, crematorium II functioned without any problems. One day, however, it was noticed that the sliding dampers were malfunctioning. A more thorough investigation revealed that the internal lining was collapsing and that the underground connecting flues were not in much better shape. The Zentralbauleitung telephoned Prüfer and asked him what to do. The engineer promised to send new blueprints for the smokestack and went off on a business trip to the Rhineland, as he felt that it was not really Topf's problem: his firm had not built the smokestack. When the blueprints failed to arrive, the Bauleitung sent telegram after telegram to demand them. It also requested a study of whether heat released by the refuse furnace in crematorium III could be used to warm the water for 100 showers. On April 15, Prüfer returned to Erfurt and promised to leave for Auschwitz two days later. He got there on April 19,[88] calmed down the SS, promised blueprints for a new smokestack, and noted with feigned sadness that the guarantee of crematorium IV's furnace had expired and that he could no longer repair a furnace built with second-class materials. He nonetheless estimated that its gas chambers were still usable, provided they were ventilated mechanically; he pocketed an order for two deaeration systems for crematoria IV and V, amounting to 2,510 RM,[89] and returned to Erfurt on April 20.

Crematorium II was stopped on May 22 or 23, and the Köhler company began to clear away the rubbish from the smokestack. This job was completed on May 29,[90] yet Köhler could not begin the repairs because Prüfer's blueprints still had not arrived. They did not arrive until a month later, at the end of a bittersweet correspondence between the Zentralbauleitung, Topf, and Köhler, in which each side cast blame on the other for the damages and delays.

The delays in the completion of crematorium II in March had made crematorium IV the first to be officially handed over to the camp administration, on March 22. It had cost 203,000 RM (1992: $810,000).[91] Again there are leaks that inform us about the use of the building. On February 28, an overseer from Riedel and Son, whose crew was finishing the interior of the west section, had to put in "windows" of solid wood with the chinks filled up. In his daily report, he wrote, "Putting in gas-tight windows." On March 2, when he had to asphalt the ground of the area where the gas-tight windows had been put in, he wrote at the end of the day: "Ground to be asphalted in gas chamber."[92]

The first gassing in crematorium IV did not go well. An SS man, wearing a face mask, had to climb a little ladder to get to a "window," then open it with one hand and pour in the Zyklon B with the other. This acrobatic routine had to be repeated six times. When the gas-tight doors were opened to evacuate the gas, it was noticed that the natural aeration was ineffective; a door had to be cut immediately into the north corridor to get an air current flowing.[93]

The double four-muffle furnace in crematorium IV functioned well for only a short time. It soon began to show problems because Prüfer, in his haste to lower its price, had oversimplified it. After only two weeks of intensive operation, the furnace split open. Koch filled in the cracks with fireproof rammed earth, but they reappeared. By mid-May the furnace was again out of service, and crematorium IV ceased to be used, once and for all.

Prüfer blamed the mediocre quality of the materials, yet he knew that he himself was responsible. In fact, Prüfer had known that the furnace was going to produce problems for more than a month before its inauguration. In February, Prüfer had been informed that the Mogilev prototype had developed cracks due to the overly centralized structure of the furnace. In the component unit of this model furnace, two muffles and a generator (figure 5), the muffle (M1) between the generator and the central duct for evacuating smoke got considerably hotter than the other muffle (M2), which was farther away from the generator. The thermal distortion gave rise to tensions in the fireclay, which eventually broke and split open.

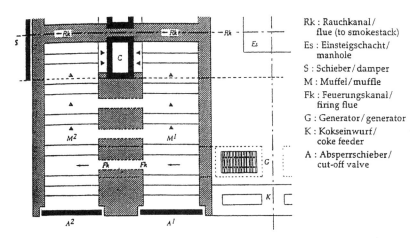

Figure 5. Diagram of a component unit of the eight-muffle furnace, initial type, for crematorium IV at Birkenau. C—central duct for evacuating smoke, connecting the two muffles to the underground smoke flue.

Unable to do anything about the furnace in crematorium IV, Prüfer decided to modify the furnace in crematorium V. He redesigned its structure, regrouping the muffles and surrounding them with two ducts placed around the edge. This new arrangement "thickened" and "reinforced" the furnace.[94] But Prüfer was unable to remedy the principal cause of the cracks, the lateral generator. Crematorium V was delivered on April 4, although the gas-tight doors of its gas chambers were not put in until April 16–17.[95]

Work progressed in the meantime on crematorium III. At the beginning of May, Messing fitted its gas chamber. There was great urgency to complete it, as the incinerating capacity of the concentration camp had plummeted drastically with crematorium IV out of service and II stopped. Only crematorium I in the main camp and V, which had a fragile furnace that might quit at any moment if pressed too hard, were in operation. Crematorium III was finally delivered on June 24.[96] The detailed invoice mentions that its morgue 1 contained a gas-tight door and 14 (false) showers, two features incompatible with its function as a morgue.[97] As in crematorium II, no motor was put in for deaerating morgue 2 (the undressing room, labeled as such twice by Messing).

Within a week, crematorium II had been brought back into operation, and the Zentralbauleitung submitted a report to the WVHA showing the camp's daily incinerating output, calculated by taking as a "unit" 70 to 100 kg of animal remains. There seems to be a large discrepancy between these official figures and the potential output: 340 kg versus 250 kg for crematorium I; 1,400 kg versus 1,000 kg for crematoria II and III; and 768 kg versus 500 kg for crematoria IV and V. (Real output, of course, was considerably less, since all the crematoria were not in use.) Nevertheless the figures were valid in a way: the time it took to incinerate two children weighing 10 kg each and a woman weighing 50 kg was equal to that for a man weighing 70 kg. This introduces a multiplying factor varying from one to three and makes all the statistics of crematorium output a matter of chance. The estimated yield of crematoria IV and V had been calculated on the basis of crematorium II, assuming that each muffle had the same capacity as one in crematoria II and III.

But the estimate was more than optimistic. At the end of June, crematorium IV was out of service and crematorium II was stopped. At the end of July, crematorium I was neutralized at the request of the Political Department. As for crematorium V, it would not be used after September because crematoria II (repaired) and III would thereafter suffice to "treat" the daily flow of convoys of Jews. . . .

Relations between Topf and the Zentralbauleitung sharply deteriorated after September. Both parties felt uncomfortable with the other. The Bauleitung criticized Topf for the failure of the furnace in crematorium IV and for the trouble with the smokestack of crematorium II, and Topf was beginning to realize what a quagmire it had gotten into. As the military situation of the Axis was getting very shaky, certain Topf officials began to consider what the future of the firm might be after an Allied victory. They realized that the outlook was bleak.

Above all, Topf realized that working with the SS had been no sinecure. First of all, the SS had picked over the smallest bill. Then it had paid slowly. On August 20, 1943, the Zentralbauleitung owed Topf almost 90,000 RM.[98] Dozens of follow-up letters were sometimes necessary before the company could get what it was owed. Finally, the SS had been capricious and inconsistent, making Topf wrack its brains for days on end over a project that the SS would then abandon without explanation, such as, for example, crematorium VI, which never saw the light of day, and the preheating of morgue 1 in crematoria II and III, and the 100 showers in crematorium III, which never got past the drawing board. Or else it ordered installations that, once built, it had no further need of, such as the ventilation system in crematorium I.

The last chapter in relations between Topf and Auschwitz occurred in 1944. Planning the imminent arrival of Hungarian Jews, the new head of the Bauleitung, SS-Obersturmführer Werner Jothann, wanted to ensure that crematoria II and III were in top order; he also hoped to reactivate crematoria IV and V, which had not been used since September 1943. He asked Topf to install permanent elevators in crematoria II and III and to set up deaeration systems for the gas chambers in crematoria IV and V to allow for massive gassings. After enormous difficulties and direct intervention from the WVHA with the Reich Ministry for Arms and Munitions, the two elevators were delivered to Auschwitz in May 1944.[99] But time was running out to set them up. Installation of the deaeration system in crematorium V, the parts of which had been in the warehouse since January, was done in May.[100] For the two gas chambers and the corridor, which represented a volume of 480 cu m, almost equal to that of morgue 1 in both crematoria II and III, Schultze had planned a deaeration system of the same power: a number 450 blower with a 3.5-hp motor extracting 8,000 cu m an hour.[101] A second ventilation system was not set up.

The massacre of Hungarian Jews in May and June 1944 was carried out principally in crematoria II, III, and V. The furnace of crematorium V was rapidly overwhelmed, and pits were dug alongside its gas chambers to incinerate the victims in the open air. Also, bunker 2 was reactivated for the occasion to handle small groups, whose bodies were burned in an incineration pit measuring 30 sq m.[102] Toward the end of the summer, when Zyklon B began to run short, victims were flung headlong into the burning pits of crematorium V and bunker 2.

As thousands of women, children, and old people disappeared into the flames, the Zentralbauleitung and Topf were settling their accounts. The Zentralbauleitung had paid practically all its outstanding bills during the last trimester of 1943 and at the beginning of February 1944. But it wanted Topf to pay for the jobs it had commissioned the metalwork shop of the DAW to do and for various little things that Topf needed on the work sites and that the Zentralbauleitung had procured. For example, the cost of a cylinder of oxygen, lent for two months, amounted to 2.10 RM; borrowed motor oil came to 8.25 RM. Topf challenged these bills, which totaled 9,000 RM. The total then was reduced to 7,500. . . .

On October 7, 1944, members of the Sonderkommando at Birkenau revolted. Crematorium IV, where most of them were lodged, was set on fire. The insurrection was put down violently by the SS. The building was then torn down, and the metal elements from the stoves were retrieved and stored in the Bauhof.[103]

At the end of November, on a verbal order from Himmler, the gassings were halted. A demolition commando, formed at the beginning of December, then dismantled crematoria II and III. Crematorium V continued to be used, but henceforth in a "normal" fashion, for the incineration of persons who died "naturally."

By mid-January 1945, nothing was left of crematoria II and III but their asphalted carcasses. The camp complex was evacuated on January 18. At noon on January 20, the SS blew up the resistant structures of crematoria II and III. Crematorium V, still intact, was dynamited at 1:00 A.M. on January 22, and on January 27, Soviet soldiers arrived at the snow-covered rubble of the four structures.

The United States Third Army liberated Buchenwald less than three months later, on April 11. On the 12th, Eisenhower visited that camp. The two triple-muffle furnaces of the Buchenwald crematorium ensured Topf's immediate celebrity. The Third Reich surrendered on May 8. On May 30, after a botched investigation, the U.S. Military Police arrested Prüfer.[104] Ludwig Topf committed suicide on the night of May 30–31[105]— needlessly, as it turned out, since on June 13, Prüfer was set free, even managing to come away with an order for a furnace from the Americans. The U.S. investigators, failing to search the company's home offices, did not understand Topf's role in setting up the gas chambers at Auschwitz.

From June 14 to 21, Ernst-Wolfgang Topf and Prüfer apparently destroyed all the contracts the firm had signed with the SS at Auschwitz.[106] As the U.S. army was withdrawing from Erfurt, which was to be part of the Soviet zone, the younger Topf brother moved west with the Americans on June 21, carrying no wealth with him other than technical and industrial documents.[107]

On July 3, the Soviets occupied Erfurt. On October 11, Gustav Braun, Topf's director of development, was questioned by the Soviet military about Prüfer and the Topf brothers.[108] On March 4, 1946, the Soviets arrested Braun (who had become temporary director), Sander, Prüfer, and Schultze.[109] Erdmann escaped internment because he was registered in a communist union.[110] Braun was condemned to 25 years in the Gulag but was freed in 1955.[111] The fate of Prüfer is unknown, but he and the other two engineers probably met the same fate as Braun. Unlike the Americans, the Soviets immediately discerned Prüfer's role in the construction of Auschwitz.[112]

Ernst-Wolfgang Topf tried to rebuild his company in Wiesbaden in 1949, but his financial means were reduced, the attempt fell short, and the Wiesbaden branch was dissolved in 1963.[113] He was never troubled by the law, despite the blunder of his only engineer, Martin Klettner, who in 1950 shamelessly submitted a patent application for an incinerating furnace. That naturally caused a stir, and was the inspiration for the play *Patent Pending* by Wim van Leer, produced in London in 1963.[114]

Bischoff led a quiet postwar life and died in 1950. Only two members of the Zentralbauleitung, Walter Dejaco and Fritz Ertl, went before a tribunal. Dejaco had personally monitored all the blueprints as head of the blueprint section. Ertl was indicted because he had presided over the infamous meeting with Prüfer and Köhler at Auschwitz on August 19, 1942, when Bischoff was in Berlin, and had countersigned a few blueprints for the new crematorium. The trial of the two "architects of the crematoria" in Vienna in January 1972 ended with the release of both.

QUESTIONS FOR DISCUSSION

1. Consider the role of Topf and Sons as a business and engineering enterprise in the design and construction of the Auschwitz-Birkenau gas chambers and crematoria. In what ways did the firm operate in a normal business manner, and in what ways did the firm operate in an illegal and/or immoral manner?

2. Pressac writes that the leaders of the SS Administrative office "began to associate the 'final solution to the Jewish problem' with the capacity of the new crematorium." Discuss the ways in which the technology of the crematoria and gas chambers contributed to the Nazi policy of racial extermination.

3. A key element in understanding the history of the technological development of the gas chambers is the architectural plans. Consider why the architectural and engineering changes were made when the originally designed morgue rooms adjacent to the furnace rooms were redesigned as gas chambers.

4. Although prisoners in the camps were able to build barracks and other simple structures, skilled laborers, engineers, and technicians were required to construct the crematoria and gas chambers. Consider the possible

motivations for technical and skilled laborers working on this project. Note that one construction firm, Lenz and Company, refused to bid on the project, citing a labor shortage. Could there have been other reasons that Lenz did not wish to bid on this government project? Could moral qualms have prevented the participation of Lenz and Company? What does this tell us about citizen cooperation or noncooperation with totalitarian regimes?

NOTES

The following archives were used in the preparation of this study: Central State Special Archives of Russia (Moscow); October Revolution Archives (Moscow/October Revolution); State Archives Weimar (Weimar); State Archives Katowice (Katowice); Archive of the Memorial Buchenwald (Buchenwald); Archive of the Memorial Place Dachau (Dachau); Archive Auschwitz-Birkenau State Museum (Oswiecim); Archive Yad Vashem, Jerusalem (Jerusalem); Berlin Document Center (Berlin); Federal Archives Koblenz (Koblenz); Chamber of Commerce and Industry, Wiesbaden (Wiesbaden); Centre de Documentation Juive Contemporaine, Paris (Paris); Central Committee for the Investigation of Hitlerite Crimes in Poland, Warsaw (Warsaw); National Institute for Industrial Protection, Compiegne (Compiegne); Landesgericht für Strafsachen, Vienna (Vienna).

1. Compiegne, 24d/1/506,627.
2. Weimar, dossier Prüfer 2/555a, letter of Topf to Leisse, April 14, 1936.
3. Dachau, files 943 and 2111.
4. Koblenz, letter Topf November 1, 1940. NS 4 Ma/54.
5. Weimar, 2/555a, order 39/D/1218.
6. Koblenz, letter June 18, 1939. NS 3/18–3.
7. Paris, CXXXVIII-129; Koblenz, NS 3/18–3.
8. Weimar, 2/555a, order 40/D/263 and 264.
9. Moscow, 502–1–327. Letter Topf May 31 and June 11, 1940.
10. Weimar, 2/555a, order 40/D/664 and 665.
11. Moscow, 502–1–214, weekly reports of July 5, 12, 20, 26, and August 17, 1940; Moscow, 502–1–327, letters Topf May 31 and June 11, 1940, and letter Bauleitung September 16, 1940; Koblenz, NS 4 Ma/54, letter Topf January 6, 1941.
12. Weimar, LK 6451, letter Topf July 14, 1941.
13. Moscow, 502–1–327, letters Topf September 18, 23, and 30, 1940.
14. Moscow, 502–1–327, letter Topf November 13, 1940.
15. Moscow, 502–1–312, plan Topf D 57.999 November 30, 1940.
16. Moscow, 502–1–312, letter Topf December 9, 1940.
17. Moscow, 502–1–327, letter Bauleitung January 21, 1941.
18. Moscow, 502–1–312, telegram Bauleitung January 13, 1941; 502–1–327, letter Bauleitung January 21, 1941.
19. Moscow, 502–1–214, weekly reports of Schlachter February 1, 10, 17 and 22, 1941.
20. Moscow, 502–1–214, weekly reports of Schlachter October 4, 14, and 28, 1940, which mention Boos; 502–1–214, weekly report Schlachter, March 1, 1941.

21. Moscow, 502–1–312, letter Topf February 3, 1941.
22. Moscow, 502–1–312, letter Bauleitung February 15, 1941.
23. Moscow, 502–1–327, letter Topf February 24, 1941.
24. Moscow, 502–1–327, letter Bauleitung March 15, 1941, and letter Topf February 24, 1941.
25. Katowice, PI Go/S, 467.
26. Moscow, 502–1–312, letter and telegram Bauleitung April 2, 1941; letter Topf April 2, 1941.
27. Moscow, 502–1–312, letter Grabner June 7, 1941.
28. Moscow, 502–1–214, weekly report of June 28, 1941.
29. Berlin, SSO, autobiography Karl Bischoff.
30. Oswiecim, BW 2/1 (old), negative 21135/1.
31. Moscow, 502–1–313, telegram Bauleitung October 11, 1941.
32. Moscow, 502–1–313, letter Topf October 14, 1941.
33. Oswiecim, negative 20931/4, plan of the main camp at Auschwitz, February 19, 1942.
34. Oswiecim, negative 1034/7.
35. Moscow, 502–1–313 and Oswiecim, BW 30/27 and BW 30/34.
36. Moscow, 502–1–312, letter Topf October 31, 1941.
37. Moscow, 502–1–313, letter Topf November 4, 1941.
38. Moscow, 502–1–314, letter Bischoff November 12, 1941, letter Prüfer November 21, 1941, and undated telegram.
39. Moscow, 502–1–314, letter Prüfer November 21, 1941; 502–1–327, letter Wirtz December 4, 1941.
40. Moscow, 502–1–313, letter Topf August 31, 1942.
41. Oswiecim, BW 11/1, letter Bauleitung January 5, 1942; letter Topf January 9, 1942; Moscow, 502–1–312, letter Topf November 24, 1941, letters Bauleitung November 27, 1941, December 8, 1941, January 5, 1942.
42. Degesch, *Zyklon for Pest Control* (Frankfurt am Main, 1972).
43. Moscow, 502–1–214, weekly report of July 12, 1940.
44. I reject Danuta Czech's dating of the first gassing in September 1941 in favor of one based on Jan Sehn's statement that the first gassing of Soviet prisoners took place after the month-long visit of a Gestapo team in November 1941. Sehn's account seems reliable, especially as he describes how the basement of block 11 needed two days of ventilation before it could be entered. See Danuta Czech, *Kalendarium der Ereignisse im Konzentrationslager Auschwitz-Birkenau 1939–1945* (Reinbek bei Hamburg, 1989), 117 and 119; Jan Sehn, *Concentration Camp Oswiecim-Brzezinka* (Warsaw, 1957), p. 105.
45. Moscow, 502–1–312, letter Grabner January 31, 1942.
46. Warsaw, photo taken by Stanislav Luczko, no. 5149.
47. Oswiecim, BW 30/1 to BW 30/7 (plans 932–38 and 980).
48. Oswiecim, plan 933.
49. Moscow, 502–1–313 and Oswiecim, BW 30/34, 31ff.
50. Oswiecim, BW 30/25, 1.
51. Moscow, 502–1–313, 314, letter Bauleitung March 39, 1942; Oswiecim, BW 30/34, 115.
52. Moscow, 502–1–312, bill of lading, April 16, 1942.

53. Weimar, 2/555a, letter Prüfer November 15, 1942.

54. Oswiecim, box BW 1/2, file BW 1/16, 172, box BW 1/6, file BW 1/31, 1–4.

55. Moscow, 502–1–322; G. Peters and E. Wuestinger, "Entlausung mit Zyklon-Blausaeure in Kreislauf-Begasungskamern," in *Zeitschrift für hygienische Zoologie und schaedlingsbekaempfung,* 10–11 (1940).

56. Moscow, 502–1–331, plans Boos 16.591 and 16.600.

57. Moscow, 502–1–322, report Dienstelle Arbeitseinsatz, July 2, 1942; letter public health office Bielitz, July 3, 1942.

58. Moscow, 502–4–2 to 502–4–47, the 46 death books of Auschwitz.

59. Czech, pp. 250f.

60. Jean-Claude Pressac, *Auschwitz: Technique and Operation of the Gas Chambers,* trans. Peter Moss (New York, 1989).

61. Moscow, 502–1–313, bill of lading June 18, 1942; 502–1–327, bill of lading August 6, 1942.

62. Moscow/October Revolution, 7021–108–32, 45–7, letter Bauleitung October 13, 1942.

63. Oswiecim, BW 30/30, 23; BW 30/26, 22.

64. Moscow/October Revolution, 7021–108–32, 46.

65. Weimar, 2/555a, contracts 41 D 2435 (27,600 RM), 42/1422/3 (3,258 RM), 42/1454/1 (53,702 RM).

66. Oswiecim, BW 30b–30c/22.

67. Johann Paul Kremer, *KL Auschwitz as Seen by the SS* (Oswiecim, Panstwowe Muzeum), pp. 104, 218.

68. Oswiecim, BW 30/34, 96.

69. Moscow, note by Wolter November 27, 1942.

70. Oswiecim, BW 1/19.

71. Oswiecim, BW 30/12.

72. See Pressac, pp. 481ff.

73. Oswiecim, BW 30b–30c/23.

74. Oswiecim, BW 30/30, 6 and Moscow, 502–1–313, letter Mulka January 29, 1943.

75. See Pressac, p. 370.

76. Oswiecim, BW 30/34, 84; BW 30/27, 29.

77. Oswiecim, BW 30/34, 48.

78. Oswiecim, BW 30/25, 7.

79. Moscow, 502–1–311, bill Topf May 24, 1943.

80. Oswiecim, BW 30/34, 55.

81. See Pressac, pp. 481ff.

82. Oswiecim, BW 30/41, 28.

83. Czech, p. 440.

84. Moscow, 502–2–54, 8.

85. Czech, p. 445.

86. Oswiecim, BW 30/25, 8.

87. Moscow, 502–2–54, transfer March 31, 1943; 502–1–281, letter WVHA June 23, 1944.

88. That day Prüfer signed for a blueprint made in the Zentralbauleitung.

89. Moscow, 502–2–26, letter Topf June 9, 1943.

90. Moscow, 502–2–26, letter Topf June 9, 1943; 502–1–313, letter Köhler May 21, 1943.
91. Moscow, 502–2–54, transfer agreement March 19/22, 1943; 502–1–281, letter WVHA June 24, 1944; also Oswiecim, BW 30/43, 31f.
92. Oswiecim, BW 30/28, 73, 68.
93. *Auschwitz Album* (New York, 1980), photo 112.
94. Deduction based on the roughly 50 cm difference in spacing between the axes of the two crucibles of the basic element of the eight-muffle furnace placed in crematoria IV and V. The measurements were taken from the remains of the furnace in the ruins of crematorium V in Birkenau, and from photo Oswiecim negative 888.
95. Oswiecim, BW 30/25, 14; BW 30/26, 27.
96. Moscow, 502–2–54, transfer June 24, 1943.
97. Moscow, 502–2–54, 87.
98. Moscow, 502–1–313, letter Topf August 20, 1943.
99. Oswiecim, BW 30/34, 18; Moscow, 502–1–313 telegram Bauleitung May 12, 1944; 502–1–327, letter Betzinger June 15, 1944.
100. Moscow, 502–1–327, letter Betzinger June 13, 1944.
101. Moscow, 502–1–327, bill Topf December 23, 1943.
102. Moscow/October Revolution, Russian plan of bunker 2, scale 1:1000 of March 3, 1945.
103. Oswiecim, photo negative 888.
104. Weimar, 2/555a, note June 18, 1945.
105. Weimar, 211, 3; LK 4651, letter February 7, 1946.
106. Study of the personnel file of Prüfer shows that it lacks all contracts negotiated after March 1941.
107. Buchenwald, 64–0–2, letter Topf September 25, 1945; Wiesbaden, dossier Topf, letter January 6, 1948.
108. Weimar, 2/555, report Gustav Braun October 11, 1945.
109. Weimar, 2/555 (Prüfer) and 2/381 (Braun), notes of April 26, 1946 of Machemehl, secretary of the firm.
110. Weimar, 2/938 and 2/938a, personnel file Erdmann.
111. Moscow, internment file 236334, Braun.
112. Cf. Pravda, no. 109, May 7, 1945; French translation in *Forfaits hitleriens* (Geneva and Paris, 1945), p. 309.
113. Wiesbaden, dossier Topf, ordinance of March 19, 1963.
114. Compiegne, German patent, 24/d/1, no. 861.731.

CHAPTER 4

Technology and Politics in Totalitarian Regimes: Nazi Germany

———————————— \/ ————————————

This chapter presents an analysis of the characteristics of technology in autocratic, totalitarian regimes, such as Germany under the rule of the Nazi party, by an expert on the history of science and technology, Paul R. Josephson. The discussion of Nazi technology is derived from a more in-depth study by Josephson that compares it to the technology and science that developed in the Soviet Union under Stalin, another totalitarian regime. Here we focus on Nazi technology as representative of essential characteristics that Josephson determines to be associated with totalitarian political systems: (1) the state is the prime mover in the creation of technology, which leads to both the development of large-scale "big science" projects that only governments can fund, and to the establishment of technologies that are unresponsive to market forces and the needs of the public; (2) technological expertise is subjugated to the interests of the state through overly centralized and bureaucratic control of research and development; and (3) emphasis is placed on massive projects, a gigantomania of scale designed for the display value of the political ideals of the regime. All three characteristics are seen in Josephson's brief review of the history of Nazi technological achievements, especially in the architectural debates in Weimar and Nazi Germany and in the development of the V-2 rockets. Technology in the

Nazi regime was a means of furthering the ideology of Nazism and its racist, anti-Semitic world view. Modernist Bauhaus architectural design, even though it had originated in Germany, was thought to be Jewish and Bolshevist (i.e., communist), and thus was banned. Hitler and his architect, Albert Speer, dreamt of massive building projects and urban redesign to demonstrate the superiority of Aryan culture (see chapters 6–8). This political use of ideology casts doubt on the traditional idea that technology (and science) are value-neutral, that there is "one best way" to design and develop a technological artifact or system. As the history of technology in Nazi Germany demonstrates, political, economic, and social criteria strongly influence the developments and achievements of science and technology in a particular society.

From *Totalitarian Science and Technology*

Paul R. Josephson

Technologies are symbols of national achievement. They demonstrate the prowess of the nation's scientists and engineers. They are central to national security strategies. They serve foreign policy purposes through technology transfer. They entrance a public who can become intoxicated with the artifact's symbolism and overlook its potential dangers to society (and at other times provoke fear and dislike). We need only think of the space race between the United States and the USSR, or other technological posturing between the two superpowers, to comprehend the importance of technology in securing a regime's legitimacy at home and abroad.

Skyscrapers and apartment housing, subway systems, assembly lines, canals and bridges, hydropower stations, and nuclear reactors have an imposing physical presence. They also have what has been called "display value" (Smith 1983; Frost 1991; Hughes 1989b). Display value includes the social, cultural, and ideological significance of technology. While countries differ in terms of economic and political organization—market or centrally planned economy, single-party or multiparty system, centralized or decentralized decision-making apparatus—the display value of large-scale technologies applies to all.

Yet surely the place of technology in totalitarian regimes differs from that in pluralist regimes. [Because of] economic, political, and social concerns, . . . technology . . . has a particular style in [totalitarian] regimes. At first glance technology would seem to be value-neutral, serving the rational ends of achieving a desired outcome in the "one best way." This way means efficiency maximization. Technologies are various devices, techniques, or systems intended to give us control over the natural environment—and also over our political, economic, and social structures. The latter include scientific management for industry, the gathering, collating, and analysis of data for national planning, and so on. Engineers strive for efficiencies in production by optimizing the use of labor and capital inputs. They work toward these ends through planning to set prices, allocating raw materials and market share, and designing shop layouts and material flows (Ellul 1964).

The "one best way" distinction is crucial, for it implies that given any engineering problem the solution will be universal, based on engineering calculations that employ the scientific method. The "one best way" means that rockets and jets the world over resemble each other because other designs would not fly. All hydroelectric stations, subways, bridges, and skyscrapers share essential materials, structural elements, and components, or they would not stand. The first-glance differences between technologies in different settings reflect, literally, superficial elements: the skin of glass and steel or aluminum and plexiglas of a skyscraper, for example. You could go so far as to say that functional efficiency determines design. Yet technologies are more than components assembled in the "one best way" to create a large system. Economic and social obstacles as much as technical ones must be overcome to ensure successful diffusion of technology. Capital, political and human organizations are vital to technology (Hughes 1989a).

Engineers trained in a given milieu tend to accept the broader cultural values of their system. What are rational means for achieving desired ends in one society may be abhorrent in another. For example, the mass production of consumer goods through the "American system" of interchangeable parts and Fordism (standardized production; a controlled and steady flow of energy and materials in production processes from acquisition to the assembly line; and mass production to lower unit costs) will be crass materialism to conservative German engineers. The factory assembly line symbolized the exploitation of the proletariat to Soviet engineers. On the other hand, Soviet leaders idealized Taylorism (a doctrine of scientific management in industry) and established an officially sponsored materialism. And when the ends are full employment, social welfare, inexpensive housing, or universal health care (and not *simply* the design of a jet engine!), disagreements over the means and ends pour forth.

Take the example of public housing. Recognizing that their expertise could be used to achieve social goals, and responding to housing needs, engineers in Nazi Germany and the Stalinist USSR sought a prominent role in factory organization, housing, and urban planning. In the USSR, a Marxist urban industrial ideology held sway. Urban centers swelled in the 1920s and 1930s as peasants streamed into cities. Stalin encouraged this behavior by cutting capital investment in the countryside to focus on the creation of heavy industry and by forcing the peasantry into hated collected farms. Planners' preferences held sway in this centrally planned economy. Housing had to be built rapidly. Why not use inexpensive, standardized designs based on prefabricated forms that could be assembled rapidly by unskilled and illiterate workers into dwellings?

Soviet housing was proletarian in its minimal space, threadbare appointments, and shared bathrooms. This housing frequently incorporated the "collectivist" ethos in communal kitchens, child care facilities, and rooms for workers' clubs, but these were introduced more often to cut costs than to uphold a proletarian social ideal. The apartments and clubrooms, like the factory itself, also had a political function as the appropriate setting for the Communist Party to employ various media (radio, film, mass publications, meetings) to educate the masses about Stalin's programs. In Nazi Germany, these communal means and ends were rejected out of hand as anathema to the *völkisch* peasant and reviled as "Bolshevist." More appropriate for the German were thatched-roof cottages that showed his organic and blood ties to the soil.

THE TOTALITARIAN MACHINE

Does the machine, the symbol of the engineer, have the same effect on societies everywhere? Do all of the world's engineers employ machines for the same ends? Is the universal goal of the machine such efficiencies as increased output per unit of input, economies of scale through mass production, and speed of output? More to the point, can the engineer make rational, optimalistic choices in a totalitarian system? The answer is often yes, but the path to that answer has been arduous in every system.

Yet the ideological underpinnings of National Socialism and Soviet Marxism differed significantly. Nazism was an antiurban, racially based ideology. According to its myth, Aryan "settlers" whose blood rooted them organically in the German soil created a technology that served *völkisch* needs, not the profit motive of international capitalists. At the same time, German technological achievements—for example, in the chemical and automotive industries—were pioneering efforts that displayed complex elegance. So there was a disjunction between the advanced state of German technology and the Nazi myth, described by historian Jeffrey Herf as "reactionary modernism" (Herf 1984).

Soviet technologies were intended to reflect the collectivist ethos of serving the basic housing, transport, and food demands of the masses. Simultaneously, they served state goals of economic self-sufficiency and military might. The construction sites were also forums for educating the unskilled workers, not only about technical details but also in the messages of Stalinism. The result was bland, functional designs in which workers' safety and environmental concerns played a secondary role.

In spite of these differences, several features distinguish technologies in totalitarian regimes from those in pluralist regimes. The most obvious is the fact that the state serves as prime mover behind development and diffusion. Whether in Soviet research institutes or Nazi ordnance laboratories, this engenders "big science" approaches to research and development. The absence of market forces and the exclusion of the public from decisions about how or whether to diffuse a technology permits the development of technologies that persist no matter their questionable efficacy or environmental soundness. These characteristics also apply in the nonmarket sectors of democracies, notably defense industries, which are infamous for projects that waste billions of dollars.

A second feature of totalitarian technology is overly centralized administration of research and development. This is not surprising in countries of state socialism, such as the former USSR, where the state owns most of the means of production. But in fascist regimes, too, the persistence of private property is tempered by centrally funded projects that rely on the state for their impetus. Major industrialists prosper in close cooperation with the state, while smaller businesses are subjugated to the "national good." This leads to irrational use of resources, as the case . . . of Albert Speer's monumental plans to rebuild Berlin will demonstrate. To be sure, decision making about which projects to fund involves give-and-take among engineers, economic planners, and party officials. Naturally, officials stress the interests of the state. Hence engineers in totalitarian regimes tend to be more accountable to the state; those in pluralist regimes find greater autonomy in setting the research agenda. Their professional societies sell expertise, receiving the exclusive right to practice their professions through licenses granted by the state: for example, as medical doctors. In totalitarian regimes, societies, clubs, and associations for architects, scientists, lawyers, and doctors are subjugated to single-party organizations ruled from above.

Third, technologies in totalitarian regimes are characterized by gigantomania: for example, Speer's plans for wide-gauge (four-meter) railroad track with two-story-high cars or Stalin's seven "wedding-cake" Moscow skyscrapers and the world speed and distance records that were set in aviation (Bailes 1978, 381–406). This scale concerns both physical parameters and the display value of the technology. Gigantomania often results in waste of labor and capital resources, especially in centrally planned economies where the state is the prime mover behind every project. In totalitarian regimes projects seem to take on a life of their own, so important are they for cultural and political ends as opposed to the ends of engineering rationality. . . .

WEIMAR CULTURE AND TECHNOLOGY

National Socialist ideology was ambivalent about modern technology. On the one hand, technology was central to efforts to rearm Germany and secure the new empire's glorious future. The superweapons its army leaders sought during the war required the input of technological experts. Its Four-Year Plan, adopted on the eve of World War II to prepare the economy for the *Blitzkreig*, was an agglomeration of macroeconomic techniques and state-supported projects geared to produce a great industrial power. Many engineers welcomed the strong central government of the National Socialists for its ability to support modern technology more efficiently than the Weimar regime, which had been plagued by an inexperienced liberal parliamentary government and the chaos of the free market. In 1914, imperial Germany had been the leading scientific and industrial nation in the world. Its engineers saw the new chemical weapons and airplanes of World War I as signifying the glories that might be achieved by wedding technical knowledge to a strong state power (Herf 1984, 152–62).

On the other hand, German engineers on the whole were conservative individuals who rejected the rationality of Enlightenment social progress. They believed in the ability to understand physical processes empirically, but not in the extension of empirical methods to human problems. Nazi ideologists, for their part, detested the modern symbols of Weimar technology. They perceived in its spare, utilitarian architecture "Bolshevist" designs, which abandoned the natural antiurbanist aesthetic that should have characterized *völkisch* technology. Nazi Germany needed modern technology to achieve its imperial ends but rejected this technology on anachronistic ideological grounds and found great fault with Soviet technological style. Yet the Nazi technological style—characterized by a preference for centralized project management with attendant social and political control and by gigantomania—was paradigmatic for totalitarian regimes. . . .

The hyperinflation, unemployment, and leftist and rightist uprisings of the early Weimar years gave way to economic prosperity and economic stability in the late 1920s. Efforts to employ Fordism and Americanism for higher productivity and industrial rationality reached their zenith. But as the Great Depression of the early 1930s set in, the political parties on the extremes grew, with the Nazis the ultimate beneficiaries. Throughout the period, the conservatives blamed the lost war, the unfavorable terms of the Versailles treaty, and economic instability on Jews and liberals. They viewed cosmopolitan mass culture as decadent and attacked political liberalism as "Bolshevist" (Herf 1984, 18–22). The engineers among them saw the left as promoting technological stagnation through their fear of rearmament and criticized liberal political and social programs for promoting "cultural Luddism"; this meant they believed the liberals would destroy *völkisch* culture as the anti-industrial Luddites of early nineteenth-century England had smashed machines to bits. National Socialism gave them hope of fulfilling self-interest and state service, unleashing technology from the bonds imposed by the Weimar Republic. Engineers eventually talked themselves into believing that the Nazis had abandoned the anti-industrial themes of *völkisch* thought (Herf 1984, 152–62).

What was it about Weimar that raised the specter of Bolshevist technology? To many German engineers such vibrant cultural phenomena as the Bauhaus, an artistic and technological movement born in the Weimar Republic, symbolized everything that was non-German about modern technology. Like other modernist architects such as Le Corbusier and Frank Lloyd Wright, Bauhaus architects transformed the house or other building into a tool. They sought to integrate craft, art, and industry in one modern aesthetic. They appealed to such ideals as democracy, optimality, and efficiency in their designs. For Le Corbusier, the park and the skyscraper were united to exalt rational power. Wright, in his utopian vision Broadacre City, saw the telephone and automobile as contributing to the disappearance of the city because these technologies were inherently democratizing in their decentralizing force and their ability to diffuse population, wealth, and power (Fishman 1982; Whitford 1984; Banham 1986). The democratic ends of such architecture disturbed the conservative Germans.

Bauhaus artists such as Walter Gropius and Ludwig Mies van der Rohe seized upon the aesthetic of the machine, its embodiment of speed, efficiency, and clean lines, in every thing they produced: office buildings and apartments, chairs and other furnishings, even utensils and vases. They took inspiration from factory design. They sought to bring together artists, craftsmen, sculptors, and architects in the common endeavor of tying crafts to industry and mass producing craftwork. Architects secured funding from the Weimar and municipal governments for many of their projects for mass housing and concentrated on the technical aspects of construction technology and planning. Some of them claimed "that construction methods determined style itself," with standardization of building parts— prefabricated concrete forms and modular construction—essential for a uniform aesthetic. They believed that mass housing was not different from mass transportation or any other problem of urban planning (Lane 1985,

128–30). Bauhaus supporters believed that technology could be employed to achieve a diversity of modernist social ends—inexpensive housing, rapid mass transit, etc., and their implicitly democratic ends—through standardized means. No matter what Bauhaus architects believed, socialist, modernist, or totalitarian ends can be achieved through the application of standardized construction techniques.

Most German engineers, however, believed that this style of technology could not be reconciled with German culture in a nationalist ideology. In spite of the fact that the Bauhaus style was recognized internationally as an achievement of German culture, for conservative elements it was "un-German," based on a uniform industrial aesthetic, a proletarian social policy, and a "Bolshevist" political program of helping the masses. They attacked its prefabricated housing and standardized building methods. Conservative architects appealed to national building traditions. They considered that flat roofs, for example, provided inadequate draining of rain and melting snow and were inappropriate to the German climate; according to one, the flat roof was an "oriental form" and equated with flat heads. Other architects declared that standardized building techniques produced "'nomadic architecture,' leading to 'uprootedness, spiritual impoverishment and proletarianization.'" Still others adopted an antiurban theme, attacking skyscrapers and calling for a return to the German soil. Eventually, this kind of criticism of the Bauhaus was incorporated into racial arguments, where the origin of the Bauhaus style was attributed to cultural decadence that had its roots in biological causes. These kinds of explanations, of course, won support in Nazi circles (Lane 1985, 132–40).

NAZI TECHNOLOGY

Were National Socialism a consistent ideology, we would expect efforts to create an agrarian society in which the *Volk* could best prosper. But the Nazi rise to power did not give way to rural nostalgia or to an antimodernist technological ethos that supported the peasant's organic tie to the soil. Rather, Nazism combined anti-Semitism and the embrace of modern technology in a myth, according to which technological advance grew out of a racial battle between Aryan and Jew, blood and gold. The engineer would assist the regime in destroying an unhealthy urban atmosphere, liberating the nation from the "fetters of Jewish materialism. The Nordic race was ideally suited to use technology; the Jew misused it." . . . Nazi technology embodied service to the nation, not pursuit of profit. Service to the nation meant joining with the state to achieve economic independence. State trade, tariff, tax, price, and wage policies would help to underwrite technological development to achieve autarky and enable the nation to engage in war when cut off from the import of raw materials (Herf 1984, 189–93).

For Hitler himself there was no *völkisch* rejection of technology. If in life and politics the strongest won, so among nations the technologically weak would be defeated. Hitler advocated rearmament and, like Stalin, national autarky. He used new media such as radio and film to praise *völkisch* technology for propaganda ends and sponsored modern highways—the autobahn—and other modern artifacts for economic and military ends (Herf 1984, 194–96). And when the war effort bogged down, Hitler hoped for a technological savior in the form of a new superweapon like the V-2 rocket.

Hitler's writings and speeches criticized Weimar culture for its weaknesses, its decadence, its materialism, its "lack of an heroic ideal," its "Bolshevist" art. He singled out its architecture as the epitome of these problems. Hitler supported gigantomania in Nazi architecture. The Nazi leaders built massive monuments to their rule whose neoclassical style and scale were neither *völkisch* nor humanistic. Hitler believed that a "great" architecture was needed in the Third Reich, since architecture was a vital index of national power and strength. There had to be monuments in cities, not symbols of cultural decay.

When the Nazis began vigorously to oppose the Bauhaus in the 1930s, the foremost party philosopher, Alfred Rosenberg, led the charge. Rosenberg had joined the Nazi Party in 1920 and became editor of *Völkischer Beobachter* in 1921, through which he attacked the Bauhaus. His career had ups and downs, but in 1933 he was put in charge of ideological training of Nazi Party members. From this position, Rosenberg hoped to see the Nazi Party university create a place for natural science, especially to study the biological laws of races to reveal the poisonous influence of the Jews. In 1941, Rosenberg became the Reich's minister for the eastern occupied territories, a position from which he could see Nazi racist policies of *Lebensraum* and the "final solution" put into action. He was hanged for war crimes in 1946 (Rosenberg 1970; Pois 1970).

In 1929, Rosenberg founded the Kampfbund to spread a Nazi gospel of virulent Christian anti-Semitism and racial doctrines. Many of these doctrines were based on the writings of Count Gobineau, who had argued that the rise and fall of civilizations is connected to their racial composition. Those of Aryan stock flourish, while those diluted through miscegenation decline. Rosenberg embraced conspiracy theories and feared the "international Jew," freemasonry, and Jewish control of banking and the media. The Kampfbund was central in spreading Rosenberg's message of the *völkisch* aesthetic. Initially, the Kampfbund had the strong political backing of the Nazi Party. In the same way that Bolshevik organizations had subjugated engineers' professional associations, so the Kampfbund inexorably absorbed smaller rivals. The Kampfbund set forth the party line on cultural values. It attacked the chaos, Russian "Bolshevism," and American "mechanism" allegedly rampant in modern art, the Jewish roots of these problems, and the "Nigger-Culture" that thrived in the Weimar clubs whose excitement and decadence was so well captured in the Broadway musical, and later film, *Cabaret* (Lane 1985: 149–51). Rosenberg despised modern art. He saw in Picasso "Mongrelism," whose "bastardized progeny, nurtured by spiritual syphilis and artistic infantalism was able to represent expressions of the soul"; and he hated the work of such artists as Marc Chagall and Wassily Kandinsky, who was connected to the Bauhaus (Rosenberg 1970, 128–51).

Rosenberg argued that Bauhaus architecture was a symbol of weakened culture, of a mass society whose members had lost their historic identity through urbanization and their economic security through proletarianization and unemployment. The Bauhaus was a "cathedral of Marxism" that resembled a synagogue or a "Bolshevist" building for the nomads of the metropolis (Lane 1985, 162–63). Rosenberg constantly referred to the interconnection of race, art, learning, and moral values in his attacks on the cultural decadence of Weimar, attacks that, to the German people who were suffering through the depression, were appealing (Lane 1985, 147–49). On April 11, 1933, the Berlin police shut down the Bauhaus school by order of the new Nazi government.

Next the Nazis orchestrated the *Gleichschaltung* [coordination] of municipal building administrations and building societies by purging them of adherents to the modernist Bauhaus movement. The societies were then joined in a central organization under government control, just as all professional societies were subjugated to Communist Party organs under Stalin. In spite of their criticism of "Bolshevist" urban development, the Nazis supported programs for large-scale, low-cost public housing in their appeal for working-class support. This support of public housing resulted in part from Rosenberg's loss of influence to Joseph Göbbels. The Kampfbund was placed under Göbbels's authority, and he established the Reichskulturkammer as a branch of his Propaganda Ministry (Lane 1985, 169–71). The Kulturkammer had sections for film, literature, theater, music, the media, and visual arts, with national and regional offices. Göbbels himself hesitated to purge the new style entirely from the Third Reich. Barbara Lane writes: "If the establishment of the Reichskulturkammer cut short the purges of 1933 and prevented the original leaders of the Kampfbund from gaining control of architectural style, Göbbels's organization never explicitly repudiated the Kampfbund's attacks on the new architecture; and these attacks had a profound effect upon the careers of the radical architects" (Lane 1985, 176–84). Many modernist architects were deprived of their livelihood and had to emigrate, like physicists, biologists, and doctors. While depriving Bauhaus architects of influence and dictating issues of style, this did not prevent them from getting new commissions, and many Bauhaus assistants and students received positions in the Nazi government (Lane 1985, 171–73).

GIGANTOMANIA IN NAZI GERMANY

Nazi architectural style, like Soviet, was gigantomanic. Hitler desired immense monuments to his rule and the glory of the Third Reich for millennia to come, buildings of a scale never before seen. The party and its strong central state were the driving force of Nazi architecture. Nazi buildings were intended to express the will of the Nordic people, awaken national consciousness, and contribute to the political and moral unification of the *Volk* (Lane 1985, 185–89). In October 1935, when the major structural frame of the new Luftwaffe building was finished, Hermann Göring addressed gathered workers and functionaries to praise the structure as "a symbol of the new Reich," a building that "shakes our deepest emotions," shows German "will and strength," and would "stand forever like the union of the Volk" (Göring 193, 148–50).

Nazi architecture was not one, historicist style, nor an out and out rejection of the new style, but a variety of styles that reflected the diversity of views of the leadership: public works such as highways and bridges, government buildings, and some apartment buildings; neo-Romanesque; rustic housing projects intended to tie the urban workers to the soil; modern neoclassicism based on the Doric aesthetics of Albert Speer; and even modern (Speer 1970, 62–63; Lane 1985, 185–89).

Albert Speer was the chief architect behind many of the gigantic projects. Hitler desired Speer to make a huge field for military exercises and party rallies, with a large stadium and a hall for Hitler's addresses. While never completed, the planned Nuremburg tract embraced an area of 16.5 square kilometers (roughly 6.5 square miles). All of the structures would have been two to three times the size of the grandiose Greek and Egyptian constructions of antiquity. For example, Speer designed the Nuremburg stadium based on the ancient stadium of Athens, but far larger: six hundred yards by five hundred yards. Speer selected pink granite for the exterior, white for the stands. To the north of the stadium a processional avenue crossed a huge expanse of water in which the buildings would be reflected. When Hitler first saw the designs he was so excited, his adjutant reported, that he "didn't close an eye last night" (Speer 1970, 64–67).

In 1939, in a speech to construction workers, Hitler explained his grandiose style: "Why always the biggest? I do this to restore to each individual German his self-respect. In a hundred areas I want to say to the individual: we are not inferior; on the contrary we are the complete equals of every other nation." Hitler's "love of vast proportions," Speer commented, was connected not only with totalitarianism but with a show of wealth and strength and a desire for "stone witnesses to history" (Speer 1970, 69). Yet these structures could scarcely have instilled in the individual any personal feeling other than insignificance. For anyone but Hitler himself, any sense of glory could come only as an anonymous contributer to the all-powerful state.

Hitler wanted a new chancellery to celebrate his rise in rank to "one of the greatest men in history," with great halls and salons to make an impression on visiting dignitaries. He insisted that it be built within a year. Speer was required to raze an entire neighborhood of Berlin. Forty-five hundred workers labored in two shifts, with several thousand more scattered throughout the Reich producing building materials and furnishings. To meet Hitler's designs, Speer created a great gate, outside staircase, reception rooms, mosaic-clad halls, rooms with domed ceilings, and a gallery twice as long as the Hall of Mirrors at Versailles. The chancellery included an underground air-raid shelter. When it was finished, Hitler "especially liked the long tramp that state guests and diplomats would now have to take before they reached the reception hall" (Speer 1970, 102–3, 113–14).

The future headquarters of the Reich would have been the largest structure of all, with a volume fifty times greater than the proposed Reichstag building. It could have held 185,000 persons standing and was "essentially a place of worship." Its dome opened to admit light. At 152 feet in diameter, it was bigger than the entire dome of the Pantheon (142 feet). A three-tiered gallery was 462 feet in diameter and 100 feet tall. In order to ensure that the structure lasted into the next millenium, engineers calculated, its steel skeleton, from which solid rock walls were suspended, would have to be placed on a foundation of 3.9 million cubic yards of concrete, dozens of feet thick; the engineers did tests to determine how far the monstrous cube would sink into the sandy building site. Hitler was partly motivated by Stalin's projects. "Now this will be the end of their building for good and all," Hitler boasted (Speer 1970, 151–55).

Hitler desired to rebuild Berlin as the capital of "Germania," a new empire that would span the entire Eurasian continent and far outdistance Rome, London, and Paris in grandiosity and history. Hitler had studied the Ringstrasse in Vienna with its prominent public buildings (Schorske 1979). Speer had to order the heart of the city razed to accommodate the two new axes through the center lined with tall office buildings. Four airports were situated at the terminal points of the axes. A ring Autobahn encircled the new Berlin, incorporating enough space to double the city's population. A four-story copper and glass railway station with steel ribbing and great blocks of stone, elevators, and escalators would surpass Grand Central Station in size. The plans themselves experienced gigantomania, eventually including seventeen radial thoroughfares, each two hundred feet wide, and five rings; the land beyond the last ring would be for recreation, a woodland of artificially planted deciduous trees instead of indigenous pine. The projects required immense effort; SS head Heinrich Himmler offered to supply prisoners to increase production of brick and granite, which were in short supply. Himmler's SS concentration camp operations showed tremendous ignorance of construction techniques and often produced blocks of granite with cracks. They could supply only a small amount of the stone needed; highway construction used the wasted material as cobblestones (Speer 1970, 73–79, 134–35, 144). Only the demands of war prevented the Nazis from carrying out these radical transformation plans.

Hitler's favorite toy, it seemed, was the model city, a 1:50 scale model that was set up in the former exhibition rooms of the Berlin Academy of Arts. When Speer's father saw the mock-ups he commented, "You've all gone completely crazy." Only later, when in prison, did Speer realize the inhumanity of his designs, the "lifeless and regimented" nature of the avenues, the "complete lack of proportion" of the plans (Speer 1970, 132–39). But we should not think of Speer's designs as unique in the Western world at the time. There was a resurgence of interest in massive neoclassical forms in other Western countries: for example, Rockefeller Center in New York City, the forty-four-story gothic Cathedral of Learning in Pittsburgh, and Stalinist architecture generally.

The heroic Nazi projects pushed to the limits of technology. Very few large projects were carried out, in part because of their astronomical costs and the costs of war. Smaller, more feasible projects became showpieces of Nazi propaganda, with Hitler a prominent figure at groundbreakings. There was constant coverage of the projects, some of which took years, and this propaganda all but obscured the failings of the building program: for example, projects for the masses such as public housing never met demand. Nazi public housing retained the Weimar (and universal) practice of constructing row houses and apartment buildings on the periphery of urban population centers. Only a few projects conformed to the Nazi ideal of tiny houses with sloping roofs, sited on enormous plots of land. The surfacing of these attempted to evoke the countryside: thatched roofs, half-timbering, or vertical wood siding (Lane 1985, 190, 205–13).

There was a contradiction between the designs of the Reich's commissar for public housing to fill the world with lovely peasant houses in the postwar period and the plans of Speer as general building inspector for Berlin to undertake its rebuilding as a "world capital city" of "insane monumentality" whose buildings would be an "imperishable confirmation" of the power of the Third Reich, yet had a "nonstyle of pseudoantique form, ponderous excess and solemn emptiness." But Hitler recognized this. Referring to his government's new palace he said,

"Amid a holy grove of ancient oaks, people will gaze at this first giant among the buildings of the Third Reich in awesome wonder" (Bracher 1970, 347). But this contradiction displays a central contradiction of totalitarianism itself: the superefficient omnipotent state constructed of people kept in isolation and ignorance. . . .

"BIG TECHNOLOGY" IN NAZI GERMANY

The V-2 rocket, the first large guided rocket, was the greatest technological achievement of the Third Reich. Yet it was a poor weapon, unable to carry a large explosive payload, and diverted manpower and other resources from more sensible armaments projects. The V-2 demonstrated the importance of the leader principle in scientific success. Hitler's support set the project off; when he lost faith in the V-2, the program lost priority for material and manpower. Still, the V-2 program foreshadowed the Manhattan Project and "big science" of the postwar years as a paradigm of state mobilization to force the invention of new military technologies. The V-2 program grew out of a military bureaucracy, which rarely considered human or economic costs. This, together with the needs of secrecy and the inadequate technical basis of industry, necessitated the creation of a large government-funded central laboratory (Neufeld 1994, 51–53).

During the Weimar years, a popular fad for rocketry and space flights produced both stunts and serious liquid fuel experiments that generated national pride for the outcast nation (Neufeld 1990). With the Depression the fad ended, but experimentalists continued their trial-and-error efforts. A group that included Wernher von Braun, who would direct technical aspects of the U.S. manned space program, was established in Berlin in 1930. (Von Braun energetically promoted the U.S. program in the 1950s by touting the possibilities of the moon's colonization by millions of people; his colonization claims resembled Nazi *Lebensraum* ideology.) The Berlin group sought corporate financial backing by stressing commercial applications such as intercontinental transport. The turning point in the V-2 program was the interest of the Army Ordnance Office in the use of rockets to deliver chemical weapons. The office built a large secret facility to maintain the assumed lead in rocket development that Germany had over other nations. It used the Gestapo to impose secrecy and to drive other rocket efforts out of business. Secrecy required outside subcontracting to be abandoned and necessitated the fabrication of one-of-a-kind hardware. The program gained momentum when the Luftwaffe (air force) joined in, securing the political support and resources of Hermann Göring. The Luftwaffe underwrote a new weapons facility, Peenemünde (Neufeld 1994, 56–58).

At Peenemünde, von Braun and other scientists sought to build an in-house production line of rocket components for the finished weapons. Peenemünde had the advantage over universities in research and development in terms of concentrated scientific interest, commitment to Nazi or national ideology, stable funding, and draft exemptions for key personnel. Von Braun cultivated contacts with university scientists and engineers for manpower. He successfully created an open academic atmosphere in an environment of secrecy. In this environment "big science" was fostered. When the Nazis invaded Poland, appropriations for research rapidly expanded. Leading military figures associated with the V-2 had laid the groundwork for these increases by promising the deployment of missile weapons in short order and by fostering contacts with such high officials as Albert Speer. But at times Hitler withdrew his support, including cutting deliveries of steel in favor of other priority projects. Even relations with the Luftwaffe deteriorated as the war progressed and Germany's prospects worsened (Neufeld 1994, 59–62).

Speer secured Himmler's intervention in 1943 to push production, utilizing concentration camp labor at newly built underground facilities. In a last-ditch effort to hold off defeat, the Peenemünde facility was pushed to produce as many missiles as possible to use on England. No thought was given to the human cost, in the slaves who toiled without expression to the death in damp, disease-ridden conditions, living, working, and sleeping in the Peenemünde caves (Goebbels 1948, 286).

Hitler's arbitary and autocractic behavior had a negative effect on Nazi "big science." Speer reports that as the military situation deteriorated Hitler made a series of technological blunders: for example, ordering a fighter jet capable of shooting down American bombers to be built instead as a fast but tiny bomber, incapable of holding many bombs. Hitler then insisted that the V-2 be mass produced at a level of nine hundred per month for use as an offensive weapon. Five thousand rockets—five months' production—would deliver perhaps an effective 3,750 tons of explosives; a single combined U.S. and British bomber attack delivered 8,000 tons. But Hitler was determined that some future new weapons would decide the war. So fascinated were the Nazis with a technical fix to their military quandary that they allowed the untried, young von Braun great leeway to pursue the expensive V-2 with only long-term prospects. Yet Speer was also attracted to the romantic possibilities of a superweapon. The Nazis, he later admitted, suffered from an "excess of projects in development," not one of which could ever meet full wartime production, and many of which were rushed "from factory directly into battle" without "customary full testing time" (Speer 1970, 363–70, 409–10; Neufeld 1994, 65–66; Goebbels 1948, 219). The result, of course, was loss of young life. What is characteristically Nazi about the V-2 technology is not this loss of life but the massive build-up of state support behind the project (Neufeld 1994, 70–71).

QUESTIONS FOR DISCUSSION

1. How does the technology of Nazi Germany demonstrate that technological development is guided by political ideology? Does this history disprove the commonsense idea that the use of technology always tries to achieve the most efficient means of solving a problem?
2. Why did engineers embrace the coming of the Nazi party rule in Germany in the 1930s? In what ways was Nazi ideology compatible with the German vision of technological progress? How did German engineers conceive of their technology as being different from "Jewish" science and technology?
3. Explain Hitler's fascination with the V-2 rocket as a weapon to win the war against the Western allies.
4. Josephson notes three characteristics of the technologies developed in totalitarian political regimes: an absence of market forces, centralized administrative control, and a tendency to huge and massive projects. Consider how these characteristics influence technological development in the United States today. You may wish to consider NASA and the building of the space station, the U.S. automobile industry, computer development, and the new military technologies used in recent wars in Bosnia and Iraq.

BIBLIOGRAPHY

Bailes, Kendall. 1978. *Technology and Society under Lenin and Stalin*. Princeton: Princeton University Press.

Banham, Reyner. 1986. *Theory and Design in the First Machine Age*. 2d ed. Cambridge: MIT Press.

Bracher, Karl Dietrich. 1970. *The German Dictatorship*, tr. Jean Steinberg. New York and Washington: Praeger Publishers.

Ellul, Jacques. 1964. *The Technological Society*. New York: Vantage.

Fishman, Robert. 1982. *Urban Utopias in the Twentieth Century*. Cambridge: MIT Press.

Frost, Robert. 1991. *Alternating Currents: Nationalized Power in France, 1946–1971*. Ithaca: Cornell University Press.

Goebbels, Joseph. 1948. *The Goebbels Diaries*, tr. and ed. Louis Lochner. London: Harnish Hamilton.

Göring, Hermann. 1939. *Political Testament of Hermann Göring*, tr. H. W. Blood-Ryan. London: John Long.

Herf, Jeffrey. 1984. *Reactionary Modernism: Technology, Culture, and Politics in Weimar and the Third Reich*. Cambridge and New York: Cambridge University Press.

Hughes, Thomas P. 1989a. "The Evolution of Large Technological Systems." In *The Social Construction of Technological Systems*, ed. Wiebe E. Bijker, Thomas P. Hughes, and Trevor Pinch. Cambridge: MIT Press.

Hughes, Thomas P. 1989b. *American Genesis*. New York: Viking.

Lane, Barbara Miller. 1985. *Architecture and Politics in Germany, 1918–1945*. Cambridge and London: Harvard University Press.

Neufeld, Michael. 1990. "Weimar Culture and Futuristic Technology: The Rocketry and Spaceflight Fad in Germany, 1923–33." *Technology and Culture*, 31: 725–52.

Neufeld, Michael J. 1994. "The Guided Missile and the Third Reich: Peenemünde and the Forging of a Technological Revolution." In *Science, Technology, and National Socialism*, ed. Monika Renneberg and Mark Walker. Cambridge: Cambridge University Press.

Pois, Robert. 1970. "Introduction." In Alfred Rosenberg, *Selected Writings*, ed. Robert Pois. London: Jonathan Cape.

Rosenberg, Alfred. 1970. *Selected Writings*, ed. and introduced by Robert Pois. London: Jonathan Cape.

Schorske, Carl. 1979. *Fin-de-siècle Vienna: Politics and Culture*. New York: Knopf.

Smith, Michael L. 1983. "Selling the Atom: The U.S. Manned Space Program and the Triumph of Commodity Scientism." In *The Culture of Consumption: Critical Essays in American History, 1880–1980*, ed. Richard Fox and T. J. Jackson Lears. New York: Pantheon.

Speer, Albert. 1970. *Inside the Third Reich*, tr. Richard and Clara Winston. New York: Collier Books.

Whitford, Frank. 1984. *Bauhaus*. London: Thames and Hudson.

CHAPTER 5

Nazi Ideology, Management, and Engineering Technology in the SS

---- ❖ ----

In this chapter, an excerpt from his book *The Business of Genocide* (2002), historian of technology Michael Allen discusses the careers of the midlevel managers and engineers who served as the backbone of the SS slave-labor camps and killing centers. Allen considers the question of motivation: Why did professionally educated SS men so easily contribute to the barbaric acts of the Holocaust? Why did they believe that slave labor and mass murder were the right thing to do? To answer this question, Allen reviews the basic principles of Nazi ideology and how those principles served to create a sense of communal consensus in the enterprises controlled by the SS. The engineers and industrial managers of the SS believed that rational organization and modern management techniques would further the aims of Nazism in which they believed. The SS considered themselves the vanguard of a New World Order that would remake European civilization, and any and all means to achieve that end were acceptable. In brief, the SS engineers, architects, and other technical professionals considered the destruction of European Jewry as a fulfillment of the cultural ideals in which they had been educated. In this chapter, Allen provides incisive portraits of a midlevel SS manager, Kurt Wisselinck, and of the SS Chief of Engineering, Hans Kammler, to show how ideological considerations and beliefs guided technological and professional decisions. At the conclusion, Allen also considers the education and background of some thirty-nine SS officers in the engineering and building division, including the chief engineer at Auschwitz, Karl Bischoff. His conclusion is that there was no dissent among the SS technological elite in the construction of a system of slave labor and mass murder because they were united by a cohesive and comprehensive ideology: the "SS men were model citizens of a murderous regime."

From *The Business of Genocide: The SS, Slave Labor, and the Concentration Camps*

Michael Thad Allen

INTRODUCTION

Before January 1944 less than a fifth of all Allied bombs dropped throughout the entire course of the war had fallen on Axis targets, but in just the next six months, between January and July, the total tonnage increased by almost half again as much. The pace and ferocity of bombing only increased from that point onward, leaving the famous "rubble mountains" in every major German city. The previous summer the Red Army had lured the Germans into a trap at Kursk, after which Hitler's armies never again mounted any major offensive against the Red Army. And yet in the spring of 1944, to the Allies' great consternation, German war production continued to rise. Moreover, the Allies were yet to land at Normandy; the Soviets had yet to launch the major offensives that would lead them on to Berlin; Wehrmacht officers had yet to stage their abortive assassination of Adolf Hitler; and Hitler and his leading paladins were increasingly enthusiastic about "wonder weapons" like the V-2 rockets and the V-1 cruise missile. These proved vain hopes, but especially for those who wished to remain blind, obvious signs of utter collapse were still several months away.

German engineers and midlevel managers were chief among those who refused to give up. Not the least of their contributions was the oversight of millions of forced laborers who had come to make up one-fourth of Germany's total work force. To German management fell the daily task of reconfiguring modern production around these laborers in a last-ditch effort to match the Allies tank for tank and plane for plane.[1] Foreign civilians made up the majority of this compulsory labor force.

Limited recruitment campaigns for foreign workers had started as early as 1940, but after March 1942 a special "General Plenipotentiary for the Labor Action" began large roundups of "Eastern Workers" to ship west to German factories. Over 700,000 concentration camp prisoners labored under the most brutal conditions, and even if they formed only a small part of the overall German war economy, by 1944 hardly a single locale with any factory of note lacked a contingent of prisoners. Every morning columns of somber workers, starving and bruised, could be seen marching from fenced enclosures down the streets of ordinary German towns. By 1944 Heinrich Himmler's SS (Schutzstaffel) was parceling out these inmates by the thousands for everything from aircraft factories to chain-gang-style construction.

This [essay] is about the managers of that process. They worked in a special division of the SS called the SS Business Administration Main Office (Wirtschaftsverwaltungshauptamt, or WVHA). This office spread a network of slavery across German-occupied Europe. From its pool of prisoners came the bulk of the work force for the V-2 rockets as well as other "wonder weapons." Most concentration camp prisoners, however, worked under the WVHA's elite corps of civil engineers, which specialized in breakneck construction projects, among them the conversion of underground tunnels into factories such as the eerie caverns where V-2 rocket assembly took place.…

As this [essay] examines the management of slave labor and murder, it questions not how modern structures divested Nazi "technocrats" of moral agency but rather how perpetrators endowed their institutions with personal significance.[2] Much scholarship that seeks to understand the barbarity of the SS begins by asking the question, Why were those involved not repulsed by their actions? or, to quote Hans Mommsen, "Why did so many who participated in the series of events that led directly and indirectly to the extermination of the Jews fail to withdraw their contribution either through passive resistance or any form of resistance whatsoever?"[3] Entire books are dedicated to explaining how Nazi perpetrators were able to overcome repugnance for their deeds, which presupposes that they indeed found them repugnant.[4] Historians essentially ask why SS men did not have the good sense to act as we hope we would have acted in their position, that is, as moral, upstanding citizens who would have saved fellow human beings. But the SS confronts us with a world of murderers, not good citizens; more precisely, SS men were the model citizens of a murderous regime. Instead of asking why SS men did not feel what they did not feel or why they failed to act as they might, should, or could have done, I pose the question, Why did they believe it was the right thing to do?…

Why did the SS set out to broker hundreds of thousands of prisoners to Hitler's war industries? Many speculate that the SS wanted to gain "control over the economy." To me this answer is unsatisfactory, for it discounts any real motivation. The image of banal careerists immersed in the office work of murder too often dovetails with such an image of institutions in which a purely pragmatic "will to power" supposedly eclipsed decisions about moral right and wrong. Although the Third Reich, like any complex state, played host to numerous conflicts, we should not be too hasty to label it, as did Franz Neumann, as a Behemoth, eaten up from within by a war of all against all in a raw bid for power. Who would ever deny that the Third Reich was exceptionally fragmented? Neumann's great service was to point this out. Two executive organs existed for agricultural policy; there were two justice systems (SS and civilian), two armies (Waffen SS and Wehrmacht), two chancelleries (party and state). Sometimes three or four institutions overlapped, and they fought each other incessantly. But histories of the Third Reich have dwelt too much on struggles for power; likewise, they have too readily attributed inefficiency and conflict to what is commonly known as "polycracy," defined as the "rule of many" and first established by the German historian Peter Hüttenberger. The historian Peter Hayes once remarked that, on one hand, we are led to believe that Hitler's Germany was polycratic and thus incapable of concerted organizational effort because everyone struggled against his fellows; on the other hand, this small country in central Europe kept the entire world at bay well through 1942, even into 1943, while losing about the same number of soldiers in combat (3–4 million) over the course of the whole war as the number of Red Army prisoners the Wehrmacht captured in the first six months of the Soviet invasion.[5]

Beyond the Nazis' startling efficiency at many different tasks, it is in the very nature of multiple, overlapping institutions that they created as many venues for cooperation as for infighting. I would argue that "polycracy" relied on cooperation, and that this followed ideological consensus precisely because—with so many agencies—the historical actors had to constantly exercise their initiative and conscious choice. Motivation mattered more, not less, due to the higgledy-piggledy nature of National Socialist organizations. In fact, the progressive rationalization of the camps could not have proceeded without the help and encouragement of Reich ministries, private industrialists, and civilian managers. . . .[6]

MODERN MANAGEMENT AND NAZI IDEOLOGY:
THE CASE OF KURT WISSELINCK

Kurt Wisselinck serves as a brief introductory example of how this modern management operated within the SS. First, there is no denying that power struggles marked Wisselinck's career with the WVHA, as Neumann and Hüttenberger would quickly point out. In 1944

Wisselinck was Chief Factory Representative (*Hauptbetriebsobmann*) within the SS to a rival institution, the German Workers Front (Deutsche Arbeitsfront, or DAF). The DAF had crushed the German trade unions in the first year of Hitler's seizure of power, but it also demanded social welfare programs and appointed representatives like Wisselinck to enforce its decrees. Private industry disliked many of these policies. Management often viewed DAF representatives as usurpers who sought to trample its prerogatives. The DAF had also founded industries of its own, which posed unwanted competition to private corporations. (The most famous was Volkswagen, organized to manufacture the Beetle, the "people's car.") Beyond claiming the right to place representatives in SS companies, the DAF had set up its Volkswagen plant as a model of technological efficiency and National Socialist principles.[7] The WVHA—which managed state rather than private corporations—had cause to fear the DAF's encroachment, for the WVHA's own corporations also posed as beacons of Nazi ideals. Robert Ley, head of the DAF and by all accounts an ambitious and fanatic Nazi, might well have perceived the SS as a threat to his own industrial empire and vice versa. And if it came to a pitched bureaucratic struggle, Wisselinck, as SS officer and DAF representative simultaneously, held key leverage. He might undermine the SS from within; on the other hand, he might act as an agent of the SS and undermine DAF intervention. Yet when conflict erupted, as it did in February 1944, the issue did not turn on the extension of bureaucratic influence but on ideological principle, and the outcome differed from that which orthodox interpretations of "polycracy" might lead us to expect.

Wisselinck had heard of misconduct at the SS Granite Works of Gross-Rosen. The Granite Works had started as one of the SS's first large-scale industrial projects in the concentration camps, founded to provide stone for the Nuremberg Party Rally Grounds. After the advent of total war, the SS also tried to convert its facilities to take in armaments production. Wisselinck routinely visited such SS factories on rotation, but this time his trip was different. He had put through a special request to the WVHA to inspect Gross-Rosen because he sensed a severe transgression of DAF policies toward civilian employees. Since its inception, the quarries had worked prisoners to death, but this was not what Wisselinck considered unjust. Rather, his interest had been piqued by rumors that Gross-Rosen was not exploiting the prisoners enough. Thus, when he heard that no one had distributed clothing confiscated from Jews to SS manager-trainees as specified, he acted quickly to make the factory conform to Nazi policy. What he learned upon arrival further appalled him. Trainees complained that their instructor was a drunk and was sleeping with his secretary. Wisselinck also suspected embezzlement. In addition, he alerted the headquarters of the WVHA that one cook seemed to favor the prisoners: "The apprentices complain that they are being withheld additional portions of potatoes with the justification that there are no more left, while it can be observed that the prisoners receive the food as additional rations."[8]

Anyone who has seen documentary footage of the camps knows what the prisoners began to look like in 1944, emaciated skins stretched over skeletal bodies. Mortality statistics, which fluctuated wildly, were running at about 10 percent a year at Gross-Rosen. The WVHA tracked them carefully.[9] Something as simple as an occasional potato could have made the difference between surviving the last year of war or perishing of starvation and disease within a few weeks. Furthermore, a steady diet—even of leftovers—might have even benefited production. Gross-Rosen's managers in fact mentioned this in their own defense. They complained that Wisselinck's presence endangered efficiency. To no avail. The head of the entire WVHA, Oswald Pohl, personally communicated his "sharpest disapproval" to the Granite Works.[10] The message was clear: nothing should be given to starving prisoners. So important were the issues involved that the chief of the WVHA backed Wisselinck, a DAF representative, against others in the SS's own management.[11]

If a war of all-against-all defined the Nazi period, does this explain Pohl's and Wisselinck's deeds? After all, polycratic interpretations of National Socialism can account for cooperation. Institutions often worked together to eliminate mutual rivals and thus increase their own influence. Alliances of convenience were indeed common. But Wisselinck's trip to Gross-Rosen did nothing to enhance the DAF's or the WVHA's authority, nor did the pursuit of power seem to define his purpose. Wisselinck neither extended the DAF's reach nor advanced the WVHA's factory operations. At stake was not the expansion of bureaucratic authority; rather these events proceeded along ideological lines in which the DAF and WVHA shared common commitments. Within the WVHA—and other Reich institutions as well—most believed that the bereavement of concentration camp prisoners was just. Although one cook at Gross-Rosen saw things somewhat differently, Wisselinck mobilized the entire apparatus of SS bureaucracy against her: he wrote reports, compiled statistics, called in his superior. In the end he actually demanded the "rationalization" of the camp's kitchen. More strict bookkeeping would ensure that such "embezzlement" could not happen again.[12] Moreover, if Wisselinck had "just followed orders" as a man constrained to an "iron cage," he might have overlooked the camp entirely. His visit was a matter of personal initiative, . . . [acting] on principle. He went out of his way to ensure that Gross-Rosen's management *did not* help prisoners to survive, to insure that it *did* give confiscated Jewish belongings to SS recruits; and he carried through with his inspection in spite of complaints that he was actually endangering efficiency.

Skeptical readers will doubt that Wisselinck was really ideologically engaged in the whole matter. Might he not simply have been striving for his superiors' attention? Yet at about this time, at no one's bidding, he wrote a lengthy memorandum with no apparent reader other than himself: "The business undertakings of the Schutzstaffel are the best means to breath new life into National Socialist ideals, to let them become reality, to blaze new trails in the area of applied socialism. We must live socialism as the deed! Our example must spur other corporations forward to emulate us in order to see the growth of a healthy, satisfied, and happy *Volk.*" Wisselinck operated neither as an agent of the DAF nor as an agent of the SS but as both, for he went on to express spontaneous enthusiasm for a plexus of ideologies that formed the raison d'être of the SS's business enterprises *and* those of the DAF as well. Every SS company should offer its German employees generous social benefits (programs championed by the DAF). In turn, he connected these to Nazi racial imperialism. Affordable SS housing should encourage Aryan families "rich in children" and tie them to their "Motherland." "Blood and Soil" should unite the Nazi homestead and further garner loyalty to the factory community, a microcosm of the larger national community of Nazism. Before Hitler's rise to power, Wisselinck claimed, "primitive housing" had proved a "breeding ground of immorality" and a "feeding trough [*Nährboden*] of Marxism."[13] He also blamed banks, thus condemning communism and capitalism in the same breath. Ideals like these could make the distribution of leftover potatoes seem like an issue of national security and cultural renaissance. . . .

While no one should discount the Nazis' rabid suppression of communism, their hatred of Jews, their fantasies of a romantic German past, and their intervention in the national economy, Wisselinck did not apply himself so energetically merely because he feared this or that. It is well to remember the words of Richard Evans regarding right-wing violence: "The murderers' actions, and the brutal language accompanying their deed, suggest that it was not fear, but loathing and contempt, which motivated them."[14] Wisselinck's proactive assertion of identity filled his prose and his actions. This was Nazi activism, not reaction: "The SS . . . must be an example and ever again an example in social policy."[15] Even in 1944, when the Reich was already beyond saving, he still saw himself in the vanguard of social change.

I have used the admittedly awkward term "plexus of ideologies" because I believe the image of a complex network, one with branching, even partial systems of ideals, provides a better understanding of how organization men like Wisselinck worked. They operated within a broad current whose tenets sometimes ran together, sometimes followed parallel courses, and sometimes collided. Wisselinck did not become an accomplice to murder by following any single tributary but by working within the whole. He felt competent to switch and modify his course continually and was encouraged by the National Socialist emphasis upon passion and activism over logic and consistency, upon syncretism over synthesis. On the other hand, this did not mean that the WVHA, or any other National Socialist institution for that matter, acted arbitrarily. The organization as a whole tended toward efficient action when multiple ideals, individuals, and institutions reinforced each other. In the case of Gross-Rosen, Wisselinck was able to mobilize his superior officers through the WVHA's bureaucratic edifice in favor of DAF policies. The outcome was no accident. Shared ideals reached into constituencies outside the WVHA and lent coherency to this collective action. A useful metaphor is perhaps a river delta in which currents may eddy or alter direction but nevertheless eventually and inevitably issue into the ocean. Precisely because of the importance of consensus, Nazi ideology issued, finally, in one massive sea of blood. Understanding the multiple valence of ideological tributaries, their conjunctions and contradictions, best explains why SS men like Wisselinck chose to do what they did.

Questioning why they did what they did brings us directly to the junction of modern organization and ideological motives. I argue that ideology is embedded in the quotidian tasks of bureaucratic operations because it lies at the root of collective identity and consensus. The function of consensus is best understood by considering the nature of modern management, whose techniques transform local, particular experiences and artifacts into fungible information amenable to collation, interchangeability, and abstract transfer. Above all modern organizations do so through statistics. At issue here is the role of consensus in evoking individuals' identification with impersonal institutions and abstract information. The most banal statistics have always depended upon the input, trust, and collective work among white-collar workers.[16] At the juncture of personal as well as collective trust among managers, ideological consensus has always played an indispensable role by helping render the information they worked with fungible. Information could be more readily transferred when SS officers trusted each other than when they had cause to doubt each others' motives. Ideals also served a function by animating large bureaucratic hierarchies—which are otherwise impersonal and even alienating—with a sense of individual purpose, a sense of personal mission. SS men worked harder and information within the WVHA flowed better when they believed in what they did. Again, I do not argue that one motive inspired all SS men; likewise no one individual needed to identify with each and every principle of the SS. Above all, ideology cannot be reduced to a single-minded goal, which organizations then set about to instrumentalize. But the WVHA functioned best when it succeeded in evoking the active identification of its officers—for whatever reason—with elements of its social cause. Once officers identified with the institution and their fellows, if only with fragments of larger, grander visions, their specialized skills could be mobilized in unison for the whole.[17]

Managing concentration camp industry involved three separate professional communities, each with its own distinct style and career patterns. Their interconnections, conflicts, and consensus all shaped the brutality of the concentration camps and slave labor. Two developed internally to the SS. First were the managers of the WVHA—businessmen, accountants, and engineers, among them Kurt Wisselinck. Second were the Kommandanten, the leadership core of the Inspectorate of Concentration Camps. The third community was external to the SS and entered only when the German economy plunged into total war late in the winter of 1941–42, namely, the state planners and industrialists within the Reich Ministry for Armaments and Munitions. Each community had its own vision of how to foster managerial teamwork and marshal "organization men." In general, these overseers of forced labor considered themselves idealists and wished to convert their visions into reality. Their ideals were manifold, as Wisselinck's manifesto has already hinted.

Some currents developed uniquely within the SS. First, the SS consciously set out to remake Europe in its own image. Police surveillance of the private and public lives of citizens in the name of "German values" was only one aspect of this drive. The SS also wished to build what came to be known as the "New Order," a program both to extirpate "unworthy" races from eastern Europe and to place model Nazi communities in their stead. Wisselinck's manifesto referred to this program when he wrote of "settlement houses . . . to maintain a perpetual stream of fresh [Aryan] blood."[18]

Second, a strong commitment to the Führer principle—a doctrine of Nazi leadership and national unity—drove decision-making and organizational structure. The Führer principle was Janus-faced, as much a communitarian ideology as a spur to "internecine strife," for it stressed unity and individual initiative at one and the same time. It did so by emphasizing that individual leadership grew out of collective identity. Every "Führer" conceived himself as the manifestation of the "will" of his subordinates; likewise, he conceived himself as a man in confluence with the will of his own "leaders." Adolf Hitler sat at the top, nothing less than the supposed embodiment of the historical mission of the German will. The Führer principle prompted individuals both to act spontaneously *and* to close ranks obediently, to act out *but also* to act in communion with other like-minded men. This dovetailed with the very structures of modern, centralized bureaucracy, which depend on the creative initiative of organization men but which focus that initiative upon collective endeavor in order to accomplish what no single individual can do alone. As Ronald Smelser has elegantly put it, "One could hope for success not as an isolated atom in a highly individualistic society, where failure or bad luck could bring precipitate social destruction, but rather as an integral part of a dynamic organization reaching out in an almost chiliastic fashion for total transformation of the world."[19] Oswald Pohl, the chief of the WVHA, made the very structure of his institutions and corporations reflect this goal.

Third, as we have seen, the SS emphasized the socialism in National Socialism. WVHA managers wished their businesses to serve goals of Nazi community without regard for pecuniary gain. They resented the threat that international markets posed to homogeneous "German" culture. Whether profitable or not, the SS wanted to manufacture a National Socialist renaissance, and they suspected businessmen of being loyal only to their purse strings. If we were to describe this as an anti-ideology, cultural anticapitalism is perhaps least awkward. It differed from anticapitalism of other stripes. The SS did not oppose monopolies or joint-stock companies, as did many liberal critics, because of the threat they posed to individualism; nor did the SS wish to redistribute the means of production to the working class, as did many socialists and communists; rather the WVHA opposed capitalism because of the threat that it posed to a homogeneous German culture.

For this doctrine, "productivism" serves as a better label. Productivist ideology meant that companies should not so much do business and make products as make Germans and Germanness. It promised to make the factory floor into a system with which to stamp managers and workers alike with an indelible national harmony. In industrial terms, this meant an elevation of factory organization and technology as a supreme concern over consumption, marketing, or distribution, which both Richard Overy and Mary Nolan have noted from quite different methodological approaches.[20] As Detlev Peukert pointed out, "The consumer-goods market promotes the individualism and freedom of movement that the political system [attempted] to obliterate."[21] This was another reason why liberal capitalism disgusted SS men like Wisselinck: it had spawned the "vulgar" street life of the Weimar Republic, materialistic pursuits, and a corresponding proliferation of tastes. When Nazis imagined revolutionizing consumption, rigidly standardized products like the VW Beetle or the Volks Radio were the result. These foresaw little room for consumer choice. The national organization in charge of distribution in Nazi Germany actually advertised its services as delivering the "IMPULSES OF THE ECONOMY to the daily life of the people" (emphasis in original).[22]

By contrast to the varieties of consumer impulse and expression, a well-run factory displayed unified organization and bent the material world to a collective human will. Specialized machine tools, standardization, and assembly lines had captured the fantasy of Hitler in the 1920s. The SS followed this lead. In 1924, just a month before delivering his first political speech, Heinrich Himmler had written to a close friend, "So you're reading Henry Ford . . . one of the most worthwhile, weighty, and most spirited predecessors in our fight."[23] It is significant that Himmler praised Ford for his "spirit" and not his wealth. To many ardent National Socialists, Ford's River Rouge was not so much a business as a manifestation of supreme will and the harbinger of a new world. To the WVHA, production was the forge of national identity, not first and foremost an act of economic output. . . .

By praising Ford, who had popularized these techniques, Himmler was merely echoing the widespread enthusiasm for the visionary potential of modern production. Nazi productivism reinforced a strong current of modernization, a fourth mission within the multivalent ideology of the WVHA. Even in seemingly old-fashioned industries like stone quarrying, the SS tried to introduce modern machines, despite their unsuitability to the conditions of forced labor. Modern factories may be defined by their operations, which took in raw materials and yielded finished product in a continuous stream, displacing traditional, small-scale batch or craft production. New technologies had made this possible by substituting machines for the work of human hands as well as for the human regulation of labor. As a vanguard of National Socialism, the SS wished to claim such futurism for itself. Jeffrey Herf has coined the phrase "reactionary modernism" to describe this impulse. In his view, the Nazis sought to reject Enlightenment doctrines of reason and individualism while using technological rationality in order to pursue their preposterous, irrational dreams. Who could deny this was true? But Herf also proposes that this represented a burdensome ideological contradiction. How can one reject the Enlightenment, equated more or less straightforwardly with modernity, but then champion technological prowess? This is a dilemma, however, only if we mistake the Enlightenment for modernity in general and mistake technological rationality as the pinnacle of all human reason derived from the Enlightenment. By and large, National Socialists were not among those who indulged in these assumptions. Moreover, the supposed contradiction between technical rationality and romanticism never bothered industrialists in Germany or anywhere else. As such it was never unique to the German engineering profession or National Socialism and seems to have manifested itself already during the French Revolution as well.[24] At least in the way that SS men spoke and acted, modernity had less to do with eighteenth-century political philosophy and more to do with a claim to futurism staked in terms of their mastery of the machines and modes of organization new to the twentieth century. . . .

One last ideal appears in this study only in context with the other four, not because it is of lesser significance but because it pervaded all other ideological currents. Its separate treatment could not do justice to its influence. Namely, those who led SS technological enterprise shared a deep-seated belief in their own racial supremacy. They therefore believed in the legitimacy of murder and the forced labor of Jews and whoever did not count as "Aryan." Describing their sentiments as racial supremacy in no way downplays their anti-Semitism. Rather Nazi racial supremacy was much more prodigious in generating contempt for human life than an anti-ideology alone can account for. If we hold, as does Elie Wiesel, that "those who speak about the 11,000,000 [total victims of Nazi extermination] do not know what they are talking about . . . it is 6,000,000 Jews," we can never explain why the WVHA worked myriad concentration camp inmates to death and not only Jews.[25] There were differences of degree and number, to be sure, but slave labor was not a discriminating business in the fate that awaited the SS's victims. . . .

Within the WVHA a distinct community of officers inhabited each departmental division. Each depended on its members to solve problems with expert knowledge and to forge a working consensus—that is, on the ability to act on ideals as well as mere issues of problem solution. Failure could result from a deficit of either sound business skills or consensus, while neither alone sufficed in and of itself to ensure success. The WVHA's construction corps presents an example of managerial success in which both consensus and skill coincided. Here Oswald Pohl recruited a tightly knit cadre of civil engineers and architects who had already worked together in a parallel branch of the state, the German Air Force. They represented the highest concentration of technically trained officers within the WVHA and, in all likelihood, within the SS as a whole. Not insignificantly, they came from an engineering tradition with the longest-standing connection to state service and the military. Further, a significant proportion had overt commitments to the Nazi cause. Many were activists. Their chief, Hans Kammler, was able to inspire their cooperation, and their success during the war was horrific for its brutal efficiency. Here "extermination through work" became a reality as civil engineers managed productive labor and genocide on the same projects.

If the WVHA's corps of engineers fostered concerted action through shared goals, other managerial echelons proved dysfunctional due to ideological strife. For example, during the general shortage of all white-collar personnel in Germany after 1936, Oswald Pohl had to look for competent factory managers outside his close circle of SS ideologues but failed to elicit their dedication to the plexus of ideological goals embedded in the SS's prison factories. As a result, dedicated managers soon complained that they could not work with the newcomers; meanwhile, the newcomers complained about the hostility of the old guard. No one worked together, and their enterprises fell apart accordingly.

It was part of the absurdity of Nazi Germany that prisoners paid most dearly for such mismanagement. Among Kommandanten, the commanders of the concentration camps, and their staffs a core had formed who shared a homogeneous sense of purpose, albeit one that demanded the brutalization of prisoners. On the other hand, the Kommandanten had few managerial skills, administrative or technical. They excelled only at terror and wreaked havoc on industrial production. In fact, industries proved successful in utilizing the SS's slaves only when they removed concentration camp guards from the direct technical supervision of production. Most SS factories crumbled along fault lines of managerial inconsistency and conflicting commitments. They failed, however, not because rational managers cannot operate under fanatic ideological influences, as is commonly held. Rather, SS industry broke down because SS managers came to loggerheads over antinomic issues, issues in which they believed. . . .

The SS Business Administration Main Office is of twofold importance. First, it reveals the historically unique use of modern means in slave labor and genocide. Second, this institution operated with the same basic structure as any other modern organization in the West. In this sense its managers were "ordinary men." Because the WVHA worked in such familiar ways, here the Nazi catastrophe cannot be conceived as an unfathomable exception in Western history.[26] "I suppose you would feel better if I told you all those who implemented the holocaust were demented," Raul Hilberg once remarked.[27] Had they been, the task of maintaining a just and equitable society would certainly be much easier. We would only have to round up the cretinous madmen who conform to the caricatures of evil presented as the bad guys in American Saturday morning cartoons. Sadly, however, the task is much more difficult and requires understanding how men and institutions that differed little from those found in any other modern industrialized society became the eager tools of genocide. . . .

HANS KAMMLER: MODERN ENGINEERING IN THE SS

Although Oswald Pohl (head of WVHA) was a competent financial administrator, he could have never mastered the technical details of building the New Order alone. At the end of 1940, he therefore courted Dr. Hans Kammler, an engineer from the German air force, who would quickly prove one of the most capable and dedicated men ever to make his career under Himmler. The chief of Himmler's Personal Staff requested Kammler's release as "general adviser for settlement in the staff of the Reichskommissar for the Reinforcement of Germandom" and did not hesitate to allude to the "German building program of the Führer," a clear sign that winning the peace and constructing the New Order, not wartime concerns, dominated the SS's intentions at the time.[28] Kammler went to work for the SS on 1 June 1941. Now the pace and scale of the New Order demanded a different organization, and . . . Pohl and Himmler turned to a modern technical manager.

In Kammler technological competence and extreme Nazi fanaticism coexisted in the same man, a historical warning against the facile belief that technological rationality is the "highest" form of reason. For his intensity, his mastery of engineering, his organizational genius, and his passion for National Socialism, SS men esteemed Kammler as a paragon. The afterglow of this awe lingered well after the war, as Pohl testified:

> Not only was he a wonderful construction engineer but also a son of an old Pomeranian officer's family. And as a cavalry officer [in the First World War] he was an excellent soldier and was also an honorary professor at the technical school at Charlottenburg [the Polytechnic University in Berlin] in scientific matters. Physically, he was tall, slim, with a haughty nose; he was elastic just like a bow which is eternally strong. Quite often I could not understand how this man coped with the tasks to which he was assigned in as short a time as one day. He was everywhere! Apparently he slept only during official trips in his car at night. And neither did he float over the surface of matters but somehow managed to know all tasks to the very bottom. . . . He was possessed of an agility which could not be explained. He called his men . . . to his office at any time of the day or night regardless of whether it was noon or at three o'clock in the morning. . . . In his manners he was very ambitious—but in a good sense because he never aspired to become important.[29]

Albert Speer later came to fear the chief SS engineer and numbered him among the calm, cool, and inscrutable experts who served Himmler: "Nobody would have dreamed that some day he would be one of Himmler's most brutal and most ruthless henchmen."[30] Most who worked with Kammler directly, however, including Speer's own subordinates, did not fear but admired him. "He thought his mind could encompass and master all problems," said one SS building engineer. "Far from regarding the enormous load of assignments which gradually came his way as a burden, he rather felt them to be an adequate appreciation of his personality."[31]

Kammler came from a privileged if not elite background. Pohl stated that Kammler's father was an officer and Kammler a cavalryman, almost certainly a romanticization. Kammler's father had been a gendarme of Stettin. Kammler himself must have felt a personal identification with the military either through his father's profession, patriotism, or both. He was born in 1901 into that generation of World War I latecomers that included Heinrich Himmler. Kammler never saw action, but he did claim to have mobilized with a cavalry regiment in May 1919. The German military effort had long collapsed. Nevertheless, Kammler participated in the Free Corps Rossbach, one of the right-wing paramilitary units full of older, disgruntled soldiers and nostalgic young men like himself. He eventually dropped out of the paramilitary scene to finish his studies, and, after passing through several humanistic high schools (*Gymnasien*), he completed a Diploma Engineer in architecture in 1923 at the Polytechnic University of Danzig. Even at this early date, he sought out practical experience in Danzig's Municipal Settlement Office and dedicated his thesis to techniques for surveying, cost-calculation, and housing development. His studies concentrated on the modern management of construction—not the aesthetics of form—and testified to the convergence of architectural and engineering practice at this time. Kammler also made himself familiar with industrial processes. During one semester break, he acted as a supervisor for a sugar factory in Hanover, where he managed transport work at the river docks. After graduation, he began work as a civil servant drafting and reviewing blueprints for the municipal government of Berlin and immediately began managing settlement projects in Zehlendorf.[32]

In 1928 Kammler passed his civil service exams. Up till then he had worked as an assistant in state offices; now he was qualified to lead one. As the scope of his professional tasks grew, the ideological character of his work came increasingly to the fore. Kammler's Diploma thesis of 1923 had dispassionately discussed left-leaning architects like Walther Gropius.[33] After 1928, his interests in settlement building converged with the particular advocacy of the garden city movement celebrated among right-wing architects who wished to unite German families with the "German soil." By 1930 Kammler was organizing settlements for agrarian communities, and in 1932 he joined the Nazi Party. Shortly after the seizure of power, he began work in the Reich Agriculture and Food Ministry (Reichs Ernährungsministerium), led by Richard Walther Darré, who had framed the rhetoric of "Blood and Soil" adopted by Himmler himself. Kammler rose to lead his own Garden Settlement Division by 1935 "at the expressed wish of the Reich Leader Darré," whom he had obviously impressed.[34] Kammler first donated his time to the SS in 1933 as an adviser to the Race and Settlement Office, also led by Darré, and three years later sought to serve his country as a military engineer for the air force, which, like the SS, owed its existence to National

Socialism. In all these endeavors he rehearsed the organizational abilities that he later put to use under Pohl.

Not unlike Pohl's business experts, Hans Hohberg or Erduin Schondorff, Kammler shared a lust for complex organization. Pohl likely sensed this, admired it, and recognized in Kammler a kindred spirit, a man above the petty pursuit of authority who nevertheless reveled in the mastery of organizational dynamism. Kammler's tale is the tale of a man who mobilized the creativity of others outside himself, and for that reason the SS civil engineering corps depended on a shared consensus of purpose. A well-defined mission was essential in recruiting many of the talented officers upon whom Kammler relied. By and large, his top officers signed up because they believed in what they were doing. The mythology created by Albert Speer and historians after the war that technical work distanced such men from moral considerations does not bear out in scrutiny of their daily tasks, and Kammler would have strenuously rejected the label of "technocrat" applied to him after the war.[35] To him . . . modern technology, organization, and ideologies of German supremacy were one and the same . . . and . . . Kammler knew how to mobilize them in unison. The engineers under Kammler gave vent to their contempt for "typically Polish" misrule in matters of technical and organizational proficiency, just as the SSPF [SS Police Force] staff of Lublin associated poor organization with degeneracy.[36] Likewise, in the slang of engineers at Flossenbürg, inferior building stones were referred to as "Jews."[37] Given the glorification of the "German inventive spirit," it is not too much to assume that many of them believed that the "German will" was the wellspring of technological progress and sound organization and, conversely, that efficient institutions and machines were evidence of the restless action of the German will.

Nothing expressed Kammler's own ambitions in these matters more clearly than the book that he brought out jointly in 1934 with a docent at the Technical University in Berlin (Edgar Hotz). The authors concentrated on technical information, including guides to Tayloristic time-motion studies, modern bureaucratic hierarchies, and statistical methods of surveillance. But Kammler and his coauthor also raised their voice in a litany of productivism and racial supremacy. . . . They wished to produce national culture instead of profits. They cried down the Weimar Republic, for "the man and the soil did not stand at the center . . . but rather materialism, bureaucratic technicalities, legalities, and the salesman's point of view."[38] Kammler, like many engineers, believed that the methods of modern management and organization were part and parcel of the new society he wished to construct. Romantic belief that contact with the German soil was necessary to make good Germans existed side by side with this enthusiasm. Even banal bookkeeping, in this light, became an arena of political rejuvenation: "We are certain," states his introduction, "that a precondition for the unification of cost and price accounting between firms and customers is a complete change from liberal capitalism to a National Socialist economic order."[39] Whereas, in their eyes, the Weimar Republic had stifled the best methods of organization, the authors complimented the Nazi regime for committing itself to the unfettered release of those institutions and technological developments new to the twentieth century. Modernity and National Socialism mutually reinforced each other.

Many during and after the Second World War expected engineers to have been natural resisters of Nazi rule due to their "rational" profession. Not even Franz Neumann was free of this romanticization of technical knowledge as an inherently moral force: the engineer, he wrote, "will later constitute . . . the most serious break in the regime. The engineer exercises the most rational vocation and he knows what beneficent powers the productive machinery can wield. Every day sees how this machinery becomes an instrument of destruction rather than of welfare."[40] Nevertheless, as difficult as it is to believe, many young, intelligent, idealistic engineers, especially the most educated and elite among them, looked to National Socialism to fulfill their visions of progress. At the Polytechnic University of Munich, for example, the Nazis carried fifteen of thirty seats in November 1932. These were the last elections for student body representatives before Hitler's seizure of power. The voter turnout reached 90 percent, and a further ten seats were carried by other radical right representatives. Liberals or socialists carried not a single one. Nine years earlier, Polytechnic students had held rallies just days after the "Beer Hall Putsch" of November 1923, and fully 70 percent of those present had spoken out in favor of Hitler and demanded leniency.[41]

Since the turn of the century, professional engineering education taught students to draw a direct causal line between industrial growth and social progress, between the steady promotion of technical innovation and the betterment of humankind. Viewed abstractly, this drive is perhaps laudable, but the moral crux lies in *what kind of society* lay at the center of their vision. Increasingly in the late 1920s the extreme right succeeded in mobilizing the activism of Germany's elite engineering students. It is small wonder that engineers generally loathed the Weimar Republic, for they identified democracy and free markets with the wreck of German industry and a stunted economy at the very time when advances in modern production and management techniques opened unprecedented opportunities to increase distribution and production. The prostration of the Weimar economy not only blighted the career chances of engineers; it withered their vision of what a progressive Germany should be and do.[42]

Of course, economic disaster did not automatically turn engineers into goose-stepping Nazis. But it is significant that the support of engineers for Hitler's regime increased over time as the Nazis succeeded in sustaining industrial growth. From the vantage point of the present, historians now know that the Third Reich's boom years of 1933–36 rested on high deficit spending and choked-off investment in the consumer sector. Historians like Richard Overy are correct to warn that the sometime lingering admiration for the Nazis' "economic efficiency" (preserved in statements like "they built roads and got people working again") is hollow, ignorant, and facile, but the engineers of the 1930s were contemporary observers without the luxury of well-informed historical research. Who could deny that they were finding jobs again? No less, these jobs were exciting. While the Western democracies continued to flounder through the Great Depression, the Nazis' message of productivism and their promotion of technological prowess as a wellspring of identity made the engineer seem like a poet: the smithy of the German soul.[43]

Kammler quickly set out to construct the New Order by applying the panoply of modern managerial methods that had enjoyed their first widespread popularization in Germany in the 1920s. Here again his academic writings shared much in common with the work of Erduin Schondorff, the SS's expert in brick manufacture. Both ridiculed old-fashioned building masters (a guild title) who based management on "rules of thumb" instead of systematic bookkeeping and proven, scientific methods.[44] And yet Schondorff had concentrated on theoretical engineering science and neglected the factory floor—the arena of direct control over the material world. By contrast, Kammler and his coauthor Hotz had pointed out that no automatic machinery or scientific knowledge could substitute for clear-eyed foremen and keen managers who kept statistics on what workers were doing, when raw materials were coming in, or how their building sites progressed. The greatest demon of the work site was in all cases time, whose waste was always the guilty party whenever anything disrupted the steady confluence of construction or prevented the utilization of all resources at full capacity. Idle machinery, laborers, or materials, in the eyes of Kammler, wasted the potential, so crucial to the productivist aesthetic, to push the pace and yield of industry to its outer limits. They proposed managerial hierarchies and schedule plans written up in bar graphs in order to render the complexities of a large building site in simple, visual form. Reading them at a glance, any civil engineer could become the master of time. . . .

Thus as timing and implementation of the New Order became a pressing concern to Himmler, Pohl, and the RKF, it was no accident that the SS turned to Kammler. One officer testified that almost no one could keep track of Kammler's flurry of activity in 1941 and 1942. He stormed in almost daily with new organizational charts and revisions of old ones. He also lured a cadre of civil engineers and architects away from the German air force to the SS and made sure that they were much like himself: they had elite education and careers managing large-scale construction projects. Before mid-1941, only a handful of high-ranking, technically trained officers had sat in the Office II [SS Construction]. That number now doubled, the number of lower-level drafters and technicians quintupled, and Kammler made plans to increase the size of the Office II even further.[45]

In addition, Kammler did not simply lay out a national administrative structure and then expect it to run automatically. . . . Kammler enforced his managerial system through methodical surveillance. He distributed over forty standardized forms to all levels of the SS construction corps. Thereafter he could track the daily material conditions of on-site construction at remote locations and made sure to replace existing chiefs of Construction Directorates who had been exposed as incompetent. On the other hand, capable officers like Gerhard Weigel, who had led SS construction since the early 1930s, stayed on. Kammler was quickly convinced of their technical knowledge and dedication.

Kammler also dissolved the "New" Construction Directorates and effectively lifted building out of the Kommandanten's hands by creating Building Inspections (SS-Bauinspektionen, or BIs). . . . Previously the engineers at Flossenbürg had worked differently from those at Buchenwald, Sachsenhausen, or Auschwitz. From now on, they executed their tasks in the same way, using the same forms, subject to the same audits. Now any engineer could move from directorate to directorate and find colleagues who were used to working the same way within the same system. Their activities—and thus their experiences within the Office II—became normalized and subject to interchangeability. . . .

ENGINEERING IDEOLOGY

Kammler's branching Building Inspections with their nested Construction Directorates and mobile Building Brigades extended over the whole of central Europe, and the nature of their technological work on this scale necessarily demanded that Kammler place trust in technical men at building sites beyond his direct, personal control. Considering Kammler's insistence on rigid structure, it may seem that SS engineers were becoming mere cogs in the wheels of a giant bureaucracy. But Kammler underscored the fact that bureaucratic duties are double-edged: they demand subordination to large, impersonal organizations but also bestow the power to exploit the capacity of collective work. There can be no doubt that Kammler demanded subordination: "The Building Inspectors [the chiefs of the Building Inspections] are not to develop or to design but to audit, supervise, and compare." Nevertheless, he also stressed that within each engineer's domain, "he has to decide for himself and represents the Office II in all construction affairs with local Waffen SS and police authorities as well as the army and civilian authorities."[46] The memorandum of one Central Construction Directorate officer clearly shows his awareness of control and initiative: "In a recent meeting the chief of the office [Kammler] . . . has ordered that the head of each service division take responsibility in the future for all work in his division, likewise departments, and will be held responsible."[47] Far from being cogs in a machine, the SS civil engineers were the big fish in their ponds of regional authority, and they were conscious of their command.

In the SS companies, conflicts over the multiplicity of meanings within Nazi ideology had caused turmoil and failure, even when Pohl had recruited competent managers. The SS civil engineering corps was a marked contrast. Kammler knew that his appeals to responsibility and accountability would ring hollow . . . without the amalgamation of initiative *and* competence. In the absence of energetic participation from dedicated subordinates, his administrative hierarchy would remain a creature of SS filing cabinets. Kammler therefore sought to build a modern hierarchy of like-minded men in which consensus might act as a further stimulant to initiative and the fungibility of experience. All SS personnel sheets included a category for the estimation of "ideology" (*Weltanschauung*). Typically, this slot was filled with perfunctory statements like "longtime National Socialist" whose importance should not be exaggerated. Nevertheless, Kammler took the evaluation of dedication seriously. He even barred some from advancement on ideological grounds. Regarding one officer Kammler wrote, "Not fit for office chief." One of the reasons given was the lack of "ideological equipment."[48] In other cases, Kammler emphasized the dedication of those he wished to promote, often praising technical and ideological capacity in the same sentences. Kammler once wrote of an officer, "[He] is especially eager for action, has an outstanding comprehension of how to exploit developing possibilities, and possesses the old Staffel spirit."[49] By "Staffel spirit" Kammler meant the Schutzstaffel. He was referring to the collective identity which, as the chief of Office Group C, he wished to create and uphold. In this environment, the organization was the ideology and vice versa.

Did Kammler's corps heed that "spirit"? Careful study of collective biographies suggests his officers' identification with their work. (I have found data on thirty-nine, at least two-thirds of the elite.) Conscious ideological engagement can be proved for nearly half, eighteen in all. Engagement denotes those who made conscious statements or decisions of ideological sympathy. This number may plausibly be extended to twenty-six if one counts an additional eight officers who joined the Nazi Party before January 1933; for early membership implies identification with National Socialism before membership was fashionable. Naturally, this qualitative evidence must be carefully weighted. A large difference may be drawn between officers who promoted National Socialism and those who only sympathized or participated. Some SS construction officers gave mild but nonetheless unmistakable signs of sympathy but cannot, by any stretch of the imagination, count as overt fanatics; on the other hand, a full quarter were proven activists. Several officers participated in agrarian settlement clubs, others in overtly National Socialist organizations; others sat in jail for their political beliefs. . . . They did more than just participate in the Nazi movement. Either by building organizations or by promulgating ideology, they put their time, creativity, and knowledge at the disposal of National Socialism and consciously sought to propel the movement forward. Because they are such obvious cases, like the activism of Kammler himself, let us start with a weaker case. . . .

Take for example the thirty-two-year-old former Organization Todt engineer, Heinrich Courte. Courte was like many new officers of the total war era: Kammler did not recruit him directly to the Office Group C-Construction; rather, the Office Group C snapped him up out of the mass of men who enrolled in the Waffen SS in 1942. Kammler bestowed the title of "expert leader" upon him, and he distinguished himself in the deployment of slave labor in the Building Brigades.[50] Courte's personnel file yields various indicators that he found himself at home among ideologically driven men like Kammler; on the other hand, *absolutely no evidence* suggests that he was alienated. At the Polytechnic University of Aachen, during what was probably the beginning of his political consciousness, he joined the Student Platoon of the SA and then switched after a few months to the SS. Here he took time out from studies to participate in special training for military construction. Second, after receiving his diploma in engineering, Courte went to work for the Organization Todt. Part of the "social structure" of the German engineering profession included a traditional association of the full mobilization of the nation's technical capacity with social progress (a sentiment by no means unique to engineers in Germany). It is therefore probably safe to assume that Courte believed Nazi construction projects such as those under the Organization Todt and the full employment of civil engineers they helped create were positive contributions to German society. Third and last, his curriculum vitae contains another hint of ideological sympathy. He took pains to explain his father's suicide as the result of the "general disintegration" of the Weimar Republic.[51]

Taken together Courte's biography remains ambiguous evidence. As a student, he may have succumbed to peer pressure and joined the SA. Ulrich Hartung, Thomas Zeller, and Franz Seidler have pointed out that

Organization Todt engineers discussed the very form of bridges, the vistas offered by parkways, the architecture of rest stops, and plantings on medians as symbols of a Nazi renaissance. Thus the "structure" of these organizations almost inevitably included exposure to such ideals, literally in the blueprints; nevertheless, even if Courte would have had to be extremely obtuse to miss the meanings attributed to his work in the Nazi media or among colleagues, the historian must still admit to such possibilities: perhaps Courte was oblivious. In addition, even his condemnation of the Weimar Republic may have been disingenuous, for SS racial theories linked the German "will" and racial supremacy to bloodlines, and suicide in the family could be viewed as a sign of poor genetic or spiritual mettle. Courte had an interest in explaining away his father's death in a way that would appeal to his superiors. Further, even if Courte held a wholehearted, genuine disgust for the Weimar democracy—a disgust widespread among technical men in the 1920s and 1930s—this would prove only a certain affinity for Nazism but not necessarily active belief.[52] In light of available evidence, one can only wager the conclusion that men like Courte interpreted aspects of their lives in ideological terms, and, judging from their service, they also willingly participated in Kammler's organization.

For twelve officers there is no hard evidence of ideological engagement. They may have been dedicated participants (although not activists) or they may have been mere fellow travelers. Nevertheless, the success of the Office Group C depended equally on cooperation and the *absence* of any counteractive dissent. It is therefore also significant that, in contrast to, say, the dissent of those within the SS companies, *no evidence* reveals any similar friction within the organizational structures initiated by Kammler, nor did anyone seek to undermine them. Because, as Kammler well knew, formal bureaucratic directives alone could provide only slender ties within his institution, at the very least it is safe to say that the vast majority of officers in the Office Group C had nothing against radical SS ideology.

For instance, as is hardly atypical in any large, impersonal bureaucracy, Kammler's subordinates broke and bent the rules. But they consistently did so to reinforce their organization. The Central Construction Director of Auschwitz, Karl Bischoff, defied the orders of his regional Building Inspector in order to deal directly with the Ministry of Armaments and War Production. He did so, however, to speed up the construction of Auschwitz and secure key raw materials.[53] It is important to remember that he could have chosen to act otherwise. Had he merely "followed orders" as his institutional niche formally prescribed, Bischoff could have easily chosen to let schedules fall by the wayside and might have even pointed out his fidelity to formal instructions by way of deflecting blame from his own office. In other bureaucratic niches of the WVHA occupied by individuals who did not readily identify with the SS, this is exactly what happened. For example, the chief engineer at an SS-owned factory near Auschwitz, a civilian and not an SS man, refused to deliver shipments to Bischoff's construction corps and based this obstruction on petty state and municipal regulations that prohibited such transactions—regulations over which the SS routinely ran roughshod.[54] By contrast, Bischoff ignored a steady stream of complaints from the municipality of Auschwitz in order to push ahead with the construction of the concentration camp.[55]

Bischoff himself belongs among the "participants" like Courte, not the "activists." While he had worked for the German air force, he had also served the German Workers Front as a Cell Leader. Ronald Smelser has noted the general ideological commitment of those who usually served as Cell Leaders.[56] Thus the structure of this organization would lead us to suspect Bischoff's commitment, but nevertheless no evidence speaks of his activism. At Auschwitz, on the other hand, he clearly refused to go out of his way to support the cause of Nazi fundamentalism. When queried by the Regional Party Leader (*Ortsgruppenleiter*) of the NSDAP and the Kommandant staff of Auschwitz whether his subcontractors were "free from foreign and Jewish capital" and if "the owners of the firms and their wives are of Aryan descent and Reich German," Bischoff blandly replied that he did not know and the Regional Party Leader should seek such information elsewhere.[57] The engineer was not exercised by such issues, yet when this same engineer requested the Gestapo to arrest some civilian workers for shirking, he added that they were "for the most part lazy Poles" (the German is somewhat stronger: *polnischeBummelanten;* an American construction site manager might use "jerk-offs"). Likewise others in Bischoff's command referred to foreign workers as worthless loafers who shirked "in order to live in their homeland of donothingness or alms and handouts."[58] Of note, the letters requesting Gestapo intervention to punish workers were very standardized. Not only the SS but also its civilian subcontractors routinely issued them. The most usual practice was merely to copy the same paragraph over and over while filling in new names. Those petitions to the Gestapo quoted earlier differed, however; Bischoff and his subordinates added unbidden slurs to existing stock phrases, a sort of racist flourish upon otherwise fungible information.

This unusual deployment of racial stereotypes cuts to the crux of issues surrounding human agency in bureaucratic structure. Earlier, Bischoff had lifted not a finger to "prove" the Aryan character of his subcontractors. Regarding workers, on the other hand, he and his subordinates were ready and willing to add extra slurs to routine requests to the Gestapo. Why? One answer has recently been advanced by Wolfgang Seibel, who stresses the ways in which bureaucratic context structures agency. Even when those structures represent established pathways of action, they are inert without the activation energy provided by initiative, motivation, and interest. Thus, at one level, even when ideological consensus exists that "something must be done" but institutionalized pathways are absent, little is likely to happen. At another level, however, when institutions and intentions reinforce each other—even competing institutions or otherwise contradictory intentions—the consequences are usually swift and decisive.[59] In other words, ideology mattered more, not less, because of the nature of National Socialist organizations.

When the Regional Party Leader appealed to Bischoff to uphold the racial hierarchy of National Socialism among his contractors, the engineer found himself called upon to take initiative that lay far beyond the bounds of his normal activity. In the Central Construction Directorate he already had plenty to do and no time to chase down what must have seemed extraneous gossip. Prying into the private lives of other engineers and businessmen was police work, work for which he and his staff had neither training nor resources. But this hardly meant that racial identity did not matter to him as soon as "business" made it relevant, and there seems to have been a consensus in his office that poor performance among prisoners or civilian workers was due to their nature as Poles, Jews, Czechs, or whatever "racial" category could be made to fit. Bischoff did not hesitate to mobilize bureaucratic organization by appealing to this consensus, and his office seems to have added racial slurs in its arrest requests to get prompter action or harder punishment; at the very least, the added sentences would have differentiated these requests in the eyes of local SS officials from otherwise standardized formulations.

Some may ask whether Bischoff really believed in such stereotypes or whether he merely used them cynically to "fit in." The point seems moot to me. He worked within a radicalized institution (the SS) within an already radical political movement (National Socialism) that associated efficiency with racial supremacy and inefficiency with "ballast existences" and "unnecessary eaters." If such appeals could and did incite the Gestapo to a prompter response, this could only have served as "evidence" to confirm belief in racial tautologies. There is no necessary dividing line between pragmatism and fanaticism in such a context. These officers had clearly internalized Nazi racial supremacy to some degree (and likely to a much greater degree—they were, after all, engineering genocide). Bischoff was not a man to demonstrate in the streets on behalf of Nazi ideals; on the other hand, everything suggests that he had nothing against the most radical Nazi policies, and some evidence suggests he identified with them passively.

Perhaps nothing was more powerful than this passive acceptance and the lack of any contravening dissent in Kammler's organization, dissent that officers could have otherwise found ample opportunity to express in petty administrative obstruction. The actions of officers who did not express their ideological engagement still spoke volumes about their dynamic initiative in an organization that could construct gas chambers and manage slavery only through collective action. Ideology facilitated operations precisely because the maintenance of consensus never needed to be a heated topic of daily declarations and contention. It had become a matter of their collective identity as engineers of the New Order.

QUESTIONS FOR DISCUSSION

1. One popular idea about the Nazis involved with the death camps is that they were men who focused solely on the technical aspects of their jobs. How does Allen's analysis of engineers and managers in the SS show that this popular idea is less than the whole truth?

2. Hans Kammler, the chief engineer for the SS, was a highly cultured man with a firm belief in the social progress to be achieved by technological development. How then can we explain his zealous participation in the design and development of the death camps? What does his career demonstrate about the education of engineers and technological professionals, both in Nazi Germany and in contemporary society?

3. Is engineering the most rational of the professions? Is there a necessary connection between engineering technology and social progress? Why did the technological professionals of the SS—men such as Kurt Wisselinck and Karl Bischoff—believe that their actions were commendable, that they were advancing the goals of humanity?

4. Is there a way to structure the education of engineers and other technological professionals so as to avoid the horrors of the Holocaust? What concrete proposals can you recommend for implementation in the university education of engineers in our society today? Would courses in "engineering ethics" serve to prevent technological genocide?

ABBREVIATIONS

In addition to the abbreviations found in the text, the following abbreviations are used in the notes.

BAK Bundesarchiv Koblenz
BDC Berlin Document Center
NO Nazi Organization (Nuremberg Trials Documents)
RG Record Group
RuSHA Rasse- und Siedlungshauptamt (Race and Settlement Main Office)
USHMM United States Holocaust Memorial Museum, Washington, D.C.

NOTES

A number of documents cited in the notes can be found in multiple archives, particularly those related to the Nuremberg Trials, and thus are not cited to a particular archive below. I have used the standard designation of Nuremberg documents (NO, NG, NI, PS, etc.) when it was known to me. References to Defense Document Books, Prosecution Document Books, and Protocol are to Trial IV vs. Oswald Pohl et al., held at Nuremberg. I have carried out research in these various document collections in different locations at different times. In any case where an English title is given for a German document, I have relied upon Nuremberg translations. I have used documents at the National Archives, Washington, D.C.; the Imperial War Museum, London; the Institut für Zeitgeschichte, Munich; and the Bundesarchiv Potsdam and Koblenz, now located at the Bundesarchiv Lichtefelde, Berlin.

1. Herbert, *Fremdarbeiter,* 270, gives the exact statistic of foreign workers in the overall German work force as 26.5 percent in August 1944. Regarding the loyalty of German midlevel management, see Prinz, *Vom Mittelstand zum Volksgenossen.*

2. Giddens, *The Consequences of Modernity,* esp. 137–44; Bourdieu, *Outline of a Theory of Practice,* 72–95; Habermas, *Theorie des kommunikativen Handelns,* 1:209–368 and esp. 2:459–61; Zunz, *Making America Corporate,* esp. 55–58, for the careers of engineers as midlevel managers; Zeitlin and Tolliday, "Employers and Industrial Relations between Theory and History," 1–34. Discussion of the role (or its absence) that ideology played in the genocide has erupted again in the wake of Daniel Goldhagen's *Hitler's Willing Executioners.* Although Goldhagen's critics are right to point out the book's methodological and substantive flaws, there can be little doubt that Goldhagen has gained such wide acclaim because he addressed the role of ideology, which many historians have neglected. Many recent works have begun to put ideology back into the picture, among them Bartov, *Hitler's Army;* "Passing into History," 162–88; and *Murder in Our Midst;* Herbert, *Best;* Orth, *Die Konzentrationslager-SS.*

3. Mommsen, "Die Realizierung des Utopischen," 186.

4. Lifton, *The Nazi Doctors,* argues that SS men were forced to lead double lives to overcome their repulsion for their work, a quandary that in fact few ever faced.

5. Hayes, "Polycracy and Policy in the Third Reich," 190–210.

6. Hüttenberger, "Nationalsozialistische Polykratie," 417–42, quotation from 421. Neumann prefigured Hüttenberger's theory in *Behemoth.* Allen, "The Banality of Evil Reconsidered."

7. Smelser, *Robert Ley,* 155, and on DAF ideology, 174–79. Mommsen and Grieger, *Das Volkswagenwerk,* is discussed extensively in n. 8, pp. 322–23, and n. 3, p. 331.

8. Quotation from Wisselinck, "Ernährung und Ausbildung der Lehrlinge: Deutsche Erde- und Steinwerke Granitwerk Gross-Rosen," 2–7 Mar. 1944, T-976/18. See also Wisselinck, "Aktenvermerk Granitwerk Gross-Rosen,"

30 Mar. 1944, T-976/18, and another similar case, Opperbeck to Chef W Baier, "Bericht des Hauptbetriebobmannes SS-Ostuf. Wisselinck vom 13 Sep. 44 über den Besuch im Werk Butschowitz am 31 Aug. 44," 3 Oct. 1944, T-976/18. By contrast Wisselinck praised SS companies that withheld rations from their prisoners and made efforts to secure extra rations for civilians (see Wisselinck to Chef W Baier, "Granitwerk Gross Rosen," 29 Feb. 1944, T-976/18, and Wisselinck's reports throughout this collection). Jaskot, "The Architectural Policy of the SS," 100–159, contains excellent analysis of the SS's stone quarries. See also NO-2132, Dr. Claussen, directive of Reichsminister für Ernährung und Landwirtschaft, 7 Apr. 1942.

9. Karny, "'Vernichtung durch Arbeit.' Sterblichkeit in den NS-Konzentrationslagern," 140–47.

10. Pohl to Obersturmf. Ketterer, Betriebsobmann der Granitwerk Gross-Rosen, "Gross-Rosen/Striegau," 24 Mar. 1944, T-976/18.

11. At around this time, correspondence begins to refer to Wisselinck as the Sonder-Reichstreuhänder der Arbeit für sämtliche SS-Wirtschaftsbetriebe (Special Reich Trustee of Labor for all SS Business Operations). He was obviously being promoted for excelling at his job. This title appears on various reports in T-976/18.

12. Wisselinck to Stab W, "Vorschläge zur weitgehendsten Ausschaltung von Veruntreuungen in der Gemeinschaftsverpflegung," unspecified, sometime in March 1944, T-976/18. Compare a similar case at Jonastal/Ohrdruf labor camp, Remdt and Wermusch, *Rätsel Jonastal,* 52.

13. All quotations from Wisselinck, "Die SS-Siedlungen bzw. die Werksiedlungen in den wirtschaftlichen Unternehmungen der Schutzstaffel," 17 May 1944, T-976/18.

14. Evans, *In Hitler's Shadow,* 36.

15. Wisselinck, "Die SS-Siedlungen."

16. Beniger, *The Control Revolution;* Zunz, *Making America Corporate;* Chandler, *The Visible Hand,* and, for a comparative perspective that includes Germany, see *Scale and Scope.* Regarding the German case in particular, see Kocka, *Die Angestellten,* and "Scale and Scope," 711–16. Regarding the Weimar and Nazi period, see Prinz, *Vom Mittelstand zum Volksgenossen.*

17. Gellately in particular has warned against rigid causal explanations that invoke ideology; see "'A Monstrous Uneasiness,'" 180. Allen, "Technocrats of Extermination."

18. Wisselinck, "Die SS-Siedlungen."

19. Smelser, *Robert Ley,* 19.

20. Nolan, *Visions of Modernity;* Overy, *The Nazi Economic Recovery,* "Mobilization for Total War in Germany, 1939–1941"; "Germany, 'Domestic Crisis' and War in 1939"; and "'Blitzkriegswirtschaft'?"

21. Peukert, *Inside Nazi Germany,* 193.

22. Advertisement, *Der Vierjahresplan: Zeitschrift für Nationalsozialistische Wirtschaftspolitik* 3 (1939): 235. This was a special issue and the advertisements were extremely glossy. Compare Overy, "'Blitzkriegswirtschaft'?," with Ritschl, "Die NS-Wirtschafts-ideologie," 48–70, and Mason, "Domestic Dynamics of Nazi Conquests: A Response to Critics," 161–89; "Labour in

the Third Reich, 1933–39"; and "Some Origins of the Second World War," 67–87.

23. Quoted after Ackermann, *Heinrich Himmler als Ideologe*, 37.

24. See Herf, *Reactionary Modernism.* MIT's engineering faculty in the interwar period was just as enamored of reactionary "antimodern" architecture as were the worst Nazi hacks. See Sinclair, "Inventing a Genteel Tradition: MIT Crosses the River," 1–18. Compare Alder, "Innovation and Amnesia," esp. 300, and *Engineering the Revolution.* On the case of German engineering during the Enlightenment, see Brose, *The Politics of Technological Change in Prussia.* Recently David Lindenfeld has pointed out that "interpretation of the Holocaust rests on a double caricature—of the Third Reich on the one hand, and of the legacy of the Enlightenment on the other," in "The Prevalence of Irrational Thinking in the Third Reich," 368. The history of technology can make a significant contribution to Herf's interesting beginnings precisely by departing from these caricatures. See also Latour, *We Have Never Been Modern,* esp. 67–70; Dietz, Fessner, and Maier, "'Der Kulturwert der Technik,'" 24; and Zilt, "'Reactionary Modernism' in der westdeutschen Stahlindustrie?," 191–202.

25. Abrahamson, *Against Silence,* 42.

26. Some very sophisticated historians of Nazism believe the exceptionalism of National Socialism should always be highlighted above its common roots in Western culture; for example, Friedländer, "West Germany and the Burden of the Past"; Maier, *The Unmasterable Past,* 66–99.

27. Hilberg, "Significance of the Holocaust," 101.

28. Wolff to Gen. Kastner-Kirdorf, Chef d. Luftwaffenpersonalamtes, 6 Mar. 1941, BDC SS Personal-Akte Hans Kammler; "Gutachten" from 31 May 1941 signed by the Reichsminister der Luftfahrt und Oberbefehlshaber der Luftwaffe, Luftwaffenverwaltungsamt, BDC SS Personal-Akte Hans Kammler. Kammler must have agreed to work for the HAHB immediately (for his official personnel card lists him as an officer of the Amt II already in August 1940).

29. Testimony of Oswald Pohl, Protocol: 1281–82.

30. Speer, *Slave State,* 12.

31. Affidavit of Heinrich Werner Courte, Defense Document Book of Max Kiefer.

32. BDC SS Personal-Akte Hans Kammler, esp. Lebenslauf. Kammler must have been aware of the SS's Berlin, Krumme Lanke settlement in this capacity, for it lay in his region of Zehlendorf.

33. Hans Kammler, "Zur Bewertung von Geländeerschliessungen für die grossstädtische Siedlung" (Engineering diss., Hanover, 1931), "Bibliographischer Anhang."

34. Lebenslauf, BDC Personal-Akte Hans Kammler.

35. See the discussion of Speer's and Joachim Fest's construction of the Nazi technocrat as a literary trope in Van der Vat, *The Good Nazi,* 330–32; Agoston, *Teufel oder Technokrat?*

36. Edgar Hotz and Hans Kammler, *Grundlagen der Kostenrechnung und Organization eines Baubetriebs für den Wohnungs- und Siedlungsbau in*

Stadt und Land (Berlin: Verlagsgesellschaft R. Müller, 1934), 1; Kammler, "Zur Bewertung von Geländeerschliessungen," 37. See the anonymous report, 22 May 1943, "Besprechung mit dem Amtsgruppenchef C. Besuch am 21.5.43," USHMM RG-11.001M.03: 20 (502-1-25).

37. Amt II to Neubauleitung Flossenbürg, 10 Aug. 1940, BAK NS4/59. This slur was apparently common in the building trades. Wolschke-Bulmahn, "Biodynamischer Gartenbau," 640.

38. Hotz and Kammler, *Grundlagen,* 1.

39. Ibid., vii.

40. Neumann, *Behemoth,* 472.

41. Durth, *Deutsche Architekten,* 23–40, 65–86, 102–3; Ludwig, *Technik und Ingenieure,* 20–35, 105–9; Wengenroth, "Zwischen Aufruhr und Diktatur," 215–23; Gispen, *New Profession, Old Order,* 48–51; Bolenz, *Vom Baubeamten,* 33–39, and regarding housing, 85–86.

42. Durth, *Deutsche Architekten,* 23–40, 65–86; Ludwig and König, *Technik, Ingenieure und Gesellschaft;* Ludwig, *Technik und Ingenieure,* 20–35, 105–9; Hortleder, *Das Gesellschaftsbild des Ingenieurs,* 111. James, *The German Slump,* 148, points out that the lack of any vision of the future was also a general sentiment among businessmen and financiers. Prinz, *Vom Mittelstand zum Volksgenossen,* 134–36.

43. James, *The German Slump,* 370–72, and in general 343–419; Overy, "'Blitzkriegswirtschaft'?," 370–435. For an excellent example of one consumer-durable industry, see Sudrow, "Das 'deutsche Rohstoffwunder' und die Schuhindustrie," 63–92. Prinz, *Vom Mittelstand zum Volksgenossen,* 175–81.

44. Hotz and Kammler, *Grundlagen,* 41–47.

45. Testimony of Karl Fanslau, Protocol: 2562; Testimony of Oswald Pohl, Protocol: 1303–5, 1743; NO-1922, Affidavit of Max Kiefer; Affidavit of Heinz Schürmann, Defense Document Books of Franz Eirenschmalz; NO-2613, Affidavit of Franz Eirenschmalz; Kammler, end of Dec. 1941, "Bericht des Amtes II—Bauten über die Arbeiten im Jahre 1941," USHMM RG-11.001M.03: 19 (502-1-13); Kammler, "Hauptamt Haushalt und Bauten Amt II—Bauten. Geschäftsverteilungsplan vom 20.6.41," USHMM RG-11.001M:19 (502-1-9).

46. Quotation from Kammler, 17 Nov. 1941, "Organization der SS Bau-dienststellen" (prepared for Pohl), USHMM RG-11.001M.03: 19 (502-1-12), which contained "Dienstanweisungen für den Leiter einer Bauinspektion," "Dienstanweisung für den Leiter einer ZBL," and "Dienstanweisung für den Leiter der Bauleitung."

47. Werner Jothann to all Bauleitungen, 2 Aug. 1944, "Geschäftsbetrieb bei den ZBL mit den angegliederten Bauleitungen und Abteilungen," USHMM RG-11.001M.03: 24 (502-1-84).

48. Kammler, evaluation of Franz Eirenschmalz, 17 Nov. 1944, BDC SS Personal-Akte Franz Eirenschmalz.

49. Kammler evaluation, 26 Apr. 1944, BDC SS Personal-Akte Robert Riedl.

50. BDC Personal-Akte Heinrich Courte.

51. BDC RuSHA Akte Heinrich Courte.

52. Hortleder, *Das Gesellschaftsbild des Ingenieur*, 111; Hartung, "Bauästhetik im Nationalsozialismus," 71–84; Zeller, "Landschaften des Verkehrs," 323–40; Seidler, *Fritz Todt.*
53. Regarding Bischoff's altercation with his immediate superior Gustav Rall, see the correspondence Bischoff to Kammler, Rall to Bischoff, and Kammler to Rall, July–Sept. 1942, USHMM RG-11.001M.03: 23 (502-1-82).
54. See Allen, "The Puzzle of Nazi Modernism."
55. On the ongoing feud between the municipality of Auschwitz and the SS building authority at the concentration camp, see Polenz, 3 Dec. 1942, "Besprechung am 3.12.42 in Kattowitz," USHMM RG-11.001M.03: 23 (502-1-78); Amtskommissar Butz der Stadt Auschwitz to ZBL Auschwitz, 7 July 1942, USHMM RG-11.001M.03: 23 (502-1-72); and same to ZBL Auschwitz, 13 July 1942, with Bischoff's reply, 13 July 1942, USHMM RG-11.001M.03: 23 (502-1-76).
56. BDC Personal-Akte Karl Bischoff. He was *Zellenleiter* from 1936 to 1938 in Munich. Smelser, *Robert Ley*, 155, and on DAF ideology of organization; 98–179 in general.
57. Ortsgruppenleiter der NSDAP bei Kommandantur Auschwitz to Bischoff, 24 Apr. 1942, and reply of 29 Apr. 1942, USHMM RG-11.001M.03: 25 (502-1-99).
58. The first quotation is from Karl Bischoff to HUTA AG, 18 Mar. 1943, "Verhaengung von Strafen ueber Zivilarbeiter," USHMM RG-11.001M.03: 22 (502-1-58); the second is from Werner Jothann to Gestapo Auschwitz, 2 Aug. 1944, "Wiederbeibringung von 2 auslaendischen Arbeitern," USHMM RG-11.001M.03: 22 (502-1-70).
59. Seibel, "Staatsstruktur und Massenmord," 539–69.

BIBLIOGRAPHY

Abrahamson, Irving. *Against Silence: The Voice and Vision of Elie Wiesel.* New York: Holocaust Library, 1985.

Ackermann, Josef. *Heinrich Himmler als Ideologe.* Göttingen: Musterschmidt, 1970.

Agoston, Tom. *Teufel oder Technokrat: Hitlers graue Eminenz.* Berlin: Verlag E. S. Mittler & Sohn, 1993.

Alder, Ken. *Engineering the Revolution: Arms and Enlightenment in France.* Princeton: Princeton University Press, 1997.

——. "Innovation and Amnesia: Engineering Rationality and the Fate of Interchangeable Parts Manufacturing in France." *Technology and Culture* 38 (1997): 273–311.

Allen, Michael Thad. "The Banality of Evil Reconsidered: SS Mid-Level Managers of Extermination through Work." *Central European History* 30 (1997): 253–94.

——. "The Puzzle of Nazi Modernism: Modern Technology and Ideological Consensus in an SS Factory at Auschwitz." *Technology and Culture* 37 (1996): 527–71.

———. "Technocrats of Extermination: Engineers, Modern Bureaucracy, and Complicity." In *Lessons and Legacies of the Holocaust,* edited by Ronald Smelser. Evanston: Northwestern University Press, forthcoming.

Bartov, Omer. *Hitler's Army: Soldiers, Nazis, and War in the Third Reich.* Oxford: Oxford University Press, 1992.

———. *Murder in Our Midst: The Holocaust, Industrial Killing, and Representation.* Oxford: Oxford University Press, 1996.

Beniger, James. *The Control Revolution: Technological and Economic Origins of the Information Society.* Cambridge: Harvard University Press, 1986.

Bolenz, Eckhard. *Vom Baubeamten zum freiberuflichen Architekten: Technische Berufe im Bauwesen (Preussen/Deutschland, 1799–1931).* Frankfurt am Main: P. Lang, 1999.

Bourdieu, Pierre. *Outline of a Theory of Practice.* Cambridge: Cambridge University Press, 1977.

Brose, Eric. *The Politics of Technological Change in Prussia: Out of the Shadow of Antiquity, 1809–1848.* Princeton: Princeton University Press, 1993.

Chandler, Alfred. *Scale and Scope: The Dynamics of Industrial Capitalism.* Cambridge: Harvard University Press, 1990.

———. *The Visible Hand: The Managerial Revolution in American Business.* Cambridge: Harvard University Press, 1977.

Dietz, Burkhard, Michael Fessner, and Helmut Maier. "'Der Kulturwert der Technik' als Argument der Technischen Intelligenz für sozialen Aufstieg und Anerkennung." In *Technische Intelligenz und "Kulturfaktor Technik": Kulturvorstellungen von Technikern und Ingenieuren zwischen Kaiserreich und früher Bundesrepublik Deutschland,* edited by Dietz, Fessner, and Maier, 1–34. Münster: Waxmann, 1996.

Durth, Werner. *Deutsche Architekten Biographische Verflechtungen, 1900–1970.* Braunschweig: Friedr. Vieweg & Sohn, 1986.

Evans, Richard. *In Hitler's Shadow: West German Historians and the Attempt to Escape from the Nazi Past.* New York: Pantheon, 1989.

Friedländer, Saul. "West Germany and the Burden of the Past: The Ongoing Debate." *Jerusalem Quarterly* 42 (1987): 3–18.

Gellately, Robert. "'A Monstrous Uneasiness': Citizen Participation and Persecution of the Jews in Nazi Germany." In *Lessons and Legacies: The Meaning of the Holocaust in a Changing World,* edited by Peter Hayes, 178–95. Evanston: Northwestern University Press, 1991.

Giddens, Anthony. *The Consequences of Modernity.* Stanford: Stanford University Press, 1990.

Gispen, Kees. *New Profession, Old Order: Engineers and German Society, 1815–1914.* Cambridge: Cambridge University Press, 1989.

Goldhagen, Daniel. *Hitler's Willing Executioners: Ordinary Germans and the Holocaust.* New York: Alfred A. Knopf, 1996.

Habermas, Jürgen. *Theorie des kommunikativen Handelns.* Vols. 1, 2. Frankfurt am Main: Suhrkamp, 1981.

Hartung, Ulrich. "Bauästhetik im Nationalsozialismus und die Frage der Denkmalwürdigkeit." In *Raktionäre Modernität und Völkermord: Probleme des Umgangs mit der NS-Zeit in Austellungen und Gedenkstätten*, edited by Bernd Fankenbach and Franz-Josef Jelich, 71–84. Essen: Klartext-Verlag, 1994.

Hayes, Peter. "Polycracy and Policy in the Third Reich: The Case of the Economy." In *Reevaluating the Third Reich*, edited by Thomas Childers and Jane Caplan, 190–210. New York: Holmes & Meier, 1993.

Herbert, Ulrich. *Best: Biographische Studien über Radikalismus, Weltanschauung und Vernunft 1903–1989*. Bonn: Dietz, 1996.

———. *Fremdarbeiter: Politik und Praxis des "Ausländer-Einsatzes" in der Kriegswirtschaft des Dritten Reiches*. Bonn: Verlag J. H. W. Dietz Nachf., 1986.

Herf, Jeffrey. *Reactionary Modernism: Technology, Culture, and Politics in Weimar and the Third Reich*. Cambridge: Cambridge University Press, 1984.

Hilberg, Raul. "Significance of the Holocaust." In *The Holocaust: Ideology, Bureaucracy, and Genocide*, edited by Henry Friedlander and Sybil Milton, 101. Millwood, N.Y.: Kraus International Publications, 1980.

Hortleder, Gerd. *Das Gesellschaftsbild des Ingenieurs: Zum politischen Verhalten der Technischen Intelligenz in Deutschland*. Frankfurt am Main: Suhrkamp, 1970.

Hüttenberger, Peter. "Nationalsozialistische Polykratie." *Geschichte und Gesellschaft* 2 (1976): 417–42.

James, Harold. *The German Slump: Politics and Economics, 1924–1936*. Oxford: Clarendon Press, 1986.

Jaskot, Paul. "The Architectural Policy of the SS, 1936–45." Ph.D. diss., Northwestern University, 1993.

Karny, Miroslav. "'Vernichtung durch Arbeit': Sterblichkeit in den NS-Konzentrationslagern." In *Sozialpolitik und Judenvernichtung: Gibt es eine Ökonomie der Endlösung?*, edited by Götz Aly and Susanne Heim, 133–58. Berlin: Rotbuch Verlag, 1987.

Kocka, Jürgen. *Die Angestellten in der deutschen Geschichte 1850–1980*. Göttingen: Vandenhoeck & Ruprecht, 1981.

———. "Scale and Scope, a Review Colloquium." *Business History Review* 64 (1990): 711–16.

Latour, Burno. *We Have Never Been Modern*. Cambridge: Harvard University Press, 1993.

Lifton, Robert Jay. *The Nazi Doctors*. New York: Basic Books, 1986.

Lindenfeld, David. "The Prevalence of Irrational Thinking in the Third Reich: Notes Toward the Reconstruction of Moden Value Rationality." *Central European History* 30 (1997): 365–84.

Ludwig, Karl-Heinz. *Technik und Ingenieure im Dritten Reich*. Düsseldorf: Droste Verlag, 1974.

Ludwig, Karl-Heinz, and Wolfgang König. *Technik, Ingenieure und Gesellschaft: Geschichte des Vereins Deutscher Ingenieure 1856–1981*. Düsseldorf: VDI-Verlag, 1981.

Maier, Charles. *The Unmasterable Past: History, Holocaust, and German National Identity*. Cambridge: Harvard University Press, 1988.

Mason, Timothy. "Domestic Dynamics of Nazi Conquests: A Response to Critics." In *Reevaluating the Third Reich*, edited by Thomas Childers and Jane Caplan, 161–89. New York: Holmes & Meier, 1993.

——. "Labour in the Third Reich, 1933–39." *Past and Present* 33 (1968): 112–41.

——. "Some Origins of the Second World War." *Past and Present* 29 (1964): 67–87.

Mommsen, Hans. "Die Realizierung des Utopischen: Die 'Endlösung der Judenfrage' im 'Dritten Reich.'" In *Der Nationalsozialismus und die deutsche Gesellschaft*, 184–232. Reinbek bei Hamburg: Rowohlt, 1991.

Mommsen, Hans, and Manfred Grieger. *Das Volkswagenwerk und seine Arbeiter im Dritten Reich*. Düsseldorf: Econ Verlag, 1996.

Neumann, Franz. *Behemoth: The Structure and Politics of National Socialism, 1933–1944*. New York: Harper and Row, 1994.

Nolan, Mary. *Visions of Modernity: American Business and the Modernization of Germany*. Oxford: Oxford University Press, 1994.

Orth, Karin. *Die Konzentrationslager-SS: Sozialstrukturelle Analysen und biographische Studien*. Göttingen: Wallstein Verlag, 2000.

Overy, Richard. "'Blitzkriegswirtschaft'? Finanzpolitik, Lebensstandard und Arbeitseinsatz in Deutschland 1939–42." *Vierteljahreshefte für Zeitgeschichte* 36 (1988): 370–435.

——. "Germany, 'Domestic Crisis' and War in 1939." *Past and Present* 116 (1987): 138–68.

——. "Mobilization for Total War in Germany, 1939–1941." *English Historical Review* 88 (1988): 613–39.

——. *The Nazi Economic Recovery, 1932–1938*. Cambridge University Press, 1982.

Peukert, Detley. *Inside Nazi Germany: Conformity, Opposition, and Racism in Everyday Life*, 1982. Reprint, New Haven: Yale University Press, 1987.

Prinz, Michael. *Vom Mittelstand zum Volksgenossen: Die Entwicklung des sozialen Status der Angestellten von der Weimarer Republik bis zum Ende der NS-Zeit*. Munich: R. Oldenbourg Verlag, 1986.

Remdt, Gerhardt, and Günter Wermusch. *Rätsel Jonastal: Die Geschichte des letzten Führerhauptquartiers*. Berlin: Christoph Links Verlag, 1992.

Ritschl, Albrecht. "Die NS-Wirtschaftsideologie—Modernisierungsprogramm oder reaktionäre Utopie?" In *Nationalsozialismus und Modernisierung*, edited by Rainer Zitelmann and Michael Prinz, 48–70. Darmstadt: Wissenschaftliche Buchgesellschaft, 1991.

Seibel, Wolfgang. "Staatsstruktur und Massenmord: Was kann eine historisch-vergleichende Institutionenanalyse zur Erforschung des Holocaust beitragen?" *Geschichte und Gesellschaft* 24 (1998): 539–69.

Seidler, Franz. *Fritz Todt: Baumeister des Dritten Reiches*. Frankfurt am Main: Verlag Ullstein, 1988.

Sinclair, Bruce. "Inventing a Genteel Tradition: MIT Crosses the River." In *New Perspectives on Technology and American Culture*, edited by Sinclair, 1–18. Philadelphia: American Philosophical Society, 1986.

Smelser, Ronald. *Robert Ley, Hitler's Labor Front Leader*. New York: Berg, 1988.

Speer, Albert. *Slave State: Heinrich Himmler's Masterplan for SS Supremacy*. London: Weidenfeld and Nicolson, 1981.

Sudrow, Anne. "Das 'deutsche Rohstoffwunder' und die Schuhindustrie: Schuhproduktion unter den Bedingungen der nationalsozialistische Autarkiepolitik." *Blätter für Technikgeschichte* 60 (1998): 63–92.

Van der Vat, Jan. *The Good Nazi: The Life and Lies of Albert Speer.* New York: Houghton Mifflin, 1997.

Wengenroth, Ulrich. "Zwischen Aufruhr und Diktatur: Die Technische Hochschule 1918–1945." In *Die Technische Universität München: Annährungen an ihre Geschichte,* edited by Wengenroth, 215–23. Munich: Faktum, 1993.

Zeitlin, Jonathan, and Steven Tolliday. "Employers and Industrial Relations between Theory and History." In *The Power to Manage? Employers and Industrial Relations in Comparative-Historical Perspective,* edited by Zeitlin and Tolliday. 1–34. New York: Routledge, 1991.

Zeller, Thomas, "Landschaften des Verkehrs Autobahnen im Nationalsozialismus und Hochgeschwindigkeitsstrecken für die Bahn in der Bundesrepublik." *Technikgeschichte* 64 (1997): 323–40.

Zilt, Andreas. "'Reactionary Modernism' in der westdeutschen Stahlindustrie? Technik als Kulturfaktor bei Paul Reusch und Hubert Hauttmann." In *Technische Intelligenz und "Kulturfaktor Technik": Kulturvorstellungen von Technikern und Ingenieuren zwischen Kaiserreich und früher Bundesrepublik Deutschland,* edited by Burkhard Dietz, Michael Fessner, and Helmut Maier, 191–202. Münster: Waxmann, 1996.

Zunz, Olivier. *Making America Corporate, 1870–1920.* Chicago: University of Chicago Press, 1990.

CHAPTER 6

Architectural Aesthetic and Political Ideology in Nazi Germany

---------------- ᐅ ----------------

In this chapter, art historian Paul B. Jaskot considers the social and cultural importance of the art and aesthetics of architecture in the Holocaust. Jaskot believes that art and culture cannot be distinguished from the social, political, and economic forces in the history of a nation. Focusing on the role of architecture, he argues that the oppressive and genocidal Nazi regime was not merely a political response to social and historical problems in Germany but was an outgrowth of and a statement of a particular cultural mind-set. Decisions about art and architecture are a reflection of a society and its intellectual and political leaders, and such decisions have significant social and political consequences for a people and a nation. The architectural design of the labor and extermination camps, for example, was merely the culmination of a cultural process that began with Hitler's overt depiction (in *Mein Kampf*) of Jewish building design as being the cause of problems in the modern world. This essay summarizes Jaskot's book-length treatment of the subject (*The Architecture of Oppression: The SS, Forced Labor and the Nazi Monumental Building Economy*; 2000)—here he emphasizes four aspects of the history of Nazi Germany: (1) the use of architecture as a form of anti-Jewish propaganda during the early years of the Nazi regime (1933–38); (2) the increasing anti-Jewish policies of the regime after *Kristallnacht* (November 9, 1938) and the use of architectural plans for Berlin in these new anti-Jewish activities; (3) the murderous slave labor camps, particularly the stone quarries that produced the raw materials for the monumental Nazi building projects; and (4) the architectural design of Auschwitz as a camp for the development of efficient, mass-produced death. A key player in the architectural plans of the Third Reich was Hitler's chief architect and master builder, Albert Speer, who later served as Armaments Minister during the war. In the next chapter (Chapter 7), we will read excerpts from Speer's diaries about his role in the Nazi regime. We must bear in mind the precise ways in which architectural designs helped to perpetuate and to advance the political and social goals of the Third Reich.

Architecture and the Destruction of the European Jews

Paul B. Jaskot

Possibly no single political event has affected the development of modern European society more than the rise to power of the National Socialist German Workers' Party (NSDAP) in 1933. Most emblematic of the brutality of this fascist regime was the destruction of the European Jews. The intentional and systematic murder of a people using modern technology makes this genocide unique to the twentieth century.

Yet this aspect of Nazi society has played little role in the history of art. The few scholars who have looked at anti-Semitism and National Socialist art and architecture have most often turned to the modernist artists who were denigrated in racist terms at the infamous Degenerate Art Show in Munich. Further, art historians have begun to look at academic Nazi painters like Adolf Ziegler and architects like Albert Speer to show how they institutionally responded to the emerging anti-Semitic policies. Having discussed the exile of modernist artists from Germany and Europe, and having cited a few prominent examples of artists active in National Socialist institutions, most twentieth-century art historians then turn to the postwar expansion of the art market, especially in the United States. Auschwitz does not figure in this history of art.

What I would like to argue is that any modern art history that does not include a more comprehensive understanding of the policies that led to Auschwitz is a misleading art history. Because the history of art is the history of society, if we are to understand the significance and meaning of works of art, we must also understand their function in particular societies at particular times. Social art historians certainly do emphasize how specific formal decisions, markets and audiences have been mobilized or manipulated by patrons, artists and critics in an attempt to communicate a specific meaning. But we must also analyse how these decisions (aesthetic and otherwise) have ramifications outside the artistic institutions usually identified as the subject of art history, or even independent from the particular meaning of specific art works. While I will discuss aesthetic developments, form will be only one category amongst many used to understand these works of art. Expanding the categories of analysis not only helps attain a more complete knowledge of the work of art, but also allows a critique of the standard art histories that would exclude the genocide from an account of modern European art. Such an expanded account of culture and cultural policy also contributes to a more comprehensive knowledge about the genocide and its status as an oppressive extreme. But further, it emphasizes how this event can help us understand other modes and conditions of oppression in modern industrial life and culture, some of which developed from the remnants of National Socialist politics into the cold war and remain depressingly present in our own time.

This, as I see it, is the principle function of an overview of architecture and the destruction of the European Jews. Analyzing how architecture was used to further anti-Semitic goals is a way of arguing that oppressive policies are not just a matter of a few elite politicians making certain decisions in isolation. Rather, these policies are enacted and sometimes made possible by their integration into all areas of society, including culture. To make this argument, I will present the variety of ways that architecture played a part in developing the policies against the Jews. This essay will deal with how the chronology of anti-Semitic practices is parallel to and part of a complementary chronology of architectural projects and their construction. This chronology can be roughly organized into four, sometimes overlapping, sections.

First, I will address the initial stages of anti-Semitic propaganda and cultural practices leading up to the election of the National Socialist Party in 1933 and through the first years of its consolidation of power in Germany. My second concern will be the radicalization of anti-Semitic policy, above all following the pogrom of 9 November 1938 (the so-called *Kristallnacht*). These years as well saw an intensification of the integration of architectural goals with measures aimed against the Jewish community, particularly in Berlin. German Jews were, however, not just subject to the broad policy of the state, but also to specific policies of particular Nazi institutions (above all the SS). Hence, third, I want to address the way in which many German Jewish citizens after 1938 were not only denied basic political, economic and social rights, but were also rigorously suppressed and policed in the SS-controlled forced labour concentration camps, especially after the outbreak of World War II. Here, too, we find a connection to architectural policy. In the forced labour camps at the stone quarries of Flossenbürg and Mauthausen, the practice of murdering prisoners came together with the SS interest in the production of stone to complete the monumental building projects commissioned by the Party and State.

And finally, the development of the death camps, beginning in 1941, as the most grotesque extreme of Nazi anti-Semitic policy must also be analysed as partially a result of the brutally capable architectural staff who constructed these facilities. These four aspects of National Socialist architecture correspond to the radicalization of anti-Semitism from its ideological basis to its role as propaganda, from its use as the impetus for state regulation to its institutionalization as a policy of destruction. Hence, looking at these four moments in the development of anti-Semitism helps to clarify how specific policies were carried out with or legitimated by the aid of architecture in National Socialist Germany.

The point of such an endeavour is to raise the key historical themes that ground the integration of architecture and anti-Semitism in National Socialist Germany and, thereby, provide the basis for further study of the genocide. Simultaneously, this is meant as a critique of the art-historical discipline which has ignored the study of the genocide or relegated it to a side-issue of the history of modern European and North American art. The absence of Auschwitz from art history points to the strong influence of the private art market within the discipline. That is to say, art that has been considered prominent or critical (i.e., art that has been historically analysed), remains predominantly art that has been defined and valued by the marketplace which was centred in Paris prior to World War II and, after the war, in New York. While these market dynamics are crucial for explaining the historical valuation of art and its institutions, they of course should not be crucial in defining the parameters of historical analysis. An analysis of architecture and the genocide shows how flawed such a limitation can be and how necessary it is to see art as connected to broader aspects of society (not just the marketplace and cultural institutions). It is only with such a revaluation that we can comprehend the importance of anti-Semitic policy to an analytic assessment of National Socialist art.

ARCHITECTURE AS PROPAGANDA: ANTI-SEMITISM AND THE CONSOLIDATION OF POWER, 1925–1937

The integration of architecture with the Nazi anti-Semitic programme began almost with the foundation of the Party itself. Hitler solidified the connection between his anti-Semitic views and architectural goals through certain key passages in *Mein Kampf* (1925). In his book, Hitler promoted the pseudoscientific racial theory that Germans were superior "Aryan" people and that only a people of supposedly pure blood had the political will to create a strong society; this political will would in turn be reflected in their architecture. Specifically, Hitler praised ancient classical architecture and the architecture of the Ringstrasse in Vienna, and condemned Berlin architecture which, to him, emphasized only financial institutions and Jewish-owned department stores. By equating the positive expression of political power with certain kinds of monumental architectural traditions, and by relating the negative problems of modern society to buildings constructed or owned by Jews, Hitler early on set the stage for architecture to be a component of the Nazis' racist and anti-Semitic propaganda.[1]

As part of their election strategies in the late 1920s and early 1930s, National Socialist ideologues emphasized a negative evaluation of architecture, modern architecture representing a supposedly racial corruption of Germanic and *völkisch* values; they did not promote any particular example of contemporary architecture as representing a positive expression of Nazi ideas. There were two reasons behind this negative campaign. First, the Nazi Party was trying to gain electoral success by critiquing the dominant party of the Weimar years, the Social Democratic Party (SPD). Since the SPD had been associated with promoting and sometimes funding certain architectural projects designed by modernist architects or members of the Bauhaus, Nazi cultural critics could use the flat-roofed, concrete-walled buildings as a foil for their critique of what they characterized as the essentially internationalist and non-German policies of the SPD. Such criticism usually took on a clear anti-Semitic or racist cast, the architecture being connected to a specious argument about a Jewish communist conspiracy or about its essentially "Semitic character."[2]

The second reason for the negative campaign, however, was internal to the Nazi Party itself. While architectural criticism did *not* dominate the propaganda tactics of most of the Party elite, Alfred Rosenberg did champion the critique of modernist architecture in his role as editor of the *Völkischer Beobachter*, the main Party newspaper. Traditionalist architects such as Paul Schultze-Naumburg found an outlet for both their architectural and racist views in the pages of this newspaper. Schultze-Naumburg came to the attention of Rosenberg because of his talks and publications on the supposed racial character of architecture and, particularly, the un-Germanic and decadent forms of modernist architects like Mies van der Rohe and Walter Gropius. Such sentiments appealed to the *völkisch* Rosenberg and he enlisted the architect as one of the leading spokespersons for his *Kampfbund für deutsche Kultur* (Combat League for German Culture [KDK]). In 1931, the KDK sponsored Schultze-Naumburg on a highly publicized lecture tour of his racist ideas on art and architecture. For this wing of the NSDAP, anti-Semitic, anti-Marxist and racist propaganda was firmly attached to functionalist architecture, even though architects like Mies and Gropius claimed that their work was essentially apolitical.[3]

But it should be emphasized that anti-Semitic architectural criticism was only a small part of a much larger propaganda campaign to bring the National Socialists to power. In negative assessments of modern architecture, the Nazi critic was often just as likely to emphasize such architecture's imagined political ties to the SPD or Communist Party, by labelling it "cultural bolshevism," as to see it in racist or anti-Semitic terms. In this sense, architectural criticism followed the more dominant propaganda trends of the pre-1933 NSDAP: attacking the existing political parties and parliamentary system while promoting specific economic and social solutions to the chaos in Germany after the onset of the 1929 Depression. Such a campaign often included vague notions of an "ideal" Germany and Germanic culture that would materialize after Hitler came to power. Anti-Semitism in architectural criticism, as in other areas of Nazi propaganda, was a strategic tool to be emphasized or de-emphasized depending on the shifting political landscape of the late Weimar Republic.[4]

Once Hitler was in power, however, the importance of architecture became much more evident. Hitler began to support particular architects and made it clear that architectural projects were key to the development of a National Socialist culture. It was at this point that the negative criticism of modern architecture was complemented by the official sanctioning of positive architectural expressions with supposedly Germanic political and racial characteristics. For official state and Party buildings, Hitler favoured the stripped-down neoclassicism of Paul Ludwig Troost and, after Troost's death in 1934, that of Speer. Such an aesthetic formed the backdrop upon which Nazi ideologues projected a racist and politically loaded interpretation of Germany under Hitler.[5]

Speer's *Zeppelinfeld* (Photo 1) at the Nuremberg Party Rally Grounds exemplifies these ideological considerations. The *Zeppelinfeld* project included a large viewing stand facing an open field and surrounded by pylons topped with flag stands. The focus of the field was clearly on the viewing stands themselves, which Speer in his memoirs claimed to have modelled on the Pergamum Altar (exhibited in the Pergamon Museum in Berlin).[6] This claim is substantiated by formal similarities between the two, including the long, sweeping travertine staircase (here functioning as seats for viewers) leading up to a colonnade and bracketed by two perpendicular pylons. The fact that the Pergamum Altar was also a Hellenistic victory altar further connects the Nuremberg building site with claims of Greek precedence and Nazi dynastic ambitions. But not all the project's sources are Greek for, like all major buildings at Nuremberg, the *Zeppelinfeld* also included a central podium with a pulpit from which Hitler could

*Photo 1. Albert Speer, Zeppelinfeld, Party Rally Grounds in Nuremberg.
c. 1935. (Troost,* Bauen im neuen Reich.)

speak. This central podium is essentially a Roman Imperial device, used by emperors like Augustus to hold the attention of the people gathered. Hence, the *Zeppelinfeld* incorporated the two dominant strains of interpretation of official state and Party architecture: Roman to emphasize the expansionist and militarist goals of the Party; and Greek to emphasize a supposed racial connection between the "pure" German race and the ancestry of the Germanic *Volk*.[7] However contradictory the ideological associations, this architecture, like other monumental state and Party buildings, supported the emphasis on permanence which Hitler associated with specific types of classical public architecture, as well as with the strength of a legitimate political regime.[8] It provided the site upon which a racist view of Germanic culture could be projected, and is consistent with this highly ideological stage of anti-Semitic policy.

But while Speer's and Troost's buildings formed the stage for the projection of conflicting Nazi ideological positions, these buildings were the exception to Party and state construction. That is to say, there was never a coherent National Socialist architectural policy. While specific buildings like the *Zeppelinfeld* were approved in the early years of Nazi rule as examples of the racial superiority of Nazi society which other architects might emulate, no systematic attempt was made to formulate and institutionalize one particular style. In spite of this lack of a coherent National Socialist aesthetic, however, critics and politicians alike continued their negative campaign about "degenerate" and so-called Jewish artistic and architectural styles.

While the propaganda campaign continued, specific anti-Semitic policies also began to affect architectural practice. Between 1933–1937, the National Socialist government increasingly sought to define exactly who was Jewish (most infamously in the 1935 Nuremberg Laws) and to regulate this population by exclusion from publicly sponsored and Party-influenced institutions, including architectural schools and institutions (such as the Prussian Academy of Art and the *Werkbund*) and commissions throughout the country. Backing up the ideologically driven demonization of Jews were specific laws and policies aimed at distancing them from the dominant institutions and social groups in Germany. The process began with the Law for the Reestablishment of the Professional Civil Service of 7 April 1933, which excluded Jews from holding state positions including all posts in public building administrations. This law became the basis of Paragraph 10 of the First Decree for the Implementation of the Reich Chamber of Culture (*Reichskulturkammer*) Law passed on 1 November 1933. While the decree does not explicitly mention Jews, its wording allowed for the dismissal of Jews in all cultural professional organizations under the control of Goebbels's *Reichskulturkammer*, including the fields of architecture and fine arts. Up until 1938, the institutional exclusion of Jews from German society and, consequently, from architectural practice, formed the political focus of National Socialist policy. At the same time, the public vilification of Jews and vague and often contradictory ideological claims about un-German architecture continued.[9]

ARCHITECTURE AND THE ENACTMENT
OF ANTI-SEMITIC POLICY, 1938–1941

Regulatory policies aimed at specific segments of the Jewish population (such as professionals) gave way after the pogrom of 9 November 1938 to much more sweeping and radicalized anti-Semitic policies meant to control the economic, political and social rights of German Jews. November of 1938 forms a point of no return, a point prepared by the anti-Semitic propaganda ánd legislation which preceded it and legitimized by that which came after. From this moment and intensifying into the war years, we can analyse how government policy became increasingly restrictive in regards to what *any* German Jew could do and thus, targeted the entire community. The result included policies to limit the physical freedom of the Jews, concentrate them, deprive them of a means of subsistence and, ultimately, completely separate them from German society. This was a different and active anti-Semitism, one that could be legitimized through architecture and, in key locations such as Berlin, was sometimes affected through architectural policy developed even before the November pogrom.

The plans for the rebuilding of Berlin give some insight into this phase of anti-Semitic policy and architecture. Through the late 1930s and into World War II, Berlin was Germany's preeminent building site. Its position as the centre of state and Party architectural policy was achieved both through Hitler's direct interest in the redesign of the capital and through the centralization and extension of Speer's control over architectural policy as inspector general of building for the Reich Capital Berlin (*Generalbauinspektor für die Reichshauptstadt Berlin* [GBI]). Speer's proposal was the largest single architectural project in the German building economy. The actual plan, announced publicly on 28 January 1938, included a north-south and east-west axis at the heart of the city, a concentration of subway and train facilities, a redesign of the Königsplatz and a major housing programme. The north-south axis became the core of the urban design and was meant to function as the main ceremonial boulevard of the new Berlin.[10]

To grasp how the decisions made concerning the formal design of a monumental urban plan for Berlin functioned as part of the developing anti-Semitic policy, one must go beyond an account of anti-Semitic ideology or an analysis of the architectural profession and concentrate on the implementation of particular economic and social policies aimed at the Berlin Jewish population. Specifically, as I have argued elsewhere, anti-Semitic housing policy (concerned as it was with controlling and then removing the Jewish population) became the focus of Speer's efforts to complete the monumental plans for the rebuilding of Berlin.[11]

As Speer and his staff began finalizing their designs around two monumental intersecting axes for the heart of Berlin, they focused on several preconditions for the construction process; among them, the procurement of materials, property and substitute housing for those displaced by the project. These preconditions for construction were determined by the formal choices that Speer and his architects made in terms both of particular buildings and the urban plan as a whole. Wilhelm Kreis's *Soldiers' Hall* (Photo 2), a large neoclassical masonry structure designed to memorialize the German soldier and the war dead, exemplifies these architectural choices. On the north-south axis, Kreis's building functioned as the symbolic facade of the new headquarters of the Army High Command. The stripped-down classicism and granite stone of the facade would tie the building to its surroundings, while its massive scale and location in proximity to the Runder Platz would separate it from other administrative headquarters on the axis in keeping with its function

Photo 2. Wilhelm Kreis, Model of the Soldiers' Hall. Berlin. c. 1938.
(*Troost*, Bauen im neuen Reich.)

as an important propaganda site for the commemoration of the military
martyr. After the outbreak of war on 1 September 1939, the symbolic significance of this ceremonial building increased; as a result, work continued on the site and in the collection of materials for the project until at
least the early months of 1944.[12]

What becomes clear from the example of the *Soldiers' Hall* is the way
in which the GBI considered the emphasis on particular buildings part of
a massive urban scheme, a scheme developed in terms of key sites chosen
on the basis of the changing conditions of prewar and wartime Germany.
This also meant that such factors as the scale of a building (the *Soldiers'
Hall* alone was to be built with over 96,000 cbm of granite) and its location would influence other contingencies of the building process, such
as whether and how much of a potential site was to be cleared of its
housing.[13] As much as their aesthetic concerns, architects at the GBI
involved themselves in precisely these elements of urban planning in
order to achieve their design decisions. Their formal choices for buildings
and the geographic layout of the plan led to their broader involvement in
state and Party policy.

One of the immediate policies of interest to the GBI was, of course,
housing and property ownership, precisely because these issues inter-
sected with the site-specific demands of such massive projects as the

Soldiers' Hall. The need to address the laws governing property ownership and to create substitute housing for those displaced formed two key components of Speer's early strategy to complete the plan. The GBI had the authority to direct all buying and selling of properties in this district and construction on the site also had to be approved by the architectural administration. Concomitantly, the GBI could direct the city to purchase, sell or build on the lands under its influence.[14] Protected by Hitler and independent of other government administrations, the GBI acted in an executive capacity and ignored the established state administrative hierarchy, and hence was relatively free to set property acquisition policy.

In connection with its executive capacity to acquire property, the GBI found several solutions to the problem of acquiring adequate substitute housing for those who were displaced by site clearing near the *Soldiers' Hall* and elsewhere on the two axes of the Berlin plan. Prominent among such solutions was depriving Jews of, first, their tenant rights and then, during the war, their property rights. In 1933, when Hitler came to power, this area bordered on and partially included the district of the Tiergarten, a district that contained approximately nine per cent of the total residential population of Berlin Jews. A significant section of the Jewish population thus had interests in the renting of housing and ownership of land connected with the proposed building site.[15]

Before the pogrom in November 1938, attempts in the private sector to isolate Jews from the economy and the government's exclusion of Jews from certain professions resulted in many practical restrictions of Jewish rights. Nevertheless, no systematic policy was in place to limit the rights of Jews to own and rent property. Hence, at the time when Speer was working to deprive Berlin Jews of their housing in mid-1938, he was taking part in one of the most advanced stages of anti-Semitic policy aimed at excluding Jews from German society. In 1938, the execution of millions of Jews was not yet an issue; the denial of their claims to political, social and economic rights was, however, of central concern.[16]

How the GBI planned to formulate and take advantage of anti-Semitic policy became clear in a meeting between representatives of the GBI and the Berlin City Planning Office (*Stadtplanungsamt*) called by Speer's office on 14 September 1938. Speer began by asking the assembled administrators what problems had been created by the lack of substitute housing for those displaced by rebuilding projects. The next item on the agenda provided a solution for these administrative difficulties. In a proposal that must have originated significantly before the date of the meeting, Speer suggested the new idea that substitute housing could be found by displacing Berlin Jews from their homes. This proposal would allow completion of the architectural plans and save the German state the costs of constructing new housing. Though consistent with the general anti-Semitic fervour of the Party and state bureaucrats of the time, Speer's suggestion went well beyond even the plans of the Gestapo to that date.[17] He proposed depriving Jews of property and tenant rights and placing them in designated blocks of small dwellings to be closed off as a form of ghetto. The necessary laws and regulations could be created after Speer had gained Hitler's approval of the project. He went on to note the economic advantage of not having to build large dwellings as substitute housing (alleviating pressure on the building economy) and the fact that his proposal would clear the way for completion of his architectural plans. The success of Speer's plan depended on the trenchant anti-Semitism of Nazi Germany, the effectiveness of the Gestapo as a police enforcer of anti-Semitic policy and the ability of the GBI to take advantage of policy goals seemingly outside its area of authority.

Yet the GBI architects were not operating in a vacuum, and the question of the next step against the Jews was being discussed among many (often competing) administrative bodies.[18] Just how complex the interconnection of the interests of various administrative bodies was appears in the minutes of a confidential meeting at the *Stadtplanungsamt* on 27 September 1938. At this meeting, representatives of the *Stadtplanungsamt*, the German Labour Front (*Deutsche Arbeitsfront* [DAF]), the Berlin police, the Party's District Leadership of Berlin (*Gauleitung Berlin*), the Statistical Office and the GBI planned how they could work together to solve the problems surrounding the eviction of Jews. Two parallel concerns guided the discussion: the GBI's great interest in gaining control of large dwellings as quickly as possible and the efforts already begun by the Ministry of Justice to relax tenant protection for Jews. In their desire to move the two goals forward, those at the meeting combined these two concerns. The gathering of statistical information on Jewish dwellings in Berlin was seen as crucial for both cases. With these statistics (and Hitler's approval), the implementation of anti-Semitic housing policy could begin by identifying and evicting particular segments of the Berlin population. The GBI argued that this information had to be collected as soon as possible in order to move the architectural plans forward. Under the guise of the needs of the GBI, all Jews at or bordering key architectural sites would be registered and Berlin's Jews separated from the rest of city's population.[19]

In 1938, after the GBI had determined the main elements of the rebuilding plan, Berlin architectural policy was used to push the rapid development of anti-Semitic policy and was easily tied to the complex goals of other administrations. The pogrom of 9 November 1938 made further secret administrative meetings and complicated justifications unnecessary. Until this event, the Ministry of Justice and the GBI had worked intensely via bureaucratic channels to push through the housing policy changes they sought. After the pogrom, the highest officials in the Party and state swept aside an administrative conclusion to the debate and formulated a policy meant to be enacted from the top down. But even then, the initial interests of the GBI were picked up and incorporated in the final policy. While the pogrom sped up the enforcement of eviction measures, the move against Berlin's Jewish tenants was already well underway before November 9 and had the support of administrations already mobilized by the actions of the Ministry of Justice and the GBI.

The participation of the Nazi political elite did not mean, however, that Speer's interest in using anti-Semitic policy to clear such massive sites, including that of the *Soldiers' Hall*, was no longer a part of state housing initiatives. By 30 April 1939, when the decree on Jewish housing was finally issued by Hitler,[20] any Jewish tenant could be evicted if the landlord could show that the tenant had replacement housing somewhere else. The decree also stated that homeless Jews had to be taken in by other Jews and that all subsequent rental or owner laws were to be the responsibility of the Ministries of Justice and Labour. Yet the retreat from a general eviction of Jews to eviction only in specific cases was hardly a blow to the GBI. With over 50,000 Jewish families in Berlin, Speer had ample room from which to select the 2500 to 3000 houses that he needed. To handle this selection, he created a special office on Jews in the GBI (the Main Resettlement Division) and kept a roster of registered Jewish housing in Berlin.[21] In fact, after the meeting at which the decisions concerning Jewish tenant rights had been made, Hermann Göring required, in a letter of 26 November 1938, that all appropriated Jewish dwellings in Berlin be registered with and at the disposal of the GBI as a related issue of the upcoming April decree.[22] Thus, although larger concerns ultimately defined the tenant law, Speer's interests nevertheless contributed to the development of the debate after the pogrom. Göring took these interests up and made them into a specific component of the new measures against the Berlin Jews.

The involvement of the GBI with anti-Semitic housing policy shows the integration of architectural goals with the stepped-up measures against the German Jews in 1938 and after. Such manoeuvring by the GBI to make its architectural goals commensurate with state anti-Semitic policy continued well into World War II and as long as the privileging of monumental architecture and German military victories would allow. Architectural planning was not merely a convenient means to address the ideological goals of the state. Rather, Speer and his staff were involved in influencing the timing and the active pursuit of a more brutal anti-Semitic policy in order to realize their plans for the rebuilding of Berlin.

ANTI-SEMITIC POLICY AND THE PRODUCTION OF BUILDING MATERIALS IN THE FORCED LABOUR CAMPS, 1938–1942

Through such means as the expropriation of Jewish housing, the GBI managed to continue significant architectural activity well into 1942, particularly for the prestige projects along the north-south axis and at the Runder Platz. But architect involvement with the oppressive practices of the National Socialist state was by no means limited to anti-Semitic housing policy. The need for materials for specific building sites led GBI administrators and others to take advantage of SS control over forced labour concentration camps which were set up around quarrying and brick-making facilities. Kreis's *Soldiers' Hall*, for example, with its massive granite requirements, became one of the projects around which the SS organized its forced labour operations. While the Tiergarten site, on which the *Soldiers' Hall* was partially to be built, was very much part of the coerced displacement of Jews from their property, the *Soldiers' Hall* was also a focus of SS attempts to build an economic empire through the output of forced labour concentration camps which had been established at stone quarries to punish and kill the state's political and ideological enemies. The production of granite under the brutal working conditions of labour camps such as Flossenbürg and Mauthausen contributed not only to the physical suppression of designated prison populations but the building of major architectural projects even during the war. At the stone-quarry labour camps, death for Jewish inmates and thousands of others (those whom the SS had imprisoned because of their actual or perceived social and political affiliations) was not unrelated to the camps' role in supplying material for the architectural projects of the Party and state.[23]

Beginning in 1938, SS administrators, at the height of their optimism, pursued stone orders from Berlin and Nuremberg and, through their firm, the German Earth and Stone Works (*Deutsche Erd- und Steinwerke, GmbH* [DEST]), identified specific forced labour camps to serve the monumental building economy. In the period between 1938 and early 1942, when SS political authority increased with its control of more and more people throughout occupied Europe, its economic enterprises also peaked. Through the DEST, the SS used its forced labour economic enterprises to link its steadily increasing political authority over Jews and other groups to the privileged position of architectural policy in National Socialist Germany. At the quarry sites, political suppression, productive labour and the needs of the monumental building economy all came together.

It is important to note that punishment at the stone-quarry labour camps was often determined according to the prisoners' political, social or national affiliations. In this sense, unlike other designated populations, Jewish prisoners were rarely abused for their productivity, especially in the early war years. That is to say, aesthetic choices based on particular kinds of high-quality granite provided the preconditions for an emphasis on productive forced labour at the camps for most general categories of inmates. But such aesthetic choices formed the precondition only for the type of punishment of the Jewish inmates, as well as some other exceptions including the Spanish communists at Mauthausen. Although many fewer Jews were sent to the forced labour camps than to the even more extreme death camps in the eastern occupied territories, those who did end up in Flossenbürg or Mauthausen were often murdered. The practice of murdering Jews in the quarry camps became an important precedent to the policy of destroying Jews in the death camps. The artistic decisions that became preconditions for killing at Flossenbürg and Mauthausen indicated a radicalization of anti-Semitic policy which culminated by the end of 1941 in the institutionalization of destruction at the death camps.[24]

The SS use of forced labour stone quarries was the result of aesthetic decisions made by Hitler and Speer (e.g., the use of particular materials like granite) and the willingness of architects to become involved with the organization of SS economic operations. Of course, it also relied on the expanding prison populations that formed the labour force which the SS controlled. With the coming of the war and Germany's territorial expansion, the prison populations increased exponentially. In April 1940, the first non-German prisoners arrived in Flossenbürg. These included Czech students and intellectuals as well as Poles, the largest group of non-German prisoners. In addition to these groups, two thousand Soviet prisoners of war (Jewish and non-Jewish) were sent to the camp in October 1941, kept in a special section to themselves and not included in the general SS camp registration lists. By February 1943, the camp held over four thousand inmates. Camp populations reflected the military advances of the German army through Europe and Soviet territory, as well as the expanded authority of the SS to control ever larger groups of people. They also reflected the SS interest in using forced labour to fill supply orders from the state's monumental building projects.[25]

From at least mid-1940, the SS sent some German, Polish and Czech Jews to the Flossenbürg camp. They were given especially cruel treatment. For Flossenbürg and the other stone-quarry work camps, Jews in these years were rarely inmates solely because of their ethnicity (the ghettos and, after 1941, the death camps served that function) but rather because of their ethnicity *and* a particular "crime" or nationality with which they were affiliated. These inmates were Jewish communists, homosexual Jews, Dutch Jews or Jews incarcerated for hard crimes. Nevertheless, Jewish inmates were usually treated differently from non-Jewish inmates. By the time Himmler enacted his order of October 1942, which sent any remaining Jews to Auschwitz or Lublin, only twelve Jews remained at Flossenbürg to be transported to the death camps. Most Jews sent to Flossenbürg were either immediately executed or died within the first week from the abuse they suffered. This situation did not change until 1944 when the necessity of mobilizing labour for armaments also included Jewish labour for Flossenbürg.[26]

The concentration camp population at the other well-established forced labour quarry camp of Mauthausen (in present-day Austria) was somewhat different from that of Flossenbürg. Foreign prisoners began arriving in early summer 1940 and, as with Flossenbürg, Poles formed the largest national group that was not German or Austrian. Almost to a person, Polish nationals were placed in the worst work commandos, including site clearing. Beginning in October 1941, Mauthausen also received major transports of Soviet prisoners of war who were given the most difficult work assignments. Unlike at Flossenbürg, another national group almost as large as the Poles was formed by Spanish communists and Republicans who had been trapped in France after the German invasion in 1940. Until 1940, Jews made up an even smaller percentage of the camp than at Flossenbürg. Indeed, only one, a homosexual Jew, is known to have been in the camp as of 1940. But Jewish transports began arriving in greater numbers in 1941, the majority of which came from Holland. Of the nine hundred Dutch Jews incarcerated in that year, only eight were still alive in December.[27]

In the early war years, the punishment of prisoners was inseparable from the development of SS economic policy. Of the five camps existing at the beginning of the war in which economic concerns played a significant role, Flossenbürg was the first and most consistent producer of stone. Though the quarries had been worked from the opening months of the camp, it was not until January 1940 that orders began to be filled and deliveries made. In this period, the most consistent stone orders for the high-quality granite of the quarries were for rebuilding efforts in Berlin, guaranteeing contracts for camp production as long as architectural policy was still a priority at the state level. In November 1940, stone-mason workshops set up to train prisoners also began providing limited amounts of cut stone for the Party Rally Grounds at Nuremberg, another priority wartime building site. The four quarries and stone-mason training programme remained in full production until May 1943, when the first quarry was closed and its workers shifted to the manufacture of armaments. Before this date, the SS could pursue its work orders through connections to the major state architectural commissions and the expansion of production to include stone-cutting needed by the German economy.[28]

Production for the DEST was successful in these years because it was based on the exploitation of a large camp labour force that, at this stage in the war, seemed unlimited to the SS administrators. The contradiction of killing labourers being used to create an economic empire was maintained as long as the SS continued to increase its political authority over prisoners in the early war years. The DEST's unwillingness to address the labour conditions during this period meant that both intentional and unplanned injuries and deaths frequently occurred in the stone quarries, particularly among Jewish inmates. Along with the constant beatings used to make the labourers work harder, the brutal weather conditions during the winter months and the lack of basic nutrition and health care set one prisoner against the next in a struggle for survival. Quarry commandos were used to carry out reprisals against specific prisoners. Prisoners marked for punishment were often forced to carry unusually heavy stones on their backs from the quarries to the camp at the end of a day, often causing them to collapse with fatigue or die of heart failure. Because of the control over ever larger numbers of prisoners (particularly from the occupied territories), camp administrators managed to maintain and even increase levels of production in spite of the brutal conditions experienced in the camps.

Even more so than at Flossenbürg, quarry labour at Mauthausen took a heavy toll on the lives of the prisoners. Because Reinhard Heydrich had designated that the camp was for individuals who would never be released, the Mauthausen quarries had the highest mortality rate of any of the labour camps. But, to repeat, for Jewish inmates, even if production levels were met, the inmates would still suffer heavy punishment. The anti-Semitism of the guards and the SS camp administrators meant that Jewish inmates were not used for their labour but rather were marked for murder. The work environment, however, provided the killing ground for these victims. At Mauthausen, multiple testimonials and records attest to the quarry site (and particularly the one hundred and eighty-six steps leading out of the quarry) as the place where most of the Jewish prisoners were killed. One Polish Jewish inmate was forced to carry a stone weighing one hundred and forty kilos from the quarry, up the steps and to the camp; he collapsed and died from the exertion. Further, Jews were forced to jump from the sides of the quarry or committed suicide in the same way to avoid an even more painful and drawn-out death. While other Jews were simply shot when they arrived at the camp or died because of the poor conditions within the first week, the quarry was still an effective tool for intimidation and execution for the extreme anti-Semitism at Mauthausen.[29]

The effectiveness of using a forced labour site to murder Jewish inmates is indicated by the SS's own records. To take a five-month example from the SS registration lists, the first large transport of Jews came to Mauthausen on 23 May 1941 with the arrival of 341 Dutch Jewish inmates mostly from Amsterdam. Ninety-two more Dutch Jews arrived on 23 June, ninety-five on 24 June, and ninety-one on 25 June (all referred to as

Aktion A'dam). One hundred and three more Jewish inmates were sent to Mauthausen on 17 September for a total of 619 in these transports. Considering that in all of 1940, only about ninety Jews had been inmates in the camp, these numbers represented a significant increase in the Jewish population.[30] In the same period (from May to the end of September 1941), almost all deaths recorded in an additional SS list were those of Jewish prisoners (356 total deaths listed, of which only 21 were non-Jewish inmates).[31] Even with a conservative estimate, this means that almost fifty per cent of the Jewish population at Mauthausen was destroyed within months if not days of arriving in the camp. By October 1942, only thirty Jews remained to be sent from Mauthausen to Auschwitz. While the details of their deaths are not clear, from what we know of the camp and its means of execution, it is beyond a doubt that many of the murders of Jewish inmates took place in the quarry or in the process of carrying stone.

Death at Mauthausen and Flossenbürg often came together with the orientation of the camp economy to the architectural projects of the Party and state. For Jewish prisoners, the quarries were significant in contributing to the conditions that led to physical and psychological break-down and exposed all inmates to the vagaries of the SS and its designated *Kapos*. It was not without reason that, in both camps, a prisoner feared being assigned to the stone-quarry work details of DEST, for it implied almost certain death. In the early stages of the war, the symbolic importance of Hitler's building programmes could be maintained at the expense of the prisoners' lives. In these years, the development and conditions of the quarries at Flossenbürg and Mauthausen indicate the connection of architectural policy and SS economic policy; further, the history of the quarries underlines the means by which the radicalized anti-Semitic policy of murdering Europe's Jewish population could function in these camps. By the early years of the war, the relation of anti-Semitic policy and architecture was not limited to propaganda, regulation, appropriation of property, or concentration, but had been extended to include excessive destructive measures.

ARCHITECTURE AND THE DEATH CAMPS, 1941–1945: THE EXAMPLE OF AUSCHWITZ

Finally, if our interest is in the relationship between architecture and the genocide, we need to consider those sites which were the brutal extreme of SS political power, i.e., the death camps. For, while the abuse of Jewish forced labour at the quarry camps was tied to the SS economic administrators' interest in the building materials market, so too was the architecture of the major death camps a matter of careful consideration, although for very different if contiguous political reasons. Bluntly stated, at the extermination camps, architects played a crucial role. But the architectural considerations were not aesthetically driven but rather technologically based. Construction of buildings was functionally determined in terms of the massive and complex process of organizing the deaths of millions of people. This grotesque functional requirement means that we need to consider the political goals of the SS in relation to architecture as significantly different at the sites of the mass destruction of the European Jews.

Deborah Dwork and Robert Jan van Pelt's book, *Auschwitz: 1270 to the Present* (1996), is the first scholarly work to take seriously the purpose of architects within the construction process of the death camps. The basic question which Dwork and van Pelt attempt to answer is why Auschwitz? Why this particular town and this particular camp? To get at this question, they propose that the death camps in general and Auschwitz in particular must be seen not as a result of a few fanatical Nazis who controlled a small cadre of devoted followers, but rather as a consequence of a complex of everyday organizational requirements and decisions made by "ordinary people"—transport permissions, material requisitions, real estate transactions, etc. However, they also argue that these bureaucrats, administrators, architects, and others, were active at the camp site because they were driven by deep ideological goals that made them particularly suitable for developing the destruction process in the early years of the camp.[32]

The ideological goals served by architecture and urban planning at Auschwitz had deep roots in the SS mentality that projected a connection between the SS dominance in eastern Europe and a racist view of the history of Germanic expansionist progress in the middle ages. That is to say; SS ideologues continued to promote the projection of anti-Semitic ideology onto the built environment, a move we have seen as consistent with earlier stages of architectural criticism. SS architect Hans Stosberg, appointed to oversee the expansion of the site after 1941, made this connection explicit in his specially-made Chirstmas card for December 1941. On the card, Stosberg had printed the following: "In the year 1241 Silesian knights, saviours of the Reich, warded off the Mongolian assault at Wahlstatt. In that same century Auschwitz was founded as a German town. Six hundred years later [*sic*] the *Führer* Adolf Hitler fends off the Bolshevik menace from Europe. This year, 1941, the construction of a new German city and the reconstruction of the old Silesian market was planned and initiated."[33] Auschwitz, as a camp and as a general urban site, would be redesigned by the SS architects and planners with the justification that they were enacting the fulfilment of the German destiny as articulated by Himmler and other SS ideologues.[34]

But, as with other SS sites, it is important to understand not only the ideological claims, but also the practical development of urban planning and construction. Segments of the town were certainly laid out with a notion of Germanic medieval rural settlement forms in mind. But the camp itself, after the initial industrial forced labour goals of the SS were frustrated, relied less on realizing a centuries-old Germanic mission than it did on the cold-blooded requirements of the process of Jewish geno-cide. Auschwitz-Birkenau did serve the stop-and-start goals of provid-ing labour for the developing IG Farben chemical plant also at the site. But by late 1941, the camp's function was increasingly turned away from a centre of forced labour to one of mass destruction.[35]

In this sense, the layout of the camp and its buildings, all architect-designed, followed institutional and functional requirements in which aesthetic goals took second place. The camp itself was organized around the typical pavilion plan, centred as it developed through 1943 on several large roll-call plazas.[36] Due to the sheer number of prisoners and the variable policies that controlled those prisoners (from forced labour to extermination), multiple roll-call plazas were required in order to main-tain order and a functional separation of prison populations according to the SS's political goals.

Photo 3. Main rail entrance of Auschwitz-Birkenau, 1945. (YIVO Institute for Jewish Research, courtesy of United States Holocaust Memorial Museum Photo Archives.)

By the end of 1943, Auschwitz-Birkenau was functioning as the only extermination camp still open and its architecture had been turned over almost completely to serving this goal. Gone were many of the plans to turn the town into an "ideal" German settlement, only to be replaced by the administrative and policy-driven focus on the camp and its function. That meant that the newly reconstructed entrance pavilion did not form the same kind of focus as in the dramatic fortified facade of such SS labour camps as Mauthausen, but rather was designed as a frame for the rail spur that led directly into the Appellplatz of Birkenau. In addition to its monumental size and permanent materials, the structure also served as a watch tower for SS personnel guarding the entrance of the trains. Its shape and form were standard institutional design originating in the architecture office of the camp itself. While in the postwar period this entrance pavilion has taken on massive symbolic importance as a sign of SS goals and brutality, in the period of its use its symbolic significance was secondary to its function as part of the very real and horrifying destruction of the European Jews around which the site was organized.[37]

The political goal of destroying the European Jews, enacted in late 1941, required architecture that facilitated the huge bureaucratic process and architects that were ideologically or professionally willing to turn their trade to functionalist purposes. These preconditions meant that the architecture of Auschwitz-Birkenau—whatever the SS claims to its symbolic content—was designed first and foremost as an architecture that enabled these policy decisions. Distinct from the forced labour camps, the political goal of extermination required different types of architectural forms that became a necessary component of the functioning of the camp. As with the general development of anti-Semitic policy in National Socialist Germany, so too can the particular relation of architecture to anti-Semitism be traced from its beginnings as part of an ideological campaign to its brutal conclusion in the industrially organized destruction of the European Jews.

CONCLUSION

In May 1945, after Allied and Red Army offensives from the west and east had sealed the fate of National Socialist Germany in the last struggles of World War II, the short-lived Donitz Government attempted to establish a transitional German cabinet. As one of the candidates for the Minister of Economics, Albert Speer wrote the following to acting Foreign Minister Lutz Schwerin von Krosigk:

> I am . . . not in the position in my technical knowledge to carry out the
> duties of the Reich Minister of Economics, which at the present

moment must deal to a large degree with the problems of the economy of finance, credit and currency.

I am an architect. And it is exactly such an unthinkable undertaking to engage an artist to do debt repayment as—in the past—to assign a champagne dealer [Joachim von Ribbentrop] the Reich Foreign Ministry.[38]

It is at this time that Speer began to emphasize the distinction between his qualifications as Hitler's favoured architect before 1942 and his political and administrative skill as head of the Ministry of Armaments and Munitions after 1942. By depicting himself as an artist who after 1942 was just following orders, Speer succeeded in focusing his trial at Nuremberg solely on his technocratic role in organizing the armaments industry. Art historical and historical scholarship has generally respected this split in Speer's biography between his artistic and political concerns.

But this analysis of Albert Speer's career in Nazi Germany exposes the heart of the historical problem which I have addressed in these pages. The architectural history of National Socialism has largely been represented as separate from a comprehensive analysis of its political history. That is, art historians have focused on the interpretation, reception and propagandistic use of formal techniques, but have avoided a thorough investigation of the function of building for Party and state policy. An account of architecture as contiguous with Party and state policy takes us beyond a limited focus on ideological considerations to a more complete understanding of the function of art. Here, anti-Semitic policy becomes a necessary part of the art historical project.

What this overview of architecture and the genocide has shown is that we decidedly cannot separate political history from art history. Rather, if our goal is to determine how an extreme ideological anti-Semitism could lead to such destructive policies, then we need to look not only at those Party leaders and ideologues who were formulating and promoting anti-Semitic ideas and practices. We need to analyse as well all the means that were used either to promote anti-Semitic ideas or to formulate and implement anti-Semitic political goals. It is in this sense that we realize why looking at propaganda concerning finished monuments was so important, or how an architect's ideas about housing policy in Berlin became relevant for other policies. Further, we can analyse how the development of SS forced labour camps served architectural and anti-Semitic interests, and how even the death camps themselves have an architectural history. Each of these components of architectural history deserves further and more detailed study than is possible here. Nevertheless, an overview of the developing relationship between architecture and anti-Semitic policy helps to lay the foundation for a broadly based and analytically complex extension of our cultural understanding of National Socialist Germany. That these artistic components end in the genocide further marks the importance of seeing the complexity of the destruction process and also how such a process increasingly developed from a systematic and wide-spread policy of oppression.

QUESTIONS FOR DISCUSSION

1. Architecture, more than any other technological development, consciously considers aesthetic ideals in the creation of its projects. Consider the role of aesthetics in the design of the built environment of the Auschwitz death camp. Focus on the famous image of the entrance to Birkenau, the tower building, and the railway.
2. How was architectural design used to advance the Nazi goals of anti-Semitism and race purification? Consider the choice of stone as a primary building material and its sometimes contradictory effects on the Nazi policy of extermination.
3. What were the ideological goals of Nazi architecture and urban planning? What lessons should contemporary architecture and urban design students learn from the Nazi era of architectural history?
4. Is architecture a form of propaganda? Consider the debate over the designs for a memorial at the site of the World Trade Center in New York City and compare this debate to the purposes envisioned by the Nazi building project of the *Soldiers' Hall.*

NOTES

My thanks for the editorial interest of Bernard Schwartz and the critical comments of Deborah Mancoff and Robert Buergiener. Additional thanks to David Mickenberg for supporting the original version of this article as a talk co-sponsored by the Block Gallery (Northwestern University) and the Spertus Institute of Jewish Studies. Many aspects of this analysis were first presented to the DePaul students in my course on art and the Holocaust (1997). I am grateful for their interest, their criticisms and their enthusiasm.

1. Hitler, A., *Mein Kampf,* Ludwig Lore trans. (Munich: Zentralverlag der NADAP, 1939) at 257–63.
2. For a discussion of the politicization of modernist architecture in the Weimar era, see R. Pommer and C.F. Otto, *Weissenhof 1927 and the Modern Movement in Architecture* (Chicago: University of Chicago Press, 1991) at 145–66.
3. Schultze-Naumburg, P., *Kunst und Rasse* (Munich: 1928). See the discussion of the architectural debates in the late Weimar Republic in B. Miller Lane, *Architecture and Politics in Germany 1918–1945* (Cambridge, MA: Harvard University Press, 1968) at 125–67. For a discussion of the fate of the Bauhaus in relation to Rosenberg and Schultze-Naumburg's campaign, see E.S. Hochman, *Architects of Fortune: Mies van der Rohe and the Third Reich* (New York: Weidenfeld & Nicolson, 1990) at 73–105.

4. For a succinct overview of pre-1933 propaganda themes and tactics, see D. Welch, *The Third Reich: Politics and Propaganda* (London: Routledge, 1993) at 8–16.

5. For a forceful discussion of the "artistic transformation of politics" evident in Hitler's political development, see O.K. Werckmeister, "Hitler the Artist," 23 *Critical Inquiry* 270 (1997).

6. Speer, A., *Inside the Third Reich* (New York: Macmillan, 1970) at 55–56.

7. See the discussion of the *Zeppelinfeld,* its architectural sources and its ideological significance, in A. Scobie, *Hitler's State Architecture: The Impact of Classical Antiquity* (University Park: Penn State University Press, 1990) at 85–92.

8. The best overview of the competing ideological claims made for architecture in this period remains the first significant study of Nazi architecture's political function: Miller Lane, supra note 3 at 169–216.

9. On the exclusion of German Jews from arts organizations, see in particular A.E. Steinweis, *Art, Ideology and Economics in Nazi Germany: The Reich Chambers of Music, Theatre and the Visual Arts* (Chapel Hill: University of North Carolina Press, 1993) at 32–49, 103–46. For an overview of economic regulations against the German Jews, see A. Barkai, *From Boycott to Annihilation: The Economic Struggle of German Jews 1933–1943,* William Templer trans. (Hanover, NH: University Press of New England, 1989).

10. For the development of the Berlin plan, see H. Reichhardt and W. Schäche, *Von Berlin nach Germania: Über die Zerstörungen der Reichshauptstadt durch Albert Speers Neugestaltunasplanungen* (Berlin: Transit Buchverlag, 1986) at 97–108; and Scobie, supra note 7 at 97–108. See also the excellent case studies of, respectively, the city building administration and the construction of the New Reich Chancellery in W. Schäche, *Architektur and Städtebau in Berlin zwischen 1933 und 1945: Planen und Bauen unter der Ägide der Stadtverwaltung* (Berlin: Gebr. Mann Verlag, 1991); and A. Schonberger, *Die Neue Reichskanzlei von Albert Speer: Zum Zusammenhang von nationalsozialistischer Architektur und Ideologie* (Berlin: Mann Verlag, 1981).

11. This section is adapted substantially from my article, "Anti-Semitic Housing Policy and Albert Speer's Plans for the Rebuilding of Berlin," *Art Bulletin* LXXVII no. 4 (1997) at 622–32. In relation to Speer and anti-Semitic housing policy, see also the essay by K. Kurvers and J.F. Geist, "Tatort Berlin, Pariser Platz," in *1945: Krieg. Zerstörung. Aufbau; Architektur und Stadtplanung, 1940–1960,* exh. cat., *Akademie der Künste* (Berlin: Henschel Verlag, 1995) at 55–118. For a parallel example of the development in 1938 of anti-Semitic housing policy, see G. Botz, "National Socialist Vienna: Antisemitism as a Housing Policy" reprinted in *The Nazi Holocaust. Historical Articles on the Destruction of European Jews,* M.R. Marrus ed. (Westport, CT: Meckler Corp., 1989) at 640. Note, however, that it was only in Berlin that anti-Semitic housing policy was so closely tied to monumental architectural plans.

12. For a more comprehensive analysis of the *Soldiers' Hall* in relation to the material needs of the Berlin plan, see P. Bourquin Jaskot, "The Architectural Policy of the SS, 1936–1945" (PhD Diss., Northwestern University, 1993) at 161–233. See also Scobie, supra note 7 at 37–68.

13. Kreis's report of May 1939 in BA Potsdam, 46.06 GBI/772 19. The Potsdam documents, as with those in Koblenz, have now been relocated to the Bundesarchiv Berlin (BA). Research for this article was completed before the move and, hence, I have maintained the Potsdam file designations.

14. See the documents on financing and compensation of owners displaced from their property in BA, R43II/1176a. For a summary of the jurisdictional authority of the GBI over the city of Berlin, see Reichhardt and Schäche, supra note 10 at 47–49.

15. Although the number of Jews dropped significantly between 1933 and 1938 (from 160,504 to 127,600), their concentration in any one sector of Berlin remained relatively consistent in this period. The largest concentration was in Berlin Mitte (17.9 per cent of the Jewish population), while the greatest percentage in any one area of the city was in Wilmersdorf (12.9 per cent of the total population of the district). See the excellent summary of the demographic development and geographic distribution of the Berlin population in G. Alexander, "Die Entwicklung der judischen Bevölkerung in Berlin zwischen 1871 und 1945," 20 *Tel Aviver Jahrbuch für Deutsche Geschichte* 287 (1991).

16. For a detailed analysis of this process, see esp. Barkai, supra note 9 at 56–77.

17. For the developing policy and actions of the Gestapo, see R. Gellately, *The Gestapo and German Society: Enforcing Racial Policy 1933–1945* (Oxford: Clarendon Press, 1990).

18. The competing and complementary interests of individuals and groups within the Party and state for jurisdiction over anti-Semitic measures are well documented in the historical literature (excluding, of course, a discussion of the role of Speer and his architectural interests); see, e.g., the discussion of the policy of forced Jewish resettlement, 1939–1941, in C. Browning, "Beyond 'Intentionalism' and 'Functionalism': A Reassessment of Nazi Jewish Policy from 1939 to 1941" in *Reevaluating the Third Reich,* T. Childers and J. Caplan eds. (New York: Holmes & Meier, 1993) at 213–21.

19. BA Potsdam 46.06 GBI/157, at 195–97.

20. *Reichsgesetzblatt* I (30 April 1939) at 864–65.

21. Schmidt, M., *Albert Speer: The End of a Myth* (London: Harrap Ltd., 1985) at 182.

22. BA Potsdam, 46.06 GBI/157, at 145.

23. For a full analysis of the connection of SS concentration camps to state architectural policy, see Jaskot, supra note 12.

24. Whether National Socialist officials valued or did not value Jewish labour is subject to debate in Nazi studies. However, convincing arguments have been brought forth to suggest that Jewish forced labour was variably valued depending on the location of the Jewish population and the changing needs of the German war economy. See, for example, G. Aly and S. Heim, "The Economics of the Final Solution: A Case Study from the General Government," 5 *Simon Wiesenthal Centre Annual* 3 (1998).

25. Siegert, T., "Des Konzentrationslager Flossenbürg" in *Bayern in der NS-Zeit,* vol. 2, M. Broszat and E. Fröhlich eds. (Munich: R. Oldenbourg Verlag, 1979) at 461.

26. Siegert ibid. at 461–74. See also, the discussion of social life and existence in the camps in F. Pingel, *Häftlinge unter SS-Herrschaft. Widerstand. Selbstbehauptung und Vernichtung im Konzentrationslager* (Hamburg: Hoffman und Campe Verlag, 1978).

27. Rabitsch, G., "Des KL Mauthausen" in *Studien zur Geschichte der Konzentrationslager* (Stuttgart: Deutsche Verlags-Anstalt, 1970) at 61.

28. See the summary of the development work at Flossenbürg through 1943 in BA, NS3/32: 13–14. Discussion of the stone-mason programmes and mention of patrons for Mauthausen and Flossenbürg can be found in BA, NS3/1346: 149–56.

29. Horwitz, G.J., *In the Shadow of Death: Living Outside the Gates of Mauthausen* (New York: Free Press, 1990) at 7–22; D.W. Pike, *In the Service of Stalin: The Spanish Communists in Exile 1939–1943* (Oxford: Clarendon Press, 1993) at 132–36. While Pike is weak in his analysis of the SS, his account of the experience of Spanish inmates and others including Jews at Mauthausen is a solid summary of the evidence of life in the camp.

30. Horwitz, ibid, at 13–14. See the registration lists (*Zugänge Listen*) for 1941 in Archivum Glówna Komisja Badania Zbrodni Hitlerowskich w Polsce: Konzentrationslager Mauthausen, 5.

31. See the death list (*Verstorben*) from 1939–1941 in Archivum Glówna Komisja Badania Zbrodni Hitlerowskich w Polsce: Konzentrationslager Mauthausen, 46.

32. See Dwork and van Pelt, *Auschwitz: 1270 to the Present* (New York: Norton, 1996) at 10–12. For a review and critical assessment of Dwork and van Pelt, see P.B. Jaskot, "Art and Politics in National Socialist Germany," *Oxford Art Journal* (forthcoming).

33. Dwork and van Pelt at 19.

34. For a broader discussion of SS ideological goals in the eastern territories, see J. Wolschke-Bulmahn and G. Groning, "The National Socialist Garden and Landscape Ideal: *Bodenständigkeit* (Rootedness in the Soil)" in *Culture and the Nazis*, R. Etlin ed. (forthcoming).

35. Dwork and van Pelt at 197–225; P. Hayes, *Industry and Ideology: IG Farben in the Nazi Era* (Cambridge: Cambridge University Press, 1987) at 319–76.

36. An analysis of the development of penal and institutional architectural types in modern Europe and the United States can be found in T.A. Markus, *Buildings and Power* (London: Routledge, 1993) at 95–145.

37. See the discussion of the ideological and political importance of forced labour camp construction at Mauthausen, Flossenbürg and Buchenwald in Jaskot, supra note 12 at 234–74. For the symbolic significance of the architecture of Auschwitz (particularly the entrance pavilion in the postwar period), see Dwork and van Pelt at 354–78; D. Hoffmann, "Auschwitz im visuellen Gedächtnis" in *Auschwitz: Geschichte. Rezeption und Wirkung*, Fritz Bauer Institut ed. (Frankfurt: Campus Verlag, 1996) at 223.

38. Speer letter of 15 May 1945, BA, R3/1587.

CHAPTER 7

Architecture and Technology in Nazi Germany: Memoirs

—— ⋁ ——

Albert Speer (1905–1981) was one of the most powerful men in the Nazi regime that ruled Germany from 1933 until 1945. He began as Hitler's architect, designing new buildings for the Nazi party and for the German empire envisioned by the Führer. In January 1942 he became Armaments Minister of the Reich, in charge of all military production; by the end of the war (1944–45) he oversaw all industrial output in the German empire. Speer was one of the highest ranking Nazis to escape execution after the war; at the Nuremberg Trials of the Nazi leadership, he was convicted of war crimes (because his factories had used slave labor) and sentenced to twenty years' imprisonment. He served his sentence at Spandau prison, and while there he wrote *Inside the Third Reich,* published in Germany in 1969 and in the United States in 1970. These memoirs are an inexhaustible source of detailed information about the operations, lifestyles, and thought processes of Hitler and his high-level associates, men such as Joseph Goebbels (Minister of Propaganda), Hermann Goering (Reich Marshall and Commander in Chief of the Air Force), Martin Bormann (Party Chairman and Hitler's chief aide), and Heinrich Himmler (Leader of the SS). In this chapter are several short selections from Speer's memoirs that focus on his training and career as an architect and the relationship between his professional life and his work for

Hitler and the Nazi regime. In the first group of entries, which Speer himself entitled "Architectural Megalomania," we have his account of some of his early success as Hitler's architect designing buildings and even outdoor presentations for the party rallies at Nuremberg. In the second selection, we have Speer's thoughts about the events of *Kristallnacht* (November 9, 1938) when the Nazi party organized a countrywide violent pogrom against all the remaining Jews of Germany. The final group of entries concern his time as Armaments Minister and reveal his participation in the German missile program with its use of forced slave labor from the SS concentration camps. In all of these selections, Speer is acutely aware of his role as a professional expert in a technological discipline, as he tries to explain and to justify his participation in the evils of the Nazi regime. We must remember, however, that Speer, as all men, is inclined to put the most favorable interpretation on his thoughts and actions.

From *Inside the Third Reich: Memoirs*

Albert Speer

TRANSLATED BY RICHARD AND CLARA WINSTON

ARCHITECTURAL MEGALOMANIA

Speer Tells of His First Commissions for Hitler and the Nazi Party

Early in 1934 Hitler surprised me with my first major commission. The temporary bleachers on the Zeppelin Field in Nuremberg were to be replaced by a permanent stone installation. I struggled over those first sketches until, in an inspired moment, the idea came to me: a mighty flight of stairs topped and enclosed by a long colonnade, flanked on both ends by stone abutments. Undoubtedly it was influenced by the Pergamum altar. The indispensable platform for honored guests presented problems; I tried to place it as unobtrusively as possible midway in the flight of stairs.

With some trepidation I asked Hitler to look at the model. I was worried because the design went far beyond the scope of my assignment.

The structure had a length of thirteen hundred feet and a height of eighty feet. It was almost twice the length of the Baths of Caracalla in Rome.

Hitler took his time looking at the plaster model from all sides, professionally assuming the proper eye level, silently studying the drawings, and remaining totally impassive through it all. I was beginning to think he would reject my work. Then, just as he had done that time at our first meeting, he tersely said, "Agreed," and took his leave. To this day I am not sure why, given as he was to long-winded comments, he remained so terse about such decisions.

Where other architects were concerned, Hitler usually rejected the first draft. He liked an assignment to be worked over several times and even during construction would insist on changes in detail. But after this first test of my ability he let me go on without interference. Henceforth he respected my ideas and treated me, as an architect, as if I were his equal.

Hitler liked to say that the purpose of his building was to transmit his time and its spirit to posterity. Ultimately, all that remained to remind men of the great epochs of history was their monumental architecture, he would philosophize. What had remained of the emperors of Rome? What would still bear witness to them today, if their buildings had not survived? Periods of weakness are bound to occur in the history of nations, he argued; but at their lowest ebb, their architecture will speak to them of former power. Naturally, a new national consciousness could not be awakened by architecture alone. But when after a long spell of inertia a sense of national grandeur was born anew, the monuments of men's ancestors were the most impressive exhortations. Today, for example, Mussolini could point to the buildings of the Roman Empire as symbolizing the heroic spirit of Rome. Thus he could fire his nation with the idea of a modern empire. Our architectural works should also speak to the conscience of a future Germany centuries from now. In advancing this argument Hitler also stressed the value of a permanent type of construction.

The building on the Zeppelin Field was begun at once, in order to have at least the platform ready for the coming Party Rally. To clear ground for it, the Nuremberg streetcar depot had to be removed. I passed by its remains after it had been blown up. The iron reinforcements protruded from concrete debris and had already begun to rust. One could easily visualize their further decay. This dreary sight led me to some thoughts which I later propounded to Hitler under the pretentious heading of "A Theory of Ruin Value." The idea was that buildings of modern construction were poorly suited to form that "bridge of tradition" to future generations which Hitler was calling for. It was hard to imagine that rusting heaps of rubble could communicate these heroic inspirations which Hitler admired in the monuments of the past. My "theory" was intended to deal with this dilemma. By using special materials and by applying certain principles of statics, we should be able to build structures which even in a state of decay, after hundreds or (such were our reckonings) thousands of years would more or less resemble Roman models.[1]

To illustrate my ideas I had a romantic drawing prepared. It showed what the reviewing stand on the Zeppelin Field would look like after generations of neglect, overgrown with ivy, its columns fallen, the walls crumbling here and there, but the outlines still clearly recognizable. In Hitler's entourage this drawing was regarded as blasphemous. That I could even conceive of a period of decline for the newly founded Reich destined to last a thousand years seemed outrageous to many of Hitler's closest followers. But he himself accepted my ideas as logical and illuminating. He gave orders that in the future the important buildings of his Reich were to be erected in keeping with the principles of this "law of ruins." . . .

After January 30, 1934, at the suggestion of Robert Ley, head of the Labor Front, a leisure-time organization was created. I was supposed to take over the section called Beauty of Labor; the name had provoked a good deal of mockery, as had the title Strength through Joy itself. A short while before, on a trip through the Dutch province of Limburg, Ley had seen a number of mines conspicuous for their neatness and cleanliness and surrounded by beautifully tended gardens. By temperament Ley always tended to generalize, and he now wanted to have all of German industry follow this example. The project turned out to be an extremely gratifying one, at least for me personally. First we persuaded factory owners to modernize their offices and to have some flowers about. But we did not stop there. Lawn was to take the place of asphalt. What had been wasteland was to be turned into little parks where the workers could sit during breaks. We urged that window areas within factories be enlarged and workers' canteens set up. What was more, we designed the necessary artifacts for these reforms, from simple, well-shaped flatware to sturdy furniture, all of which we had manufactured in large quantities. We provided educational movies and a counseling service to help businessmen on questions of illumination and ventilation. We were able to draw former union leaders and some members of the dissolved Arts and Crafts Society into this campaign. One and all devoted themselves to the cause of making some improvements in the workers' living conditions and moving closer to the ideal of a classless People's Community. However, it was somewhat dismaying to discover that Hitler took hardly any interest in these ideas. He who could lose himself in the details of an architectural project proved remarkably indifferent when I came to him with reports of my progress in this social area. The British ambassador in Berlin, at any rate, thought better of it than Hitler.*

It was due to my new party rank that in the spring of 1934 I received my first invitation to an official evening reception that Hitler gave as party chief, one to which wives were also invited. We were seated in groups of six to eight persons at round tables in the large dining hall of the Chancellor's residence. Hitler went from table to table, said a few friendly words, and made the acquaintance of the ladies. When he came up to us I introduced my wife, whom I had hitherto not mentioned to him. "Why have you deprived us of your wife for so long?" he commented privately a few days later, obviously much taken with her. In fact one reason I had avoided introducing her earlier was my dislike for the way Hitler treated his mistress. Moreover, it seemed to me that it should have been the business of the adjutants to invite my wife or to call Hitler's attention to her existence. But you could not expect any sense of etiquette from them. In the final analysis Hitler's own petit-bourgeois origins were reflected in the behavior of the adjutants.

That first evening they met, Hitler said to my wife with a certain solemnity: "Your husband is going to erect buildings for me such as have not been created for four thousand years."

Every year a rally was held at the Zeppelin Field for the assemblage of middle and minor party functionaries, the so-called *Amtswalter,* who were in charge of the various organizations affiliated with the NSDAP. While the SA, the Labor Front, and, of course, the army tried to make a good showing at its mass meetings and impress Hitler and visitors by their bearing and discipline, it proved a rather difficult task to present the Amtswalter in a favorable fashion. For the most part they had converted their small prebends into sizable paunches; they simply could not be expected to line up in orderly ranks. There were conferences about this problem in the Organization Section for Party Rallies, for the appearance of the Amtswalter had already provoked some sarcastic comments on Hitler's part. The saving idea came to me: "Let's have them march up in darkness."

I explained my plan to the organization leaders of the Party Rally. The thousands of flags belonging to all the local groups in Germany were to be held in readiness behind the high fences surrounding the field. The flagbearers were to divide into ten columns, forming lanes in which the Amtswalter would march up. Since all this was to take place

*Sir Neville Henderson, *Failure of a Mission* (New York, 1940), p. 15: "There are, in fact, many things in the Nazi organization and social institutions, as distinct from its rabid nationalism and ideology, which we might study and adapt to our own use with great profit both to the health and happiness of our own nation and old democracy."

at evening, bright spotlights would be cast on these banners, and the great eagle crowning them all. That alone would have a dramatic effect. But even this did not seem sufficient to me. I had occasionally seen our new anti-aircraft searchlights blazing miles into the sky. I asked Hitler to let me have a hundred and thirty of these. Goering made a fuss at first, since these hundred and thirty searchlights represented the greater part of the strategic reserve. But Hitler won him over: "If we use them in such large numbers for a thing like this, other countries will think we're swimming in searchlights."

The actual effect far surpassed anything I had imagined. The hundred and thirty sharply defined beams, placed around the field at intervals of forty feet, were visible to a height of twenty to twenty-five thousand feet, after which they merged into a general glow. The feeling was of a vast room, with the beams serving as mighty pillars of infinitely high outer walls. Now and then a cloud moved through this wreath of lights, bringing an element of surrealistic surprise to the mirage. I imagine that this "cathedral of light" was the first luminescent architecture of this type, and for me it remains not only my most beautiful architectural concept but, after its fashion, the only one which has survived the passage of time. "The effect, which was both solemn and beautiful, was like being in a cathedral of ice," British Ambassador Henderson wrote.[2]

When it came to cornerstone layings, there seemed no way to blot out the dignitaries, ministers, Reichsleiters, and Gauleiters,* although these too were a less than impressive bunch. The parade marshals had all they could do to teach them to line up properly. When Hitler appeared they stiffened to attention and raised their arms in salute. At the cornerstone laying of the Nuremberg Kongresshalle, Hitler saw me standing in the second rank. He interrupted the solemn ceremonial to extend his hand to me. I was so overwhelmed by this unusual sign of favor that I let my own hand, raised in salute, fall with a loud smack on the bald head of Julius Streicher, the Gauleiter of Franconia, who stood just front of me.

During the Nuremberg Party Rallies, Hitler remained out of sight most of the time, as far as his intimates were concerned. He withdrew either to prepare his speeches or to attend one of the numerous functions. He took special satisfaction in the foreign visitors and delegations who came each year in growing numbers, especially when these were from the democratic West. During his hasty lunches he asked to have their names read and was obviously pleased at the interest shown by the world at large in National Socialist Germany.

I too had a strenuous time of it in Nuremberg, having been made responsible for all the buildings in which Hitler would appear in the course

---

* [Reichsleiters are government officials and Gauleiters are Nazi Party officials. -Ed.]

of the rally. As "chief decorator" I had to check on the arrangements shortly before the beginning of the function, then rush along to see to the next. At that time I dearly loved flags and used them wherever I could. They were a way of introducing a play of color into somber architecture. I found it a boon that the swastika flag Hitler had designed proved more amenable to these uses than a flag divided into three stripes of color. Of course it was not altogether consonant with the flag's dignity to use it mostly for decorative effect, for accenting the pleasing harmonies of certain façades or covering ugly nineteenth-century buildings from eaves to sidewalks. Quite often I added gold ribbons to the flag to intensify the effect of the red. But it was always scenic drama I was after. I arranged for veritable orgies of flags in the narrow streets of Goslar and Nuremberg, with banners stretched from house to house, so that the sky was almost blotted out.

With all this to attend to, I missed most of Hitler's rallies except for his "cultural speeches," as he himself called these major oratorical flights. He used to draft these while he was at Obersalzberg. At the time I admired the speeches not so much, I thought, for their rhetorical brilliance as for what I felt to be their incisive content, their intellectual level. In Spandau I decided I would reread them, once my prison term was over, on the theory that I would find in them one element in my former world which would not repel me. But my expectations were disappointed. In the context of that time they had said a great deal to me; now they seemed empty, without tension, shallow and useless. What was more, in them Hitler openly aired his intention to pervert the very meaning of the concept of culture by mobilizing it for his own power goals. I found it incomprehensible that these tirades should once have impressed me so profoundly. What had done it? . . .

During the preparations for the Party Rallies I met a woman who had impressed me even in my student days: Leni Riefenstahl,* who had starred in or had directed well-known mountain and skiing movies. Hitler appointed her to make films of the rallies. As the only woman officially involved in the proceedings, she had frequent conflicts with the party organization, which was soon up in arms against her. The Nazis were by tradition antifeminist and could hardly brook this self-assured woman, the more so since she knew how to bend this men's world to her purposes. Intrigues were launched and slanderous stories carried to Hess, in order to have her ousted. But after the first Party Rally film, which convinced even the doubters of her skill as a director, these attacks ceased.

---

*[Leni Riefenstahl was a famous (female) German film director, specializing in documentaries. Her film, *Triumph of the Will*, set at the Nuremberg rally of 1934, is a masterpiece of pro-Hitler propaganda. -Ed.]

When I was first introduced to her, she took a yellowed newspaper clipping from a little chest. "Three years ago, when you reconstructed the Gau headquarters, I clipped your picture from the newspaper," she said. Why in the world had she done that, I asked in astonishment. "I thought at the time that with your head you might well play a part. . . . In one of my movies, of course."

I recall, incidentally, that the footage taken during one of the solemn sessions of the 1935 Party Congress was spoiled. At Leni Riefenstahl's suggestion Hitler gave orders for the shots to be refilmed in the studio. I was called in to do a backdrop simulating a section of the Kongresshalle, as well as a realistic model of the platform and lectern. I had spotlights aimed at it; the production staff scurried around—while Streicher, Rosenberg, and Frank could be seen walking up and down with their manuscripts, determinedly memorizing their parts. Hess arrived and was asked to pose for the first shot. Exactly as he had done before an audience of 30,000 at the Party Congress, he solemnly raised his hand. With his special brand of ardor, he turned precisely to the spot where Hitler would have been sitting, snapped to attention and cried: "My Leader, I welcome you in the name of the Party Congress! The congress will now continue. The Fuehrer speaks!"

He did it all so convincingly that from that point on I was no longer so sure of the genuineness of his feelings. The three others also gave excellent performances in the emptiness of the studio, proving themselves gifted actors. I was rather disturbed; Frau Riefenstahl, on the other hand, thought the acted scenes better than the original presentation.

By this time I thoroughly admired the art with which Hitler would feel his way during his rallies until he had found the point to unleash the first great storm of applause. I was by no means unaware of the demagogic element; indeed I contributed to it myself by my scenic arrangements. Nevertheless, up to this time I had believed that the feelings of the speakers were genuine. It was therefore an upsetting discovery, that day in the studio, when I saw that all this emotion could be represented "authentically" even without an audience.

For the buildings in Nuremberg I had in mind a synthesis between Troost's classicism and Tessenow's simplicity.* I did not call it neoclassicist, but neoclassical, for I thought I had derived it from the Dorian style. I was deluding myself, deliberately forgetting that these buildings

---

*[Paul Ludwig Troost and Heinrich Tessenow were architects who influenced Speer's early career. Tessenow was Speer's principle mentor at university; he taught architecture "in the spirit of simple craftsmanship . . . [with] . . . a minimum of pomp" (Speer, p. 11). Troost was a professor of architecture in Munich, and a favorite of Hitler's despite his bare and economical style. -Ed.]

had to provide a monumental backdrop such as had already been attempted on the Champs de Mars in Paris during the French Revolution, although the resources at that time were more modest. Terms like "classical" and "simple" were scarcely consonant with the gigantic proportions I employed in Nuremberg. Yet, to this day I still like my Nuremberg sketches best of all, rather than many others that I later prepared for Hitler and that turned out considerably more practical.

Because of my fondness for the Doric, when I went on my first trip abroad in May 1935, I did not go to Italy to see the Renaissance palaces and the colossal buildings of Rome, although these might have served me better as prototypes for what was wanted. Instead, I turned to Greece—a sign of where I considered my architectural allegiance to lie. My wife and I sought out chiefly examples of Doric buildings. I shall never forget how overwhelmed we were by the reconstructed stadium of Athens. Two years later, when I myself had to design a stadium, I borrowed its basic horseshoe form.

In Delphi I thought I discerned how the purity of Greek artistic creativeness was speedily contaminated by the wealth won in the Ionian colonies in Asia. Didn't this prove how sensitive a high artistic consciousness was and how little it took to distort the ideal conception to the point of unrecognizability? I happily played with such theories; it never occured to me that my own works might be subject to these same laws.

When we came back in June 1935 my own house in Berlin-Schlachtensee was completed. It was of modest dimensions, 1345 square feet of living space comprising one dining room, one living room, and minimal bedrooms—in deliberate contrast to the recent habit among the leaders of the Reich, who were moving into huge villas or acquiring palaces. We wanted to avoid all that, for we had observed that in surrounding themselves with pomp and stiff officialism, these people were condemning themselves to a slow process of "petrifaction"—which involved their private lives as well.

In any case I could not have built on any greater scale, since I lacked the means. My house cost seventy thousand marks; in order to swing it I had to ask my father to take a mortgage of thirty thousand marks. Although I was acting as a free-lance architect for the party and the state, my income remained low. For in an idealistic spirit which seemed to accord with the temper of the time, I had renounced any architect's fees for all my official buildings.

This attitude, however, caused some amazement in party circles. One day in Berlin, Goering said to me in high good humor: "Well, Herr Speer, you have a great deal to do now, of course. You must be earning plenty." When I said that was not the case, he stared incredulously at me. "What's that? An architect as busy as you? I figured you for a couple of hundred thousand a year. That's all nonsense, this idealistic business. You must make money!" Thereafter I accepted the architect's fee, except for my Nuremberg buildings, for which I received a thousand marks a month. But it was not only on financial grounds that I clung to my professional independence and fended off an official post. Hitler had, I knew, much greater confidence in nonofficial architects—his prejudice against bureaucrats colored his views in everything. At the end of my career as an architect my fortune had increased to about one and a half million marks, and the Reich owed me another million that I did not collect.

My family lived happily in this house. I wish I could write that I had a share in this familial happiness, as my wife and I had once dreamed. But by the time I arrived home, it would be late in the evening and the children would have long since been put to bed. I would sit with my wife for a while—silent from exhaustion. This kind of rigidity became more and more the norm, and when I consider the matter in retrospect, what was happening to me was no different from what was happening to the party bigwigs, who ruined their family life by their ostentatious style of living. They froze into poses of officialism. My own rigidity sprang from excessive work.

In the autumn of 1934 Otto Meissner, state secretary in the Chancellery, who had served under Ebert and Hindenburg and now was working for his third Chief of State, telephoned me. I was to come to Weimar the next day in order to accompany Hitler to Nuremberg.

I sat up until the wee hours sketching out ideas that had been exciting me for some time. More major construction for the Party Rallies was wanted: a field for military exercises, a large stadium, a hall for Hitler's cultural addresses and for concerts as well. Why not concentrate all that, together with what already existed, into a great center? I thought. Until then I had not ventured to take the initiative on such questions, for Hitler kept this sort of decision for himself. I therefore went about drafting this plan with some hesitation.

In Weimar, Hitler showed me a sketch for a "Party Forum" by Professor Paul Schultze-Naumburg. "It looks like an oversized marketplace for a provincial town," he commented. "There's nothing distinctive about it, nothing that sets it off from former times. If we are going to build a party forum, we want people centuries hence to be able to see that our times had a certain building style, like Königsplatz in Munich, for example." Schultze-Naumburg, a pillar of the League of Struggle for German Culture, was given no chance to defend his proposal; he was not even called into Hitler's presence. With total disregard for the man's reputation, Hitler threw away the plans and ordered a new competition among various architects of his choice. . . .

To build this giant complex an Association for the Nuremberg Party Rally Site was created. The Finance Minister of the Reich reluctantly assumed the duty of funding the project. Out of some whimsical impulse Hitler appointed Minister of Churches Kerrl to take charge of the association, and as the latter's deputy, Martin Bormann, who thus received his first important assignment outside the party secretariat.

The plan called for an expenditure of between seven and eight hundred million marks on building, which today would cost three billion marks [$750,000,000]—eight years later I would be spending such a sum every four days on armaments.[3] Including the camping grounds for participants, the tract embraced an area of 16.5 square kilometers (about 6.5 square miles). Under Kaiser Wilhelm II, incidentally, there had been plans for a "Center for German National Festivals" with an area 6600 by 2000 feet.

Two years after Hitler had approved it, my design was exhibited as a model at the Paris World's Fair of 1937 and won the Grand Prix. At the southern end of the complex was the Marchfield; the name was intended not only as a reference to the war god Mars, but also to the month in which Hitler introduced conscription.* Within this enormous tract, an area of 3400 by 2300 feet was set aside where the army could practice minor maneuvers. By contrast, the grandiose area of the palace of Kings Darius I and Xerxes in Persepolis (fifth century B.C.) had embraced only 1500 by 900 feet. Stands 48 feet high were to surround the entire area, providing seats for a hundred and sixty thousand spectators. Twenty-four towers over a hundred and thirty feet in height were to punctuate these stands; in the middle was a platform for guests of honor which was to be crowned by a sculpture of a woman. In A.D. 64 Nero erected on the Capitol a colossal figure 119 feet high. The Statue of Liberty in New York is 151 feet high; our statue was to be 46 feet higher.

To the north, in the direction of the old Nuremberg castle of the Hohenzollerns, which could be seen in the distance, the Marchfield opened out into a processional avenue a mile and a quarter long and 264 feet wide. The army was to march down this avenue in ranks 165 feet wide. This avenue was finished before the war and paved with heavy granite slabs, strong enough to bear the weight of tanks. The surface was roughened to provide a secure footing for the goose-stepping soldiers. On the right rose a flight of stairs from which Hitler, flanked by his generals, would review such parades. Opposite was a colonnade where the flags of the regiments would be displayed.

This colonnade with its height of only sixty feet was to serve as a foil for the "Great Stadium" towering up behind it. Hitler had stipulated that

---

*It probably also referred to the National Assembly of the Franks, which was likewise called the Marchfield.

the stadium was to hold four hundred thousand spectators. History's largest precedent was the Circus Maximus in Rome, built for between one hundred and fifty and two hundred thousand persons. Modern stadiums in those days contained about a hundred thousand seats.

The pyramid of Cheops, with a base of 756 feet and a height of 481 feet, measured 3,277,300 cubic yards. The Nuremberg stadium would have been 1815 feet long and 1518 wide and could have enclosed a volume of over 11,100,000 cubic yards, some three times more than the pyramid of Cheops.[4] The stadium was to be by far the largest structure on the tract and one of the hugest in history. Calculations showed that in order to hold the required number of spectators the stands would have to be over three hundred feet high. An oval would really have been out of the question; the resultant bowl would not only have intensified the heat, but produced psychological discomfort. I therefore turned my thoughts to the Athenian horseshoe shape. We took a hillside of approximately the same shape and smoothed out its irregularities by temporary wooden structures; the question was whether sporting events would be visible from the upper rows. The results of our study were more positive than I had expected.

Our rough estimate of the costs of the Nuremberg stadium came to between two hundred and two hundred and fifty million marks—approximately a billion marks [$250,000,000] at present-day construction costs. Hitler took this calmly. "That is less than two battleships of the *Bismarck* class. How quickly a warship can be destroyed, and if not, it is scrap-iron anyhow in ten years. But this building will stand for centuries. When the Finance Minister asks what it will cost, don't give him any answer. Say that nobody has any experience with building projects of such size." Granite to the value of several million marks was ordered, pink for the exteriors, white for the stands. At the site a gigantic pit for the foundation was dug; during the war it became a picturesque lake, which suggested the proportions of the structure.

Farther to the north of the stadium the processional avenue crossed an expanse of water in which the buildings would be reflected. Then, concluding the complex, came a square, bounded on the right by the Kongresshalle, which still stands, and on the left by a "Kulturhalle" meant specifically for Hitler's speeches on cultural matters.

Hitler had appointed me the architect for all these buildings except the Kongresshalle, which had been designed in 1933 by Ludwig Ruff. He gave me a free hand with plans and execution and participated every year in a ceremonial cornerstone laying. However, these cornerstones were subsequently moved to the municipal buildings and grounds yard to wait until the building had made further progress and they could be incorporated in the wall. At the laying of the cornerstone for the stadium on September 9, 1937, Hitler solemnly shook hands with me before the assembled party bigwigs. "This is the greatest day of your life!" Perhaps I was something of a skeptic even then, for I replied: "No, not today, my Fuehrer, but only when the building is finished."

Early in 1939 Hitler, in a speech to construction workers, undertook to justify the dimensions of his style: "Why always the biggest? I do this to restore to each individual German his self-respect. In a hundred areas I want to say to the individual: We are not inferior; on the contrary, we are the complete equals of every other nation."[5]

This love for vast proportions was not only tied up with the totalitarian cast of Hitler's regime. Such tendencies, and the urge to demonstrate one's strength on all occasions, are characteristic of quickly acquired wealth. Thus we find the largest buildings in Greek antiquity in Sicily and Asia Minor. It is an interesting corollary that those cities were generally ruled by despots. But even in Periclean Athens the statue of Athena Parthenos by Phidias was forty feet high. Moreover, most of the Seven Wonders of the World won their repute by their excessive size: the Temple of Diana at Ephesus, the Mausoleum at Halicarnassus, the Colossus of Rhodes, and the Olympian Zeus of Phidias.

Hitler's demand for huge dimensions, however, involved more than he was willing to admit to the workers. He wanted the biggest of everything to glorify his works and magnify his pride. These monuments were an assertion of his claim to world dominion long before he dared to voice any such intention even to his closest associates.

I, too, was intoxicated by the idea of using drawings, money, and construction firms to create stone witnesses to history, and thus affirm our claim that our works would survive for a thousand years. But I found Hitler's excitement rising whenever I could show him that at least in size we had "beaten" the other great buildings of history. To be sure, he never gave vent to these heady feelings. He was sparing in his use of high-sounding words to me. Possibly at such moments he actually felt a certain awe; but it was directed toward himself and toward his own greatness, which he himself had willed and projected into eternity.

At the same Party Rally of 1937 at which Hitler laid the cornerstone of the stadium, his last speech ended with the ringing words: "The German nation has after all acquired its Germanic Reich." At dinner afterward Hitler's adjutant, Brückner, reported that at these words Field Marshal von Blomberg had burst into tears from sheer emotion. Hitler took this as evidence of the army's assent to what was being promised in this slogan.

At the time there was a great deal of talk to the effect that this mysterious dictum would be ushering in a new era in foreign policy; that it would bear much fruit. I had an idea of what it meant, for shortly before the speech was given, Hitler one day abruptly stopped me on the stairs to his apartment, let his entourage go on ahead, and said: "We will create a great empire. All the Germanic peoples will be included in it. It will begin in Norway and extend to northern Italy. I myself must carry this out. If only I keep my health!"

That was still a relatively restrained formulation. In the spring of 1937 Hitler visited me at my Berlin showrooms. We stood alone in front of the nearly seven-foot high model of the stadium for four hundred thousand people. It had been set up precisely at eye level. Every detail had been rendered, and powerful spotlights illuminated it, so that with only a little imagination we could conceive the effect of this structure. Alongside the model were the plans, pinned up on boards. Hitler turned to these. We talked about the Olympic Games, and I pointed out, as I had done several times before, that my athletic field did not have the prescribed Olympic proportions. Without any change of tone, as if it were a matter settled beyond the possibility of discussion, Hitler observed: "No matter. In 1940 the Olympic Games will take place in Tokyo. But thereafter they will take place in Germany for all time to come, in this stadium. And then we will determine the measurements of the athletic field."

According to our carefully worked out schedule this stadium was supposed to be completed in time for the Party Rally of 1945. . . .

Speer Tells of the Design for the New Reichstag, or People's Hall

Whenever he came to see my models of the Berlin buildings, Hitler would particularly brood over one part of the plan: the future headquarters of the Reich which was meant to manifest for hundreds of years to come the power that had been attained in the era of Hitler. Just as the Champs Elysées finds its dramatic focus in the residence of the French kings, so the grand boulevard was to culminate in a group of buildings which Hitler regarded as central to his political activities. These were the Chancellery, where the affairs of government were conducted; the High Command of the Armed Forces, where the power of command over the three branches of the services was concentrated; and a secretariat for the party (Bormann), for protocol (Meissner), and for Hitler's personal affairs (Bouhler). The Reichstag building also formed part of this complex, but this in no way signified that Hitler meant the German parliament to play any important part in the exercise of power. It was mere chance that the old Reichstag building happened to be situated there.

I proposed to Hitler that Paul Wallot's Reichstag, built in Wilhelmine Germany, be razed. But here I met unexpected resistance. Hitler liked the structure. However, he intended to use it merely for social purposes. Hitler was usually taciturn about his ultimate goals. When on this and some other occasions he spoke rather candidly to me about the background of his building plans, he did so out of that intimacy that almost always crops up in the relationship between an architect and his client. "In the old building we can set up reading rooms and lounges for the deputies. For all I care the chamber can be turned into a library. With its five hundred and eighty seats it's much too small for us. We'll build a new one right beside it. Provide a chamber for twelve hundred deputies!"[6] That assumed a population of one hundred and forty million, and so in saying this Hitler was revealing the scale on which he was thinking. Partly he had in mind a rapid natural increase of the Germans, partly the incorporation into the Reich of other Germanic peoples—but he was not including the population of subjugated nations, for these would not have any voting rights. I proposed that he simply increase the number of voters whom each deputy represented, and thereby make the old Reichstag chamber still usable. But Hitler did not want to alter the proportion of sixty thousand voters for each deputy which had been set by the Weimar Republic. He never explained his reasons; but he was as firm on this matter as he was firm about nominal retention of the traditional electoral system with its fixed dates for elections, rules of franchise, ballot boxes, and secret ballot. On this matter he evidently wanted to preserve a tradition which had brought him to power, even though his introduction of the one-party system had made the whole thing pointless.

The buildings which were intended to frame the future Adolf Hitler Platz lay in the shadow of the great domed hall. But as if Hitler wanted by architecture alone to denigrate the whole process of popular representation, the hall had a volume fifty times greater than the proposed Reichstag building. He had asked me to work out the designs for this hall as early as the summer of 1936.[7] On April 20, 1937, his birthday, I gave him the renderings, ground plans, cross sections, and a first model of the building. He was delighted and only quarreled with my having signed the plans: "Developed on the basis of the Fuehrer's ideas." I was the architect, he said, and my contribution to this building must be given greater credit than his sketch of the idea dating from 1925. I stuck to this formula, however, and Hitler was probably gratified at my refusal to claim authorship for this building. Partial models were prepared from the plans, and in 1939 a detailed wooden model of the exterior some ten feet high and another model of the interior were made. The floor could be removed in order to test the future effect at eye level. In the course of his many visits to the exhibit Hitler would unfailingly spend a long time contemplating these two models. He would point triumphantly to them as an idea that must have struck his friends fifteen years ago as a fantastic quirk. "In those days who was prepared to believe me when I said that this would be built some day!"

This structure, the greatest assembly hall in the world ever conceived up to that time, consisted of one vast hall that could hold between one hundred fifty and one hundred eighty thousand persons standing. In spite of Hitler's negative attitude toward Himmler's and Rosenberg's mystical notions, the hall was essentially a place of worship. The idea was that over the course of centuries, by tradition and venerability, it would acquire an importance similar to that St. Peter's in Rome has for Catholic Christendom. Without some such essentially pseudoreligious background the expenditure for Hitler's central building would have been pointless and incomprehensible.

The round interior was to have the almost inconceivable diameter of eight hundred and twenty-five feet. The huge dome was to begin its slightly parabolic curve at a height of three hundred and twenty-three feet and rise to a height of seven hundred and twenty-six feet.

In a sense the Pantheon in Rome had served as our model. The Berlin dome was also to contain a round opening for light, but this opening alone would be one hundred and fifty-two feet in diameter, larger than the entire dome of the Pantheon (142 feet) and of St. Peter's (145 feet). The interior would contain sixteen times the volume of St. Peter's.

The interior appointments were to be as simple as possible. Circling an area four hundred sixty-two feet in diameter, a three-tier gallery rose to a height of one hundred feet. A circle of one hundred rectangular marble pillars—still almost on a human scale, for they were only eighty feet high—was broken by a recess opposite the entrance. This recess was one hundred and sixty-five feet high and ninety-two feet wide, and was to be clad at the rear in gold mosaic. In front of it, on a marble pedestal forty-six feet in height, perched the hall's single sculptural feature: a gilded German eagle with a swastika in its claws. This symbol of sovereignty might be said to be the very fountainhead of Hitler's grand boulevard. Beneath this symbol would be the podium for the Leader of the nation; from this spot he would deliver his messages to the peoples of his future empire. I tried to give this spot suitable emphasis, but here the fatal flaw of architecture that has lost all sense of proportion was revealed. Under that vast dome Hitler dwindled to an optical zero.

From the outside the dome would have loomed against the sky like some green mountain, for it was to be roofed with patinated plates of copper. At its peak we planned a skylight turret one hundred and thirty-two feet high, of the lightest possible metal construction. The turret would be crowned by an eagle with a swastika. . . .

Hitler was obsessed with the idea for this domed building. We had already drawn up our designs when he heard that the Soviet Union was also planning an enormous assembly building in Moscow in honor of Lenin. He was deeply irked, feeling himself cheated of the glory of building the tallest monumental structure in the world. Along with this was an intense chagrin that he could not make Stalin stop by a simple command. But he finally consoled himself with the thought that his building would remain unique. "What does one skyscraper more or less amount to, a little higher or a little lower. The great thing about our building will be the dome!" After the war with the Soviet Union had begun, I now and then saw evidence that the idea of Moscow's rival building had preyed on his mind more than he had been willing to admit. "Now," he once said, "this will be the end of their building for good and all.". . .

During my imprisonment, this design, with its red mosaics, its pillars, its bronze lions and gilded silhouettes, had assumed in my memory a bright, almost pleasant character. But when I once again saw the color photographs of the model, after a lapse of more than twenty-one years, I was struck by the resemblance to a Cecil B. De Mille set. Along with its fantastic quality I also became aware of the cruel element in this architecture. It had been the very expression of a tyranny.

Before the war, I had laughed at an inkwell which the architect Brinckmann (who like Troost had originally designed steamship décor) had presented Hitler as a surprise gift. Brinckmann had made a solemn construction out of this simple utensil. It was a mass of ornamentation, scrolls and steps—and then, alone and forlorn amid all the magnificence of this "inkwell for the Chief of State," there was a tiny pool of ink. I thought I had never seen anything so abnormal. But contrary to my expectations Hitler did not disdain the object. In fact he praised this bronze inkwell immoderately. Brinckmann was no less successful with a desk chair he had designed for Hitler. It was veritably of Goeringesque proportions, a kind of throne with two oversized gilded pine cones topping the back. These two items, with their inflated bombast, seemed to me to reek of the parvenu. But from about 1937 on Hitler furthered this tendency toward pomposity by showing increasing approval of it. He had come round again to Vienna's Ringstrasse, where he had once begun. Slowly but steadily he moved even further away from the doctrines of Troost.

And I moved with him. For my designs of this period owed less and less to what I regarded as "my style." This estrangement from my beginnings was revealed in other ways besides the wildly excessive size of my buildings. For they also no longer had any of the Dorian character I had originally tried to achieve. They had become pure "art of decadence." Wealth, the inexhaustible funds at my disposal, but also Hitler's party ideology, had led me along the path to a style which drew its inspiration rather from the show palaces of Oriental despots.

At the beginning of the war, I had formed a theory which I explained at a dinner in Maxim's in Paris to a group of German and French artists.

Cocteau and Despiau were among the latter. The French Revolution, I said, had developed a new sense of style which was destined to replace the late rococo. Even its simplest furniture was beautifully proportioned. This style, I argued, had found its purest expression in the architectural designs of Boullée. The Directoire that followed this revolutionary style had still treated their more abundant means with lightness and good taste. The turning point, I said, had come with the Empire style. From year to year new elements were introduced; elaborate ornamentation had been lavished upon the still classical basic forms until, at the end, Late Empire had achieved a resplendence and wealth that could scarcely be surpassed. Late Empire had expressed the end point of a stylistic evolution which had begun so promisingly with the Consulate. It had also expressed the transition from Revolution to the Napoleonic Empire. Within it were revealed signs of decay which were a forecast of the end of the Napoleonic era. Compressed within the span of twenty years, I said, we could observe a phenomenon that ordinarily took place only over centuries: the development from the Doric buildings of early antiquity to the fissured baroque facades of Late Hellenism, such as was to be seen in, say, Baalbek; or the Romanesque buildings at the beginning of the medieval period and the playful Late Gothic at its end.

Had I been able to think the matter out consistently, I ought to have argued further that my designs for Hitler were following the pattern of the Late Empire and forecasting the end of the regime; that, therefore, Hitler's downfall could be deduced from these very designs. But this was hidden from me at the time. Probably Napoleon's entourage saw in the ornate salons of the Late Empire only the expression of grandeur. Probably only posterity beholds the symptoms of downfall in such creations. Hitler's entourage, at any rate, felt the towering inkwell to be a suitable prop for his genius as a statesman, and similarly accepted my hulking dome as the symbol of Hitler's power.

The last buildings we designed in 1939 were in fact pure neo-Empire, comparable to the style that prevailed a hundred and twenty-five years before, shortly before Napoleon's fall. They were marked by excessive ornamentation, a mania for gilding, a passion for pomp, and total decadence. And not only the style but the excessive size of these buildings plainly revealed Hitler's intention.

One day in the early summer of 1939, he pointed to the German eagle with the swastika in its claws which was to crown the dome nine hundred fifty-seven feet in the air. "That has to be changed. Instead of the swastika, the eagle is to be perched above the globe. To crown this greatest building in the world the eagle must stand above the globe." There are photos of the models in which this revision is plainly to be seen.

A few months later the Second World War began. . . .

THOUGHTS ON NAZI ANTI-SEMITISM

Speer Remembers His Thoughts after the November 1938 Pogrom

On November 10 [1938], driving to the office, I passed by the still smoldering ruins of the Berlin synagogues. . . . Today, this memory is one of the most doleful of my life, chiefly because what really disturbed me at the time was the aspect of disorder that I saw on Fasanenstrasse: charred beams, collapsed façades, burned-out walls—anticipations of a scene that during the war would dominate much of Europe. Most of all I was troubled by the political revival of the "gutter." The smashed panes of shop windows offended my sense of middle-class order.

I did not see that more was being smashed than glass, that on that night Hitler had crossed a Rubicon for the fourth time in his life, had taken a step that irrevocably sealed the fate of his country. Did I sense, at least for a moment, that something was beginning which would end with the annihilation of one whole group of our nation? Did I sense that this outburst of hoodlumism was changing my moral substance? I do not know.

I accepted what had happened rather indifferently. Some phrases of Hitler's, to the effect that he had not wanted these excesses, contributed to this attitude. Later, in private, Goebbels hinted that he had been the impresario for this sad and terrible night, and I think it very possible that he confronted a hesitant Hitler with a *fait accompli* in order to force him to take the initiative.

It has repeatedly surprised me, in later years, that scarcely any anti-Semitic remarks of Hitler's have remained in my memory. Out of the scraps that remain, I can reconstruct what crossed my mind at the time: dismay over the deviation from the image I wanted to have of Hitler, anxiety over the increasing deterioration of his health, hope for some letup of the struggle against the churches, a certain puzzlement at his partiality for utopian-sounding remote goals, all sorts of odd feelings—but Hitler's hatred for the Jews seemed to me so much a matter of course that I gave it no serious thought.

I felt myself to be Hitler's architect. Political events did not concern me. My job was merely to provide impressive backdrops for such events. And this view was reinforced daily, for Hitler consulted me almost exclusively on architectural questions. Moreover, it would have been regarded as self-importance on the part of a man who was pretty much of a latecomer in the party had I attempted to participate in the political discussions. I felt that there was no need for me to take any political positions at all. Nazi education, furthermore, aimed at separatist thinking. I was expected to confine myself to the job of building. The grotesque extent to which I clung to this illusion is indicated by a memorandum of mine to Hitler as late as 1944: "The task I have to fulfill is an unpolitical one. I have felt at ease in my work only so long as my person and my work were evaluated solely by the standard of practical accomplishments."[8]

But fundamentally the distinction was inconsequential. Today it seems to me that I was trying to compartmentalize my mind. On the one hand there was the vulgar business of carrying out a policy proclaimed in the anti-Semitic slogans printed on streamers over the entrances to towns. On the other hand there was my idealized picture of Hitler. I wanted to keep these two apart. Actually, it did not matter, of course, who mobilized the rabble of the gutter to attack synagogues and Jewish businesses, it did not matter whether this happened at Hitler's direct instigation or merely with his approval.

During the years after my release from Spandau I have been repeatedly asked what thoughts I had on this subject during my two decades alone in the cell with myself; what I actually knew of the persecution, the deportation, and the annihilation of the Jews; what I should have known and what conclusions I ought to have drawn.

I no longer give the answer with which I tried for so long to soothe the questioners, but chiefly myself: that in Hitler's system, as in every totalitarian regime, when a man's position rises, his isolation increases and he is therefore more sheltered from harsh reality; that with the application of technology to the process of murder the number of murderers is reduced and therefore the possibility of ignorance grows; that the craze for secrecy built into the system creates degrees of awareness, so it is easy to escape observing inhuman cruelties.

I no longer give any of these answers. For they are efforts at legalistic exculpation. It is true that as a favorite and later as one of Hitler's most influential ministers I was isolated. It is also true that the habit of thinking within the limits of my own field provided me, both as architect and as Armaments Minister, with many opportunities for evasion. It is true that I did not know what was really beginning on November 9, 1938, and what ended in Auschwitz and Maidanek. But in the final analysis I myself determined the degree of my isolation, the extremity of my evasions, and the extent of my ignorance.

I therefore know today that my agonized self-examinations posed the question as wrongly as did the questioners whom I have met since my release. Whether I knew or did not know, or how much or how little I knew, is totally unimportant when I consider what horrors I ought to have known about and what conclusions would have been the natural ones to draw from the little I did know. Those who ask me are fundamentally expecting me to offer justifications. But I have none. No apologies are possible. . . .

ARMAMENTS MINISTER

Speer Reflects on His Technological Management Style

Within half a year after my taking office we had significantly increased production in all the areas within our scope. Production in August 1942, according to the *Index Figures for German Armaments End-Products,* as compared with the February production, had increased by 27 percent for guns, by 25 percent for tanks, while ammunition production almost doubled, rising 97 percent. The total productivity in armaments increased by 59.6 percent.[9] Obviously we had mobilized reserves that had hitherto lain fallow.

After two and a half years, in spite of the beginning of heavy bombing, we had raised our entire armaments production from an average index figure of 98 for the year 1941 to a summit of 322 in July 1944. During the same period the labor force expanded by only about 30 percent. We had succeeded in doubling the output of labor and had achieved the very results Rathenau had predicted in 1917 as the effect of efficiency: doubling production without increasing equipment or labor costs.

It was not that any genius was at work here, though that has often been asserted. Many of the technicians in my office would undoubtedly have been more fit for the job, as far as knowledge of the fields involved is concerned. But none of them could have thrown the nimbus of Hitler into the balance as I could, and that made all the difference. The backing of the Fuehrer counted for everything.

Aside from all organizational innovations, things went so well because I applied the methods of democratic economic leadership. The democracies were on principle committed to placing trust in the responsible businessmen as long as that trust was justified. Thus they rewarded initiative, aroused an awareness of mission, and spurred decision making. Among us, on the other hand, all such elements had long ago been buried. Pressure and coercion kept production going, to be sure, but destroyed all spontaneity. I felt it necessary to issue a declaration to the effect that industry was not "knowingly lying to us, stealing from us, or otherwise trying to damage our war economy." . . .[10]

We owed the success of our programs to thousands of technicians with special achievements to their credit to whom we now entrusted the responsibility for whole segments of the armaments industry. This aroused their buried enthusiasm. They also took gladly to my unorthodox style of leadership. Basically, I exploited the phenomenon of the technician's often blind devotion to his task. Because of what seems to be the moral neutrality of technology, these people were without any scruples about their activities. The more technical the world imposed on us by the war, the more dangerous was this indifference of the technician to the direct consequences of his anonymous activities. . . .

Speer Tells of the German Rocket Program and Slave Labor

Ever since the winter of 1939, I had been closely associated with the Peenemünde development center,* although at first all I was doing was meeting its construction needs. I liked mingling with this circle of nonpolitical young scientists and inventors headed by Wernher von Braun—twenty-seven years old, purposeful, a man realistically at home in the future. It was extraordinary that so young and untried a team should be allowed to pursue a project costing hundreds of millions of marks and whose realization seemed far away. Under the somewhat paternalistic direction of Colonel Walter Dornberger these young men were able to work unhampered by bureaucratic obstacles and pursue ideas which at times sounded thoroughly utopian.

The work, mere glimmerings of which were being sketched out in 1939, also exerted a strange fascination upon me. It was like the planning of a miracle. I was impressed anew by these technicians with their fantastic visions, these mathematical romantics. Whenever I visited Peenemünde I also felt, quite spontaneously, somehow akin to them. My sympathy stood them in good stead when in the late fall of 1939 Hitler crossed the rocket project off his list of urgent undertakings and thus automatically cut off its labor and materials. By tacit agreement with the Army Ordnance Office, I continued to build the Peenemünde installations without its approval—a liberty that probably no one but myself could have taken.

After my appointment as Minister of Armaments, I naturally took a keener interest in this great project. Hitler, however, continued to be exceedingly skeptical. He was filled with a fundamental distrust of all innovations which, as in the case of jet aircraft or atom bombs, went beyond the technical experience of the First World War generation and presaged an era he could not know.

On June 13, 1942, the armaments chiefs of the three branches of the armed forces, Field Marshal Milch, Admiral Witzell, and General Fromm, flew to Peenemünde with me to witness the first firing of a remote-controlled rocket. Before us in a clearing among the pines towered an unreal-looking missile four stories high. Colonel Dornberger, Wernher von Braun, and the staff were as full of suspense over this first launching as we were. I knew what hopes the young inventor was placing on this experiment. For him and his team this was not the development of a weapon, but a step into the future of technology.

*[Peenemünde was a special research center for the development of military rockets, headed by Wernher von Braun. -Ed.]

Wisps of vapor showed that the fuel tanks were being filled. At the predetermined second, at first with a faltering motion but then with the roar of an unleashed giant, the rocket rose slowly from its pad, seemed to stand upon its jet of flame for the fraction of a second, then vanished with a howl into the low clouds. Wernher von Braun was beaming. For my part, I was thunderstruck at this technical miracle, at its precision and at the way it seemed to abolish the laws of gravity, so that thirteen tons could be hurled into the air without any mechanical guidance.

The technicians were just explaining the incredible distance the projectile was covering when, a minute and a half after the start, a rapidly swelling howl indicated that the rocket was falling in the immediate vicinity. We all froze where we stood. It struck the ground only a half a mile away. The guidance system had failed, as we later learned. Nevertheless the technicians were satisfied, since the thorniest problem had been solved: getting it off the ground. Hitler, however, continued to have the "gravest doubts" and wondered whether a guidance capability could ever be developed.[11]

On October 14, 1942, I was able to inform him that his doubts could be over. The second rocket had successfully flown the prescribed course of one hundred and twenty miles and had struck within two and a half miles of the target. For the first time a product of man's inventive mind had grazed the frontiers of space at an altitude of sixty miles. It seemed like the first step toward a dream. Only at this point did Hitler, too, show lively interest. As usual, his desires underwent instant inflation. He insisted that before the rocket was put into action a flock of five thousand missiles was to be ready, "available for wholesale commitment."*

I now had to make arrangements for mass production. On December 22, 1942, I had Hitler sign an order to this effect, although the rocket still needed considerable development before it could lend itself to mass manufacture.[12] I thought I could risk rushing matters in this way. Based on the progress already made and the promises from Peenemünde, the final technical data was to be available by July 1943, at which point we could go right into production.

On the morning of July 7, 1943, I invited Dornberger and von Braun to headquarters at Hitler's request. The Fuehrer wanted to be informed on the details of the V-2 project. After Hitler had finished with one of his conferences, we went together over to the movie hall, where some of Wernher von Braun's assistants were ready. After a brief introduction the

---

*See *Führerprotokoll,* October 13–14, 1942, Point 25. Even 5000 long-range rockets, that is more than five months' production, would have delivered only 3750 tons of explosives; a single attack by the combined British and American air forces delivered a good 8000 tons.

room was darkened and a color film shown. For the first time Hitler saw the majestic spectacle of a great rocket rising from its pad and disappearing into the stratosphere. Without a trace of timidity and with a boyish sounding enthusiasm, von Braun explained his theory. There could be no question about it: From that moment on, Hitler had been finally won over. Dornberger explained a number of organizational questions, while I proposed to Hitler that von Braun be appointed a professor. "Yes, arrange that at once with Meissner," Hitler said impulsively. "I'll even sign the document in person."

Hitler bade the Peenemünde men an exceedingly cordial good-by. He was greatly impressed, and his imagination had been kindled. Back in his bunker he became quite ecstatic about the possibilities of this project. "The A-4 is a measure that can decide the war. And what encouragement to the home front when we attack the English with it! This is the decisive weapon of the war, and what is more it can be produced with relatively small resources. Speer, you must push the A-4 as hard as you can! Whatever labor and materials they need must be supplied instantly. You know I was going to sign the decree for the tank program. But my conclusion now is: Change it around and phrase it so that A-4 is put on a par with tank production. But," Hitler added in conclusion, "in this project we can use only Germans. God help us if the enemy finds out about the business."[13]

There was only one point on which he pressed me, when we were alone again. "Weren't you mistaken? You say this young man is thirty-one? I would have thought him even younger!" He thought it astonishing that so young a man could already have helped to bring about a technical breakthrough which would change the face of the future. From then on he would sometimes expatiate on his thesis that in our century people squandered the best years of their lives on useless things. In past eras an Alexander the Great had conquered a vast empire at the age of twenty-three and Napoleon had won his brilliant victories at thirty. In connection with this he would often allude, as if casually, to Wernher von Braun, who at so young an age had created a technical marvel at Peenemünde.

In the autumn of 1943 it turned out that our expectations had been premature. The final blueprints had not been delivered in July, as promised, so that we were not able to go into mass production immediately. A great many sources of error had been discovered. In particular, when the first rockets with warheads were fired, there were inexplicable premature explosions when the missile reentered the atmosphere.[14] There were still many questions unsolved, I warned in a speech on October 6, 1943, so that it would be premature "to count with certainty on this new weapon." I added that the technical difference between individual manufacture and mass production, considerable enough in itself, would involve special difficulties in the case of these highly complicated mechanisms.

Almost a year passed. At the beginning of September 1944 the first rockets were fired at England. Not, as Hitler had imagined, five thousand at one blow, but twenty-five, and then not at one blow but over a period of ten days.

After Hitler had become excited over the V-2 project, Himmler entered the picture. Six weeks later he came to Hitler to propose the simplest way to guarantee secrecy for this vital program. If the entire work force were concentration camp prisoners, all contact with the outside world would be eliminated. Such prisoners did not even have any mail, Himmler said. Along with this, he offered to provide all necessary technicians from the ranks of the prisoners. All industry would have to furnish would be the management and the engineers.

Hitler agreed to this plan. And Saur and I had no choice, especially since we could not offer a more persuasive arrangement.[15]

The result was that we had to work out guidelines for a joint undertaking with the SS leadership—what was to be called the Central Works. My assistants went into it reluctantly, and their fears were soon confirmed. Formally speaking, we remained in charge of the manufacturing; but in cases of doubt we had to yield to the superior power of the SS leadership. Thus, Himmler had put a foot in our door, and we ourselves had helped him do it. . . .

Himmler promptly made every effort to push his way into the field of armaments production. He readily offered countless prisoners and as early as 1942 began placing pressure on a number of my assistants. As far as we could make out, he wanted to turn the concentration camps into large modern factories, especially for armaments, with the SS continuing to have direct control of them. General Fromm at the time called my attention to the perils of this for orderly production of armaments, and Hitler made it clear he was on my side. After all, we had had certain dismal experiences before the war with such SS projects, which had promised us bricks and granite. On September 21, 1942, Hitler ruled on the matter. The prisoners were to work in factories under the direction of the industrial armaments organization. Himmler's expansionist drive had been curbed for the present, at least in this field.[16]

At first the factory managers complained that the prisoners arrived in a weakened condition and after a few months had to be sent back, exhausted, to the regular camps. Since their training time alone required several weeks and instructors were scarce, we could not afford to train a new group every few months. In response to our complaints the SS made considerable improvements in the sanitary conditions and rations of the camps. Soon, in the course of my rounds through the armaments plants, I saw more contented faces among the prisoners and better fed people.[17]

Our hard-won independence in matters of armaments was broken by Hitler's order to erect a large rocket-production plant dependent on the SS.

In a lonely valley in the Harz Mountains a widely ramified system of caves had been established before the war for the storage of vital military chemicals. Here, on December 10, 1943, I inspected the extensive underground installations where the V-2 was to be produced. In enormous long halls prisoners were busy setting up machinery and shifting plumbing. Expressionlessly, they looked right through me, mechanically removing their prisoners' caps of blue twill until our group had passed them.

I cannot forget a professor of the Pasteur Institute in Paris who testified as a witness at the Nuremberg Trial. He too was in the Central Works which I inspected that day. Objectively, without any dramatics, he explained the inhuman conditions in this inhuman factory. The memory is especially painful, the more so because he made his charge without hatred, sadly and brokenly and also astonished at so much human degeneracy.

The conditions for these prisoners were in fact barbarous, and a sense of profound involvement and personal guilt seizes me whenever I think of them. As I learned from the overseers after the inspection was over, the sanitary conditions were inadequate, disease rampant; the prisoners were quartered right there in the damp caves, and as a result the mortality among them was extraordinarily high.* That same day I allocated the necessary materials and set all the machinery in motion to build a barracks camp immediately on an adjacent hill. In addition, I pressed the SS camp command to take all necessary measures to improve sanitary conditions and upgrade the food. They pledged that they would do so.

Up to this time I had actually paid almost no attention to these problems, and the assurances of the camp commanders persuaded me that matters would be corrected. I did not take action again until January 14, 1944. On January 13, Dr. Poschmann, the medical supervisor for all the departments in my Ministry, described the hygienic conditions at the Central Works in the blackest colors. The next day I sent one of my department heads to the plant.[18] Simultaneously, Dr. Poschmann started taking various medical measures. A few days later my own illness partially put a halt to these actions.* But on May 26, soon after I was back at

---

*The shocking effect the camp had on us is indicated in the deliberately veiled phraseology of the *Office Journal* entry for December 10, 1943: "On the morning of December 10 the minister went to inspect a new plant in the Harz Mountains. Carrying out this tremendous mission drew on the leaders' last reserves of strength. Some of the men were so affected that they had to be forcibly sent off on vacations to restore their nerves."

*[Speer was hospitalized for exhaustion for over two months beginning on January 18, 1944. -Ed.]

my post, Dr. Poschmann told me that he had arranged for the assignment of civilian doctors to many of the labor camps. But there were difficulties. On the same day, I received a rude letter from Robert Ley in which he protested against Dr. Poschmann's interference on formal grounds. Medical treatment in camps was his province, he declared, and angrily demanded that I reprimand Dr. Poschmann, forbid him any further meddling, and discipline him for the steps he had already taken.

I answered immediately that I had no reason to meet his demands, that on the contrary we had the greatest interest in adequate medical treatment for the prisoners.[19] That same day I discussed further medical measures with Dr. Poschmann. Since I was making all these arrangements in cooperation with Dr. Brandt, and since apart from all humanitarian considerations, the rational arguments were on our side, I did not give a hang about Ley's reaction. I was confident that Hitler would rebuke the party bureaucracy which we had passed over and would even make scornful remarks about the bureaucrats. . . .

Speer Considers His Guilt Over His Connection to the SS Death Camps

Himmler had long been striving to set up a business firm which would be the property of the SS. Hitler, or so it seemed to me, was cool to the idea, and I did my best to reinforce him in this. Perhaps this conflict was one of the reasons for Himmler's strange conduct during my illness. For during those months he had at last managed to persuade Hitler that a large-scale SS business enterprise would offer numerous advantages. At the beginning of June 1944, Hitler asked me to assist the SS in its efforts to build up an economic empire extending from raw materials to manufacturing. He had a strange reason, now, for furthering this enterprise: The SS must be strong enough so that under his successors it would be able, for example, to oppose a Finance Minister who wanted to cut its funds. . . .

Himmler presented me with a well-thought-out and wide-ranging plan. During my illness the SS, in spite of all Saur's efforts to oppose it, had acquired the Hungarian concern of Manfred-Weiss, an important armaments company. With this as a core, Himmler explained, he wanted systematically to construct a steadily expanding cartel. Would I suggest a specialist to help with the construction of this giant enterprise? After reflecting briefly, I proposed Paul Pleiger, who had set up large steel mills for the Four-Year Plan. Pleiger was an energetic and independent man who, with his manifold ties to industry, would be able to ensure that Himmler did not expand his concern too vigorously and too unscrupulously. But Himmler did not like my nominee. That was the last time he asked me for advice.

Himmler's close associates Oswald Pohl, Hans Jüttner, and Gottlob Berger were tough and ruthless in negotiation, but moderately good-natured. They had that kind of banality which seems quite tolerable at first sight. But two of his other men were surrounded by an aura of iciness like that of their chief: Both Reinhard Heydrich and Hans Kammler were blond, blue-eyed, long-headed, always neatly dressed, and well bred. Both were capable of unexpected decisions at any moment, and once they had arrived at them they would carry them through with a rare obstinacy. Himmler had made a significant choice in picking Kammler as his aide. For in spite of all his ideological crankiness, in matters of personnel Himmler was not overly concerned about lengthy party membership. He was more interested in such qualities as energy, swift intelligence, and extreme zeal. In the spring of 1942, Himmler had appointed Kammler, who had previously been a high-ranking construction employee in the Air Ministry, to head the SS construction operations, and in the summer of 1943 he chose him to handle the rocket program. In the course of my enforced collaboration with this man, I discovered him to be a cold, ruthless schemer, a fanatic in the pursuit of a goal, and as carefully calculating as he was unscrupulous.

Himmler heaped assignments on him and brought him into Hitler's presence at every opportunity. Soon rumors were afloat that Himmler was trying to build up Kammler to be my successor.[20] At the time I had seen only the best side of Kammler, and I rather liked his objective coolness. In many jobs my partner, in his intentions possibly my rival, he was in his career as well as his manner of work in many ways my mirror image. He too came from a solid middle-class family, had gone through the university, had been "discovered" because of his work in construction, and had gone far and fast in fields for which he had not been trained.

During the war the supply of labor became the key factor in any industrial unit. At the beginning of the forties, and subsequently at a faster and faster pace, the SS began secretly building labor camps and making sure they were kept full. In a letter of May 7, 1944, Walter Schieber, one of my department heads, called my attention to the efforts of the SS to use its powers over labor in order to promote its economic expansion. Moreover, the SS was casting eyes on the foreign workers in our factories and became more and more zealous in arresting them for trivial violations of rules and transferring them to its own camps.* My

---

*Dr. Schieber states further: "The SS siphons off by now a significant number of the many foreign and especially Russian workers who man the armaments plants. This drain is caused by the constant growth of the extensive SS economic interests, which is being prompted with particular zeal by Obergruppenführer Pohl." At the meeting of the Armaments Staff on May 26, 1944, Kammler had boasted that he had "simply placed fifty thousand persons in protective custody in order to obtain the necessary labor" for the SS enterprises.

assistants estimated that by this technique we were being deprived of thirty to forty thousand workers a month during the spring of 1944.

At the beginning of June 1944, I protested to Hitler that I could not "stand a loss of half a million workers a year . . . all the more so because a majority of them were skilled workers trained with considerable effort." I said that they simply had to be "returned to their original occupations as quickly as possible." Hitler told me to discuss the problem with Himmler; he would then make a decision in my favor.[21] But in defiance of the facts Himmler denied both to me and to Hitler that any such practices were being pursued.

The prisoners themselves, as I sometimes had a chance to observe, also feared Himmler's growing economic ambitions. I recall a tour through the Linz steelworks in the summer of 1944 where prisoners were moving about freely among the other workers. They stood at the machines in the lofty workshops, served as helpers to trained workers, and talked unconstrainedly with the free workers. It was not the SS but army soldiers who were guarding them. When we came upon a group of twenty Russians, I had the interpreter ask them whether they were satisfied with their treatment. They made gestures of passionate assent. Their appearance confirmed what they said. In contrast to the people in the caves of the Central Works, who were obviously wasting away, these prisoners were well fed. And when I asked them, just to make conversation, whether they would prefer to return to the regular camp, they gave a start of fright. Their faces expressed purest horror.

But I asked no further questions. Why should I have done so; their expressions told me everything. If I were to try today to probe the feelings that stirred me then, if across the span of a lifetime I attempt to analyze what I really felt—pity, irritation, embarrassment, or indignation—it seems to me that the desperate race with time, my obsessional fixation on production and output statistics, blurred all considerations and feelings of humanity. An American historian has said of me that I loved machines more than people.[22] He is not wrong. I realize that the sight of suffering people influenced only my emotions, but not my conduct. On the plane of feelings only sentimentality emerged; in the realm of decisions, on the other hand, I continued to be ruled by the principles of utility. In the Nuremberg Trial the indictment against me was based on the use of prisoners in the armaments factories.

By the court's standard of judgment, which was purely numerical, my guilt would have been greater had I prevailed over Himmler and raised the number of prisoners in our labor force, thus increasing the chances of more people for survival. Paradoxically, I would feel better today if in this sense I had been guiltier. But what preys on my mind nowadays has little to do with the standards pf Nuremberg nor the figures on lives I saved or might have saved. For in either case I was moving within the system. What disturbs me more is that I failed to read the physiognomy of the regime mirrored in the faces of those prisoners—the regime whose existence I was so obsessively trying to prolong during those weeks and months. I did not see any moral ground outside the system where I should have taken my stand. And sometimes I ask myself who this young man really was, this young man who has now become so alien to me, who walked through the workshops of the Linz steelworks or descended into the caverns of the Central Works twenty-five years ago.

One day, some time in the summer of 1944, my friend Karl Hanke, the Gauleiter of Lower Silesia, came to see me. In earlier years he had told me a great deal about the Polish and French campaigns, had spoken of the dead and wounded, the pain and agonies, and in talking about these things had shown himself a man of sympathy and directness. This time, sitting in the green leather easy chair in my office, he seemed confused and spoke falteringly, with many breaks. He advised me never to accept an invitation to inspect a concentration camp in Upper Silesia. Never, under any circumstances. He had seen something there which he was not permitted to describe and moreover could not describe.

I did not query him, I did not query Himmler, I did not query Hitler, I did not speak with personal friends. I did not investigate—for I did not want to know what was happening there. Hanke must have been speaking of Auschwitz. During those few seconds, while Hanke was warning me, the whole responsibility had became a reality again. Those seconds were uppermost in my mind when I stated to the international court at the Nuremberg Trial that as an important member of the leadership of the Reich, I had to share the total responsibility for all that had happened. For from that moment on, I was inescapably contaminated morally; from fear of discovering something which might have made me turn from my course, I had closed my eyes. This deliberate blindness outweighs whatever good I may have done or tried to do in the last period of the war. Those activities shrink to nothing in the face of it. Because I failed at that time, I still feel, to this day, responsible for Auschwitz in a wholly personal sense.

QUESTIONS FOR DISCUSSION

1. How does Speer use his role as a technological professional (an architect) to justify his actions during the Nazi regime, and in particular, that he was ignorant of (or oblivious to) the plight of the Jews of Germany and Eastern Europe? Are his rationalizations persuasive? How do your answers to these questions affect your view of contemporary technological professionals who may be engaged in illegal or immoral activities?

2. Consider how Speer's theories of architecture—especially the "theory of ruin value"—support the ideological positions of the Nazi regime. Do Speer's theories of architecture demonstrate that architecture is a technology that is embedded with political values? Note that in later years Speer claims to be amazed that he had been so influenced by the speeches and ideas of Hitler and claims that he disdains the designs and architectural plans of his youth.

3. Why did Speer (and Hitler) want to design everything on such a large scale? What does this teach us about the political and social function of architecture and of technological professionals?

4. Speer claims that it was easy to manage scientists and technicians because they have a "blind devotion to [their] task" regardless of the moral dimensions of their work. Is this true about technological professionals in general? What does Speer reveal about himself and his motivations when he describes the personality of the technician in such a way?

NOTES

Unless otherwise indicated and with the exception of family letters, all documents, letters, speeches, and such, as well as the *Office Journal*, are in the Federal Archives (Bundesarchiv) in Koblenz, catalogued under the inventory number R 3 (Reich Ministry of Armaments and War Production).

The *Office Journal* is a day-by-day record kept in my department from 1941 to 1944. It covered my activities first as Inspector General of Buildings and later as Armaments Minister. [References in text to "the Minister" indicate author.–*Translators' Note*]

The *Führerprotokoll* is the record of Hitler's activities.

1. To this end we planned to avoid, as far as possible, all such elements of modern construction as steel girders and reinforced concrete, which are subject to weathering. Despite their height, the walls were intended to withstand the impact of the wind even if the roofs and ceilings were so neglected that they no longer braced the walls. The static factors were calculated with this in mind.

2. Sir Neville Henderson, *Failure of a Mission* (New York, 1940), p. 72.

3. According to Rolf Wagenführ, *Die deutsche Industrie im Kriege 1939–1945* (Berlin, 1954), p. 86, German expenditures for war production in 1944 amounted to seventy-one billion marks. *Die deutsche Bauzeitung*, Vol. 1898, Nos. 5, 9, 26, and 45, contain details about the future site for German national celebrations.

4. The Olympic Stadium built in Berlin in 1936 had a volume of only 9,886,800 cubic feet.

5. From an unpublished speech delivered by Hitler on January 9, 1939 to the workers constructing the new Chancellery building.

6. According to the preserved plan, the new assembly hall was to have an area of 22,596 square feet.

7. Working sketches for the project, drawn up at the time, are still in existence. On November 5, 1936, Hitler did the sketches based on the preliminary plans I had presented.

8. From my memorandum to Hitler, September 20, 1944.
9. From the *Indexziffern der deutschen Rüstungsfertigung,* January 1945. The statistics were based on the prices of the individual items of military hardware; price increases were not taken into account to avoid inflating the statistics. The monetary value that munitions production represented within the total armaments outlay for the three branches of the armed forces amounted to 29 percent; therefore, when this monetary value was doubled, it had a strong impact on the total armaments index.
10. Speech delivered April 18, 1942. By employing the principle of trust, "something which may strike administrative bureaucrats as a sheer impossibility," I continued, "we may succeed in destroying a system which, if it were allowed to continue, would increasingly become a serious drag on the whole war economy." Doubtlessly I was exaggerating when, two years later, on August 24, 1944, I told my assistants in the armaments organization "our placing of so much trust in factory managers and technicians is absolutely unique."
11. See *Führerprotokoll,* June 23, 1944, Point 21.
12. This December 12, 1942 order empowered the planners to finish the designs for the project and to order the machine tools, which required a lead time of many months. The designers could also initiate negotiations with the suppliers and rush the necessary allotments into the production process.
13. See *Führerprotokoll,* July 8, 1943, Points 18, 19, and 20.
14. Further details may be found in David Irving, *Die Geheimwaffen des dritten Reiches* (Gütersloh, 1965).
15. See *Führerprotokoll,* August 19–22, 1943, Point 24.
16. See *Führerprotokoll,* September 20–22, 1942, Point 36.
17. The head of the Armaments Delivery Office, Dr. Walter Schieber, asserted in a letter dated May 7, 1944 (Nuremberg Document 104 PS) that establishment of the concentration camp annexes called "labor camps" was justified, despite much friction with the SS, because "the technical and the human success would outweigh the drawbacks."
18. See *Office Journal,* January 13, 1944.
19. See Ley's letter dated May 26, 1944 and my reply written the following day.
20. See E. Georg, *Die wirtschaftlichen Unternehmungen des SS* (Stuttgart, 1963).
21. See *Führerprotokoll,* June 3–5, 1944, Point 21.
22. Eugene Davidson, "Albert Speer and the Nazi War Plans," *Modern Age,* No. 4 (1966).

CHAPTER 8

Albert Speer: Ethics, Architecture, and Technology

※

In this chapter, law professor Jack L. Sammons, Jr., considers the professional ethics of Albert Speer, Hitler's architect and armaments minister during the war, whose diaries were excerpted in Chapter 7. As we saw in Chapter 7, Speer claims in his memoirs that his moral failure consisted of the separation of his skills as a trained architect from the overall goals and consequences of Nazism. Sammons discusses this traditional defense of Speer, that he was a "Pure Technician" solely concerned with his technical skill—in this case, architecture—and thus unaware of the moral and political values that provided the environment for his expertise. Under this traditional view, the only moral course of action is what Sammons calls "rebellious ethics"—a person must rebel against his technical expertise and reassert himself as a moral being. Speer himself used this traditional argument in his own defense, as a way of rationalizing his guilt for the atrocities of the Nazi regime; he claimed that he neglected his humanity and focused only on his role as Hitler's architect. But law professor Sammons cross-examines Speer's memoirs and argument, and rejects the defense of the Pure Technician. According to Sammons, Speer chose the immoral life not because he focused too much on his technical role as an architect, but because he betrayed the true values of architecture. He abandoned the craft of architecture in the pursuit of power. Speer saw that Hitler's architectural vision was out of proportion to human life, gigantic, monstrous, a betrayal of both German cultural history and a sensitivity to human civilization— yet this did not stop him from working toward that vision. The aesthetic and spiritual aspects of architecture, its unique place as a technology and art form that practically situates humans in their built environment, should have been a guide for Speer's moral and spiritual life, but he ignored his ideals of architecture in exchange for power, wealth, and fame. Sammons correctly sees Speer's case as a paradigm for all technical professionals—not just architects, but also lawyers, doctors, industrial managers, and engineers—all who must find a way to integrate the ideals and goals of their technical craft with their ideals of a moral life. Thus Speer's life is a moral lesson for us all.

From "Rebellious Ethics and Albert Speer"

Jack L. Sammons, Jr.

Every task, however simple, sets the soul who does it free.
        —*Henry Van Dyke* (Episcopal Hymnal #586)

According to the familiar story, Albert Speer failed to avoid complicity in the Nazi evil surrounding him by not rebelling against his role as Hitler's architect. We teach, preach, and practice professional ethics in this country by holding on to such stories about the morally corrupting effects of our professional roles and the concomitant need to rebel against them. As ethical people, we say, we must stand apart from our professional roles in personal moral judgment of them, in order to avoid becoming an Albert Speer. This is the dominant paradigm for the ethics of our professions. I call this paradigm rebellious ethics, and I want to challenge it by offering a truer telling of the life of Albert Speer and then examining an implication of this truer telling for professional ethics.

THE PURE TECHNICIAN AND A NEED TO REBEL

The paradigmatic version of Speer's story started, oddly enough, when members of the British press recognized that Speer was very much like what most British professionals wanted to be: superbly educated, intelligent, prosperous, powerful, and well bred from good professional stock. He was an effective professional—even an insightful and perceptive one.[1] What the British press saw in Speer in the 1940s, we still see in him today. The traits he displayed as an architect and, later, as Minister of Armaments, are the traits we continue to admire in our professionals.

Because Speer is so much like the professionals we admire, we feel a need to explain his moral failure, and to do so in a way different from our explanations of the moral failure of a Himmler or a Goering or a thousand other petty criminals. By being so like us and yet such a conspicuous moral failure, the story of Speer drives us to define professional ethics in reaction to him. We want professional ethics to be able to separate us from this Speer as easily as we can separate ourselves from a Himmler or a Goering.

The seminal piece for this ethical separation from Speer was written by an English journalist for the British newspaper *The Observer* on April 9, 1944.

> Speer is, in a sense, more important for Germany today than Hitler, Himmler, Goering, Goebbels, or the generals. They all have, in a way, become the mere auxiliaries of the man who actually directs the giant power machine—charged with drawing from it the maximum effort under maximum strain. . . . In him is the very epitome of the "managerial revolution." Speer is not one of the flamboyant and picturesque Nazis. Whether he has any other than conventional political opinions at all is unknown. He might have joined any other political party which gave him a job and a career. He is very much the successful average man, well dressed, civil, noncorrupt, very middle-class in his style of life, with a wife and six children. Much less than any of the other German leaders does he stand for anything particularly German or particularly Nazi. He rather symbolizes a type which is becoming increasingly important in all belligerent countries: the pure technician, the classless bright young man without background, with no other original aim than to make his way in the world and no other means than his technical and managerial ability. . . . This is their age; the Hitlers and Himmlers we may get rid of, but the Speers, whatever happens to this particular special man, will long be with us.

After this article, Speer is no longer Hitler's architect; he is the Pure Technician. But this character is poorly named. The Pure Technician is not a product of technology, although technology may increase his number. His title has much more to do with accountability. The Pure Technician is the expert who is not accountable beyond his area of expertise.[2] His technique, he claims, is morally neutral and he asks to be judged only by whether his means are the most efficient ones toward whatever end is given to him.

By thus characterizing Speer as the Pure Technician we provide a way to separate ourselves from him. We also make clear our motivation for doing so because the Pure Technician is the personification of the moral disease awaiting us if we continue to be like him—that is, if we continue to be wholly captured by our professional roles. Speer the Pure Technician, we know, never reflected beyond what his role as Hitler's architect required of him until it was far too late for a life well lived (if not for his soul), and by not doing so he failed repeatedly to see as people those affected by his acts. Because Speer is so much like us, however, our faith in who we are tells us that Speer the person, as opposed to Speer the professional architect, would have seen as people those affected by his acts if only he had reflected *as a person*. This, however, the Pure Technician cannot do because the Pure Technician always wears the moral blinders of his role. Thus, Speer's moral vision was so impaired by being the Pure Technician that he could not, in a phrase Hauerwas and Burrell use to describe Speer in their perceptive article about him, ". . . spell out [this ethical] feature of his engagement with the world."[3] So Speer, this story tells us, was far too integrated in his role as architect and not well enough integrated in himself for a successful ethical life. If we are to separate ourselves from Speer, then, we must avoid this degree of role integration.

Speer accepted this story about himself in a poignant autobiography he labored over for twenty years in Spandau during his imprisonment after the Nuremberg Trials and finished soon after his release. He was, he said, "above all an architect"[4] who came to think that being Hitler's architect was a sufficient description of a way of life. Because he did, he said, he shut his eyes to the horror around him.[5] So lost in this role was he that he saw no grounds outside the system—a system that was Hitler—where he could take his moral stand.[6] Meditatively, the imprisoned Speer expanded upon his story:

> The nightmare shared by many people . . . that some day the nations of the world may be dominated by technology—that nightmare was very nearly made a reality under Hitler's authoritarian system. Every country in the world today faces the danger of being terrorized by technology, but in a modern dictatorship this seems to me to be unavoidable. Therefore, the more technological the world becomes, the more essential will be the demands for *individual freedom and the self awareness of the individual human being as a counterpoise to technology.*[7]

This, then, is how we are to separate ourselves from Speer. We will not be like him if we take our professions much less seriously than he did and ourselves much more seriously, but to do this, we must do what Speer did not: We must consciously maintain a personal and psychological detachment from our professional roles. By doing so, we free ourselves for the personal reflection so plainly missing from Speer's life. For it is in our personal detachment from role that we find the moral distance needed for spelling out our full engagement with the world.

But our roles are very imposing, and preserving our personal moral freedom from them is an extremely difficult moral task. If we want to avoid the morally corrupting forces of professional role Speer suffered, we must consciously adopt and steadfastly maintain the personal and psychological stance of the *moral rebel* against our professions. Thus, the answer professional ethics gives to the challenge presented by Speer's life, and the paradigm in which professional ethics works, is for professional ethics to be rebellious.

There is a long and complex history behind the development of the moral psychology of the rebel—it is, perhaps, a reflection of art's much earlier association with self-projection and the singular voice—but the extreme degree of its current manifestation in professional ethics (the extent, that is, to which Speer the Pure Technician haunts us) is surely a recent phenomenon. Over the past one hundred and twenty years, the ethics of the legal profession, for example, have evolved quickly from the professional to the personal, from an internal source for ethical judgments to a purely external source for conduct.

Despite the recentness of its current domination, however, this rebellious stance has now become so ingrained in our ethical thinking about professional roles that to challenge it is to risk great misunderstanding, if not moral condemnation. But this risk we must take, because there is a truer telling of the story of Speer's moral failure, one which challenges the rebellious ethics paradigm. This telling of his life teaches us that professionals should be good at what they do—better than Speer was. It says that Speer's moral failure was *as an architect*[8] and that it is in greater, not lesser, integration with his role that Speer could have had the moral resources—the distance, the vision, and the courage—he needed to see that he, too, released the gas and fired the ovens. This truer telling condemns Speer more strongly than the story of Speer the Pure Technician because it asks about moral resources available to Speer, in the story of the architect he professed to live by. It also condemns him by being more consistent with his autobiography than his own conclusions were. From this, we can see that Speer's self-deception—for this is how Hauerwas and Burrell describe his being dominated by his role[9]—continued in Spandau on Speer's own terms; that is, on terms he could have accepted as Hitler's architect. This version of Speer's life condemns us, too, by revealing how much like Hitler's architect we continue to be, and how we cannot separate ourselves from him by a facile rebellion against our professional roles. It says we are failing, as Speer failed, because we do not take our professions seriously enough.

THE FAILED ARCHITECT

The familiar story of Speer is right when it says that Speer came to rely on his role as an architect as a sufficient morality. (Later, as I shall describe, he discovered that his morality was also based on a story about the German people, a story he seldom understood as an architect although, ironically, this story was part of his understanding of good architecture.) There were other moralities available to the young Speer, but Speer rejected the moralities of his parents, as did so many young Germans of the time, along with much of his past,[10] and the older Speer never reconciled himself to them or to the moral stories in which his family had lived for generations. He did not understand himself as being in these stories or "see their relevance to the chaos around him."[11] Nor could the older Speer find a relevant morality as a husband or as a father sufficient to challenge his self-deceptions as Hitler's architect. A different person, perhaps, could have judged his life as a Nazi with an understanding of himself as a good husband or as a good father, but Speer needed more of a community for his moral reflections (as I believe most Germans did) than the family could provide. It would have been extremely difficult for Speer to understand the relationship between the practical and the spiritual—as he so needed to do to see his situation truthfully—in the community of his family. But it should have been far easier for him to do so in the community of the practical and the spiritual that good architecture can be. And this was the community in which Speer located himself. This is what he meant when he said he was "above all an architect."

While the familiar story is right about Speer's reliance on role as a sufficient morality, the implication of this reliance should not be the one rebellious ethics draws, that is, that this reliance limited Speer's moral reflections. For to deny to Speer a deep engagement with architecture, to ask him to take his profession less seriously, would be to deny him the only morality he had that could place him outside Hitler's system for reflection and thus provide him with something moral to proclaim from that external stance. We can see that this is true by looking at his life as an architect more closely.

THE MORAL LESSONS OF ARCHITECTURE

Until very near the end of the war, Speer's only moments of moral insight into the truth of his situation as Hitler's architect—the only times he came close to spelling out his full engagement with the world—were those of architectural insights.[12] As an architect, Speer began to see in Hitler's obsession with huge dimensions,[13] his "violation of the human scale,"[14] his lack of proportion, his lack of concern for the social dimension of architecture,[15] his use of architecture as only an expression of his strength, and the pomposity and decadence of his style, a dictator bent on world domination for the sole purpose of his own glorification—a megalomaniacal tyrant, full of hubris and entirely lacking in compassion and balance. Architecture also revealed to Speer the horrifying contradictions in Hitler's life, contradictions that later gave Speer the strength to oppose him.

What architecture offered Speer, however, was more than just a different perception of the person to whom he had turned over his life. Architecture also began to tell Speer who *he* had become as Hitler's architect. As with many of his architectural insights into reality, this lesson came first to Speer while he was on an art tour gathering ideas for his designs. Describing the Escorial, a complex comparable to Hitler's Fuhrer Palace in its proportions, he said:

> What a contrast with Hitler's architectural ideas: in the one case, remarkable conciseness and clarity, magnificent interior rooms, their form perfectly controlled; in the other case, pomp and disproportionate ostentation.[16]

Speer saw this contrast as expressing an impulse underlying the Escorial "quite different and far more spiritual," he said, than the impulse underlying his own work. Following this visit, he had an epiphany: "In hours of solitary contemplation it began to dawn on me for the first time that my recent architectural ideals were on the wrong track."[17]

Thus architecture offered Speer a truer perspective on Hitler and on himself, for the moral vision this German and this Nazi needed to criticize the acts of the popular hero who ruled his country, and to understand himself, could come best from the only separate community available to him in which the virtues could still be defined and understood. It was in a practice in which the practical and the spiritual could be combined, as they are when architecture is good, that he could see the limitations of Hitler's insistence upon the primacy of the practical. (As Hitler once stated: "For there can be only one single rule, and this rule, put succinctly, is: That is correct which is useful in itself.")[18]

By being an architect, Speer could continue an imaginary conversation within a community of architects extending over time (and a conversation with his mentor, a person I will describe later). This public-private conversation requires a more explicit spelling out of engagements; it requires more explanations than the private conversation of rebellious ethics— the conversation of the "two-in-one" in Hannah Arendt's phrase. This architectural conversation continues eternally as a dialogue that reveals the teleology of architecture. It continues because the good architect knows it would be the death of architecture, as others have said it would be the death of religion, to cling to the last revelation.

The public-private conversation of architecture differs sharply from what remained of true public conversations in Hitler's system. As told by Speer:

> The ordinary party member was being taught that grand policy was much too complex for him to judge it. Consequently, one felt one was being represented, never called upon to take personal responsibility. The whole structure of the system was aimed at preventing conflicts of conscience from even arising. The result was the total sterility of all conversations and discussions among these like-minded persons. It was boring for people to confirm one another in their uniform opinions. . . . What eventually developed was a society of totally isolated individuals.[19]

The public-private conversation Speer could have as an architect could place him in a community outside this "society of totally isolated individuals" in which he could only see himself. By doing so, it could give him a moral distance from Hitler, and the skills he needed to spell out his full engagement with the world. At its best, architecture could have been for Speer the "good companion" that David Kolb claims it can be:

> So architecture makes a good companion. Architects have grappled in detail with problems of rootedness and continuity. The surrounding environment cannot be wished away; the ways people live cannot be arbitrarily changed; all this must be taken into account, which is not to say it must be passively accepted. We can learn from the discipline and facticity of architecture not to be taken in by extreme positions that claim for us a freedom either wider or more narrow than the freedom we have. The difficulties of creating good architecture can illuminate our tasks in building cultures and worlds together amid the products of our past.[20]

As Speer himself knew, for example, it was only through his preliminary architectural studies—and through none other—that he had acquired the ability to examine various points of view with a lack of conscious bias.[21]

SPEER'S FAILURE TO LEARN

Writing in Spandau, however, Speer failed to understand the morality that architecture could have been for him. Instead, he accepted the way others had characterized him:

> I so rarely—in fact almost never—found the time to reflect about myself or my own activities, that I never gave my own existence a thought.

Today, in retrospect, I often have the feeling that something swooped me up off the ground at the time, wrenched me from all my roots, and beamed a host of alien forces upon me. In retrospect, what perhaps troubled me most is that my occasional spells of uneasiness during this period were concerned mainly with the direction I was taking as an architect, with my growing estrangement from [my mentor's] doctrine.[22]

It was not until after he left Spandau that the now pensive Speer, looking back at his work, could see more clearly what had been the obvious lessons of architecture. The Nazi style, he saw now, was "decadent baroque, comparable to the style that accompanied the decline of the Roman Empire . . . ," and "neoclassicism . . . multiplied, altered, exaggerated, and sometimes distorted to the point of ludicrousness."

Speer's failure to learn the moral lessons of architecture, and, accordingly, his failure as an architect, are symbolized in the gilded eagle he designed for the great domed hall that was to be the architectural center of Hitler's power. For the post-Spandau Speer, this eagle became the symbol of what architecture could have taught him about Hitler, but did not, and of the person he could have been, but was not:

Had I been able to think the matter out consistently, I ought to have argued further that my designs for Hitler were following the pattern of the Late Empire and forecasting the end of the regime; that, therefore, Hitler's downfall could be deduced from these very designs. But this [decadence] was hidden from me at the time. And not only the style but the excessive size of these buildings plainly revealed Hitler's intention. One day in the early summer of 1939, he pointed to the German eagle with the swastika in its claws which was to crown the dome nine hundred fifty-seven feet in the air. "That has to be changed. Instead of the swastika, the eagle is to be perched above the globe." There are photos of the models in which this revision is plainly to be seen. A few months later the Second World War began.[23]

Surveying his life, he knew now what he did not know then:

What is more, by my abilities and my energies I had prolonged that war by many months. I had assented to having the globe of the world crown that domed hall which was to be the symbol of the new Berlin.[24]

After Spandau, Speer could also see what being Hitler's architect had done to him as an architect:

And I moved with [his tendency towards pomposity]. For my designs of this period owed less and less to what I regarded as "my style." This estrangement from my beginnings was revealed in other ways beside the wildly excessive size of my buildings. They had become pure "art of decadence." Wealth, the inexhaustible funds at my disposal, but also Hitler's party ideology, had led me along the path to a style which drew its inspiration rather from the show palaces of Oriental despots.[25]

Thus Speer knew he had turned his back on reality, something he knew a good architect must never do in his work.[26] But, as he also understood, the eyes he had used as an architect were not his own: he saw all his buildings with Hitler's political eyes. Because he did, Speer, too, came to be ruled by the practical and, as a result, "on the plane of feeling only sentimentality emerged. . . .[27] This was a utility that swept aside his architectural sense. He did not just turn his back on reality; he brushed it away. "In the euphoria of history-making activity, unpleasant facts were ignored; they were no more than obstacles to the achievement of the grand design."[28]

And so Speer failed to learn the moral lessons architecture offered him. But why? In May 1935, when Speer visited Delphi, the model for his work for Hitler, on his first trip abroad, he made a discovery:

The purity of Greek artistic creativeness was speedily contaminated by the wealth won in the Ionian colonies in Asia. Didn't this prove how sensitive a high artistic consciousness was and how little it took to distort the ideal conception to the point of unrecognizability? I happily played with such theories; it never occurred to me that my own works might be subject to these same laws.[29]

But why did it not occur to him? Why had he come to see the world with his client's eyes and not his own architecturally trained ones? We can account for this failure, as we always should in the case of professions, by looking for corruption. When we do, we see Speer as something far different from Speer the Pure Technician, and we see something far different from a Speer who is "above all" an architect. We see, instead, Speer the Failed Architect.

THE CORRUPTION OF A PROFESSION

Speer failed architecture by corrupting his craft in a very common way. It is the old story of hubris, as Davidson calls it in his discerning foreward to Speer's autobiography.[30] As an architect, Speer sought pride and position and the opportunity to create on a heroic scale. In doing so, he defined success as an architect only in terms of the external goods it could provide, the ones that have little to do with the craft itself. As Speer said: "After years of frustrated efforts I was wild to accomplish things—and twenty-eight years old. For the commission to do a great building, I would have sold my soul like Faust." The soul he offered to his Mephistopheles was not just the one he was referring to; he offered his architectural soul as well. By seeking only the external goods of his profession, Speer eventually denied himself the moral distance and the moral direction it could provide.

Speer's corruption of architecture began in his break with his architectural mentor, Professor Heinrich Tessenow, a man whose work Speer described as "a champion of the spirit of simple craftsmanship in architecture and belief in architectonic expressiveness by severely delimited means. 'A minimum of pomp is the decisive factor.'"[31]

Tessenow taught the young Speer: "Style comes from the people. It is our nature to love our native land. There can be no true culture that is international. True culture comes only from the maternal womb of a nation." Speer and other students saw parallels between Tessenow's doctrine and the ideology of the National Socialists, but Tessenow did not, and he remained firmly opposed to Hitler. Despite his mentor's opposition, however, Speer, influenced by his National Socialist colleagues, joined the Party.

A few years later, when Speer showed Tessenow drawings he had done for an enthusiastic Hitler, Tessenow responded: "Do you think you have created something? It's showy, that's all."[32] Tessenow must have known that Hitler's cultural expressionism was mere ostentation, vanity, and pride and not a truthful reflection of the people at all. This was a style of architecture that could not spell out the uniqueness of the German people's engagement with the world, which is what Tessenow thought architecture should be doing. It was, instead, a mirrored reflection of Hitler, used as a cheap trick to manipulate those it claimed to represent. But the young Speer missed this lesson from his mentor. Grand praise from the Fuhrer more than compensated for his mentor's lack of respect for his work. By this move, Speer came to see his success as an architect as indistinguishable from recognition by the State and this, then, in the dictatorship that was Germany, reduced to recognition by Hitler alone. Speer became an architect obsessed with a single, immensely powerful and violent client whose pleasure defined success for him. Necessarily, as he sought self-respect as an architect from Hitler's praise, he rejected his craft.

For Hitler to serve well in its place, Speer needed desperately to admire this man who affirmed his being.[33]

> Only a few months before I had been carried away by the prospect of drafting and executing buildings. Now I was completely under Hitler's spell, unreservedly and unthinkingly held by him. I was ready to follow him anywhere. Yet his ostensible interest in me was only to launch me on a glorious career as an architect.[34]

This Speer mimics the infamous hired gun of legal ethics defining success by doing well whatever the client wants. As is true for the hired gun, however, Speer was not dominated by his client on architectural matters.[35] As he said: "If the architect's ideas ran counter to his own, Hitler was not stubborn: 'Yes, you're right, that's better.' The result was that I too was left with the feeling of creative independence." But also as is true for the hired gun, Speer tried to separate his architectural function from all others and, thus, his understanding of architectural matters—the grounds on which he was free to think for himself were very limited. "I am only concerned with what is legal," the hired gun says, "the rest is none of my business." And Speer echoes:

> I felt myself to be Hitler's architect. Political events did not concern me. My job was merely to provide impressive backdrops for such events. And this view was reinforced daily, for Hitler consulted me almost exclusively on architectural questions. . . . I felt that there was no need for me to take any political position at all. Nazi education, furthermore, aimed at separatist thinking; I was expected to confine myself to the job of building. The grotesque extent to which I clung to this illusion is indicated by a memorandum of mine to Hitler as late as 1944: "The task I have to fulfill is an unpolitical one. I have felt at ease in my work only so long as my person and my work were evaluated solely by the standard of practical accomplishments."[36]

Within the limited range in which he understood his work, Speer thought he retained his judgment. But it was not judgment he retained; it was only expertise. For Speer's problem was not that he could not judge what his client was doing, it was that he did not see such judgments as within his role. Speer thought that architecture could be separated from all else; he thought that the practical and the spiritual could be held apart, as he tried to hold politics apart from "practical accomplishments." But the world cannot be dissevered this way and neither can architecture, as Speer knew when he later looked upon the vast gilded eagle with its claws over the globe.[37]

Speer's drive to get ahead and what became of it—his corruption of his profession by seeking only external goods, in MacIntyre's now classic terms—is a very common form of corruption. It was a corruption of architecture by Speer as it would be a corruption of law, of medicine, of engineering, of business, of art, or of religion. This commonplace corruption best explains Speer's failure to reflect and not some lack of personal moral distance from his profession. The moral distance Speer needed for reflection was there to be found within the profession itself. The truth for Speer, something that sounds ironic only from the perspective of rebellious ethics, is that it was in further integration with architecture that he could have seen his responsibility for the world around him.

This truer story of Albert Speer is closer to home for us than the story of Speer the Pure Technician. Speer the Failed Architect draws us into his story in a way that rebellious ethics cannot. It says: We cannot escape the ghost of Speer by not taking our jobs so seriously. We can do so only by taking them more seriously in the right way.

Near the end of the war, Speer left his position as Hitler's architect to become Minister of Armaments. There was no discontinuity in this for him because he could achieve the external goods he sought as an architect just as well as a bureaucrat. By understanding success as tied to Hitler's approval, he was trying to live, as some other professionals do, by the prestige and power of his client rather than by the excellence of his craft. Accordingly, architecture itself became irrelevant and only Hitler's approval ultimately mattered. Speer, however, thought of his position as Minister of Armaments as a temporary departure from architecture. He continued to see himself as an architect because, as he put it, "I saw the possibility of winning a reputation, and even fame, as Hitler's architect whereas whatever even a prominent minister could accomplish would necessarily be absorbed in Hitler's glory." At this stage of his life, Speer could see no reason for being an architect other than the external goods it could provide.[38]

Ironically, it was as a bureaucrat, the archetypical role for the Pure Technicians we fear, that Speer turned upon Hitler. He did so for reasons that return us by an interesting route to his former mentor, Professor Tessenow. Speer began his separation from Hitler when he heard Hitler discussing the devastation of Warsaw. He saw Hitler "wantonly and without cause annihilating the city which he himself had called the most beautiful in Europe. . . . Within a few days," Speer goes on, "some of the contradictions in Hitler's nature had been revealed to me, although at the time I certainly did not perceive them in anything like their full intensity."[39]

From this point on, Speer turned steadily against Hitler. Later, he thought the morality he relied upon to support his opposition was a morality he learned from Hitler—one taken almost directly from the text of *Mein Kampf*, a text Speer had paid little attention to before. From *Mein Kampf* and from his colleagues, Speer began to understand the story in which he lived as one about the German people. He saw that the essential element of all he had done was that he was doing it for them. This element, this one remaining piece of integrity that made any sense of Speer's life at all, Hitler violated when he turned on the German people as the world began to corner him. Finally Speer was learning the lesson his mentor had offered so many years before: the difference between Tessenow's architectural need to spell out truthfully the German culture and the German people, and Hitler's use of the ideas of a culture and a people for personal political power. At the end of the war, we can see as Speer could not an immanent integrity in what could have been his life as an architect and how this would have shaped him and saved him from himself.

I am tempted to stop here. If I have told this story well, it makes my point, and if I have not, I probably will only make it worse with further explication. But if Suzi Gablik is right (and I believe she is) when she describes in *Has Modernism Failed?*[40] what happened to art when it adopted the artistic equivalent of rebellious ethics—how the practice of art became corrupted as artists sought only external success and security—and if art is our miner's canary, then what I have described as Speer's corruption of architecture may be what lies just ahead for all professions (if it has not yet arrived) as we continue within the paradigm of rebellious ethics. Rebellious ethics, in its effort to separate us from Speer, seems to leave us as morally exposed as Speer became. Are we not as obsessed with pride and position—or their more timid relative, security—as the young Speer was in rejecting his craft? Now I must wonder why this is so. Why does rebellious ethics fail us? The answer to this is, of course, a large task, too large for one article, but one component of the answer is that rebellious ethics cannot provide a conception of the self that rebels adequate to protect us from becoming as self-deceived as Albert Speer.

To return to our starting place, according to rebellious ethics, Speer the person, unlike Speer the Pure Technician, would have seen the horror around him. Rebellious ethics proclaims this because Speer is so much like us and we have faith in who we are. Speer needs to take his profession less seriously—far less seriously—and himself far more seriously. He performs this difficult moral task by constantly rebelling against his role as an architect. But who is this self that rebels? Who is this self that we must take so seriously? And who is this self that is so like us that we trust it?

THE ROLELESS PERSON

One answer is that this self is the authentic self of existentialist thought. To reflect from the broadest, and therefore the least limiting, perspective possible, the authentic self must not identify itself with any role. This moral rebel could not be Speer the German, nor Speer the Christian, nor Speer the citizen, nor Speer the father or husband, nor Speer as *a* Speer nor even Speer as Speer, because these are just other blinding roles, equally relativistic, reflection-limiting choices of a way of life—especially so, for some of them, in Nazi Germany. The moral rebel of rebellious ethics whose reflections we trust is Speer the Roleless Person. This, then, is one possible "self" rebellious ethics tells us to become for our reflections upon our professional roles if we are to avoid becoming Speer the Pure Technician.

If we have learned anything at all from postmodern philosophy, however, it is that our reflections always come from a particular perspective and both imply and need a teleology. Because this way of identifying the moral rebel does not examine the perspective or the teleology, it becomes not a faith in the moral rebel, but a faith in reflection alone. It is reflection, then, and not ourselves, that we must take more seriously. This faith in reflection is what Stanley Fish has called the "anti-foundationalist theory hope," and it is a bad faith because it leaves us as vulnerable to self-deception as Speer was.

Hauerwas and Burrell, as I have said, tell us that the story of Speer's life is a story of self-deception,[41] a self-deception that

> . . . was correlative to his identity as he clung to the story of being Hitler's apolitical architect. . . . He had no effective way to step back from himself, no place to stand. His self-deception began when he assumed that "being above all an architect" was a story sufficient to constitute his self. He had to experience the solitude of prison to realize that becoming a human being requires stories and images a good deal richer than professional ones, if we are to be equipped to deal with the powers of the world.[42]

Hauerwas and Burrell imply that we cannot remove this risk of self-deception with a belief in reflection alone because, without a complete and truthful account of the moral rebel against which self-deception can be measured and understood, we cannot know if we are self-deceived.[43] Thus, reduced as we are by rebellious ethics, we are easy prey for the twin demons of pride and position, especially, and ironically, when they are offered by a powerful and charismatic leader for whom the world is a simple place. So, with terrible irony, these efforts within the paradigm of rebellious ethics to separate ourselves from Speer the Pure Technician leave us open to the same moral failure he suffered.

MASTER STORIES

Rebellious ethics needs not, however, find its perspective for reflection in the Roleless Person. Another answer rebellious ethics can give to the question of this self we are to take more seriously is the answer Hauerwas and Burrell gave in the quotation above when they said: "[Speer] had to experience the solitude of prison to realize that becoming a human being requires stories and images a good deal richer than professional ones, if we are to be equipped to deal with the powers of the world." This answer does not suffer from a bad faith in reflection alone and, because it does not, it is willing to abandon the claim that we must reflect from the broadest perspective possible. This answer locates the self we must take more seriously in stories and images "a good deal richer than professional ones." Instead of asking Speer to be a good person we should ask that he be a good Christian, for example. Stories such as this one, Hauerwas and Burrell tell us, are more richly connected, and, because they are, permit us to spell out our full engagement with the world more truthfully.

There is much more sophistication in this version of rebellious ethics, but it is still rebellious ethics. Hauerwas and Burrell, who would be the first to find reflection alone, and the Roleless Person, thoroughly inadequate moral groundings, complain of Speer's failure to live by a "master story"[44] capable of providing him with the moral skills he needed. It is only within a "master story" that reflection has the power to recognize alternatives. The power, that is, to criticize and change.[45]

But even for Hauerwas and Burrell, we still distance ourselves from Speer by not taking our jobs so seriously. When we do, Speer the Failed Architect awaits us. For what Hauerwas and Burrell miss is that Speer's self-deception ran deeper than his belief "that 'being above all an architect' was a story sufficient to constitute his self."[46] Speer did not live by this belief. He did not, as they describe it, turn to his profession, for a "story [with which] to articulate the engagements he would be called upon to undertake."[47] He turned away from the story his profession offered him and turned, instead, toward himself in an act of corruption of his profession. When Speer says, as he often does in his autobiography, that he was "above all an architect," he was only deceiving himself further. He was above all Albert Speer.[48]

Hauerwas and Burrell's Speer is still Speer the Pure Technician. It is still his role as architect that another Speer within an overarching narrative must rebel against. This rebellion, it is true, is now grounded in a self located within the overarching narrative, and, therefore, it has a perspective and a teleology for its reflections. There is no doubt that such a Speer could criticize and change. But we cannot stop with this solution. We have to ask: What would Hauerwas and Burrell say to the Speer who was Hitler's architect *as he was* as Hitler's architect? Would their advice to live by a richer story be as powerful for him as it is for us looking back on his life? How would they have counseled him? We must ask these questions and ask them in this way, for this is the way we ask moral questions of ourselves. We are not looking back over our lives from outside our roles or our stories, but from within them.

Would it be possible for Hauerwas and Burrell to counsel the Nazi Speer about his need to find an overarching narrative for his life? Would they be reduced to seeking to impose upon him an overarching narrative in which they have found meaning? Would they counsel Speer by their own actions—actions they are moved to by their narrative? (I am sure they would.) But, if they did, would the Nazi Speer be capable of learning this moral lesson from them? Given Speer's description of his rejection of his past, of the inadequacies of his early education for critical thinking, of Hitler's techniques for isolating and compartmentalizing, of the lack of criticism around him, of his own hubris, and so forth, and given Hitler's promise to Speer that he would design the cities of a new empire, it would have been pointless to tell Speer that he should be living by a richer story. Speer himself says as much: "In spite of all our dissensions [the thought to resign my post in order to put an end to my contribution to Hitler's regime] did not come to me then and in a similar situation probably would not come to me today."[49] Interestingly, Speer's primary reaction to reading *The Observer's* article in 1944 was Faustian pride that he had been singled out for such recognition and a fear that others would be jealous of it.[50]

But there is another way for Hauerwas and Burrell to counsel Speer. They could seek a moral meeting ground with the Nazi Speer within the practice of architecture. In its potential for combining the spiritual and the practical there lies a way—and, perhaps, the only way—for the Nazi Speer to see his life as within a narrative of the sort Hauerwas and Burrell describe. In Hauerwas and Burrell's terms, it was only in architecture that Speer could have found the imaginative and intellectual skills sufficient to overcome those he used to create a web of illusion lending plausibility to his original deceptive policy.[51] This meeting ground, however, would be lost to Hauerwas and Burrell because they join the chorus of rebellious ethics telling Speer: Do not take your profession too seriously. In doing so, they too would have unwillingly moved the Nazi Speer to further separate the spiritual and the practical. And, if we are like Speer, we must be concerned that this move in professional ethics would do the same for us.

Surely, then, what was needed for Speer—and for us—it not a hierarchy of narratives, but the moral ability to see the interconnections between one narrative and another. The truth the church—the one in which Hauerwas and Burrell's overarching narrative lives—brings to architecture is not a truth that overarches. It is a vision and imagination formed by being in that church. It is the moral ability to speak the truth of architecture to it. What is needed, then, is the vision and the imagination to see how the good architect, and the good person and, for Hauerwas and Burrell and for me, the good Christian, can be one and the same. . . .

CONCLUSION

We can let Speer teach us to rebel against all roles, or we can, with Hauerwas and Burrell, bewail Speer's failure, and our own, to live by richer stories. The Roleless Person of rebellious ethics tells us to be *nothing* too seriously, for in commitment comes a limitation on the perspective for our reflections and it is our reflections that ground our morality. Hauerwas and Burrell say be something richer than that which our professional roles can provide. But we cannot ask the Nazi Speer to do either without rewriting his biography. And we cannot do either without distancing ourselves from Speer and from our own professional lives in ways that only disserve our efforts to understand his moral failure and, by understanding his, to understand our own. We are like Speer as we are now. In our obsessions with pride, position, and security, in our hubris, we are seeing our world through the eyes of our masters—those who can provide these goods for us—and not through our own. The method we have chosen for separating ourselves from Speer, rebellious ethics, ironically, only moves us closer to him.

My thanks to Robert Audi, Joe Allegretti, Ted Blumoff, Joe Claxton, Tom Eisele, Howard Lesnick, Dave Oedel, Richard Vance, and Sidney Watson for comments, to J. Shand Watson for an ongoing conversation on similar topics, and a very special thanks to Stanley Hauerwas, Michael Goldberg, and Tom Shaffer for their comments and encouragement. As usual, thanks also to Tedham Porterhouse for inspiration. With friends like these, I should have been able to get this right and none of them is to be blamed for my failure to do so.

QUESTIONS FOR DISCUSSION

1. In this chapter, Sammons offers an alternative to the traditional view of the ethics of a technological professional. What is that traditional view, and why does Sammons call it "rebellious ethics"? Do you know any contemporary cases of this kind of rebellious ethics?
2. What are the "moral lessons of architecture," and how do they help us have a deeper understanding of Speer's failures in morality? How do the moral lessons of architecture help us to understand the ethics of professional life today?
3. Should a technological professional pursue his or her craft primarily for the external goods that are a reward for doing well—goods such as money, power, and fame? What are the other goals of a professional career? How does the life and career of Speer help us answer these questions?
4. According to Sammons, the true path to a morally sound technology is for technological professionals to take their craft more seriously. What does Sammons mean by this, and how does the life and career of Speer exemplify the wrong path?

NOTES

1. He saw, for example, as Minister of Armaments, the need to create an improvisational style for organizations if the Germans were to match the creativity of the allies. He knew enough about German authoritarianism to

understand its proclivity toward complex organizational structures that reduce efficiency by searching too hard for it. Albert Speer, *Inside the Third Reich* (New York: Avon Books, 1970), 212–13.

2. "[H]e treats ends as given, as outside his scope; his concern is with technique. . . ." Alasdair MacIntyre, *After Virtue* (Notre Dame: University of Notre Dame Press, 1984), 30. MacIntyre is describing the character "The Manager."

3. Stanley Hauerwas and David Burrell, "Self-Deception and Autobiography: Reflections on Speer's *Inside the Third Reich,*" in Hauerwas, *Truthfulness and Tragedy* (Notre Dame: University of Notre Dame Press, 1977), 83–84.

4. Speer, 21.

5. Speer, 376.

6. Speer, 375.

7. Speer, 521. This passage is from Speer's speech at Nuremberg. Emphasis has been added.

8. By condemning Speer as an architect I do not mean that he failed in ways that might be called artistic, although it is true that he did. (The relationship between artistic failure of this sort and the failure I describe is surely a very complex one.) This is not what I mean by his failure to be a good architect, for there are many good architects who fail in artistic ways.

9. "Self-Deception," *supra* n. 3.

10. Speer says that he denied "my own past, my upper-middle-class origins, and my previous environment" when he joined the Nazi party. Speer, 20.

11. The expression is Eugene Davidson's, from Speer, Introduction, p. xviii.

12. Hauerwas and Burrell notice this as well. "Self-Deception," 92.

13. "This love for vast proportions was not only tied up with the totalitarian cast of Hitler's regime. Such tendencies, and the urge to demonstrate one's strength on all occasions, are characteristic of quickly acquired wealth. . . . Hitler's demand for huge dimensions, however, involved more than he was willing to admit to the workers. He wanted the biggest of everything to glorify his works and magnify his pride. These monuments were an assertion of his claim to world dominion long before he dared to voice any such intention even to his closest associates." Speer, 69.

14. Speer, 138.

15. Speer, 79.

16. Speer, 184.

17. Speer, 184.

18. Speer, 359, quoting Hitler.

19. Speer, 33. "The departure from reality, which was visibly spreading like a contagion, was no peculiarity of the National Socialist regime. But in normal circumstances people who turn their backs on reality are soon set straight by the mockery and criticism of those around them, which makes them aware they have lost credibility. In the Third Reich there were no such correctives, especially for those who belonged to the upper stratum. On the contrary, every self-deception was multiplied as in a hall of distorting mirrors, becoming a repeatedly confirmed picture of a fantastical dream world which no longer bore any relationship to the grim outside world. In those

mirrors, I could see nothing but my own face reproduced many times over. No external factors disturbed the uniformity of hundreds of unchanging faces, all mine." Speer, 291. Here Speer is telling us quite directly that rebellious ethics' concern with people reflecting upon themselves would not have worked for him.

20. David Kolb, *Postmodern Sophistications: Philosophy, Architecture and Tradition* (Chicago: University of Chicago Press, 1990), 2.
21. Speer, 19.
22. Speer, 32.
23. Speer, 523.
24. Speer, 523.
25. Speer, 159.
26. Speer, 291.
27. Speer, 375.
28. Eugene Davidson in Speer, Introduction, p. xviii.
29. Speer, 63.
30. Eugene Davidson in Speer, Introduction, p. xviii. Understanding this as a story of hubris ties Speer more closely to Marlowe's Faust. See Christopher Marlowe, *The Tragical History of the Life and Death of Doctor Faustus.* Rollo May describes Marlowe's Faust's hubris as "the refusal to accept the human role." Rollo May, *The Cry for Myth* (New York: Norton & Co., 1991), 231.
31. Speer, 11.
32. Speer, 27.
33. Speer's architectural staff could see Hitler quite differently, but he could not. Speer described one meeting of his architects with Hitler: "Neither the environment, with its innumerable generals, adjuncts, guard areas, barriers and passes, nor the aureole that this whole apparatus conferred upon Hitler, could intimidate these specialists. Their many years of successful practice of their professions gave them a clear sense of their rank and their responsibility. Sometimes the conversation developed into a heated discussion for they quite often forgot whom they were addressing." Speer, 232. Speer could not develop a sense of his rank and responsibility other than by never forgetting who Hitler was, for his rank and his responsibility did not grow out of architecture, but out of his being Hitler's architect. During conferences such as the one just described, Speer kept himself "in the background as far as possible." Speer, 232.
34. Speer, 49.
35. Speer, 79–80. For an excellent discussion of the metaphor of the hired gun in legal ethics, see Joseph Allegretti, "Have Briefcase Will Travel: An Essay on the Lawyer as Hired Gun," 24 *Creighton L. Rev.* 747 (1991).
36. Speer, 112.
37. Speer, 120. Hitler understood the connection very well indeed. This is part of what made him so genuinely evil.
38. Speer, 198.
39. Speer, 173.
40. Suzi Gablik, *Has Modernism Failed?* (New York: Thames and Hudson, 1984).

41. "Self-Deception," *supra*, n. 3.
42. "Self-Deception," 91–93.
43. Teachers of professional ethics constantly encounter one aspect of the problem of the moral rebel—the one Hauerwas and Burrell describe—although we seldom recognize it as such. It is there in the rapidly shifting postures of our students and ourselves as we respond to the varied problems of professional life from a variety of perspectives with expressions of little more than our own prejudices. As we respond, we often do so from perspectives and with prejudices that are profoundly at odds with one another. My students sometimes answer, as I do, as Southerners; sometimes as Georgians or South Georgians; sometimes as Christians or Jews; sometimes as family; sometimes as lawyers; sometimes as gentlemen; sometimes as liberals; sometimes as students; and so on. This is what becomes of the moral rebel on whom our ethical rebellion depends because postmodern philosophy is correct and our deepest intuitions turn out not to be universal at all, but cultural and role-bound. Rather than finding one roleless moral rebel, we find, as our students do, that we are many people and that we occupy many roles. Who we are and which role we occupy as we address the problems of professional life is determined more as a reaction to the ways in which the various requirements of role are described and presented to us for moral consideration than as a reflection of any integrity in our own lives. Rebellious ethics' faith in reflection alone, then, is surely a bad faith because without a unifying understanding of the perspective from which we reflect and the teleology with which we reflect, and without some way of ordering our roles, it is very hard to understand how the product of our rebellious reflections could be anything other than the shifting prejudices of various points of view, or how these shifting prejudices could offer protection against self-deception.
44. This use of the term "master story" is from Michael Goldberg, *Jews and Christians, Getting Our Stories Straight: The Exodus and the Passion-Resurrection* (Philadelphia: Trinity Press International, 1991), pp. 13–15. By "master story" he meant "the kind of core foundational narrative that, in providing a community with its paradigmatic 'model of understanding the world . . . and guide for acting in it' (13), simultaneously gives rise to that community's most elementary, and often most distinctive, convictions about reality." See also Michael Goldberg, "God, Action, and Narrative: Which Narrative? Which Action? Which God?" *Journal of Religion*, 68, 1 (January 1988), 39–56, reprinted in Stanley Hauerwas and L. Gregory Jones, eds. *Why Narrative? Readings in Narrative Theology* (Grand Rapids: Eerdmans, 1989), 348–365. The master story Hauerwas and Burrell have in mind is the Christian one. I do not, however, mean to limit my criticism of his use of master stories to religious ones although I am certainly open to the argument that only religious stories properly qualify under Goldberg's definition of the term. I wish, instead, to criticize the method by which Hauerwas and Burrell resort to master stories to provide a perspective for moral reflection outside the professional role, and I believe this particular criticism applies more broadly and includes secular ideologies such as Marxism that perhaps would not qualify definitionally as master stories.

45. "As one architectural assignment followed another, Speer had less and less reason to spell out the engagement he had begun. He knew what he was doing; he was an architect. No more was needed." And: "So Speer's new position [as Minister of Armaments] did not require him to rethink the master image of his life: he continued to be above all an architect." "Self-Deception," 92.
46. "Self-Deception," 93.
47. "Self-Deception," 94.
48. Speer falsely made himself the center of existence, as did Hitler. By doing so, he never became a true apprentice to the craft of architecture because architecture requires that the apprentice initially submit to the authority of the craft in order to become the type of person excellence in the craft requires one to be. See Alasdair MacIntyre, *Three Rival Versions of Moral Enquiry* (Notre Dame: Univ. of Notre Dame Press, 1990), 51–81, for a description of this understanding of craft as Thomist and as emerging from the *Gorgias* and the *Republic.*
49. Speer, 339.
50. Speer, 344–45.
51. "Self-Deception," 86. Let me provide one simple example. I am a law professor, a lawyer, and a little league coach. If a friend needs to counsel me for my lawyering on the point that it is not whether you win or lose but how you play the game, they can do this best for me by reminding me that I am a little league coach. By making that connection for me, my friend would help me spell out my own self-deceptions because little league coaching within a community of good baseball people has given me some of the skill I need to see beyond the apparent seriousness of the moment.

CHAPTER 9

Genetic and Racial Theories in the Nazi War on Cancer

──────────────── \|/ ────────────────

The Nazi regime was profoundly racist. It is not an exaggeration to say that the foundation of Nazi ideology was a particular view of biology that postulated the superiority of the German (Aryan or Nordic) race and the inferiority of Jews, Gypsies, the dark-skinned, and Asians. This chapter, the first of two that consider the role of biology and medicine in the Third Reich, is an excerpt from historian of science Robert N. Proctor's book *The Nazi War on Cancer* (1999). Proctor explains how the genetic and racial theories of Nazism affected the medical research establishment in Germany before and during the war, particularly in regard to the fight against cancer. The Nazi worldview was committed to the idea of biological determinism—the theory that the genetic characteristics of race determined all traits in individuals. But the evidence for the inheritability of cancer (or the predisposition to cancer) was, at best, ambiguous. Environmental and lifestyle factors also seemed to play a part in the development and prevention of cancer (as we know today). Nazi doctors nevertheless were optimistic regarding the war against cancer: proper lifestyle changes (avoiding smoking, alcohol, and meat) and the elimination of a noxious genetic heritage (preventing the intermarriage of Aryans and Jews) could help to eradicate cancer among the "higher" civilizations, such as the Aryan empire. Nazi doctors were influenced by their racial theories to believe that Jews were the cause of cancer, particularly as merchants of tobacco and other harmful products—being merchants, of course, was a genetically based racial characteristic of Jews. The Nazi theory of biology also influenced industrial policy, for certain races—blacks, for example—were considered less prone to cancer and thus could be employed in industries where the cancer risk was high. It is interesting to see that the Nazi biological vision of Aryan racial superiority played a significant role in a public health policy that was considered important by the Nazi regime. Once again, we can conclude that scientific and technological principles are partially determined by social and political forces.

From *The Nazi War on Cancer*

Robert N. Proctor

> We have the duty, if necessary, to die for the Fatherland; why should we not also have the duty to be healthy? Has the Führer not explicitly demanded this?
>
> *Robert Hofstätter, antitobacco activist, 1939*

Biological determinism was one of the pillars of Nazi ideology. Nazi philosophers argued that biology is destiny and that "diseases" as diverse as diabetes and divorce are genetically anchored. The Nazi imagination ran wild in this territory, claiming racial, genetic, or "constitutional" predispositions for every conceivable human talent and disability. Criminality was said to be heritable—and not just criminality, but specific forms of crime (rape, embezzlement, etc.). The racial zealot Hans F. K. Günther claimed that the tendency to divorce was heritable, and Fritz Lenz of Munich went so far as to argue that the tendency to believe in Lamarckism—the doctrine of the inheritance of acquired characteristics— was inborn. The most prominent Lamarckians were Jews, he suggested, in consequence of their inborn drive to assimilate, to blend in—a kind of human variant of the "animal mimicry" common in the rest of the animal kingdom.[1]

CANCER AND THE JEWISH QUESTION

Consistent with this ideology, a number of German physicians argued that cancer, too, was a genetic disease, a disease to which different individuals and races were susceptible in differing degrees. The idea that cancer runs in families was already an old one, dating back at least to Friedrich Hoffmann's postulate, circa 1700, of a *haereditaria dispositio.*[2] Statistical explorations of cancer's heritability proliferated in the nineteenth century (always rather crude, one must say), and by the early years of the twentieth century, evidence had accumulated that certain cancers of the eye (retinoblastoma), colon cancers, and at least some breast cancers could be passed from parent to offspring via the germ cells.[3] Twin studies fueled the idea that at least some cancers might be heritable, and by the 1930s a multitude of such studies claimed to have proven a genetic predisposition.[4] Certain families were said to be immune: a 1938 study of one Croatian noble lineage claimed to have found that among 133 members of this well-documented family there was not a single instance of cancer over a period spanning nearly two hundred years.[5]

Early hints of the idea that chromosomal events might be involved in carcinogenesis began to be discussed in the 1910s and 1920s, following the rediscovery of Mendelian genetics in 1900 and the work of Theodor Boveri and others. Fritz Lenz, the Munich-based racial hygienist, suggested in 1921 that cancers must arise from the mutation of somatic cell tissues by external agents (X-rays and alcohol, for instance),[6] but the most important advocate of the mutation theory was a young Heidelberg surgeon by the name of Karl Heinrich Bauer—a man whose career reveals the forgotten but formative role played by eugenics in the progress of certain sciences.

Best known today as the first postwar president of the University of Heidelberg and founding director of Germany's National Cancer Institute (in Heidelberg in 1964), Bauer was also an avid and early supporter of eugenics, albeit of a fairly innocuous stripe. His 1926 book on racial hygiene called for sterilization of inferior stocks and marital bans, while opposing the "craziness of certain racial fanatics" who proposed the wholesale elimination of "lives unworthy of living." He was not a big believer in cancer's heritability, but his enthusiasm for more traditional eugenics—to combat the breeding of the feebleminded, for example—led him to coauthor the official technical manual for the Nazi-era Sterilization Law, published in 1936. His efforts in such areas later earned him the scorn of postwar student activists who occupied his Heidelberg office in 1968 and charged him with Nazi collaboration[7]—not entirely fairly, I would argue. Bauer never joined the Nazi party: he apparently could not have joined, given that his wife, the daughter of an admiral, was one-fourth Jewish, a particularity that also barred him from military service (and may have saved his postwar career).

In 1928, Bauer published the first book-length treatise postulating somatic mutation as the initial event in cancerous growth.[8] (Somatic mutation means changes in the body's nonreproductive cells—as opposed to changes in the "germ line" reproductive cells, like sperm and eggs.) The American geneticist Hermann J. Muller had recently shown that X-rays could cause mutations in the sperm cells of fruit flies, and Bauer used this to argue that since X-rays could cause cancer, then cancer, too, must be regarded as a product of mutation. Bauer's formulation was simple, and sweeping: "Any form of radiant energy capable of producing mutations is also capable of causing cancer." His somatic mutation hypothesis was widely accepted by the late 1930s—especially among eugenicists; Otmar von Verschuer in his racial hygiene textbook, for example, stated bluntly that malignant tumors could be regarded as "somatic mutations."[9] The mutation theory was attractive to eugenicists worrying about the corruption of the human genetic stock; some of these concerns sound plausible and or even prescient to us today (worries about X-rays and tobacco, for example); others strike us as misconceived, if not horrific (genetic harms from racial intermixing, for example).

In the common understanding of the 1920s and 1930s, genetic variation implied racial variation. It is hardly surprising, therefore, that German scientists sometimes postulated racial predispositions to account for the fact that people in different parts of the world suffered from cancer in differing degrees. Germans, Jews, and Scandinavians, for example, were said to contract cancer more readily than Latins, Slavs, and Celts.[10] Differences in cancer rates among white and black Americans were already well known (the most common view being that blacks were more "resistant"),[11] but cancer rates were also said to vary between Jews and other European peoples. Cancer studies in the Ukraine in the early 1930s, for example, seemed to indicate that elderly Jews were more than twice as likely to die of cancer as elderly Ukrainians or Russians; Jews were found to suffer exceptionally high rates of stomach cancer and low rates of uterine, genital, and breast cancer.[12]

Results such as these were sometimes used as proof of Jewish bodily inferiority. We should recall this as a time of efforts to pathologize the Jewish body: Jews were said to have bad eyes, flat feet, and bad backs, along with high rates of mental infirmity, sexual deficiency, and homosexuality.[13] Jewish diseases were alternately said to be diseases of poverty or of wealth; Jewish stomach cancer, for example, was sometimes said to be a sign, as historian Sander Gilman has noted, of the Jews' "intense striving after wealth."[14] Nazi physicians selectively drew from those parts of this literature that could be used to establish Jewish physical and mental deficiency. This was one reason Germans and Jews were instructed not to intermarry: Reich Physicians' Führer Gerhard Wagner claimed that the mixing of

Jewish and non-Jewish blood would spread the "diseased genes" of the "bastardized" Jewish race into the "relatively pure" European stocks.[15]

Today, most of the world's variation in cancer rates is recognized as due either to some kind of reporting bias (people with poor access to health care often look as if they have low cancer rates, when in fact they simply do not get fully counted in statistical surveys) or to reseachers' failure to take into account age profiles;[16] alternatively, there may be something about dietary or tobacco habits or exposure to pathogens that would explain the difference. But in the hyperracialized biologism of an earlier age, geographic and ethnic variations were often taken as proof of inborn racial predispositions. Cesare Lombroso, the Italian father of criminal biology, claimed that the Jews of Verona were twice as likely to suffer from cancer as Veronese Christians. Many Americans regarded Negroes as relatively immune[17]—a consequence, it is now recognized, of the failure properly to count all the tumors in this population. At the First International Conference on Cancer in London in 1928, Alfredo Niceforo of Naples and Eugene Pittard of Geneva claimed that *Homo alpinus* and *Homo nordicus* (the Alpine and Nordic types) had the highest rates of cancer among the "native" anthropological types in Europe, owing to their higher cancer "receptivity."[18] Italians were sometimes said to be cancer resistant—an idea that led some Americans to argue that intermarriage with Italian women would confer cancer resistance on the offspring.[19] Jews were said to be particularly susceptible to tumors of the "neuromyo-arterial glomus," while at the same time being virtually immune to cancer of the penis.[20]

In Germany, opinions differed concerning whether Jews were more or less vulnerable to cancer. Berlin's mortality tables for 1905 showed that 8.6 percent of all Jewish deaths were from cancer, compared to only 6 percent for Christians, but faith in such data was not always strong, and evidence was also growing that for some kinds of cancer, Jews were actually less vulnerable. The requirement (circa 1900) that cause of cancer deaths be recorded according to site in the body (lung, stomach, etc.), prompted new speculation about who was vulnerable or immune to particular kinds of cancer. The gynecologist Adolf Theilhaber noted that Jewish men had higher rates of stomach and intestinal cancer, but very little penis cancer. The rarity of Jewish uterine cancer was most often attributed to the ritual practice of (male) circumcision, but the Jewish neurologist Leopold Löwenfeld offered a "constitutional" explanation: Jews began their menstrual periods earlier and therefore had more blood in the uterus and were less likely, as a result, to contract uterine cancer. This was typical, he claimed, of people of the "plethoric" constitutional type.[21]

Hints of racial propensities also came from laboratory studies, which had already shown by the 1920s that strains of mice could be bred that were more or less receptive to the uptake of cancer tissue transplants, or more or less vulnerable to the agency of carcinogens.[22] SS chief Heinrich Himmler was apparently intrigued by the prospect of breeding a race of cancer-prone rats: in a 1939 meeting with Sigmund Rascher, the notorious Dachau hypothermia experimenter, the SS Reichsführer proposed breeding such a race of rodents to be released in German cities to control the rat population. It is not yet clear how far such far-fetched plans were ever carried out.[23]

Animal experimental evidence was extrapolated to humans, bolstered by the ideological push to see all aspects of human behavior—including purported racial differences—as rooted in "blood," race, or genes. Otmar Freiherr von Verschuer, director of the Frankfurt Institute for Racial Hygiene and mentor to Dr. Josef Mengele of Auschwitz, argued that Jews suffer disproportionately not just from diabetes, flat feet, hemophilia, and deafness, but also from xeroderma pigmentosum, a heritable childhood disease that results in multiple cancers of the skin, and muscular tumors (the latter ailment shared also with "coloreds" [*Farbige*]). TB, interestingly, was the only disease Verschuer considered to be less frequent in Jews, a consequence, he claimed, of the "evolutionary adaptation" of Jews to urban life.[24]

Clear-cut evidence of cancer's heritability, however, turned out to be more elusive than many cancer researchers had hoped. Karl Heinrich Bauer in 1937 used twin studies to argue that cancer was overwhelmingly a disease of "external" environmental origins: why else would identical twins so rarely have the same kind of cancer?[25] In 1940, Bauer argued that there were other reasons cancers should be regarded as exogenous in origins. For one thing, there was the fact that heritability was obvious in only a very few cancers. Xeroderma pigmentosum, neuroblastomas of the retina, and polyposis of the colon were well-known examples, but these were all quite rare. There was also the fact that men and women could have very different cancer rates. Cancer of the larynx, for example, was twenty times more common in men than in women, and lung cancer was five or ten times as likely to strike a man as a woman. Could male and female lungs really be so different—or were environmental influences involved? Lip and stomach cancers were also found more than twice as often among males, though with gallbladder cancer the ratios were reversed (women were six or seven times more likely to suffer the disease). It was hard to see how heredity could explain such differences. Male and female lungs and lips and stomachs were not obviously different in any relevant aspect; the more satisfactory explanation, Bauer suggested—correctly, as it turned out—was that something in the environments of the two sexes—smoking or drinking habits, for examples—must be responsible for the differences. He also pointed out that cancer might well "run in families" for no other reason than that people in those families may be exposed to a common environment, as in the families of Schneeberg's uranium miners, longtime sufferers from lung cancer.[26]

"Lifestyle" theories of carcinogenesis were actually quite popular in the Nazi era—even among committed Nazis. In 1939, in a long review of world cancer trends, Arthur Hintze, a leading Berlin radiologist and professor of surgery, argued that dietary habits and religious practices were important in explaining cancer rates on different parts of the planet. Stomach cancer, for example, was the most common cause of cancer death in both Europe and Japan, but the same disease was rare in Calcutta, accounting for less than 1 percent of all malignancies. The difference in the Indian case seemed to have little to do with race; rather, it appeared to stem from economic constraints and religious practices that led local populations to consume very little alcohol and almost no meat. Lifestyle factors also seemed to be at work in the rarity of stomach cancer among the Malays living in Java and Sumatra: one large autopsy study of 3,885 Malays in Batavia found only a single gastric malignancy, a fairly common disease among the Europeans and Chinese living in that part of the world. Hintze pointed out that most of the Malays were Muslims and therefore avoided alcohol and meat—habits which led to low stomach cancer rates also among the predominantly Buddhist Sinhalese of Ceylon. Lifestyle factors were similarly responsible for the high rates of genital and bladder cancers among Arabs in the Middle East, a situation that, he explained, following Sigismund Peller (a Jew whose books had been banned, interestingly), was most likely a consequence of infection by pathogens such as bilharzia and the syphilis spirochete.

Hintze did not deny that different individuals and perhaps even different races were unequally susceptible to the influence of carcinogens (he mentions the fact that light-skinned peoples are more vulnerable to sun-induced skin cancer); he simply claimed that environmental and lifestyle factors played a stronger role than was sometimes acknowledged. The upshot: we should not be fatalistic in thinking of cancer as an unavoidable accompaniment of civilization. Hintze also noted that demographic variables were the root cause of many "racial" variations: Africans, for example, were often observed to have high sarcoma rates—though part of the reason, he explained, was that these were cancers which most often struck at an early age. Africans did not live as long as some other peoples, giving rise to the (false) impression that sarcomas were a particular weakness of the Negro race. He also suggested that the idea that Africans were particularly vulnerable to benign tumors might have something to do with non-Africans' failure to appreciate the widespread cosmetic practice of ritual scarring.[27]

[Despite his interest in environmental and lifestyle factors, Hintze] was a dedicated Nazi who profited directly from the expulsion of Jews at the Rudolf Virchow Hospital. Cancer was common among the young in certain populations, he speculated, because those populations were "closer to the youth of humanity"—meaning humans' evolutionary ancestors. He also disagreed with the American Frederick L. Hoffman's perception that cancer rates as a whole were on the rise in civilized nations. Hoffman, in his view, had failed to take into account the aging of the population, whereas properly age-adjusted cancer death rates (for Switzerland in the period 1901–1933, for instance) actually showed *falling* rates. Lung cancer was the only clear-cut exception, and its rise was more than balanced by declines in other kinds of tumors. [Hellmut] Haubold—an SS man as well as a party member—was his ally in stating that cancer was not an ineluctable consequence of "culture" (or civilization). His upbeat conclusion: culture has been conquering and will continue to conquer cancer.[28]

Lifestyle cancer theories were put forward even by a number of men (and almost all were men) whose primary focus was on genetic (or "racial") disease. Otmar von Verschuer's 1941 racial hygiene textbook stated not just that cancers were "somatic mutations" but that heredity contributed only trivially to cross-cultural variations in cancer incidence. Clear-cut heritable cancer syndromes accounted for less than 1 percent of all cancers, in his view.[29] Even Jewish cancer inclinations were often explained by environmental etiologies. In 1940, Martin Staemmler and Edeltraut Bieneck—both influential Nazi physicians—noted that Jewish birthrates had declined considerably in recent years and that there was therefore a higher proportion of elderly among Jews than among non-Jews. This helped account for the higher Jewish mortality rates from disorders such as cancer, diabetes, and circulatory failure; it also helped explain their lower death rates for tuberculosis and other infectious diseases, ailments that most commonly struck the young.[30] The much-commented-upon rarity of Jewish penis and cervical cancer was sometimes given a racial explanation, though, as already noted, it was more often—and correctly—traced to the ritual practice of circumcision. (Penis cancer was also observed to be rare among Muslims who practiced ritual circumcision.) Hintze in 1939 went so far as to celebrate circumcision as "the only definite example" of how "cultural measures" could help prevent cancer; circumcision was a case where "culture has conquered cancer."[31]

How curious to hear a Nazi doctor in 1939 defending the health benefits of a Jewish ceremonial rite! Scientists at this time were in fact divided over what to attribute to nature, what to nurture—at least when it came to cancer. Generalizing, it seems that "nature" in the Nazi view of the world was looked to to explain diseases that seemed to appear in excess in Jews, while "nurture" was invoked to account for diseases from which Jews appeared to be exempt. When it came to cancer, however, opinions remained divided—for reasons I shall indicate in a moment.

More common than racial explanations were efforts to determine whether certain "constitutional body types" were predisposed to cancer, or cancer-causing behaviors—like smoking or alcohol abuse.[32] Fritz Lickint suggested that genetic factors might be involved in the addiction of certain people to tobacco or narcotics; Hans Weselmann postulated that the "vegetative-labile" type was less able to tolerate nicotine and was therefore less likely to smoke (and contract cancer).[33] Hofstätter in the 1920s put the matter bluntly, if anecdotally: "It seems to me that the Jewish race is more prone to nicotine addiction than the Aryan race. . . . Among the female smokers I know, those who smoke the most are three Jews and one Aryan woman. I know of no red-haired woman who smokes heavily, and only one blond."[34]

It was widely recognized by this time that darker skin pigmentation protected against sun-induced skin cancer; the Munich radiologist Friedrich Voltz, editor of the *Radiologische Rundschau*, took this further and proposed that the "red-blond constitutional type" was more vulnerable to cancers in general,[35] and even that the cancers of different races responded differently to X-ray therapeutics (he maintained that tumors in the "red-blond type" responded less favorably than did tumors in other races).[36] Robert Ritter, the Tübingen psychiatrist and Gypsy "expert" (read: murderer), wrote an entire essay on "red hair as a problem of racial hygiene," hinting at, among other things, a cancer predisposition.[37] The factory physician Wilhelm Hergt suggested that "blonds with delicate complexions" were more likely to fall victim to occupational cancers than were "stout and well-fed persons,"[38] and some physicians argued that the diverse races of the world harbored different predispositions to addictive drugs. Thus blacks were said to prefer hashish, Asians opium, and "Nordic" Europeans alcohol.[39] A 1940 medical thesis claimed that cigar smoking was most common among the "pyknic" and "sclerotic" types (Winston Churchill was the example given), while slender leptosomes—the typical Bavarian farmer—stood out among the users of snuff.[40]

The story of Jews and cancer is rather more subtle and scurrilous than what I have presented thus far: Jews were not just said to be either more or less prone to cancer; Jews were also said to be the *purveyors* of cancer, in various and sundry ways. The 1941 conference celebrating the founding of Jena's antitobacco institute blamed Jews for introducing tobacco into Germany, and Jews were charged with dominating the tobacco import centers of Amsterdam.[41] Jews were also said to trade in other dangerous products. Hugo Kleine in a popular book on nutrition blamed "capitalist special interests" and "masculinized Jewish half-women" (*jüdischer Emanzipierter und vermännlichter Halbweiber*) for the deterioration of German foods—one consequence of which was cancer.[42] Jews were not just disproportionately immune or susceptible to cancer; Jews were also accused of being one of its causes.

SELECTION AND STERILIZATION

One should keep in mind, of course, that there were practical, one could say surgical, implications at this time for whether a particular disease was classed as heritable. The 1933 Sterilization Law (Gesetz zur Verhütung erbkranken Nachwuchses) provided for the sterilization of a broad class of genetic defectives, and familial cancers were sometimes categorized as falling under the rubric of the law.[43] Prof. Wilhelm Clausen of Halle, for example, in 1936 argued that children suffering from retinoblastoma, a familial cancer of the eye, should be sterilized. (He did not believe that people with lesser forms of hereditary blindness—such as color or night blindness or blindness in consequence of minor albinism—should be sterilized.)[44] Fischer-Wasels was another outspoken supporter of sterilization to prevent the breeding of cancerous human stocks. In a 1934 article in *Strahlentherapie*, the Frankfurt pathologist claimed that "much that is good" could be achieved "by removing the heavily burdened families from the reproductive community, by preventing the combination and expression of afflicted genes."[45] The cancers in question included tumors of the nerve and kidney stem cells, neuroblastomas of the adrenal gland and sympathetic nerves, and certain heritable kidney cancers (nephromas) and childhood cancers of the retina (retinoblastomas). These were by no means common cancers, but the fact that they were highly heritable and often killed at an early age mandated sterilization, in his view, to prevent their being passed on into future generations.[46]

There were also implications of a more subtle nature. We do not yet know whether the notion of "red-blond" types being more vulnerable to cancer led radiologists to be less prudent in their irradiation of darker-skinned individuals, but we do have evidence that the idea of differential racial susceptibility was used to screen workers in carcinogenic industries.[47] In November of 1934, for example, at a meeting of the German Society for Industrial Hygiene, Prof. Gunther Lehmann of Dortmund's Kaiser Wilhelm Institute for Labor Physiology found that workers differed substantially in how well their noses filtered out the silica (quartz) dust known to cause silicosis, a much-feared hazard of mining, foundry work, porcelain making, sandblasting, gem cutting, and other trades where large volumes of rock dust were inhaled. Lehmann constructed an apparatus by which dust could be blown into the upper air passages of a worker, retrieving it through the mouth to see how much had been filtered out (presumably avoiding lung contamination during the test).[48]

Lehmann found that while noses with "exceptionally good filtering capacity" were able to capture 60 percent or more of the dust introduced, there were also noses that allowed almost all of the dust to enter the lungs. He used his apparatus to examine several hundred miners and found that those who had remained healthy after sixteen years tended to have much better nasal filtration than those who had fallen ill from silicosis. He also found that "mouth breathers" were more likely to contract the disease than "nose breathers." The Dortmund professor concluded that nasal filtration was probably the single most important factor predisposing an individual to silicosis, and he recommended that only persons found to have good dust-capturing capacity be allowed to work in trades where silicosis was a danger.[49] The device was apparently widely used, though not everyone agreed on its ability to identify susceptible workers.[50]

There are many similar cases of predisposition screening from this era. In 1939, when scientists from Berlin's Institute for Radiological Research conducted experiments on the human response to ultraviolet radiation, they deliberately selected "darkly pigmented brunettes" on the grounds that such people would be less susceptible to the harmful effects of the rays.[51] Miners were regularly X-rayed for early signs of lung disease, and suspect workers were dismissed. This was consistent with a paternalistic philosophy that saw workers as abstract inputs in the production process. The point in most such efforts was to adapt the worker to the workplace, rather than vice versa.

Racism played an important role in conceptions of who was vulnerable to cancer and who was not—and not just in Germany. An idea commonly heard in occupational health circles even after the war was that people of darker complexion were better suited for work in cancerous industries. Wilhelm Hueper, the American pioneer of environmental carcinogenesis and a guiding light for Rachel Carson, suggested in his 1942 magnum opus that "colored races" were "markedly refractory to the carcinogenic effect exerted upon the skin by tar, pitch, and mineral oils." Hueper argued that "the natural oiliness of the skin of Negroes seems to protect their skin against the irritative and carcinogenic action of many industrially used chemicals, as occupational dermatitis and cutaneous cancer is rarely seen in Negroes." The German expatriate admitted that the entire question of "racial resistance" was controversial and in flux, illustrating this with the example of changing views on the rarity of penile cancer among Jews. While this had originally been considered a racial characteristic, the view now accepted by "the great majority of investigators" was that the rarity was the result of the practice of circumcision.[52] Hueper nonetheless remained convinced, however, that Africans were physically less vulnerable to occupational cancers of the skin. As late as 1956, he was claiming that dark-skinned persons were more appropriate choices for work in industries with a substantial cancer danger[53]—a view at odds with the increasingly antiracialist ideas of mainstream American social science. Hueper successfully defended himself against the charge that he was a Nazi—along with charges that he was a communist—but his views on race remained strikingly similar to those of his former compatriots across the Atlantic.

Nazism transformed German cancer research and policy in many different spheres: in the language of research, in concepts of causality, in the bolstering or banishment of individuals and institutions, in the kinds of questions asked and the day-to-day ways patients interacted with their doctors. Nazism privileged the racial, the radical, and the rapid; Nazi policies would survey, sort, and screen to an extent never seen before, fighting carcinogens and cancer carriers and even "cancer fears" with the goal of creating a secure and sanitary utopia. Hans Auler, the Berlin professor who climbed in the cancer research ranks and managed to catch Goebbels's eye, saw the Nazi regime itself as anticarcinogenic:

> It is fortunate for German cancer patients, and for anyone threatened by cancer, that the Third Reich has grounded itself on the maintenance of German health. The most important measures of the government—in genetics, education, sports, postgraduate service, physical education in the Hitler Youth, SA, and SS, marital loans, home hygiene, settlements, work service, and so forth—can all be regarded as prophylactic measures against cancer.[54]

Small wonder that Auler captured the attention of Joseph Goebbels, who not only discussed his ideas with the Führer but also awarded him the hefty sum of RM 100,000 to carry on his studies.[55]

The horrendous outcomes of Nazi racial hygiene are well known, and well publicized. Less well publicized, however, is the fact that Nazi eugenics actually stimulated research into the toxic effects of mutagens and carcinogens—everything from alcohol and tobacco to workplace toxins and genotoxic contraceptives.[56] ... What we find is that Nazi ideology pushed and pulled on cancer research, sometimes for better, sometimes for worse.

QUESTIONS FOR DISCUSSION

1. What is biological determinism, and how did it influence the basic outlook governing the medical policies of the Nazi regime? Are any aspects of contemporary medical policy in the United States derived from the idea of biological determinism?

2. How did the biological theories of the Nazis affect research into the causes of cancer? Nowadays, we believe that some cancers are caused by environmental factors, but also that certain individuals are predisposed (through their genetic inheritance) to certain forms of cancer. How did the Nazi medical researchers deal with these two different causal theories?

3. Discuss how medical research during the Nazi era demonstrates that medical science and medical practice are influenced by political and social values. What current medical research in the United States is also influenced by political and social values? Is this is a good way to organize medical research?

4. With the recent success of the first phases of the Human Genome Project, some people have argued that a full map of the human genome will be useful for screening all individuals for potentially harmful or debilitating diseases and defects. Critics worry that this information can be misused, both in the area of medical treatment and in the area of industrial policy (for some people may be restricted from certain kinds of occupations). What lessons can we learn from the history of Nazi medical research to guide the formation of public policy relating to the Human Genome Project?

NOTES

1. Robert N. Proctor, *Racial Hygiene: Medicine Under the Nazis* (Cambridge: Harvard University Press, 1988), pp. 55 ff.

2. Friedrich Hoffmann, *Opera Omnia physico-medica* (Geneva, 1761), 3:446.

3. Robert N. Proctor, *Cancer Wars: How Politics Shapes What We Know and Don't Know about Cancer* (New York: Basic Books, 1995), pp. 218–22.

4. The first study of twins with cancer is apparently Tito Spannocchi's "Contributo alla ereditarietà dei fibromi dell' utero," *Archivio italiano di Ginecologia* 2 (1899): 251–54. Heinrich Kranz reviewed efforts to use twin studies to resolve the nature-nurture question for cancer in his "Tumoren bei Zwillingen," *Zeitschrift für induktive Abstammungs- und Vererbungslehre* 62 (1932): 173–81; compare also J. J. Versluys, "Zwillingspathologischer Beitrag zur Ätiologie der Tumoren," *Zeitschrift für Krebsforschung* 41 (1935): 239–59.

5. Juraj Körbler, "Zur Frage der Vererbung und der Kontagiosität bei Krebs," *Zeitschrift für Krebsforschung* 47 (1938): 86.

6. Fritz Lenz, *Menschliche Erblichkeitslehre* (Munich: Lehmann, 1921), pp. 258–62. A 1944 article in the *Zeitschrift für Krebsforschung* identified Charles Otis Whitman, Fritz Lenz, and Karl H. Bauer as the earliest pioneers of the somatic mutation hypothesis, followed later by Frederik G. Gade of Norway (Hans?) Schwarz, and Hans R. Schinz; see Ulrich Henschke, "Über Geschwulsttheorien und die Möglichkeit der Entstehung der Geschwulstzelle durch Spontanmutation," *Zeitschrift für Krebsforschung* 54 (1944): 12–14. Henschke noted the resistance in the medical community to the idea that only mutagens (*mutationsauslösende Faktoren*) could cause cancer, and that all carcinogens—e.g., X-rays, radium, ultraviolet irradiation—caused mutations (p. 15). Henschke correctly perceived that cancer was not weeded out in the

course of evolutionary history, since it tended to affect only persons past the age of reproduction. He also noted, though, that evolution was possible only through mutation, so cancer was in this sense the unfortunate consequence (*Opfer*) of the possibility of evolution (p. 23).

7. Karl Heinrich Bauer and Felix von Mikulicz-Radecki, *Die Praxis der Sterilisierungsoperationen* (Leipzig: J. A. Barth, 1936). American occupation authorities in 1945 named Bauer Rektor of the University of Heidelberg. On the 1968 accusations of Nazi collaboration, see Christian Pross, "Nazi Doctors, German Medicine, and Historical Truth," in George J. Annas and Michael A. Grodin, eds., *The Nazi Doctors and the Nuremberg Code: Human Rights in Human Experimentation* (New York: Oxford University Press, 1992), pp. 41 and 49 n. 3.

8. Karl Heinrich Bauer, *Mutationstheorie der Geschwulst-Entstehung* (Berlin: Springer, 1928).

9. Otmar Freiherr von Verschuer, *Leitfaden der Rassenhygiene* (Leipzig: Georg Thieme, 1941), p. 158. Albert Dietrich of Tübingen also followed Bauer in asserting that all mutagens are carcinogens: "Alle positiv mutationserzeugenden, strahlenden Energien sind aber zugleich krebserzeugend (K. H. Bauer)"; see his "Der Stand der Krebsforschung," in *Krebsbehandlung und Krebsbekämpfung*, ed. Landesausschuss für Krebsbekämpfung in Bremen (Berlin: Urban & Schwarzenberg, 1938), p. 15.

10. Max Schüller, "Gibt es eine Prädisposition für Krebs und worin besteht sie?" *Archiv für Rassen- und Gesellschaftsbiologie* 1 (1904): 831. Schüller himself regarded the differences as not yet proven to be racial in origins.

11. Germany's most important racial hygiene journal in 1904 reported the commonly held belief that "the white race is particularly predisposed to cancer" and that "some colored races, some of the Negro populations of Africa, for example, are entirely free of cancer and immune to it" (ibid., p. 825). Schüller maintained that recent immigrants to a country were more likely to contract cancer than persons native to that country (p. 826), a view consistent with germ theories popular at the time.

12. Ukrainian women were apparently more than four times as likely to die of genital cancer as were Jewish women living in the Ukraine; Ukrainian Jews were also only half as likely to die of breast cancer. See Arkadii M. Merkow, "Zur vergleichenden Charakteristik der Krebsaffektion der wesentlichsten nationalen und sozialen Gruppen der Stadtbevölkerung der Ukraine," *Zeitschrift für Krebsforschung* 34 (1931): 285–98.

13. Gerhard Wagner, "Unser Reichsärzteführer Spricht," *Ziel und Weg* 5 (1935): 432–33; Theobald Lang, "Die Belastung des Judentums mit Geistig-Auffälligen," *Nationalsozialistische Monatshefte* 3 (1932): 23–30; Walter Gross, "Die Familie," *Informationsdienst*, no. 58 (September 20, 1938). For a provocative critique and review, especially of pre-Nazi literature, see Sander L. Gilman, *The Jew's Body* (London: Routledge, 1992).

14. Sander L. Gilman, *Freud, Race, and Gender* (Princeton: Princeton University Press, 1993), p. 172.

15. Wagner, "Unser Reichsärzteführer Spricht," *Ziel und Weg* 5 (1935): 432; compare Walter Schottky, ed., *Rasse und Krankheit* (Munich: Lehmann,

1936), and Wilhelm Hildebrandt, *Rassenmischung und Krankheit: Ein Versuch* (Stuttgart: Hippokrates, 1935).

16. The best review of bias in cancer reporting is probably still Johannes Clemmensen, *Statistical Studies in the Aetiology of Malignant Neoplasms* (Copenhagen: Munksgaard, 1965), pp. 1–34.

17. Frederick L. Hoffman, *The Mortality from Cancer Throughout the World* (Newark: Prudential, 1915), pp. 15–16, 129. Not everyone regarded blacks as less susceptible: a professor of physiology and medical jurisprudence in the Medical College of South Carolina at Charleston in 1892 wrote: "If we look again to the accepted etiology of carcinoma of the womb we should undoubtedly consider the colored people as specially liable to it. When we remember the unbridled licentiousness of this people, their profligacy, the attendant traumatisms about the cervix in women who have borne many children, we surely find conditions that, to say the least, could scarcely be supposed to render the black race exempt." See Middleton Michel, "Carcinoma Uteri in the Negro," *Medical News* 11 (1892): 402.

18. Alfredo Niceforo, "Cancer in Relation to Race in Europe," in *Report of the International Conference on Cancer* (Bristol: J. Wright & Sons, 1928), p. 502; Eugene Pittard, "Can We Ignore the Race Problem in Connection with Cancer?" in the same volume, pp. 503–7.

19. Hermann Stahr, "Vom Lungenkrebs," *Monatsschrift für Krebsbekämpfung* 5 (1938): 212.

20. Arthur Purdy Stout, "Tumors of the Neuromyo-Arterial Glomus," *American Journal of Cancer* 24 (1935): 255–72.

21. Gilman, *Freud,* pp. 170–73. Adolf Theilhaber was one of the first to show that uterine cancer was relatively rare among Jewish women; see his "Zur Lehre von der Entstehung der Uterustumoren," *Münchener medizinische Wochenschrift* 56 (1909): 1272–73. Adolf's son, Felix, the zionist author of the Jewish *Untergangstheorie* who also studied uterine cancer, fled Germany in 1935. The best review of cancer among European Jews prior to the Nazi period is probably Sigismund Peller, "Über Krebssterblichkeit der Juden," *Zeitschrift für Krebsforschung* 34 (1931): 128–47. Peller was a Viennese Jew who left for Palestine with his wife in 1934; see his *Not in My Time.*

22. Lenz, *Menschliche Erblichkeitslehre,* pp. 264 ff.

23. Sigmund Rascher, "Denkschrift," May 1, 1939, BDC; Wolfgang Benz, "Dr. med. Sigmund Rascher: Eine Karriere," *Dachauer Hefte* 4 (1988): 193–94. The meeting described in Rascher's memorandum took place on April 24, 1939. In addition to the rat plan, Himmler apparently wanted Rascher to find out whether cancer rates in the remote villages of Memel, in eastern Prussia, were lower than elsewhere. Himmler was also interested in whether chemical fertilizers could cause cancer, especially whether the fertilizers commonly used on grass could be tied to cancers among cows. Rascher was supposed to contact local veterinary surgeons, Nazi farm leaders, and church leaders to determine local cancer rates; he was also supposed to investigate how much artificial fertilizer was being used on agricultural lands. Himmler also wanted to examine the blood of persons confined to concentration camps, to see whether a blood test could be developed that would signal cancer's early onset (ibid.).

24. Otmar Freiherr von Verschuer, *Erbpathologie, Ein Lehrbuch für Ärzte und Medizinstudierende* (Munich: Lehmann, 1937), pp. 86, 103, 159, 182, 137.

25. Karl Heinrich Bauer, "Fortschritte der experimentellen Krebsforschung," *Archiv für klinische Chirurgie* 189 (1937): 123–84; compare also his "Krebs und Vererbung," *Münchener medizinische Wochenschrift* 87 (1940): p. 479. The Berlin pathologist Robert Rössle concluded that cancer was only rarely heritable, though Wolfgang Denk in Vienna in 1939 argued from twin and genealogical evidence that heredity must account for "a minimum of 20 percent" of all cancers; see his "Zur Frage der Erblichkeit des Carcinoms," *Zeitschrift für Krebsforschung* 49 (1939): 241.

26. Bauer, "Krebs und Vererbung," pp. 475–79.

27. Arthur Hintze, "Kultur und Krebs," *Jahreskurse für ärztliche Fortbildung* 7 (1939): 67–71. Hintze was named head of radiology at the Rudolf Virchow Hospital's newly created Allgemeines Institut gegen die Geschwulstkrankheiten in 1935. He was aware that lifestyle factors could impact occupational cancers—the custom of daily bathing, for example, to which he attributed the low Japanese incidence of occupational cancers caused by oil, tar, or soot; he was also aware that anecdotal impressions of cancer incidence could be misleading if a certain class of people—Muslim women, for example—would not allow themselves to be examined by Western physicians.

28. Ibid., p. 73.

29. Otmar Freiherr von Verschuer, *Leitfaden der Rassenhygiene* (Leipzig: Georg Thieme, 1941), pp. 159–161.

30. Martin Staemmler and Edeltraut Bieneck, "Statistische Untersuchungen über die Todesursachen der deutschen und jüdischen Bevölkerung von Breslau," *Münchener medizinische Wochenschrift* 87 (1940): 447–50. The *British Medical Journal* pointed out that Staemmler and Bieneck had failed to discuss the role of state violence in producing these statistics; see "German Medicine, Race, and Religion," *British Medical Journal,* August 17, 1940, p. 230.

31. Hintze, "Kultur und Krebs," pp. 75–76.

32. A review of *Konstitutionslehre* can be found in Gerhard Koch, *Die Gesellschaft für Konstitutionsforschung: Anfang und Ende 1942–1965* (Erlangen: Palm und Enke, 1985).

33. Hans Weselmann, "Über die Nicotingastritis," *Die Genussgifte* 36 (1940): 23.

34. Robert Hofstätter, *Die rauchende Frau: Eine klinische, psychologische und soziale Studie* (Vienna: Holder-Pichler-Tempsky, 1924), p. 71.

35. Friedrich Voltz, "Pigmentbildung und Strahlenbehandlung," *Radiologische Rundschau* 1 (1933): 96.

36. Friedrich Voltz, "Biologische Probleme in der Röntgenstrahlentherapie," *Strahlentherapie* 47 (1933): 137–43.

37. Robert Ritter, "Rothaarigkeit als rassenhygienisches Problem," *Volk und Rasse* 10 (1935): 385–90.

38. Wolfgang Hien, *Chemische Industrie und Krebs* (Bremerhaven: Wirtschaftsverlag, 1994), p. 219.

39. George Reid, "Weltanschauung, Haltung, Genussgifte," *Die Genussgifte* 35 (1939): 66–67.

40. Wolfgang Klarner, *Vom Rauchen Eine Sucht und ihre Bekämpfung* (Nuremberg: Rudolf Kern, 1940), pp. 18–19. The body-type categorization mentioned here traces back to the psychiatrist Ernst Kretschmer.

41. "Erkennung und Bekämpfung der Tabakgefahren," *Deutsches Ärzteblatt* 71 (1941): 185.

42. Hugo O. Kleine, *Ernährungsschäden als Krankheitsursachen* (Stuttgart: Hippokrates, 1940), pp. 62–63.

43. The official commentary on the law specified that sufferers from retinoblastoma should be sterilized; see Arthur Gütt, Ernst Rüdin, and Falk Ruttke, *Kommentar zum Gesetz zur Verhütung Erbkranken Nachwuchses* (Munich: Lehmann, 1934).

44. August Wagenmann, ed., *Bericht über die einundfünfzigste Zusammenkunft der Deutschen Ophthalmologischen Gesellschaft in Heidelberg 1936* (Munich: Bergmann, 1936), pp. 91–102; compare also Karl A. Reiser's critique of Clausen's views in "Bemerkungen zur Erblichkeitsfrage beim Glioma retinae," *Klinische Monatsblätter für Augenheilkunde* 99 (1937): 350–55.

45. Bernhard Fischer-Wasels, "Die Bedeutung der besonderen Allgemeindisposition des Körpers für die Entstehung der Krebskrankheit," *Strahlentherapie* 50 (1934): 5–78; compare Kurt Blome's similar views in "Krebsforschung und Krebsbekämpfung," *Ziel und Weg* 10 (1940): 412.

46. Bernhard Fischer-Wasels, "Bekämpfung der Krebskrankheit durch Erbpflege." *Deutsches Ärzteblatt* 64 (1934): 92–95. The gynecologist Wilhelm Lahm prior even to 1933 argued that marital counselors should use cancer registry data to counter the pairing of persons genetically predisposed to cancer; see his "Die ärztliche Fortbildung auf dem Gebiet der Krebsbekämpfung," *Strahlentherapie* 37 (1930): 397–401; also the similar views expressed in W. Helmreich, "Erblichkeit, Rassenhygiene und Bevölkerungspolitik," *Münchener medizinische Wochenschrift* 83 (1936): 484.

47. Hien, *Chemische Industrie,* pp. 219 and 271–304.

48. Gunther Lehmann, "Die Bedeutung des Staubbindungsvermögens der Nase für die Entstehung der Lungensilicose," *Arbeitsphysiologie* 8 (1934): 218–50; also his "Untersuchungen an Staubmasken," *Arbeitsphysiologie* 9 (1936): 182–205. Rostoski, Saupe, and Schmorl in 1926 had urged Schneeberg's miners to breathe through their noses to lower their risk of developing lung cancer (by trapping carcinogenic particulates); the authors had also advised workers "not to be shy" about having their nasal passages surgically enlarged to enable better nasal ventilation ("Die Bergkrankheit," p. 375).

49. Lehmann's efforts were part of an attempted "Lösung des Staubproblems"; see Otto Schulz, "Gesundheitliche Schäden durch gewerblichen Staub," *Die Gasmaske* 11 (1939): 57–66.

50. Hans Waniek, "Die Verhütung der Staublungenkrankheiten, insbesondere der Silikose," *Klinische Wochenschrift* 23 (1944): 288–89.

51. H. Hamperl, U. Henschke, and R. Schulze, "Vergleich der Hautreaktionen beim Bestrahlungserythem und bei der direkten Pigmentierung," *Archiv für pathologische Anatomie und Physiologie* 304 (1939): 21.

52. Wilhelm C. Hueper, *Occupational Tumors and Allied Diseases* (Springfield, Ill: Charles C. Thomas, 1942), p. 765.

53. Wilhelm C. Hueper, "Causal and Preventive Aspects of Environmental Cancer," *Minnesota Medicine*, January 1956, pp. 10–11.
54. Cited in Gerhard Krug, *Die Organisation des Kampfes gegen den Krebs in wissenschaftlicher und sozialer Hinsicht.* Marburg: Med. diss., 1938, p. 21. A November 1941 article in the *Berliner Börsenzeitung* predicted that the sheer "idealism" of the Third Reich would result in a lowering of German cancer rates; see "Nationalsozialismus schützt vor Krebs," *Internationales Ärztliches Bulletin* 2 (1935): 17–18.
55. Auler met with Goebbels on February 15, 1941; the propaganda minister called his work "truly wonderful." Education minister Bernhard Rust awarded him an additional 7,000 RM; see Goebbels's *Tagebücher,* p. 504. It is not yet clear what this money was used for. It may have gone to defray some of the costs of the antiquackery film Auler was helping to make (*Jeder Achte*); this is plausible, since support of this sort was one of the primary tasks of Goebbels's ministry.
56. On genotoxic contraceptives, see Karl E. Fecht, "Über die Keimschädigung durch chemische Schwangerschaftsverhütungsmittel," *Volk und Rasse* 10 (1935): 215–17.

CHAPTER 10

Medicalized Killing
in the Nazi Death Camps

—— ❧ ——

This chapter contains excerpts from Robert J. Lifton's classic study of the role of the medical establishment in Nazi Germany, *The Nazi Doctors: Medical Killing and the Psychology of Genocide* (1986). Lifton, a professor of psychiatry and psychology, interviewed over one hundred people—both Nazi doctors and nonmedical professionals who participated in the killing operations, as well as prisoner doctors and survivors of the camps—in order to get a clear picture of the ways in which medicine was used and misused in the Final Solution. Lifton is himself a physician, a psychiatrist, and so his interviews were designed in part to uncover a psychological analysis of his subjects, especially those Nazi doctors who actively participated in the killing. Many of his interview subjects were still alive when the book was published in 1986, and so many are referred to merely by initials (Dr. Ernst B. or Dr. Wanda J., for example). Other more famous doctors whom Lifton did not interview because they were dead (such as the notorious Dr. Josef Mengele) are referred to by their full names. Lifton's book surveys the entire range of medical activities that were incorporated into the Nazi ideology of race purification, from the early programs of sterilization and euthanasia for the handicapped and mentally ill (Program 14F13), to the use of medical personnel to perform the death camp selections for the gas chambers, and to the use of the captive prisoner population for medical experiments on human subjects. The excerpts printed here are divided into three sections. In the first section, we have an introduction that places the operation of medical killing into the basic Nazi ideology of racial purification by the elimination of a racial or social disease—those non-Aryans that were corrupting civilization. Therapeutic medicine became a metaphor for the elimination of the Jewish people. The introductory section also provides an overview of all the ways in which physicians participated in the medical killing that became genocide. In the second section, we have a description—primarily based on interviews—of the role of the medical staff in the selection process. Finally, in the third section, we are told the story of the medical experiments of Dr. Carl Clauberg in Auschwitz, who attempted to find a cheap and efficient way to sterilize Jewish women. Clauberg's experiments were only one set of many different types that took place at the camps—the gruesome details are presented here as an example of a medical practice that was shockingly commonplace.

From *The Nazi Doctors: Medical Killing and the Psychology of Genocide*

Robert J. Lifton

INTRODUCTION: AUSCHWITZ AND MEDICALIZED KILLING

I gained an important perspective on Auschwitz from an Israeli dentist who had spent three years in that camp. We were completing a long interview, during which he had told me about many things, including details of SS dentists' supervision of prisoners' removal of gold fillings from the teeth of fellow Jews killed in the gas chambers. He looked about the comfortable room in his house with its beautiful view of Haifa, sighed deeply, and said, "This world is not this world." What I think he meant was that, after Auschwitz, the ordinary rhythms and appearances of life, however innocuous or pleasant, were far from the truth of human existence. Underneath those rhythms and appearances lay darkness and menace. . . .

Psychologically speaking, nothing is darker or more menacing, or harder to accept, than the participation of physicians in mass murder. However technicized or commercial the modern physician may have become, he or she is still supposed to be a healer—and one responsible to a tradition of healing, which all cultures revere and depend upon. Knowledge that the doctor has joined the killers adds a grotesque dimension to the perception that "this world is not this world." During my work I gained the impression that, among Germans and many others, this involvement of physicians was viewed as the most shameful of all Nazi behavior.

When we think of the crimes of Nazi doctors, what come to mind are their cruel and sometimes fatal human experiments. Those experiments, in their precise and absolute violation of the Hippocratic oath, mock and subvert the very idea of the ethical physician, of the physician dedicated to the well-being of patients. I shall examine those human experiments from the standpoint of the regime's medical and political ideology.

Yet when we turn to the Nazi doctor's role in Auschwitz, it was not the experiments that were most significant. Rather it was his participation in the killing process—indeed his supervision of Auschwitz mass murder from beginning to end. This aspect of Nazi medical behavior has escaped full recognition—even though we are familiar with photographs of Nazi doctors standing at the ramp and performing their notorious "selections" of arriving Jews, determining which were to go directly to the gas chamber and which were to live, at least temporarily, and work in the camp. Yet this medicalized killing had a logic that was not only deeply significant for Nazi theory and behavior but holds for other expressions of genocide as well. . . .

The very extremity of Auschwitz and related Nazi murder renders it close to unreality. A distinguished European physician, who had struggled with Nazi brutality for forty years—first as an inmate of Auschwitz and other camps and then as an authority on medical consequences of that incarceration—said to me very quietly at the end of a long interview, "You know, I still can't really believe that it happened—that a group of people would round up all of the Jews in Europe and send them to a special place to kill them." He was saying that the Auschwitz "other world" is beyond belief. The wonder is that there is not an even greater tendency than actually exists to accept the directly false contention that Nazi mass murder did not take place.

Also at issue for us here is the relationship of Nazi doctors to the human species. Another Auschwitz survivor who knew something about them asked me, "Were they *beasts* when they did what they did? Or were they *human beings*?" He was not surprised by my answer: they were and are men, which is my justification for studying them; and their behavior—Auschwitz itself—was a product of specifically *human* ingenuity and cruelty.

I went on to tell this survivor of the ordinariness of most Nazi doctors I had interviewed. Neither brilliant nor stupid, neither inherently evil nor particularly ethically sensitive, they were by no means the demonic figures—sadistic, fanatic, lusting to kill—people have often thought them to be. My friend replied, "But it is *demonic* that they were *not* demonic." He could then raise his second question, really the one he had in mind in the first place: "How did they become killers?" That question can be addressed.

What my survivor friend was struggling with—what I have struggled with throughout this study—is the disturbing psychological truth that participation in mass murder need not require emotions as extreme or demonic as would seem appropriate for such a malignant project. Or to put the matter another way, ordinary people can commit demonic acts.

But that did not mean that Nazi doctors were faceless bureaucratic cogs or automatons. As human beings, they were actors and participants who manifested certain kinds of behavior for which they were responsible, and which we can begin to identify.

There are several dimensions, then, to the work. At its heart is the transformation of the physician—of the medical enterprise itself—from healer to killer. That transformation requires us to examine the interaction of Nazi political ideology and biomedical ideology in their effects on individual and collective behavior. That in turn takes us to the significance of medicalized killing for Nazi mass murder in general—and for large-scale killing and genocide on the part of others. Finally, the work has relevance for broad questions of human control over life and death—for physicians everywhere, for science and scientists and other professionals in general, for institutions of various kinds—and also for concepts of human nature and ultimate human values. I can no more than touch on most of these general issues, having made a decision to focus on Nazi doctors and medicalized killing, and then on issues of mass murder. But my hope is that others will find here experience that might help them explore any of the searing moral issues implicit in this study.

That hope raises the important question of specificity and generality. I believe that one must stress the specificity of the Nazi killing project, especially concerning Jews: its unique characteristics, and the particular forces that shaped it. But having done that, one must also search for larger *principles* suggested by that unique project. No other event or institution can or should be equated with Auschwitz; but nor should we deny ourselves the opportunity to explore its general relevance for genocide and for situations of a very different order in which psychological and moral questions may be considerably more ambiguous. . . .

Medicalized Killing

In Nazi mass murder, we can say that a barrier was removed, a boundary crossed: that boundary between violent imagery and periodic killing of victims (as of Jews in pogroms) on the one hand, and systematic genocide in Auschwitz and elsewhere on the other. My argument in this study is that the medicalization of killing—the imagery of killing in the name of healing—was crucial to that terrible step. At the heart of the Nazi enterprise, then, is the destruction of the boundary between healing and killing.

Early descriptions of Auschwitz and other death camps focused on the sadism and viciousness of Nazi guards, officers, and physicians. But subsequent students of the process realized that sadism and viciousness alone could not account for the killing of millions of people. The emphasis then shifted to the bureaucracy of killing: the faceless, detached bureaucratic function originally described by Max Weber, now applied to mass murder.[1] This focus on numbed violence is enormously important, and is consistent with what we shall observe to be the routinization of all Auschwitz function.

Yet these emphases are not sufficient in themselves. They must be seen in relation to the visionary motivations associated with ideology, along with the specific individual-psychological mechanisms enabling people to kill. What I call "medicalized killing" addresses these motivational principles and psychological mechanisms, and permits us to understand the Auschwitz victimizers—notably Nazi doctors—both as part of a bureaucracy of killing and as individual participants whose attitudes and behavior can be examined.

Medicalized killing can be understood in two wider perspectives. The first is the "surgical" method of killing large numbers of people by means of a controlled technology making use of highly poisonous gas; the method employed became a means of maintaining distance between killers and victims. This distancing had considerable importance for the Nazis in alleviating the psychological problems experienced (as attested over and over by Nazi documents) by the *Einsatzgruppen* troops who carried out face-to-face shooting of Jews in Eastern Europe—problems that did not prevent those troops from murdering 1,400,000 Jews.[2]

I was able to obtain direct evidence on this matter during an interview with a former *Wehrmacht* neuropsychiatrist who had treated large numbers of *Einsatzgruppen* personnel for psychological disorders. He told me that these disorders resembled combat reactions of ordinary troops: severe anxiety, nightmares, tremors, and numerous bodily complaints. But in these "killer troops," as he called them, the symptoms tended to last longer and to be more severe. He estimated that 20 percent of those doing the actual killing experienced these symptoms of psychological decompensation. About half of that 20 percent associated their symptoms mainly with the "unpleasantness" of what they had to do, while the other half seemed to have moral questions about shooting people in that way.

The men had greatest psychological difficulty concerning shooting women and children, especially children. Many experienced a sense of guilt in their dreams, which could include various forms of punishment or retribution. Such psychological difficulty led the Nazis to seek a more "surgical" method of killing.

But there is another perspective on medicalized killing that I believe to be insufficiently recognized: *killing as a therapeutic imperative.* That kind of motivation was revealed in the words of a Nazi doctor quoted by the distinguished survivor physician Dr. Ella Lingens-Reiner. Pointing to the chimneys in the distance, she asked a Nazi doctor, Fritz Klein, "How can you reconcile that with your [Hippocratic] oath as a doctor?" His answer was, "Of course I am a doctor and I want to preserve life. And out of respect for human life, I would remove a gangrenous appendix from a diseased body. The Jew is the gangrenous appendix in the body of mankind."[3]

The medical imagery was still broader. Just as Turkey during the nineteenth century (because of the extreme decline of the Ottoman empire) was known as the "sick man of Europe," so did pre-Hitler ideologues and Hitler himself interpret Germany's post–First World War chaos and demoralization as an "illness," especially of the Aryan race. Hitler wrote in *Mein Kampf,* in the mid-1920s, that *"anyone who wants to cure this era, which is inwardly sick and rotten, must first of all summon up the courage to make clear the causes of this disease."*[4] The diagnosis was racial. The only genuine "culture-creating" race, the Aryans, had permitted themselves to be weakened to the point of endangered survival by the "destroyers of culture," characterized as "the Jew." The Jews were agents of "racial pollution" and "racial tuberculosis," as well as parasites and bacteria causing sickness, deterioration, and death in the host peoples they infested. They were the "eternal bloodsucker," "vampire," "germ carrier," "peoples' parasite," and "maggot in a rotting corpse."[5] The cure had to be radical: that is (as one scholar put it), by "cutting out the 'canker of decay,' propagating the worthwhile elements and letting the less valuable wither away, . . . [and] 'the extirpation of all those categories of people considered to be worthless or dangerous.'"[6]

Medical metaphor blended with concrete biomedical ideology in the Nazi sequence from coercive sterilization to direct medical killing to the death camps. The unifying principle of the biomedical ideology was that of a deadly racial disease, the sickness of the Aryan race; the cure, the killing of all Jews.

Thus, for Hans Frank, jurist and General Governor of Poland during the Nazi occupation, "the Jews were a lower species of life, a kind of vermin, which upon contact infected the German people with deadly diseases." When the Jews in the area he ruled had been killed, he declared that "now a sick Europe would become healthy again."[7] It was a religion of the will—the will as "an all-encompassing metaphysical principle;"[8] and what the Nazis "willed" was nothing less than total control over life and death. While this view is often referred to as "social Darwinism," the term applies only loosely, mostly to the Nazi stress on natural "struggle" and on "survival of the fittest." The regime actually rejected much of Darwinism; since evolutionary theory is more or less democratic in its assumption of a common beginning for all races, it is therefore at odds with the Nazi principle of inherent Aryan racial virtue.[9]

Even more specific to the biomedical vision was the crude genetic imagery, combined with still cruder eugenic visions. Here Heinrich Himmler, as high priest, spoke of the leadership's task as being "like the plant-breeding specialist who, when he wants to breed a pure new strain from a well-tried species that has been exhausted by too much cross-breeding, first goes over the field to cull the unwanted plants."[10]

The Nazi project, then, was not so much Darwinian or social Darwinist as a vision of absolute control over the evolutionary process, over the biological human future. Making widespread use of the Darwinian term "selection," the Nazis sought to take over the functions of nature (natural selection) and God (the Lord giveth and the Lord taketh away) in orchestrating their own "selections," their own version of human evolution.

In these visions the Nazis embraced not only versions of medieval mystical anti-Semitism but also a newer (nineteenth- and twentieth-century) claim to "scientific racism." Dangerous Jewish characteristics could be linked with alleged data of scientific disciplines, so that a "mainstream of racism" formed from "the fusion of anthropology, eugenics, and social thought."[11] The resulting "racial and social biology" could make vicious forms of anti-Semitism seem intellectually respectable to learned men and women.

One can speak of the Nazi state as a "biocracy." The model here is a theocracy, a system of rule by priests of a sacred order under the claim of divine prerogative. In the case of the Nazi biocracy, the divine prerogative was that of cure through purification and revitalization of the Aryan race: "From a dead mechanism which only lays claim to existence for its own sake, there must be formed a living organism with the exclusive aim of serving a higher idea." Just as in a theocracy, the state itself is no more than a vehicle for the divine purpose, so in the Nazi biocracy was the state no more than a means to achieve *"a mission of the German people on earth"*: that of *"assembling and preserving the most valuable stocks of basic racial elements in this* [Aryan] *people ...* [and] *... raising them to a dominant position."*[12] The Nazi biocracy differed from a classical theocracy in that the biological priests did not actually rule. The clear rulers were Adolf

Hitler and his circle, not biological theorists and certainly not the doctors. (The difference, however, is far from absolute: even in a theocracy, highly politicized rulers may make varying claims to priestly authority.) In any case, Nazi ruling authority was maintained in the name of the higher biological principle.

Among the biological authorities called forth to articulate and implement "scientific racism"—including physical anthropologists, geneticists, and racial theorists of every variety—doctors inevitably found a unique place. It is they who work at the border of life and death, who are most associated with the awesome, death-defying, and sometimes death-dealing aura of the primitive shaman and medicine man. As bearers of this shamanistic legacy and contemporary practitioners of mysterious healing arts, it is they who are likely to be called upon to become biological activists.

I have mentioned my primary interest in Nazi doctors' participation in medicalized or biologized killing. We shall view their human experiments as related to the killing process and to the overall Nazi biomedical vision. At Nuremberg, doctors were tried only limitedly for their involvement in killing, partly because its full significance was not yet understood.[13]

In Auschwitz, Nazi doctors presided over the murder of most of the one million victims of that camp. Doctors performed selections—both on the ramp among arriving transports of prisoners and later in the camps and on the medical blocks. Doctors supervised the killing in the gas chambers and decided when the victims were dead. Doctors conducted a murderous epidemiology, sending to the gas chamber groups of people with contagious diseases and sometimes including everyone else who might be on the medical block. Doctors ordered and supervised, and at times carried out, direct killing of debilitated patients on the medical blocks by means of phenol injections into the bloodstream or the heart. In connection with all of these killings, doctors kept up a pretense of medical legitimacy: for deaths of Auschwitz prisoners and of outsiders brought there to be killed, they signed false death certificates listing spurious illnesses. Doctors consulted actively on how best to keep selections running smoothly; on how many people to permit to remain alive to fill the slave labor requirements of the I. G. Farben enterprise at Auschwitz; and on how to burn the enormous numbers of bodies that strained the facilities of the crematoria.

In sum, we may say that doctors were given much of the responsibility for the murderous ecology of Auschwitz—the choosing of victims, the carrying through of the physical and psychological mechanics of killing, and the balancing of killing and work functions in the camp. While doctors by no means ran Auschwitz, they did lend it a perverse medical aura. As one survivor who closely observed the process put the matter, "Auschwitz was like a medical operation," and "the killing program was led by doctors from beginning to end."

We may say that the doctor standing at the ramp represented a kind of omega point, a mythical gatekeeper between the worlds of the dead and the living, a final common pathway of the Nazi vision of therapy via mass murder. . . .

The SS doctor did no direct medical work. His primary function was to carry out Auschwitz's institutional program of medicalized genocide.[14] Consider the SS doctor's activities in Auschwitz. He performed initial large-scale selections of arriving Jewish prisoners at the Birkenau camp. These selections were usually conducted according to formula: old and debilitated people, children, and women with children all selected for the gas chamber; while relatively intact young adults were permitted to survive, at least temporarily. The victim's experience, with which we begin, gives the truest picture.

After the selection, the presiding doctor was driven in an SS vehicle, usually marked with a red cross, together with a medical technician (one of a special group of "disinfectors," or *Desinfektoren,* from within the *Sanitätsdienstgrade* or SDG) and the gas pellets, to a gas chamber adjoining one of the crematoria. As *Führer,* or "leader," of the team, the doctor had supervisory responsibility for the correct carrying out of the killing process, though the medical technician actually inserted the gas pellets, and the entire sequence became so routine that little intervention was required. The doctor also had the task of declaring those inside the gas chamber dead and sometimes looked through a peephole to observe them. This, too, became routine, a matter of permitting twenty minutes or so to pass before the doors of the gas chamber could be opened and the bodies removed.

SS doctors also carried out two additional forms of selections. In one, Jewish inmates were lined up on very short notice at various places in the camp and their ranks thinned in order to allow room for presumably healthier replacements from new transports. The other type of selections took place directly in the medical blocks in a caricature of triage. Rather than simply permitting those closest to death to die—in order to use limited medical resources to treat those who might be saved—as in traditional medical triage (the meaning given the term as originally used by the French military), the Nazis combined triage with murder by sending to the gas chamber those judged to be significantly ill or debilitated, or who required more than two or three weeks for recovery.

Medical triage-murder became a standard SS policy, influenced both by the vision of the Final Solution and by I. G. Farben's economic arrangements. But an additional factor also of great importance was the residual influence of the 14f13 "euthanasia" action in the camps. In other words, the principle of killing the weak, the sick, and the generally undesirable had been established in medical circles, extended specifically to concentration camps, and then institutionalized (still within medical circles) in Auschwitz, and Auschwitz alone, on a phenomenal scale. That 14f13 influence involved both the mentality and the legality of a medical form of a triage murder, so much so that the Frankfurt court could view medical-triage killings as probably derived from 14f13 policies. In other words, the Nazi versions of "euthanasia" and the Final Solution converged on Auschwitz medical blocks, thereby rendering them an important agency of the Auschwitz ecology of murder.[15]

SS doctors also conducted murderous forms of "epidemiology": prisoners with a contagious disease, usually typhus but also scarlet fever or other conditions, would be sent to the gas chambers, sometimes together with the rest of the patients on that medical block (many of whom might have been free of the contagious disease) so that the empty block could then be completely "disinfected." (Nazi doctors played a similar role in Jewish ghettos in Poland, where they contributed to oppressive policies in the name of controlling epidemics, especially typhus.)[16]

SS doctors ordered and supervised, and sometimes themselves carried out, direct killing of debilitated patients by means of phenol injections into the bloodstream or heart given on the medical blocks. These injections were most extensive during the early years of Auschwitz (1941–43) prior to the full development of the gas chambers. They were usually performed by medical technicians or brutalized prisoners, who served as surrogates for the doctors. SS doctors had similar responsibility for another group of phenol injections ordered by the Auschwitz Political Department (actually the Gestapo) for what were known as "hidden executions": the killing of such people as Polish political prisoners or occasionally German military or other personnel condemned to death for various reasons. Doctors also attended other executions of political prisoners—usually by shooting—in order to declare the victim officially dead.

In connection with all of these killings, doctors signed false death certificates, attributing each death of an Auschwitz inmate or an outsider brought there to be killed to a specific illness (cardiac, respiratory, infectious, or whatever). Those Jews selected for death at the ramp, never having entered the camp, required no death certificates.

SS dentists, who worked closely with doctors and also performed selections, were in charge of supervising prisoner work *Kommandos* in pulling out gold teeth and fillings of dead Jews after they had been gassed.

SS doctors were supposed to perform abortions on "alien" (*fremdvölkisch*) women found to be pregnant. Whether or not that category was meant to include Jewish women (as opposed to their being in a separate category of their own), abortions were performed on them in secret by Jewish prisoner doctors when it was learned that a diagnosis of pregnancy in Jewish women meant immediate gassing.

In the case of official corporal punishment (for instance, whipping), SS doctors were required both to sign forms attesting to the physical capacity of an inmate to absorb such punishment, as well as to be present while it was administered.

SS doctors also consulted actively on determining how best to keep selections running smoothly—making recommendations, for example, about whether women and children should be separated or allowed to proceed along the line together. They also advised on policies concerning numbers of people permitted to remain alive, weighing the benefits to the Nazi regime of the work function against the increased health problems created by permitting relatively debilitated people to live.

Doctors' technical knowledge was also called upon with regard to the burning of bodies, a great problem in Auschwitz during the summer of 1944, when the arrival of enormous numbers of Hungarian Jews overstrained the facilities of the crematoria, so that bodies had to be burned in the open.

Selections, the quintessential Auschwitz ritual, epitomized and maintained the healing-killing paradox. The first selections performed by the arriving SS doctor were his ritual of initiation, his transition from ordinary life to the Auschwitz universe, and the early calling forth of his Auschwitz self.

In terms of actual professional requirements, there was absolutely no need for doctors to be the ones conducting selections: anyone could have sorted out weak and moribund prisoners. But if one views Auschwitz, as Nazi ideologues did, as a public health venture, doctors alone became eligible to select. In doing so, the doctor plunged into what can be called the *healing-killing paradox.*

For him especially, killing became the prerequisite for healing. He could arrange for medical care only so far as the slaughterhouse was kept at full function. And his healing area (the medical block) was simultaneously a clearinghouse for further killing. He became an advocate of killing on two fundamental levels: that of the ecology of the camp (selecting larger numbers at the ramp and on the medical block when the camp was overcrowded, hygienic conditions were threatened, and the quantity of sick or weak inmates strained medical facilities and lessened work efficiency) and in connection with the larger biomedical vision (curing the Nordic race by ridding it of its dangerous Jewish infection), whatever the degree of intensity or amorphousness of his involvement in that vision. The healing-killing paradox was what Dr. Ernst B. called the "schizophrenic situation." But that situation was an enduring institutional arrangement, the basis for social equilibrium in Auschwitz.

But prisoners could not be permitted to kill themselves; suicide violated the logic of the healing-killing paradox. Indeed, overt suicide, such as running into the electric fence, was considered a serious violation of discipline and often exhaustively investigated. (Suicides by Treblinka prisoners were described by one commentator as the "first affirmation of freedom" contributing to significant prisoner rebellion in that camp.)[17] More gradual submission to death, as in the case of the *Muselmänner*,* could be tolerated or even encouraged because it did not seem to challenge Nazi life-death control. The healing-killing paradox, if it was to be internalized by the Auschwitz self, required exclusive control of life and death on the part of Nazi perpetrators.

The key word in the healing-killing reversal is *Sonderbehandlung*, or "special treatment," carried over from Nazi practice and from the 14f13 project in particular. This euphemism for killing insinuated something on the order of medical therapy, along with a standing that was "more legal than legal." (In general bureaucratic usage, "special" [the prefix] was the opposite of "regular": special trains and regular trains, special courts and regular courts, etc.) Special procedures were deemed necessary because of special conditions. The word not only detoxified killing and aided in its routinization but, at the same time, infused that killing with a near-mystical priority for the "Auschwitz self" in carrying it out. Killing assumed a certain feeling of necessity and appropriateness, enhanced by the medical, as well as the military, aura surrounding it.

Sonderbehandlung was part of the mystical imperative to kill all Jews; and once Auschwitz took on that imperative, any Jewish arrival or prisoner could be experienced by the Nazi doctor's Auschwitz self as designated for death, and, psychologically speaking, as already dead. Killing someone already dead need not be experienced as murder. And since Jews, long the Nazis' designated victim, were more generally perceived as carriers of death, or bearers of the death taint, they became "doubly dead." Just as one could not kill people already dead, one could do them no harm however one mutilated their bodies in medical experimentation. The human experiments performed by Nazi doctors, while tangential

---

*[Muselmänner refers to those prisoners who were virtually dead, who seemed to have given up any hope of life, "living corpses." The term means Muslims and is based on the fact that from a distance these men, because they were constantly bent over, looked like a group of praying Arabs. It also may refer to the attitude of complete submission that these prisoners displayed. -Ed.]

to questions of ecology, were fully consistent with the regime's larger biomedical vision.

For their regulation of the Auschwitz ecology, SS doctors needed the actual medical work of prisoner doctors, who in turn needed SS doctors to make that work possible—to keep others alive and stay alive themselves. What resulted were profound conflicts within prisoner doctors concerning their relationship to the Auschwitz ecology and to their SS masters as they (the prisoner doctors) struggled to remain free of selections and to retain a genuinely healing function. There were antagonisms among these prisoner doctors along with a few examples of close identification with Nazi medical policies. But it was the SS doctors who pulled the strings, who, while not without their own significant inner conflict, managed to adapt sufficiently to the Auschwitz system to maintain its medicalized killing. Their adaptation involved the process I call "doubling," which permitted them to select for the gas chamber without seeing themselves as killers. . . .

THE SS DOCTORS AND SELECTIONS

Selections were conducted, from within a medical hierarchy, by camp physicians *(Lagerärzte)* under the direct authority of the Auschwitz chief doctor, or garrison physician *(Standortarzt)*. The latter—who was Eduard Wirths for most of the period we are concerned with—operated within two separate chains of command. He was subordinate to the chief concentration-camp physician of the SS Economic and Administrative Department, or WVHA. This position was held from 1942 by Enno Lolling, who was stationed in Berlin but came frequently to Auschwitz and other camps. At the same time, Wirths was also subject to the authority of the camp commandant, with whom he dealt regularly on a day-to-day basis.*

Other doctors had different duties and different chains of command and were not expected to perform selections. These included the troop physicians *(Truppenärzte)* who took care of SS personnel; doctors who were sent to Auschwitz specifically to do experiments on inmates (notably Carl Clauberg and Horst Schumann) and tended to have more direct ties with Himmler; and doctors who belonged to the local camp Hygienic Institute, located outside the main camp and part of a chain of command separate from either that of the camp doctors or the camp commandant. The Hygienic Institute was officially concerned with questions

---

*This double chain of authority was characteristic of Nazi bureaucracy—often involving the hierarchy of both one's immediate institution and the Party itself or an affiliate structure.

of epidemiology and bacteriology and was installed in Auschwitz after an extensive typhus epidemic in 1942.

"Medical activity in Auschwitz consisted only of selecting people for the gas chamber" was the way that Dr. Ernst B., who had been there, expressed the matter to me. Certainly what was called "ramp duty" was a central function of Auschwitz camp doctors. Generally about seven SS doctors shared that duty, and their performing selections was considered a matter of military jurisdiction: within the military-institutional structure, selections were a medical task only they were considered competent to perform.

The principle—established from above—that only doctors should select was adamantly defended by Wirths. Indeed, he himself insisted upon setting an example: not only did he himself select, when he as chief would not have had to, but he put off other obligations that might have prevented him from carrying out ramp duty for which he was scheduled.[18] His attitude was close to that of Höss, the camp commandant, who felt compelled to be present at times during not only selections but the entire sequence of killing: "I had to show them all that I did not merely issue the orders and make the regulations but was also prepared myself to be present at whatever task I had assigned to my subordinates." Significantly, he claimed that doctors had this expectation of him as well, that he felt it necessary "to look through the peephole of the gas chambers and watch the process of death itself, because the doctors wanted me to see it."[19]

The SS doctor Ernst B. thought that having a *physician* conduct selections "made it perfect"—by which he meant, "If somebody from some other place comes and says we don't have enough people or we have too many, ... then it can be claimed that the doctors have done it [the selections]—that it has been done with precise medical judgment." That "perfection" involved the appearance of appropriate medical activity— Auschwitz's "as if" situation—and that policy of doctors' doing selections was (according to Höss) largely laid down by the chief SS doctor, *Reichsarzt* SS Ernst Robert Grawitz. . . .[20]

In holding to the principle of medical efficiency for the entire operation, Wirths oversaw the selections process, including its personal arrangements, and thereby maintained the efficiency of Auschwitz killing.

Performing selections was constantly compared to being in combat. The message from Himmler, from the camp commandant, and from the medical hierarchy was that this difficult assignment had to be understood as wartime duty. Selections were often compared more directly to medical triage in war. Thus Dr. B. could quote his friend Mengele as having repeatedly said that "the selections during the war with his own people in connection with emergency care—who got care and who didn't—that these were much more problematic" than selections in Auschwitz.

Duty arrangements for selections were simple enough. The chief doctor (Wirths) provided the names of physicians—and later of pharmacists and dentists—under his jurisdiction to the ranking noncommissioned officer of the medical unit (usually a top sergeant [SS-*Stabsscharführer*] or a technical sergeant [*Oberscharführer*]) and ordered him to make up a duty roster for ramp service. The rosters included the doctor with primary responsibility for the selections on a particular day as well as a back-up doctor. The latter was supposed to be present, but was by no means always there, especially toward the last phases of the gassings in 1944. Rosters had to be signed by Wirths and posted one week in advance. Similar rosters were prepared for the ramp duty of medical corpsmen, including *Desinfektoren* who were the only ones permitted to handle the gas.

When the commandant's office was notified of the arrival of a transport, it immediately informed the SS medical division. That office in turn notified the physician on duty as well as the highest-ranking noncommissioned *Desinfektor* and the responsible people in the motor pool, from which the ambulance or other vehicle (usually bearing the Red Cross sign) was sent. This careful set of internal arrangements ensured that the selections, *from the standpoint of SS doctors and personnel,* were conducted in an orderly and proper fashion—that is according to regulations. That controlled orderliness extended to the functioning of the Jewish *Sonderkommando* in the crematoria, who were coordinated closely with this medical structure.

Each selection was greatly influenced by instructions from above concerning the relative number of arriving Jews to be killed or permitted to survive. In general terms, policy was set in Berlin by higher SS officials, including Himmler himself. But decisions were also greatly influenced by Auschwitz deliberations between the chief physician and the commandant. Overall, there was a basic conflict between the police arm of the SS, which considered itself responsible for the annihilation of all Jews; and the economic arm of the organization, which responded to the increasingly desperate wartime need for productive slave labor. Wirths and other doctors saw themselves as essentially in the second group because, in addition to performing selections, their task included maintaining the health of these slave laborers, at least to the degree of enabling them to work. But SS doctors could take the opposite view as well, claiming that overcrowding and extremely poor hygienic conditions could lead to devastating epidemics. They would therefore insist that fewer arrivals be admitted to the camp; that, in effect, a greater percentage of them be killed. Wirths and Höss constantly consulted about such matters, and there was known to be considerable disagreement and tension between the two men. Wirths constantly sought better medical facilities, while Höss was preoccupied with facilities for maximum efficiency in mass murder. According to Dr. B., they conferred on many things, including especially those that could "go wrong."

One of the things that could go wrong was for officers other than physicians to conduct selections illegally: either because they represented the Reich Security (police) position (Eichmann) and wanted to see all Jews killed, or because they represented the views of the economic and administrative division and wanted to keep as many Jews as possible alive for work. Höss claimed that medical authority supported his own police position of maximum killing:

> The *Reichsarzt* SS [Grawitz] . . . held the view that only those Jews who were completely fit and able to work should be selected for employment. The weak and the old and those who were only relatively robust would very soon become incapable of work, which would cause a further deterioration in the general standard of health, and an unnecessary increase in the hospital accommodation, requiring further medical personnel and medicines, and all for no purpose since they would in the end have to be killed. . . .
>
> I myself held the view that only really strong and healthy Jews ought to be selected for employment.[21]

The conflict within the SS was never fully resolved. In a way, it did not have to be. Advocates of maximum murder could take satisfaction in the killing of overwhelming numbers of arriving Jews; selections provided the slave-labor advocates with their slaves. And doctors' recommendations were met by both tendencies: the extensive killing prevented overcrowding; and the selections, by providing stronger inmates, eased the doctors' task of maintaining the health of the inmate population.

They could in fact come to see their physician's task, as Dr. B. said, as rendering the killing "humane": "The discussion [among doctors] was about how the matter could be carried out humanely [*die Sache human durchgeführt*]. That was the problem of the physician. . . . The discussion about the possibility of humanity [in killing], . . . [of] humanitarian [methods in the face of] . . . the general overload of the apparatus—that was the problem."

"A Regular Job"

The selections became simply "a part of their life," as a prisoner doctor, Jacob R. commented to me. And Dr. B., too, noted that, whatever reservations SS doctors had at first, they soon viewed selections as "normal duty," as "a regular job." Indeed within the Auschwitz atmosphere, as another survivor testified, "to kill a man was nothing, not worth talking about": a doctor who was perfectly polite and decent most of the time "felt no compunction about sending people into the gas."[22]

From the late spring of 1944, when an enormous influx of Hungarian Jews placed a strain on the scheduling of doctors on the duty roster, the way of conducting selections changed. Now, as Dr. B. explained, mass arrangements had to be made. At a special meeting of medical officers, Wirths announced that dentists and pharmacists were to take regular turns along with doctors in performing the selections. And selections were done by "teams": "When the train arrived, there were announcements through a loudspeaker, such as 'Mothers and children go left!'"

Although two doctors were present, neither any longer made decisions about individual arrivals. Rather, the doctor became "only a supervisor." It was still important that he be present because he had the responsibility of overseeing the behavior of noncommissioned officers, others on the selections team, and prisoners—all of whom took part in placing arriving men and women in lines according to their category. With thousands of people arriving every day—as many as ten thousand in one night—selections were done "only by groups. . . . One couldn't select individuals. . . . In the regulations it was stated that every individual must be judged capable of work—'camp-worthy'—or not on medical grounds. In practice, that was never carried out—because it was impossible. One . . . selected only according to categories." But the doctor was still central, Dr. B. emphasized: *"He stood there and led the thing."*

Doctors could become very engrossed in questions about the method or technique of selections:

> The people who participated in [a particular] selection would discuss it for days. "Which is better: to let mothers go with their children to the gas or to select the mothers later by separating them from their children?" . . . Those were the type of problems in Auschwitz—not ideological problems but purely technical problems. And wars were virtually waged over these issues.

Dr. B. explained how advice would be given to doctors and SS camp leaders by women criminal *capos* (prisoner functionaries) drawn from among actual German criminals; these *capos* found it much less difficult to handle arriving mothers whose children were still with them.

They engaged in elaborate exchanges about how many people should be killed and how many admitted to the camp, always from the standpoint of medical and hygienic considerations:

> There were numerous discussions: Should one gas more or should one [gas fewer]? Where is the limit to be set? That is, if you take more old people into the camps, then there are more diseased people, and that, for

many reasons, is the worse problem if they are in the working camp . . . where there is only so much possibility [for keeping limited numbers of people alive]. . . . Then the camp leadership comes . . . and says, "You're sending us people we can't do anything with. They'll only croak." . . . You understand that about these purely technical issues there were heated and intense discussions.

Dr. B. told me that "the doctors really became active" in confronting the overriding technical problem of burning large numbers of corpses. With the crematoria unable to take care of the enormous new load, trenches were dug and piled high with corpses.

> One had to burn . . . great piles—enormous piles. Now that is a great problem, igniting piles of corpses. You can imagine—naked—nothing burns. How does one manage this? . . .
>
> They had been through the gas chambers and now thousands were lying there and had to be burned. How does one do that? One tested numerous methods—and here the doctors were drawn in to try to solve this problem and they helped find solutions.

Ernst B. himself became a bit excited as he explained in more detail the technical problem:

> The gas chambers were sufficient, you see, that was no problem. But the burning, right? The ovens broke down. And they [the corpses] had to be burned in a big heap. . . . The problem is really a large technical difficulty. There was not too much room, so first one thought one would have to take small piles. . . . Well, . . . that would have to be tried out. . . . And then everyone contributed his knowledge of physics, about what might possibly be done differently. If you do it with ditches around them, then the air comes up from below and wooden planks underneath and gasoline on top—or gasoline underneath and wood in between—these were the problems. Well, the solution was not to let the fire die. And maintain the cooperation between the gas chamber and the crematorium. When [the fire] reached a certain intensity, then it was just right—but then you could not get to it, so it was still too hot, etc. Those were the problems.

He went on to explain how different people did different things to help:

> And the actual work was of course done by the subordinate commanders [*Unterführer*], you understand, the NCOs [*Unteroffizier*]—people who were experienced in cleaning out [*wegräumen*], who . . . had to deal with these prosaic [*hausbackenen;* literally, "home-baked"] problems. There are technically talented people . . . physicians as well as . . . NCOs and also company commanders and camp leaders. Some were . . . how

shall we say? . . . well, one cannot put it any other way—interested in it. They pressed forward, or rather they engaged themselves. . . . They said, "What those others are doing is all rubbish!" Or . . . some who had already been in other concentration camps where one was experiencing these matters because, for instance, the crematoria had been out of operation or were small. . . . Physicians and other people—all those who believed themselves to be experts—they engaged themselves there.

As Dr. B. summed up the matter: "The problem . . . was not the selections but how one can burn the colossal quantities [of corpses] if the ovens are not working. That's what was being talked about, and nothing else."

The problem led to antagonisms among doctors and other SS leaders ("Why didn't *you* have an idea?"), and to disclaimers of responsibility ("That is not *our* job—*you* go ahead and do something"). Soon discussions of the nagging problem were no longer confined to small medical or technical circles but were extended to casual off-duty moments, with such comments as, "This fool, he did such and such—how can he do that when—?" Dr. B. explained that the "best ideas" did not necessarily come from doctors or other officers but came from "very simple people" among SS personnel. And his message again and again was that the focus was always pragmatic, on what *worked*—"not [on] moral or aesthetic or any other such considerations . . . because that [area of feeling] was already blocked off [*abgeblockt*]. . . . It was purely a technical matter." And, with chilling consistency, on the subject of ethics: "No. 'Ethical' plays absolutely no [part]—the word does not exist."

B. then provided a simple but telling model:

> The whole pattern of things within the camp atmosphere . . . was just the way it is in a civilian community, with all the human squabbling, you understand. . . . It was like the planning of construction or something on that order, things you observe in any community. . . . Not only professional conflicts but also positions of power . . . were fought out just as in any civilian organization, but here it was all about the Auschwitz crematorium and such things. . . . It is exactly the same. . . . Human beings living in communities have a task, . . . administering something somewhere, and . . . they always function in the same way— according to rules—for instance, Parkinson's Law.*. . . And it was exactly that way within the concentration camp—especially so because of the secrecy and because it [the camp] had such an exceptional position [*Sonderstellung;* here suggesting "special function"]. . . . And

---

*The semi-humorous principle—put forward in C. Northcote Parkinson's 1980 book, *Parkinson: A Law*—that bureaucracy expands to fill up available space.

the extraordinary [nature] of those . . . actions [the killing], . . . that was
not a matter of debate . . . but had been accepted. For instance, the
problem of the crematorium and its capacity, etc.—that was equal to
the ordinary problem of sewerage or the like elsewhere.

One was getting rid of the waste material of a routinized communal
enterprise.

For the most part, doctors raised objections not to the project but to
being themselves victimized by violations of what they considered fair
play: "For instance, . . . one had to be on duty three nights in a row. . . .
because another . . . was shirking and organized for himself an outer
camp inspection [assignment] with which he made himself a better life."

Yet communal spirit could be mobilized: "If, for instance, doctors
were off duty and another [doctor who was on duty] wasn't able to
handle it, . . . they would have helped him, according to their [technical
ability to give advice on how to get the crematoria going again]."

The use of a vehicle marked with a red cross seemed perfectly natural:
"That was a military vehicle. What else should they have used? Gassing
was the physicians' responsibility. Physicians had only cars marked with
Red Cross markings. So what should [one expect them to use]?"

Ernst B.'s accurate description leaves out the sense of filth and evil
retained by SS doctors at some level of awareness. . . . But Dr. B. himself,
referring to ramp duty more than thirty-five years later, acknowledged,
"There is no way to describe selections in Auschwitz."

THE EXPERIMENTAL IMPULSE

Nazi doctors are infamous for their cruel medical experiments. And no
wonder: those experiments killed and maimed; as tangible medical
crimes, they were given considerable prominence at the Nuremberg
Medical Trial. Yet they were no more than a small part of the
extensive and systematic medicalized killing. And it is that aspect of the
experiments—their relation to the Nazi biomedical vision—that I shall
mainly discuss.

Generally speaking, Nazi medical experiments fall into two categories: those sponsored by the regime for a specific ideological and military purpose, and those that were done *ad hoc* out of allegedly scientific
interest on the part of an SS doctor.

For example, extensive sterilization and castration experiments in
Auschwitz, conducted mainly by doctors Carl Clauberg and Horst
Schumann, were encouraged officially as a direct expression of racial
theory and policy; the experiments with typhus contagion (injecting
people with blood from others with active typhus) and with the

effectiveness of various preparations of sera (in treating experimentally induced cases of typhus) were connected with military concerns about typhus epidemics among German troops and civilian personnel in the East;* while the study of pre-cancerous conditions of the cervix reflected a scientific interest of Dr. Eduard Wirths, the chief SS Auschwitz doctor, and his gynecologist brother Helmut. But the categories overlapped. (Mengele's research on twins grew out of his specific scientific interest but was also strongly affected by Nazi ideology.) Here we shall focus on the extensive sterilization and castration experiments, in which Auschwitz more or less specialized, and which were a direct extension of the biomedical vision. . . .

Block 10

The center for these experimental projects was the notorious Block 10, a place that could be considered to be quintessential Auschwitz. Made up mostly of women prisoners, it was located in the men's camp, and the windows were kept closed and shuttered or boarded so that communication with the outside was totally cut off. One woman prisoner doctor who spent a year there described how, from the first night, she gained a lasting impression of having been transferred to a "horror place" that resembled both hell and a mental institution. And if one could peek out, one would witness executions, prisoners being shot to death in the courtyard of the infamous Block 11.

At the same time, inmates on the block were completely vulnerable to visits and surveillance of various kinds by SS doctors and, on occasion, by nonmedical officers: "A continuous coming and going of SS . . . [so that] we never felt safe." For any visit could mean new danger, and inmates therefore "awaited with impatience . . . the evening when we would be locked up as animals in a cage but . . . nonetheless felt freer."[23]

Another woman prisoner doctor, Adelaide Hautval, told of the five hundred women "guinea pigs," all Jewish, from various countries in Europe, who were usually selected directly from transports, according to the needs of the Nazi physician experimenters: "Some required married women, others young girls, a third a mixture of all the categories." Overall conditions were superior to those in the women's camp, because there the "guinea pigs . . . would have died before the results of the experiments could have been assessed." Inmates suffered from hunger, nonetheless, and from the constant uncertainty about "What will it be

---

*Typhus experiments were conducted only to a limited degree at Auschwitz, but on a much wider scale at other camps.

this time?" For they had absorbed the Auschwitz principle that *anything is permitted*. At the same time the women deeply feared a transfer to Birkenau, where they knew death was more likely, because in Block 10 there was at least a hope that "maybe they will still let us live after this," though few believed that possible.[24]

The block was divided into separate research areas: those of Professor Clauberg, Professor Schumann (both sterilizers), Dr. Wirths and his brother (who studied pre-cancerous growths of the cervix), and a special area for studies conducted by the Hygienic Institute.

Inevitably, there was a dimension of Auschwitz schizophrenia: in this case, the twenty-two prostitutes—mostly Germans, Poles, and Russians—the only non-Jewish residents of Block 10. On Himmler's orders, the SS opened bordellos at Auschwitz and other camps. Available to élite prisoners, mostly Germans, prostitutes were meant to be a work incentive and were also intended to help diminish widespread homosexuality among male prisoners (occasionally prostitutes were assigned to known homosexuals for that purpose, with predictable results).[25] The gynecologist Dr. Wanda J. told how prostitutes were instructed to visit her if they noticed any indication of venereal disease. Camp commanders frequently appeared on Block 10 to choose particular prostitutes for their subcamps. As Dr. J. put it in discussing the prostitutes, "that was a part of everything."

Extreme rumors spread through the camp about Block 10. Prisoners considered it a "sinister place" of mysterious evil. There were widespread rumors that Clauberg was conducting experiments in artificial insemination, and women were terrified of having "monsters" implanted in their wombs. Some survivors I spoke to believed that those experiments actually occurred. Another account had Clauberg speaking of his intentions to carry out artificial-insemination experiments in the future. There were also rumors of a "museum" on Block 10: "Skulls, body parts, even mummies"; and one survivor insisted, "A friend ... saw ... our *Gymnasium* [high school] teacher stuffed [mummified] on Block 10." Again, anything was possible, and whatever occurred there was likely to be a manifestation of the Nazi racial claim.

Sterilization by Injection: "The Professor"

Block 10 was often known as "Clauberg's block," because it was created for him and his experimental efforts to perfect a cheap and effective method of mass sterilization. He was Block 10's figure of greatest authority, "the main man for sterilization" as Dr. J. put it, and the one who "has the extras in equipment and space": in addition to the wards, an elaborate X-ray apparatus and four special experimental rooms, one of which served as a darkroom for developing X-ray films. As a civilian, Clauberg was an Auschwitz outsider who rented facilities, research subjects, and even prisoner doctors from the SS. He was a powerful outsider, holding a reserve SS rank of *Gruppenführer*, or lieutenant general. Höss and everyone else were aware that Himmler was interested in the work and had given the order that brought Clauberg to Auschwitz. He began his Auschwitz work in December 1942 in Birkenau; but after persuading the authorities that his important research required a special block, he transferred his experimental setting to Block 10 in Auschwitz in April 1943.

His method was to inject a caustic substance into the cervix in order to obstruct the fallopian tubes. He chose as experimental subjects married women between the ages of twenty and forty, preferably those who had borne children. And he first injected them with opaque liquid in order to determine by X ray that there was no prior blockage or impairment. He had experimented with different substances, but was very secretive about the exact nature of the one he used, probably intent upon protecting any "medical discovery" from research competitors. Even the camp commandant, Rudolf Höss, who took a great interest in the work and witnessed several injections, later wrote, "Clauberg informed me in detail on the performance of the operation, but never revealed to me the exact chemical composition of the substance he used." That substance is now believed to have been Formalin, sometimes injected together with Novocain.[26]*

The injection was done in three stages over a few months, though some women later described four or five injections. The goal of injecting the caustic substance was to create adhesions in the fallopian tubes that would cause them to be obstructed within a period of about six weeks, as would be demonstrated by subsequent X rays. Clauberg had a prisoner nurse, Sylvia Friedmann, observe the women after the injections for symptoms of any kind.

Despite the terror induced in women victims, Marie L., a French prisoner physician, stressed that many so feared being sent back to Birkenau (where one would be "awaiting death standing in frost, mud, and swamps . . . without water or care") that they could view Block 10 as "a piece of luck and the possibility of survival." Clauberg himself encouraged this hope by his reassurances that he planned not to send them back to Birkenau (meaning the gas chamber) but to take them to his private research clinic at Königshütte, just a few kilometers from

---

*The formula was apparently developed by Clauberg and his assistant Dr. Johannes Goebel, chief chemist with the Schering pharmaceutical firm.

Auschwitz. That could well have been true because Höss later reported that "after the successful experiment, . . . Clauberg planned that everyone of the female prisoners at the end of a year undergo sexual intercourse with a male prisoner chosen especially for this purpose," in order to carry out a practical test of Clauberg's sterilization method. This test, however, was never performed "because of the course of the war."[27]

Clauberg eventually had as many as three hundred women under his control on Block 10. The experiments were supposed to be highly secret, and there was an attempt to isolate women who had been injected from those who had not. Accounts differ about the fate of the women he experimented upon. Those who refused to be experimented upon, or who were considered for one reason or another unsuitable, were sent back to Birkenau and usually gassed—as were those women who became extremely debilitated. Most women experimented upon remained on Block 10, though a considerable number developed fever and various forms of peritoneal infection.

There was the constant fear of being killed because of knowing too much. They also feared both sterilization and artificial insemination. Clauberg is reported to have told prisoners he planned artificial-insemination experiments, and there is one report of his admitting to two assistants that he had future plans for experiments in both natural and artificial insemination.

Descriptions by women experimented upon begin to tell us in human terms what Clauberg was really up to. A Czech Jew named Margita Neumann told of being taken into a dark room with a large X-ray machine:

> Dr. Clauberg ordered me to lie down on the gynecological table and I was able to observe Sylvia Friedmann who was preparing an injection syringe with a long needle. Dr. Clauberg used this needle to give me an injection in my womb. I had the feeling that my stomach would burst with the pain. I began to scream so that I could be heard through the entire block. Dr. Clauberg told me roughly to stop screaming immediately, otherwise I'd be taken back at once to Birkenau concentration camp. . . . After this experiment I had inflammation of the ovaries.

She went on to describe how, whenever Clauberg appeared on the ward, women were "overcome with anxiety and terror," as "they considered what Dr. Clauberg was doing as the actions of a murderer."[28]

Survivors also mentioned his crude and cynical "jokes," as well as the resentments of him among other Nazi camp authorities who would like to have done away with Block 10, his protection of experimental subjects being seen by some as a way of maintaining his own enterprise.

Dr. L., who for a time took care of women in Block 10, observed Clauberg closely and described him as "short, bald, and unlikable." He was in fact about five feet tall, and several inmates referred to him as a kind of "caricature." In addition he had a history of violence: as a student, later toward his wife, and on still another occasion toward a mistress. As Marie L. said, in understatement, "I think that with him there was something quite unbalanced." Similarly, Dr. Tadeusz S. invoked Clauberg as evidence for his principle that "the greatest murderers were the greatest cowards," and described him as "fat and unpleasant looking, . . . a small, ugly, funny-looking, more or less deformed person. He wanted to imitate Prussian officers but he looked like a salesman in a general's hat. . . . He was absurd."

Yet Clauberg was also a teacher and a gynecological researcher and a practitioner of considerable distinction. Long associated with the University of Kiel, his gynecological work there led to his *Habilitation* (qualification for lecturer-professorial status on the basis of advanced research and dissertation) in 1937 at the age of thirty-nine. The hormonal preparations Progynon and Proluton that he developed to treat infertility are still used today (in a letter written as early as June 1935, Clauberg discussed the former as useful for both maintaining and terminating pregnancy),[29] as is the "Clauberg test" for measuring the action of progesterone.

Clauberg's personal and ideological history, however, followed a familiar course. The oldest son of a rural craftsman who later established a weapons business, Clauberg was called to the military in 1916, saw action in France, and spent the last part of the war as a prisoner of the English. He joined the Nazi Party in 1933, became a committed Nazi who wore the Party's Golden Badge for meritorious service—while remaining personally and professionally highly ambitious—and reached his rank of reserve SS *Gruppenführer* (lieutenant general) in 1940.[30]

That same year a meeting with Himmler, arranged by a fellow SS officer, marked the beginning of a relationship based on a malignant blending of biomedical and political-racial ideologies—the initiative moving back and forth between the medical man and the SS leader, with the process culminating in "Clauberg's block" in Auschwitz. At this meeting Clauberg told Himmler of his intention to set up a research institute for reproductive biology, which would investigate both the causes and the treatment of infertility and the development of a nonsurgical means of sterilization. Himmler had first learned of Clauberg's work through the gynecologist's successful treatment of infertility in a high-ranking SS officer's wife. When Clauberg explained to the *Reichsführer* that such treatment required a preparation that could clear the fallopian tubes by softening any adhesions or substances blocking them, Himmler, whose real interest here was sterilization, was said to have suggested reversing that procedure by using agents that *produce* blocking. As a result of that conversation (whatever the sequence of who suggested what to whom), Clauberg redirected his research energies toward the explicit goal of finding an effective method of mass sterilization.

With financial support arranged by Himmler, Clauberg began animal experiments; found that a 5- to 10-percent solution of Formalin could produce the desired inflammation and blockage; sought out the highly viscous (resistant to flow) liquid that would, when containing Formalin, enable it to remain in the ovarian tubes after being introduced to the uterus; and worked on X-ray tracing techniques for monitoring effects.[31]

A year later Himmler summoned Clauberg to confer and suggested that he conduct sterilization experiments at the Ravensbrück concentration camp. But with the help of Grawitz, the chief SS doctor now involved in the matter, Clauberg eventually convinced Himmler that Auschwitz would be more practical because of its proximity to Königshütte, where Clauberg already had his clinical facilities. On 30 May 1942, three days after their second meeting, Clauberg wrote a letter to Himmler remarkable in its expression of the German physician's *active*, indeed determined, effort to contribute to the deadly purposes of the Nazi biomedical vision.

Clauberg makes clever obeisance not only to Himmler's overall authority but to his "scientific" concerns, by stating that he (Clauberg) had been told that "the one person in Germany today who would be particularly interested in these matters and who would be able to help me would be you, most honorable *Reichsführer.*" By mentioning proposed work on "positive population policy," Clauberg ingeniously alludes to the agricultural dimension so dear to Himmler ("The eventual or most probable importance of agriculture for the female capacity for propagation demands clarification") and then gets to the real point—the question of the "negative population policy," about which he makes the dramatic proposal that, having demonstrated the possibility of sterilization without operation on the basis of animal experiments, "now we must proceed to the first experiments on human beings." The letter goes on with this combination of flattery, slick scientific gloss, elaborate research projection (a laboratory for animal experiments, an experimental farm to investigate questions of "agriculture and fertility," etc.), and a pervasive medical focus ("The center from which all ideas start, all problems are raised . . . and finally turned over to practical use, is and remains the clinic")—all leading to the plan to "evaluate the method of sterilization without operation . . . on women unworthy of propagation and to use this method continually after it is finally proved efficient." He makes clear that Auschwitz is the ideal place for "the human material to be provided," and even proposes that it be named after Himmler as "Research Institute of the *Reichsführer* SS for Biological Propagation." The entire letter captures much of the ethos and corruption of the physician researcher within the Nazi biomedical vision.[32]

... Clauberg's assistant in Auschwitz, Dr. Johannes Goebel, worked on producing the necessary caustic substance as well as improved X-ray tracing material and, although not a physician, was given the prerogative of performing many of the injections.[33] The number of women these two men are believed to have sterilized in this fashion has been estimated from seven hundred to "several thousand."[34] According to the nurse Sylvia Friedmann, when a woman died after injection Clauberg "showed absolutely no interest, no reaction, as though the matter didn't concern him at all." There were a number of such deaths.[35]

As Russian troops approached Königshütte, Clauberg fled to Ravensbrück and arranged for some of his research victims to be sent there as well; despite the extreme chaos, he continued with his sterilization experiments. But with the approach of the Allied armies three months later, he fled again, this time to Schleswig-Holstein, seeking to join the last group of loyal SS leaders surrounding Himmler, the only Auschwitz doctor to do so. But Himmler was captured and committed suicide; and Clauberg too was captured by the Russians on 8 June 1945. Imprisoned in the Soviet Union for three years before being tried, he was then convicted of war crimes and sentenced to twenty-five years' imprisonment. But following Stalin's death (in 1953), and various diplomatic agreements, Clauberg was repatriated with other Germans in October 1955. He was not only unrepentant but grandiose and bizarre: he listed on his professional card various Nazi medical organizations, including the "City of Mothers" he had run as part of his involvement in "positive eugenics," and advertised for a secretary under his own name. When interviewed by the press, he spoke proudly of his work at Königshütte and Auschwitz and claimed, "I was able to perfect an absolutely new method of sterilization ... [which] would be of great use today in certain cases."[36]

After various pressures from survivor groups and others, Clauberg was arrested in November 1955; but for a considerable time, the German Chamber of Medicine, the official body of the profession, resisted action against him that would divest him of his title of doctor of medicine. A group of former prisoner physicians of Auschwitz issued an impressive declaration condemning Clauberg's actions there as being "in total disaccord with the sworn duty of every doctor," and bitterly decrying the fact that "such medical practitioners who ... put themselves at the service of National-Socialism to destroy human lives ... are today in a position to practice once more the profession which they have profaned in such a scandalous manner."[37] The German Chamber of Medicine finally did remove Clauberg's license. But when he died, suddenly and mysteriously, in his prison cell on 9 August 1957, the general belief was that he was in the process of naming names at the top of the Nazi medical hierarchy and that, consequently, medical colleagues helped bring about his death.[38]. . .

Removal of Limits

There is an additional Auschwitz research function: that of the camp as a constant source of victims for research done almost anywhere. Besides the Auschwitz prisoners taken to Strasbourg to be made part of Professor Hirt's skeleton collection, there are many other examples: eight prisoners from Auschwitz sent to Sachsenhausen for experiments with epidemic hepatitis, in which the possible death of the inmates was an accepted part of the arrangement; and the notorious sequence of twenty Jewish children, ages five to twelve, transferred from Auschwitz to Neuengamme in Hamburg, where they were subjected to injections of virulent tubercular serum and to other experiments, until they were removed from Neuengamme and secretly murdered just before the arrival of Allied troops.[39] Auschwitz was not just a medicalized death factory but a source of "raw materials" for everyone's deadly medical experiments.

Prisoner physicians could speak with bitter accuracy about the specific way in which their and other inmates' humanity was negated by Nazi experimenters. One observed that "man was the cheapest experimental animal. . . . Cheaper than a rat." Another declared that the experiments "had no scientific basis, and . . . that the main interest they had for those who performed them was to give Berlin, in their detailed reports, the illusion of important and continuous work, so that these brave 'researchers' might be kept far from the front in a position of sinecure."

We know that Nazi doctors partly justified the experiments by their sense that Jews were in any case doomed. While prisoner doctors made no such justification, their emotions were also affected by the Jewish death sentence. Dr. Jacob R. could remember a feeling that "the experiments were of considerably less import than the whole inferno I was viewing there."

The experiments represent, among other things, a removal of medical limits. Ordinary medical behavior is predicated upon maintaining life—and refraining from actual or potential killing or maiming one's patient in the name of enhancing the life of one's own group or people. Paradoxically, that medical vision of social cure contributed directly to using medicine to kill or injure. Hence the array of Auschwitz experiments, and others done elsewhere including artificially inflicted burns with phosphorous incendiary bombs; experiments on the effects of drinking sea water; experiments with various forms of poison, by ingestion as well as in bullets or arrows;

widespread experiments on artificially induced typhus, as well as with epidemic hepatitis and with malaria; experiments in cold immersion ("in freezing water") to determine the body's reactions and susceptibilities; experiments with mustard gas in order to study the kinds of wounds it can cause; experiments on the regeneration of bone muscle, nerve tissue, and on bone transplantation, involving removal of various bones, muscles, and nerves from healthy women. All of the experiments were related to the Nazi biomedical vision, whether they directly contributed to cultural genocide (as in the case of sterilization) or were the work of German physicians taking a leading role in biological and genetic purification.

In experiments in sterilization, of course, the ideological source and goals are clear. But all the other experiments as well reflect the Nazi image of "life unworthy of life," of creatures who, because less than human, can be studied, altered, manipulated, mutilated, or killed—in the service of the Nordic race, and ultimately of remaking humankind. One experiments without limit in order to "gather together the best blood" and "once more breed over the generations the pure type of Nordic German."[40] The task is never accomplished, so one must continue experimenting. All of Auschwitz becomes not only a vast experiment but an unending one.

QUESTIONS FOR DISCUSSION

1. How did the medical and social policy of euthanasia—the medicalized killing of the incurably sick—lead to a policy of genocide, the deliberate killing of the Jewish people? Is this particular aspect of the history of the Nazi regime relevant to current debates (in the United States and elsewhere) about the possible legalization of medical euthanasia for the terminally ill and the elderly?

2. The medical experiments by the Nazi doctors at Auschwitz—such as those performed by Dr. Carl Clauberg—were cruel and perverse, and in the end they yielded no important medical knowledge. But what if the experiments, despite their brutality, had revealed important facts for the future health of the human race? Discuss the ethical and social issues that arise in the use of medical information gleaned from immoral and cruel experiments performed on a prisoner population.

3. Lifton thinks that the key to understanding the operation of the death camp at Auschwitz-Birkenau is to see it as a "public health venture." Consider the role of the medical staff in providing the operations of mass death with a justifiable argument as a valid social policy. What different tasks did the medical staff perform, and how did each contribute to the efficiency of the camp? How did each task contribute to the appearance of an acceptable and normal social policy?

4. One surviving SS doctor, Dr. Ernst B., describes the organization and operation of the Auschwitz camp as similar to any other human organization and community—professional and personal conflicts, squabbles over power,

expanding bureaucracy. Ethics played no role in decision making, only the efficiency of the organization. The fact of mass killings lost its meaning and was considered simply as the problem to be dealt with, similar to a town board's problem with a sewage treatment plant. If this is true, what lessons can we learn for the organization of contemporary institutions and projects? What lessons must be learned for future doctors, scientists, and technological professionals?

ABBREVIATIONS

BDC	Berlin Document Center
Nuremberg	Nuernberg Military Tribunals, *United States of America v. Karl*
Medical Case	*Brandt et al., Case I ("The Medical Case")*, 2 vols. (Washington, 1947), and accompanying transcripts (National Archives, Washington).

NOTES

1. See Raul Hilberg, *The Destruction of the European Jews* (Chicago: Quadrangle, 1967 [1961]); Richard L. Rubenstein, *The Cunning of History: Mass Death and the American Future* (New York: Harper & Row, 1975); Hannah Arendt, *Eichmann in Jerusalem: A Report on the Banality of Evil* (New York: Viking, 1963). Hilberg's expanded edition of his classic work was too recent to consult fully for this book; see *The Destruction of the European Jews*, 3 vols., rev. and definitive ed. (New York: Holmes & Meier, 1985).
2. Hilberg, *Destruction*, p. 256.
3. A slightly different, published version is found in Ella Lingens-Reiner, *Prisoners of Fear* (London: Gollancz, 1948), pp. 1–2.
4. Adolf Hitler, *Mein Kampf* (Boston: Houghton Mifflin, 1943 [1925–26]), p. 435.
5. Ibid., pp. 150, 300–308, 312–13. For scholarly treatments of Hitler's (and earlier) metaphors for the Jews, see Eberhard Jäckel, *Hitler's Weltanschauung: A Blueprint for Power* (Middletown, Conn.: Wesleyan University Press, 1972 [1969]); Rudolph Binion, *Hitler Among the Germans* (New York: Elsevier, 1976); Lucy S. Dawidowicz, *The War Against the Jews, 1933–1945* (New York: Holt, Rinehart & Winston, 1975), pp. 19–21, 55–56; Uriel Tal, *Christians and Jews in Germany: Religion, Politics and Ideology in the Second Reich, 1870–1914* (Ithaca: Cornell University Press, 1975), pp. 259–89.
6. Hans Buchheim, quoted in Helmut Krausnick, "The Persecution of the Jews," in Krausnick et al., *Anatomy of the SS State* (New York: Walker, 1968 [1965]), p. 15.
7. Hilberg, *Destruction*, p. 12.
8. J. P. Stern, *Hitler: The Führer and the People* (Glasgow: Fontana/Collins, 1971), p. 70. The celebration of that religious impulse was epitomized by the gigantic Nuremberg rally of 1934, whose theme, "The Triumph of the Will," became the title of Leni Rienfenstahl's noted film. Riefenstahl, in an interview with an assistant of mine, made clear that Hitler himself provided that slogan.

9. George L. Mosse, *The Crisis of German Ideology: Intellectual Origins of the Third Reich* (New York: Grosset & Dunlap, 1964), p. 103.

10. Himmler, quoted in Krausnick, "Persecution," p. 14.

11. George L. Mosse, *Toward the Final Solution: A History of European Racism* (New York: Fertig, 1978), p. 77.

12. Hitler, *Mein Kampf*, pp. 397–98.

13. *Nuremberg Medical Case*, especially vol. I, pp. 8–17 (the indictment) and 27–74 (opening statement by Chief Prosecutor Telford Taylor, 9 December 1946); personal interview with James M. McHaney, prosecutor of the Medical Case.

14. The discussion of these medical and nonmedical activities is based on interviews with Nazi doctors and with prisoner doctors, and on the following major sources: Rudolf Höss, *Commandant of Auschwitz: The Autobiography of Rudolf Hoess* (Cleveland: World, 1959) and "Die nichtärztliche Tätigkeit der SS-Ärzte im K.L. Auschwitz" ("The Nonmedical Activity of SS-Doctors in Auschwitz"), [photo of 1947 ms. (trial document)], in *Hefte von Auschwitz* 2 (1959):81–84; Bernd Naumann, *Auschwitz: A Report on the Proceedings Against Robert Karl Ludwig Mulka and Others Before the Court of Frankfurt* (New York: Pantheon, 1966 [1965]); Herman Langbein, *Menschen in Auschwitz* (Vienna: Europaverlag, 1972) and *Der Auschwitz-Prozess: Eine Dokumentation*, 2 vols. (Frankfurt/M.: Europäische Verlagsanstalt, 1965), as well as the articles in the *Anthology* series (1971) and many of those in the journal *Hefte von Auschwitz* (from 1959 on), published by the Polish State Auschwitz Museum.

15. Majdanek bore some resemblance to Auschwitz regarding this policy but on a considerably smaller scale. See Adalbert Rückerl, *NS-Vernichtungslager im Spiegel deutscher Strafprozesse* (Munich: DTV, 1977), pp. 28–29; Josef Marszalek, *Majdanek* (Hamburg, 1982); Raul Hilberg, *The Destruction of the European Jews*, rev and definitive ed. (New York: Holmes & Meier, 1985), vol. III, pp. 899, 1219.

16. Transcript of judgment in Frankfurt Auschwitz trial, 19–20 August 1965 (4 Ks 2/63), p. 74; Raul Hilberg, *The Destruction of the European Jews* (Chicago: Quadrangle, 1967 [1961]), pp. 150–51.

17. Jean-François Steiner, *Treblinka* (New York: Simon & Schuster, 1967 [1966]), p. 110.

18. Hermann Langbein, *Menschen in Auschwitz* (Vienna: Europaverlag, 1972), pp. 420–21.

19. Rudolf Höss, *Commandant of Auschwitz: The Autobiography of Rudolf Hoess* (Cleveland: World, 1959), p. 171.

20. Ibid., p. 212.

21. Ibid., pp. 212–13; see pp. 176–79.

22. Hermann Langbein, quoted in Bernd Naumann, *Auschwitz: A Report on the Proceedings Against Robert Karl Ludwig Mulka and Others Before the Court at Frankfurt* (New York: Praeger, 1966 [1965]), pp. 102–3.

23. Unpublished testimony from Mme. Kleinova, M.D. (Prague), regarding her stay on Block 10.

24. Adelaide Hautval, "Survey of the Experiments Performed in the Women's Camps at Auschwitz and Ravensbrouck" (unpublished testimony) and personal communication.

25. On prostitution at Auschwitz, see Hermann Langbein, *Menschen in Auschwitz* (Vienna: Europaverlag, 1972), pp. 454–55.

26. Jan Sehn, "Carl Claubergs verbrecherische Unfruchtbarmachungs-Versuche an Häftlings-Frauen in den Nazi-Konzentrationslagern," *Hefte von Auschwitz* 2 (1959):3–31 (see p. 16 on the formalin formula). Höss quoted in F. K. Kaul, *Ärzte in Auschwitz* ([E.] Berlin: Verlag Volk und Gesundheit, 1968), pp. 277–78.

27. Kaul, *Ärzte*, p. 278.

28. PIIIh (Auschwitz) 863 (Wiener Library, London).

29. Sehn, "Claubergs Unfruchtbarmachungs-Versuche," p. 15.

30. BDC: Clauberg.

31. Sehn, "Claubergs Unfruchtbarmachungs-Versuche" pp. 15–16. See also Raul Hilberg, *The Destruction of the European Jews* (Chicago: Quadrangle, 1967 [1961]), pp. 605–6.

32. Clauberg to Himmler, 30 May 1942 (NO-211), *Nuremberg Medical Case*, vol. I, pp. 724–27.

33. Langbein, *Menschen*, p. 386.

34. Sehn, "Claubergs Unfruchtbarmachungs-Versuche," p. 26.

35. PIIIh (Auschwitz) 659 (Wiener Library, London).

36. Philippe Aziz, *Doctors of Death* (Geneva: Ferni, 1976), vol. II, p. 236, see also pp. 175, 235–37; Sehn, "Claubergs Unfruchtbarmachungs-Versuche," pp. 14, 26–27.

37. Aziz, *Doctors*, vol. II, pp. 240–41.

38. Sehn, "Claubergs Unfruchtbarmachungs-Versuche," pp. 31–32.

39. Günther Schwarberg, *The Murders at Bullenhuser Damm: The SS Doctor and the Children* (Bloomington: Indiana University Press, 1984 [1980]).

40. Agriculture Minister Walther Darré, quoted in Robert Cecil, *the Myth of the Master Race: Alfred Rosenberg and Nazi Ideology* (New York: Dodd, Mead, 1972), p. 144.

CHAPTER 11

IBM in Nazi Germany

---\/---

This chapter is composed of several related selections from Edwin Black's controversial book, *IBM and the Holocaust: The Strategic Alliance Between Nazi Germany and America's Most Powerful Corporation* (2001). The book is a comprehensive study of IBM's business and technological relationship with the Nazi government of Germany, beginning in 1933, when Hitler came to power, and continuing throughout World War II, when the United States was at war with Germany. IBM provided Germany a technology to manage information—not a computer, as we have today, but a sophisticated counting and sorting machine using punch cards, the Hollerith machine, named after its inventor, Herman Hollerith. Originally designed for the United States Census of 1890, the machine revolutionized the collection, tabulation, and organization of information and became the basis for the formation of the company we now know as IBM—International Business Machines. In this chapter, Black first presents an overview of the use of IBM technology in Nazi Germany. Hollerith machines were employed in the beginning to manage census information so as to identify the Jewish population of Germany and the countries it began to occupy before and during the war. Eventually, the machines were used throughout the German government and economy to manage information about industrial production, railroads, and labor in the concentration camps. This chapter also contains a section from Black's book from the perspective of one of the concentration camp prisoners who witnessed the use of the tabulating and sorting machines at the Bergen-Belsen concentration camp. A final selection details the operation of the machines during the German census of 1933 and the involvement of Thomas J. Watson, the chairman of IBM, with Dehomag, the German subsidiary of IBM. From our historical perspective, we must consider the difficulties involved in identifying the Jewish population of Germany (or any other country) without the use of sophisticated counting and sorting technologies. Did the use of IBM machines make the Holocaust's "Final Solution"—the extermination of the Jewish people—easier? Could it not be said that IBM was just following good business practice, finding technological solutions to the problems of its customers? What does this suggest about IBM's guilt or innocence in providing the Hollerith machines to Nazi Germany? Black's book has created a controversy among professional historians of the Holocaust and of business corporations, with many asserting that Black most likely overstates the degree to which IBM executives in the United States knew of the genocidal policies of the Nazi regime and the uses to which the Hollerith machines were put. Nevertheless, it is clear that IBM, under the leadership of its chairman, Thomas Watson, profited from its connection to the German government during the Nazi period.

From *IBM and the Holocaust: The Strategic Alliance Between Nazi Germany and America's Most Powerful Corporation*

Edwin Black

INTRODUCTION

Mankind barely noticed when the concept of *massively organized information* quietly emerged to become a means of social control, a weapon of war, and a roadmap for group destruction. The unique igniting event was the most fateful day of the last century, January 30, 1933, the day Adolf Hitler came to power. Hitler and his hatred of the Jews was the ironic driving force behind this intellectual turning point. But his quest was greatly enhanced and energized by the ingenuity and craving for profit of a single American company and its legendary, autocratic chairman. That company was International Business Machines, and its chairman was Thomas J. Watson.

Der Führer's obsession with Jewish destruction was hardly original. There had been czars and tyrants before him. But for the first time in history, an anti-Semite had automation on his side. Hitler didn't do it alone. He had help.

In the upside-down world of the Holocaust, dignified professionals were Hitler's advance troops. Police officials disregarded their duty in favor of protecting villains and persecuting victims. Lawyers perverted concepts of justice to create anti-Jewish laws. Doctors defiled the art of medicine to perpetrate ghastly experiments and even choose who was healthy enough to be worked to death—and who could be cost-effectively sent to the gas chamber. Scientists and engineers debased their higher calling to devise the instruments and rationales of destruction. And statisticians used their little known but powerful discipline to identify the victims, project and rationalize the benefits of their destruction, organize their persecution, and even audit the efficiency of genocide. Enter IBM and its overseas subsidiaries.

Solipsistic and dazzled by its own swirling universe of technical possibilities, IBM was self-gripped by a special amoral corporate mantra: if it *can* be done, it *should* be done. To the blind technocrat, the *means* were more important than the *ends*. The destruction of the Jewish people became even less important because the invigorating nature of IBM's technical achievement was only heightened by the fantastical profits to be made at a time when bread lines stretched across the world.

So how did it work?

When Hitler came to power, a central Nazi goal was to identify and destroy Germany's 600,000-member Jewish community. To Nazis, Jews were not just those who practiced Judaism, but those of Jewish blood, regardless of their assimilation, intermarriage, religious activity, or even conversion to Christianity. Only after Jews were identified could they be targeted for asset confiscation, ghettoization, deportation, and ultimately extermination. To search generations of communal, church, and governmental records all across Germany—and later throughout Europe—was a cross-indexing task so monumental, it called for a computer. But in 1933, no computer existed.

When the Reich needed to mount a systematic campaign of Jewish economic disenfranchisement and later began the massive movement of

European Jews out of their homes and into ghettos, once again, the task was so prodigious it called for a computer. But in 1933, no computer existed.

When the Final Solution sought to efficiently transport Jews out of European ghettos along railroad lines and into death camps, with timing so precise the victims were able to walk right out of the boxcar and into a waiting gas chamber, the coordination was so complex a task, this too called for a computer. But in 1933, no computer existed.

However, another invention did exist: the IBM punch card and card sorting system—a precursor to the computer. IBM, primarily through its German subsidiary, made Hitler's program of Jewish destruction a technologic mission the company pursued with chilling success. IBM Germany, using its own staff and equipment, designed, executed, and supplied the indispensable technologic assistance Hitler's Third Reich needed to accomplish what had never been done before—the automation of human destruction. More than 2,000 such multi-machine sets were dispatched throughout Germany, and thousands more throughout German-dominated Europe. Card sorting operations were established in every major concentration camp. People were moved from place to place, systematically worked to death, and their remains cataloged with icy automation.

IBM Germany, known in those days as Deutsche Hollerith Maschinen Gesellschaft or Dehomag, did not simply sell the Reich machines and then walk away. IBM's subsidiary, with the knowledge of its New York headquarters, enthusiastically custom-designed the complex devices and specialized applications as an official corporate undertaking. Dehomag's top management was comprised of openly rabid Nazis who were arrested after the war for their Party affiliation. IBM NY always understood—from the outset in 1933—that it was courting and doing business with the upper echelon of the Nazi Party. The company leveraged its Nazi Party connections to continuously enhance its business relationship with Hitler's Reich, in Germany and throughout Nazi-dominated Europe.

Dehomag and other IBM subsidiaries custom-designed the applications. Its technicians sent mock-ups of punch cards back and forth to Reich offices until the data columns were acceptable, much as any software designer would today. Punch cards could only be designed, printed, and purchased from one source: IBM. The machines were not sold, they were leased, and regularly maintained and upgraded by only one source: IBM. IBM subsidiaries trained the Nazi officers and their surrogates throughout Europe, set up branch offices and local dealerships throughout Nazi Europe staffed by a revolving door of IBM employees, and scoured paper mills to produce as many as 1.5 billion punch cards a year in Germany alone. Moreover, the fragile machines were serviced on site about once per month, even when that site was in or near a concentration camp. IBM Germany's headquarters in Berlin maintained duplicates of many code books, much as any IBM service bureau today would maintain data backups for computers.

I was haunted by a question whose answer has long eluded historians. The Germans always had the lists of Jewish names. Suddenly, a squadron of grim-faced SS would burst into a city square and post a notice demanding those listed assemble the next day at the train station for deportation to the East. But how did the Nazis get the lists? For decades, no one has known. Few have asked.

The answer: IBM Germany's census operations and similar advanced people counting and registration technologies. IBM was founded in 1896 by German inventor Herman Hollerith as a census tabulating company. Census was its business. But when IBM Germany formed its philosophical and technologic alliance with Nazi Germany, census and registration took on a new mission. IBM Germany invented the racial census—listing not just religious affiliation, but bloodline going back generations. This was the Nazi data lust. Not just to count the Jews—but to *identify* them.

People and asset registration was only one of the many uses Nazi Germany found for high-speed data sorters. Food allocation was organized around databases, allowing Germany to starve the Jews. Slave labor was identified, tracked, and managed largely through punch cards. Punch cards even made the trains run on time and cataloged their human cargo. German Railway, the *Reichsbahn*, Dehomag's biggest customer, dealt directly with senior management in Berlin. Dehomag maintained punch card installations at train depots across Germany, and eventually across all Europe.

How much did IBM know? Some of it IBM knew on a daily basis throughout the twelve-year Reich. The worst of it IBM preferred not to know—"don't ask, don't tell" was the order of the day. Yet IBM NY officials, and frequently Watson's personal representatives, Harrison Chauncey and Werner Lier, were almost constantly in Berlin or Geneva, monitoring activities, ensuring that the parent company in New York was not cut out of any of the profits or business opportunities Nazism presented. When U.S. law made such direct contact illegal, IBM's Swiss office became the nexus, providing the New York office continuous information and credible deniability.

NUMBERED PEOPLE

Veils of smoke hung above Bergen-Belsen concentration camp. Many of the exhausted prisoners, insensate from torture and starvation, slumped lifelessly, waiting to fade into death. But most of the 60,000 human beings squeezed into this unimaginable clearing amongst the evergreens were still running from place to place, performing assigned chores quickly, proving their strength and viability for yet another day of existence. Surviving the moment was their quest.[1] This nightmare was Bergen-Belsen concentration camp, a special Hell on Earth created by Nazi Germany.

At the rear of the camp, just meters from its back fence, stood a solitary guard tower. Its cross-barred wooden frame rose some 25 feet in the air. Looking down from this commanding perch, one saw three orderly rows of wooden barracks down to the right. Along the left lay kitchens, workshops, storage areas, and latrines haphazardly arrayed between curved, muddy lanes. This length of incarceration all terminated several hundred meters away at the gate leading to the camp commandant's office and the SS encampment. A barbed-wire perimeter gave the camp definition even as a series of internal fences straddling patrol aisles segmented the cruel confines into six sub-camps.[2]

Just below the rear watchtower, a round-topped furnace squatted atop the mud. Black and elongated, the furnace resembled a locomotive engine, but with two weighty kiln doors at the front. Its single, tall, sooty smokestack rose several meters into the air. A handmade metal stretcher of sorts, used to slide emaciated corpses into the flames, was always nearby. Here was the crematorium. Not hidden out of sight, nor obscured by structures or berms, the crematorium was close enough to burn the eyes of any SS guard stationed in the watchtower. The ominous structure and its message were visible to all as the final way station should fate falter—or deliver.[3]

Situated between two rivers and the towns Bergen and Belsen, the site was originally established in spring 1943 as a prisoner transit camp for 10,000 Jews who might be ransomed or traded. But in the last months of 1944 and early 1945, as Nazi death camps, including Auschwitz, were liberated by the Allies, Belsen became a nightmare of human consolidation, receiving transports from other sites. By spring 1945, more than 40,000 were imprisoned under indescribable conditions. Starved, worked to death, and randomly tortured, the death toll rose to nearly 20,000 just for the month of March 1945. After liberation, horrified British medical teams were unable to save some 14,000 dying souls. Eventually bulldozers were deployed to gruesomely shovel bodies into trenches of twisted rigor mortis.[4]

Just meters from the Belsen crematorium, off to the left, near the kitchens and the cisterns, down a muddy path, stood the block leader's house. Inmates sometimes called this place "the lion's den." Within "the lion's den" was a room for the *Arbeitsdienstführer*, the Labor Service Leader. That is where the Hollerith punch cards were processed. At first glance, they seemed like simple rectangular cards, five and a quarter inches long, three and a quarter inches tall, divided into numbered columns with holes punched in various rows.[5] But they were much more than simple cards.

Beginning in December 1944, a Dutch Jew, Rudolf Cheim, was assigned to work in the Labor Service Office. Hungry and desperate to stay warm, Cheim tried every cold morning to locate a bit of extra food and some matches to make a fire. Kindling was stacked in the office. But no matches. For those, Cheim needed to venture into the other room where the SS officers slouched on chairs. Invariably, they viciously punched him in the face as the price for walking near to obtain a match. But it was worth it for Cheim. He could survive.[6]

Working in the *Arbeitsdienst* was good. The Labor Service Office held the power of life or death over prisoners, including him. If an inmate could work, he could live. Cheim was happy for an office assignment working with the Hollerith punch cards and their coded numbers. But as he did, he silently observed through the corner of his eye the SS men administering the card sorting procedure. For five weeks he took mental notes.[7]

Quickly, Cheim learned the method. Every day, transports of slave laborers were received. Prisoners were identified by descriptive Hollerith cards, each with columns and punched holes detailing nationality, date of birth, marital status, number of children, reason for incarceration, physical characteristics, and work skills. Sixteen coded categories of prisoners were listed in columns 3 and 4, depending upon the hole position: hole 3 signified homosexual, hole 9 for anti-social, hole 12 for Gypsy. Hole 8 designated a Jew. Printouts based on the cards listed the prisoners by personal code number as well.[8]

Column 34 was labeled "Reason for Departure." Code 2 simply meant transferred to another camp for continuing labor. Natural death was coded 3. Execution was coded 4. Suicide coded 5. The ominous code 6 designated "special handling," the term commonly understood as extermination, either in a gas chamber, by hanging, or by gunshot.[9]

As the trains and trucks rolled in from Belgium, France, and Holland, thousands of punch cards were examined, processed, and the information fed back to the Department of Statistics at the SS Economics Office in Oranienburg. The numbered men and women were compared to a list of work needs at Bergen-Belsen and other camps. "Never a name," Cheim remembers, "only the assigned numbers." How many died was just a statistic to note, a detail for the machines to digest. That December 1944, some 20,000 prisoners were registered; 50 deaths per day, on average, were recorded on punch cards.[10]

Cheim learned that to discover the occupational make-up of a prisoner group, each inmate's individual punch card was fed into the mechanical sorter. Then the dials were adjusted to isolate certain professions, labor skills, age groups, or language abilities needed for work battalions. If prisoners were selected for work, their names appeared on a Hollerith printout for transport to nearby sub-camps, factories, and even local farms.[11]

Labor requirements were reported and then matched by Office D II of the SS Economics Office, which administered all the camps under Gen. Oswald Pohl. Pohl, creator of the "Extermination by Labor" program, ardently argued that expeditiously gassing Jews deprived the Reich of an important resource. His idea, "Extermination by Labor," quite simply meant working Jews to death. Only after outliving their usefulness would they be deported to death camps for gassing. Office D II embraced SS Chief Heinrich Himmler's declaration: "If 10,000 Russian females collapse from exhaustion while digging a tank ditch, [it] interests me only so far as the tank ditch is completed for Germany."[12]

Cheim took special notice one day when five women escaped from Bergen-Belsen. Angry SS guards vowed to recapture them. They resented reporting the prisoner departures in column 34 of the punch card forms as code 7—escaped.[13]

He became fascinated with a young Dutch seamstress. Who was she? Her journey began in the Westerbork camp. Went to Auschwitz. She was born May 10, 1924. No name. Just a number. 53752. But who was 53752, Cheim wondered? Did she not have a name, only a number?[14]

Cheim soon began to understand the truth. Hundreds of thousands of human beings were being identified, sorted, assigned, and transported by means of the Hollerith system. Numbers and punch cards had dehumanized them all, he thought. Numbers and punch cards would probably kill them all. But Cheim never understood where the Hollerith system came from.[15]

One December morning, even as the numbered man Cheim, in his tattered uniform, stepped quickly toward the Bergen-Belsen Hollerith office to stay warm and to stay alive, another man, this one dressed elegantly in a fine suit and warm overcoat, stepped out of a new chauffeured car at 590 Madison Avenue in New York. He was Thomas J. Watson. His company, IBM—one of the biggest in the world—custom-designed and leased the Hollerith card sorting system to the Third Reich for use at Bergen-Belsen and most of the other concentration camps. International Business Machines also serviced its machines almost monthly, and trained Nazi personnel to use the intricate systems. Duplicate copies of code books were kept in IBM's offices in case field books were lost. What's more, his company was the exclusive source for up to 1.5 billion punch cards the Reich required each year to run its machines.[16]

Indeed, the systems were not only used in the concentration camps, but hundreds of them had been installed for years throughout the entire commercial, industrial, war-making, and anti-Jewish infrastructure of Nazi Germany and Nazi-dominated Europe.

On this cold December day, Watson was unyielding. His German subsidiary, Dehomag, was out of control. More lawyers would be called, more telegrams would be sent, more clever maneuvering with the State Department would be undertaken—not to stop Dehomag from its genocidal partnership with the Third Reich, but to ensure that all the proceeds and profits remained with IBM NY. No matter who won, IBM would prosper. Business was its middle name.

THE CENSUS OF 1933

In mid-September 1933, 6,000 brown cardboard boxes began unceremoniously arriving at the cavernous Alexanderplatz census complex in Berlin. Each box was stuffed with questionnaires manually filled out by pen and pencil, but soon to be processed by an unprecedented automated praxis. As supervisors emptied their precious cargo at the Prussian Statistical Office, each questionnaire—one per household—was initialed by an intake clerk, stacked, and then transferred downstairs. "Downstairs" led to Dehomag's massive 22,000-square-foot hall, just one floor below, specifically rented for the project.[17]

Messengers shuttling stacks of questionnaires from the Statistical Office to Dehomag bounded down the right-hand side of an enclosed stairwell. As they descended the short flight, the sound of clicking became louder and louder. At the landing, they turned left and pushed through the doors. As the doors swung open, they encountered an immense high-ceilinged, hangar-like facility reverberating with the metallic music of Hollerith technology. Some 450 data punchers deployed in narrow rows of punching stations labored behind tall upright secretarial displays perfectly matched to the oversized census questionnaires.[18]

Turning left again, and then another right brought the messengers to a long windowed wall lined with narrow tables. The forms were piled there. From these first tables, the forms were methodically distributed to centralized desks scattered throughout the work areas. The census forms were then loaded onto small trolleys and shuttled again, this time to individual work stations, each equipped with a device that resembled a disjointed typewriter—actually an input engine.[19]

A continuous "Speed Punching" operation ran two shifts, and three when needed. Each shift spanned 7.5 hours with 60 minutes allotted for "fresh air breaks" and a company-provided meal. Day and night, Dehomag staffers entered the details on 41 million Prussians at a rate of 150 cards per hour. Allowing for holidays and a statistical prediction of absenteeism, yet ever obsessed with its four-month deadline, Dehomag decreed a quota of 450,000 cards per day for its workforce. Free coffee was provided to keep people awake. A gymnast was brought in to demonstrate graceful aerobics and other techniques to relieve fatigue. Company officials bragged that the 41 million processed cards, if stacked, would tower two and a half times higher than the Zugspitze, Germany's 10,000-foot mountain peak. Dehomag intended to reach the summit on time.[20]

As company officials looked down upon a floor plan of the layout, the linear rows and intersecting columns of work stations must have surely resembled a grandiose punch card itself animated into a three-dimensional bricks and mortar reality. Indeed, a company poster produced for the project showed throngs of miniscule people scrambling over a punch card sketch.[21] The surreal artwork was more than symbolic.

Once punched, the columns were imbued with personal information about the individual: county, community, gender, age, religion, mother tongue, number of children, current occupation, and second job, if any.[22]

"Be Aware!" reminded huge block-lettered signs facing each cluster of data entry clerks. Instructions were made clear and simple. Column 22 RELIGION was to be punched at hole 1 for Protestant, hole 2 for Catholic, or hole 3 for Jew. Columns 23 and 24 NATIONALITY were to be coded in row 10 for Polish speakers.[23]

After punching, the cards were shuttled to a separate section of the hall, where they passed through long squat Hollerith counters at the rate of 24,000 per hour. The system kept track of its own progress. Hence, Dehomag was always aware whether it was on schedule. Once counted, the cards moved to the proofing section. No errors would be tolerated and speed was essential. Proofing machines tabulated and verified proper punching for more than 15,000 cards per hour.[24]

When Jews were discovered within the population, a special "Jewish counting card" recorded the place of birth. These Jewish counting cards were processed separately.[25]

Then came the awesome sorting and resorting process for twenty-five categories of information cross-indexed and filtered through as many as thirty-five separate operations—by profession, by residence, by national origin, and a myriad of other traits. It was all to be correlated with information from land registers, community lists, and church authorities to create a fantastic new database. What emerged was a profession-by-profession, city-by-city, and indeed a block-by-block revelation of the Jewish presence.[26]

A Reich Statistical Office summary reported: "The largest concentration of Jews [in Berlin] will be found in the Wilmersdorf district. Approximately 26,000 Observant Jews account for 13.54 percent of the population within that district." Further: a total of 1,200 "Fur-Jews" accounted for 5.28 percent of the furrier trade, and nearly three-fourths of those are foreign-born. Further: based on existing emigration trends triggered by anti-Jewish persecution "only 415,000 to 425,000 Faith-Jews would remain in the German Reich by the middle of 1936."[27]

Dehomag's precious information would now help propel a burgeoning new binary of pseudo-science and official race hatred. Racial hygiene, race politics, and a constellation of related anti-Semitic disciplines were just so much talk in the absence of genuine statistics. Now a lightning storm of anti-Jewish legislation and decrees restricting Jews from all phases of academic, professional, governmental, and commercial life would be empowered by the ability to target the Jews by individual name. Moreover, by cross-sorting the Jews revealed in Column 22 row 3 with Polish speakers identified in Columns 26 and 27 row 10, the Reich was able to identify who among the Jews would be its first targets for confiscation, arrest, imprisonment, and ultimately expulsion. The so-called *OstJuden*, or Eastern Jews, primarily from Poland, would be the first to go.[28]

Friedrich Zahn, publisher of *Allgemeines Statistisches Archiv*, summed up the glee when he wrote, "In using statistics, the government now has the road map to switch from knowledge to deeds."[29]

Dehomag's census undertaking was an unparalleled accomplishment for IBM. Watson was impressed from the moment Karl Koch [an attorney with Nazi connections hired by Dehomag] secured the contract. Clearly, there was a lucrative future for IBM in Nazi Germany. At a time when other foreign companies were fleeing the Reich's violence, repression, anti-Semitism, and the inability to retrieve income from German operations, Watson moved swiftly to dramatically enlarge IBM's presence.

First, he ordered the merger of several small IBM subsidiaries in Germany. Optima, Degemag, Holgemag, as well as the existing Dehomag, were folded into a new corporation also to be named "Dehomag." Through a cunning twirl of losses and profits among the four German companies, and then manipulating balances owed by those subsidiaries to IBM NY for so-called "loans," Reich profit taxes would be avoided, despite record earnings in Germany. IBM NY would simply apply the incomes to the contrived loans it had extended to its own subsidiaries. IBM's Maryland division was used as a conduit for the loan transactions. A report from IBM's accountants to the corporate treasurer was explicit: "the motive for the merger was to effect an annual savings in taxes by reducing Dehomag's net profits by the amount of the net losses of Optima and [old] Dehomag ... about $30,000 annually."[30]

[Willy] Heidinger [owner and CEO of Dehomag] confirmed in a special report to Watson, "As the merger of Degemag, [old] Dehomag, and Optima is effected . . . corporation profits tax is out of the question . . . on account of the relief from [loan] claims of IBM, as thereby no profit, but merely a reduction of losses, is obtained."[31]

Second, IBM increased its investment in Dehomag from a mere RM 400,000 to more than RM 7 million—about a million Depression-era American dollars. This would include a million Reichsmarks to purchase new land in Berlin and build IBM's first German factory. IBM was tooling up for what it correctly saw as a massive economic relationship with the Hitler regime. In the midst of America's Depression, this expansion of manufacturing base would not relieve unemployment in the United States, but actually transfer American jobs to Nazi Germany where the Hollerith machines would be manufactured.[32]

Understandably, Watson decided to visit Germany to observe conditions first hand, which he did on October 13, 1933. Despite a highly publicized boycott against German ocean liners, he ignored picket lines and sailed on the German ship *Bremen.*[33]

Watson was impressed with what he saw in Berlin. The Watsons and the Heidingers managed many happy social moments together. Mrs. Watson even asked Heidinger for a copy of his portrait as a memento of their joyous time. Heidinger sent two.[34]

Watson also visited the massive census operation at Alexanderplatz. There among the rows of data clicking clerks arrayed before their large block-letter instructions to enter Jews in Column 22 row 3, amid the clatter of shiny, black sorters flickering punch cards into a blur, Watson was moved to donate money to buy meals for everyone at IBM expense. As an added gesture, he authorized Dresden pastries for each and every member of the Statistical Office's Census Department. Heidinger later wrote to Watson that the total bill for his "bountiful gift" of 6,060 meals disbursed to 900 staffers came in at just under 4,000 Reichsmarks.[35]

More than just hot meals and baked goods, Watson wanted to make sure Dehomag was successful and effective. He personally dispatched Eugene Hartley, a top IBM census expert and manager of the firm's statistical department, to advise Dehomag. Hartley would oversee costs in Berlin and become acquainted with all details of Dehomag's census operation and its methods. These details were to be recorded in a special handbook. No copies would exist. Senior management at Dehomag sent Watson an RCA Radiogram declaring, "We especially appreciate your foresight in sending Mister Hartley who as a census expert is especially helpful to us at a time when we are undertaking greatest service job ever done by any IBM agency."[36]

Most gratifying to the Germans was the secret pact between Watson and Heidinger, entered into that October 1933, while Watson was touring Dehomag. At a time when the Hitler government was declaring its war intentions in Europe, Watson's secret deal granted Heidinger and Dehomag special commercial powers outside of Germany. Although there were IBM agencies and subsidiaries throughout Europe, Dehomag would be permitted to circumvent and supplant each one, soliciting and delivering punch card solution technology directly to IBM customers in those territories. That gave Dehomag entrée to the major foreign corporations, foreign national railroads, and foreign government offices across the Continent. IBM subsidiaries, such as those in Brussels, Paris, and Warsaw would still exist. But now Nazified Dehomag could usurp their clients and even their manufacturing base.[37]

The extraordinary arrangement virtually reinvented Dehomag as a de facto "IBM Europe." Subject to IBM NY oversight, the German subsidiary was granted free rein to cultivate its special brand of statistical services to other nearby countries, especially Austria, Czechoslovakia, Poland, Belgium, France, and Holland. Where census, registration, and other statistical operations did not exist, or where they could be updated along the lines of Germany's anti-Semitic model, Dehomag could now move in. In essence, before the Third Reich advanced across any border, its scientific soldiers would already have a vital outpost.

With its new potency to create a German sphere of statistical influence across the continent, no wonder senior management in November 1933 sent Watson a jointly signed cable proclaiming, "Your visit to Germany has brought encouragement not only to Dehomag, but to the German people."[38]

From the very first moments and continuing throughout the twelve-year existence of the Third Reich, IBM placed its technology at the disposal of Hitler's program of Jewish destruction and territorial domination. IBM did not invent Germany's anti-Semitism, but when it volunteered solutions, the company virtually braided with Nazism. Like any technologic evolution, each new solution powered a new level of sinister expectation and cruel capability.

When Germany wanted to identify the Jews by name, IBM showed them how. When Germany wanted to use that information to launch programs of social expulsion and expropriation, IBM provided the technologic wherewithal. When the trains needed to run on time, from city to city or between concentration camps, IBM offered that solution as well. Ultimately, there was no solution IBM would not devise for a Reich willing to pay for services rendered. One solution led to another. No solution was out of the question.

QUESTIONS FOR DISCUSSION

1. Consider the difficulties involved in identifying the Jewish population of Germany (or any other country) without the use of sophisticated counting and sorting technologies. How would the identification process work without an advanced technology?

2. Were there good business reasons for IBM's deal with Dehomag to facilitate its entry into other European countries? Consider what the social and political effects of this "secret deal" might be.

3. Discuss how the Hollerith machines could be used to advance the organization of slave labor in the concentration camps.

4. Are census machines that tabulate and sort information inherently evil? Could it not be said that IBM was just following good business practice, finding technological solutions to the problems of its customers? What does this suggest about IBM's guilt or innocence in providing the Hollerith machines to Nazi Germany?

NOTES

1. "Recollection of Hanna Levy-Hass" in Eberhard Kolb, *Bergen-Belsen: From "Detention Camp" to Concentration Camp, 1943–45*, trans. Gregory Claeys and Christine Lattke (Göttingen: Vandenhoeck & Ruprecht, 1985), p. 66; see *Encyclopaedia Judaica*, s.v. "Bergen-Belsen," p. 611; Kolb, pp. 29, 41, 94, 98, as well as the photos; General Glyn-Hughes, Cité in Le grand livre des témoins, FNDIRP, Ramsey, 1995, p. 291; also see photos, The Nizkor Project, www.nizkor.org; Judith Jaegermann, "Memories of My Childhood in the Holocaust," Oral History in *A History of Jews in Hamburg*, Hamburg University, www.rrz.uni-hamburg.

2. Hadassah Rosensaft Collection, United States Holocaust Memorial Museum (USHMM) Photo Archives; *Encyclopaedia Judaica*, s.v. "Bergen-Belsen," p. 611; Kolb. p. 29.

3. Hadassah Rosensaft crematorium photo, April 28, 1945, USHMM.

4. *Encyclopaedia Judaica*, s.v. "Bergen-Belsen," p. 612; Brigadier Hugh Llewelyn Glyn-Hughes in "Excerpts from *The Belsen Trial, Pt. 2 of 5: Testimony Concerning Water and Food*," The Nizkor Project, www.nizkor.org; see Raymond Philips, ed., *The Trial of Josef Kramer and 44 Others: The Belsen Trial* (London: William Hodge and Co., 1949); Kolb, p. 40.

5. Papers of Rudolf Martin Cheim, Joodsche Raad Voor Amsterdam, p. 26, YIVO [Institute for Jewish Research, New York] RG804; Kolb, p. 29; see *Encyclopaedia Judaica*, s.v. "Bergen-Belsen," p. 611.

6. Papers of Rudolf Martin Cheim, Joodsche Raad Voor Amsterdam, p. 26, YIVO RG804.

7. Papers of Rudolf Martin Cheim, Joodsche Raad Voor Amsterdam, p. 26, YIVO RG804.

8. Papers of Rudolf Martin Cheim, Joodsche Raad Voor Amsterdam, p. 26, YIVO RG804; see NA [National Archives, College Park, MD] RG242/338, T1021, Roll 5, Frame 126.

9. Papers of Rudolf Martin Cheim, Joodsche Raad Voor Amsterdam, pp. 26–27, YIVO RG804; see NA RG242/338, T1021, Roll 5, Frame 126; Testimony of and Concerning Irma Grese in "Excerpts from *The Belsen Trial, Pt. 5 of 5: The Trial of Adolf Eichmann, Session 101 (Pt. 3 of 4),* The Nizkor Project, www.nizkor.org"; Jamie McCarthy and Ken McVay, "The Meaning of Special Treatment, Pt. 1 of 3," *Deceit and Misrepresentation: The Techniques of Holocaust Denial,* The Nizkor Project, www.nizkor.org; Raul Hilberg, *Documents of Destruction: Germany and Jewry 1933–1945* (Chicago: Quadrangle Books, 1971), pp. 219–223.

10. Papers of Rudolf Martin Cheim, Joodsche Raad Voor Amsterdam, p. 28, YIVO RG804.

11. Papers of Rudolf Martin Cheim, Joodsche Raad Voor Amsterdam, pp. 27–28, YIVO RG804; Memo and Transfer List, Ravensbrück Concentration Camp Labor Deployment Office to Flossenbürg Concentration Camp Labor Deployment Office, September 1, 1944, D II NA RG242/338, T1021 Reel 17.

12. Operation of D II, *IMT*, 5:980–992; sound recording, Heinrich Himmler's Speech at Posen, October 4, 1943, NA RG238, PS 1919.

13. Papers of Rudolf Martin Cheim, Joodsche Raad Voor Amsterdam, p. 27, YIVO RG804.

14. Papers of Rudolf Martin Cheim, Joodsche Raad Voor Amsterdam, pp. 27–28, YIVO RG804.

15. Papers of Rudolf Martin Cheim, Joodsche Raad Voor Amsterdam, p. 26, YIVO RG804.

16. Thomas J. Watson, Jr., and Peter Petre, *Father, Son & Co.: My Life at IBM and Beyond* (New York: Bantam Books, 1990), pp. 29–30; CSDIC, "Secret Report: PW Intelligence Bulletin No. 2/57" April 25, 1945, p. 4, NA RG226; "Deutsche Hollerith Maschinen: Confidential Report 242," p. 8, submitted by Harold J. Carter, December 8, 1943, Department of Justice, War Division, Economic Warfare Section, NA RG60.

17. "Inventur eines Volkes," *Berliner Tageblatt* 13 (January 9, 1934); see Ludwig Hümmer, "Die Aufbereitung der Volks- und Berufszählung 1933 im Hollerith-Lochkartenverfahren," *Hollerith Nachrichten (HN)* 28 (August 1933), pp. 343–346, 347; *Illustrierter Beobachter,* January 6, 1934, p. 5.

18. Hümmer, pp. 345–347.

19. Hümmer, pp. 345–347.

20. Hümmer, pp. 345–346, 447.

21. Götz Aly and Karl Heinz Roth, *Die restlose Erfassung: Volkszählen, Identifizieren, Aussondern im Nationalsozialismus* (Berlin: Rotbuch Verlag, 1984), p. 145.

22. "Inventur eines Volkes," *Berliner Tageblatt* 13 (January 9, 1934).

23. Aly and Roth, p. 56.

24. "Inventur eines Volkes," *Berliner Tageblatt* 13 (January 9, 1934).

25. "Die Glaubensjuden im Dritten Reich," *Statistik des Deutschen Reichs* 415/5 (1936): 5 cited in Aly and Roth, p. 55.

26. Hümmer, pp. 343, 348, 351–355.

27. "Die Glaubensjuden im Dritten Reich," *Statistik des Deutschen Reichs* 415/5 (1936): 5 cited in Aly and Roth, pp. 57–59.

28. "Die Glaubensjuden im Dritten Reich," *Statistik des Deutschen Reichs* 415/5 (1936): 5 cited in Aly and Roth, pp. 57, 59; exhibit photo of Census Poster, USHMM.

29. Dr. Friedrich Zahn, "Die Statistik im nationalsozialistischen Groß-deutschland," *ASA* 29 (1939/40): 370.

30. Cablegram, Thomas J. Watson to W. Heidinger, May 19, 1933, IBM Files; also see Memorandum, W. Heidinger to W.F. Battin, July 14, 1933, IBM Files; Letter, M.G. Connally to W.F. Battin September 6, 1934, p. 3, IBM Files; Letter, F.C. Elstob to J.F. Gormley, January 19, 1934, IBM Files; Confirmation of Cable, January 20, 1934, IBM Files; Letter, J.F. Gormley to H. Karst, January 22, 1934, IBM Files.

31. Memorandum, W. Heidinger to W.F. Battin, July 14, 1933, IBM Files.

32. Letter, H.K. Chauncey to J.C. Milner, November 19, 1935, IBM Files; see Letter, O.E. Braitmayer to J.E. Holt, March 7, 1936, IBM Files; Letter, W. Heidinger to R. Kugler, December 18, 1933, IBM Files.

33. "Sails for Paris Meeting," *NYT*, October 5, 1933; Letter, W. Heidinger to Thomas J. Watson, January 2, 1934, IBM Files; also see "Sees Business Gain Generally," *NYT*, October 25, 1934.

34. Letter, W. Heidinger to Thomas J. Watson, October 31, 1933, IBM Files.

35. Letter, W. Heidinger to Thomas J. Watson, January 2, 1934; Letter, W.D. Jones to Thomas J. Watson, January 10, 1934, IBM Files.

36. Letter, Dehomag to J.T. Wilson, November 16, 1935, IBM Files; also see, "Davis Named IBM Secretary," *NYT*, February 22, 1940.

37. Cablegram, W. Heidinger to Thomas J. Watson, August 27, 1934, IBM Files; Radiogram, Thomas J. Watson to W. Heidinger, August 23, 1934, IBM Files; also see Letter and handwritten cover note on carbons, Thomas J. Watson to W. Heidinger, September 11, 1934, IBM Files.

38. Radiogram, K. Hummel and Managers to Thomas J. Watson, November 8, 1933, IBM Files.

CHAPTER 12

The Crime of I.G. Farben: Slave Labor and Mass Murder in Nazi Germany

———————————— \/ ————————————

Throughout the twentieth century, I.G. Farben has been one of the leading industrial giants, focusing on all aspects of petrochemical and pharmaceutical manufacturing. This chapter, an excerpt from the book *The Crime and Punishment of I.G. Farben* (1978) by Joseph Borkin, focuses on I.G. Farben's connection to the labor and death camps at Auschwitz. Borkin reviews the history of the business decisions that led to the alliance between the SS and I.G. Farben. As a major German industrial corporation, it is to be expected that I.G. Farben was a crucial player in the Nazi war effort, supplying synthetic oil, rubber (buna), and nitrates. Borkin notes that Hitler was determined not to repeat the mistakes of the first world war, and so he enlisted the chemical company to make sure that the German military would be supplied with the raw materials necessary for the war effort—science and technology would compensate for Germany's dearth of natural raw materials. But I.G. Farben also played a central role in the operations and development of the Auschwitz concentration camp system. The company established a factory near the main camp to produce synthetic oil and synthetic rubber, primarily because the SS would supply an almost unlimited source of slave labor. When problems arose with the transportation of the prisoners between the Auschwitz main camp and the factory, I.G. Farben constructed its own concentration camp (Monowitz) on the factory site. Primo Levi, the Italian chemist whose quotation begins this book, was employed at the Monowitz camp, where over 25,000 prisoners were worked to death. In addition, a subsidiary of I.G. Farben, Degesch (German Corporation for Pest Control), was the manufacturer of the insecticide Zyklon B (prussic acid) that was eventually used in the more efficient gas chambers of the Auschwitz-Birkenau killing center from 1942 to 1944 (see chapters 2 and 3). I.G. Farben thus played a major role in the developments of the Holocaust. Could its participation have been avoided? Or is it morally acceptable for a major industrial corporation to aid its home country in times of war, even when the war is an imperialistic war of conquest, and the victims are noncombatants singled out for their racial heritage? Did the leaders of I.G. Farben really believe in the Nazi ideology, or were they simply following good business practice? In the light of the history of the Holocaust, can we accept this type of business practice as morally permissible?

From *The Crime and Punishment of I.G. Farben: The Unholy Alliance Between Hitler and the Great Chemical Combine*

Joseph Borkin

"Without I.G.'s immense productive facilities, its far-reaching research, varied technical experience and overall concentration of economic power, Germany would not have been in a position to start its aggressive war in September 1939."[1] Such was the judgment rendered by a team of civilian and military experts assigned by General Eisenhower at the close of World War II to make an exhaustive investigation of I.G.'s contribution to the Nazi war effort. Extravagant as this conclusion may have sounded, the record sustains its accuracy.

I.G. [Farben] truly was a mighty industrial colossus. So huge were its assets admitted and concealed, so superior its technological know-how, and so formidable its array of patents that it dominated the chemical business of the world. I.G. fortified this commercial leadership by constructing a maze of cartels whose members included such industrial giants as Kuhlmann of France, Imperial Chemical Industries of Great Britain, Montecatini of Italy, Aussiger Verein of Czechoslovakia, Boruta of Poland, Mitsui of Japan, and Standard Oil (New Jersey), Du Pont, and Dow Chemical of the United States.

But I.G. was more than a corporate empire. Through the uncanny talents of its scientists and engineers, it secured the vital self-sufficiency that enabled Germany to maneuver in the world of power politics. From its laboratories and factories flowed the strategic raw materials that Germany's own territory could not supply, the synthetics of oil, rubber, nitrates, and fibers. So, too, I.G. produced vaccines, sera, and drugs such as Salvarsan, aspirin, Atabrine, and Novocain, along with sulfa drugs, as well as poison gases and rocket fuels. Few universities could match the profusion of Nobel Prizes earned by its scientists: Paul Ehrlich for Salvarsan, Fritz Haber for the fixation of nitrogen, Carl Bosch for synthesizing saltpeter and gasoline, and Gerhard Domagk for the sulfa drugs.

Gustav Stresemann, chancellor and foreign minister during the Weimar Republic, once said, "Without I.G. and coal, I can have no foreign policy." But it was for the Nazis that I.G. performed the greatest service. With I.G. and coal Adolf Hitler almost conquered the world.

Hitler was an apt student of the weaknesses that brought Germany to its knees during World War I. Defeat had drilled into him the doleful fact that Germany's impoverished land, devoid of the strategic raw materials with which modern wars are fought, had made the British blockade a decisive weapon. In planning for World War II he vowed to correct nature's imbalance with science and technology.

The result was a strange alliance between Hitler and I.G. Hitler despised I.G. for its international complexion and for its unusually large number of Jewish directors and scientists. Carl Bosch, the head of I.G. when Hitler came to power, was the most vocal anti-Nazi in the industrial community. In the light of succeeding events, it is ironic that the Nazis legally stigmatized I.G. as non-Aryan in the early years of the Third Reich. But Hitler needed I.G.'s genius and I.G. needed Hitler's support. I.G.'s first and major task for Hitler was to free German diplomacy from the bonds that shackled it to the oil wells and rubber groves of its enemies. How well it succeeded is written in the history of the world's most violent and mechanized war. For five and a half years, Hitler's tanks, trucks, and planes were propelled by I.G.'s gasoline, their wheels made of I.G.'s rubber. Success had rendered I.G. indispensable.

Mere indispensability, however, was not enough. As the war progressed, I.G.'s embrace of Hitler became more passionate. With the help of the Wehrmacht and the Nazi bureaucracy, I.G. looted the chemical properties of the defeated nations (Austria, Czechoslovakia, Poland,

Norway, and France). Moreover, it had similar plans to bring England, the United States, and the Soviet Union into its orbit.

I.G.'s moral descent did not end there. Before long it joined the Nazis in a vast forced labor program in which millions of victims from the conquered countries were enslaved in the service of German war production. But slavery was only a step in the dehumanization of victor and vanquished. I.G. found itself in the role of an industrial Faust, unable and unwilling to extricate itself from the compact it had made with Hitler to help prepare the Nazis for war. The depth of the partnership was reached at Auschwitz, the extermination center, where four million human beings were destroyed in accordance with the "Final Solution of the Jewish Question," Hitler's plan to destroy an entire people. Drawn by the almost limitless reservoir of death camp labor, I.G. chose to build a great industrial complex at Auschwitz for the production of synthetic rubber and oil. So enormous was this installation that it used as much electricity as did the entire city of Berlin. More than 25,000 camp inmates paid with their lives to construct it.

After the defeat of Germany, the horror of I.G. Auschwitz made it certain that those involved would have to face the consequences of their acts. An indictment charging twenty-four of I.G.'s highest officials with war crimes was filed with the United States Military Tribunal at Nuremberg. In the opening paragraph of his statement to the court, General Telford Taylor, the chief prosecutor at Nuremberg, summarized the spirit of the prosecution's case.

> The grave charges in this case have not been laid before the Tribunal casually or unreflectingly. The indictment accuses these men of major responsibility for visiting upon mankind the most searing and catastrophic war in human history. It accuses them of wholesale enslavement, plunder, and murder. These are terrible charges; no man should underwrite them frivolously or vengefully, or without deep and humble awareness of the responsibility which he thereby shoulders. There is no laughter in this case; neither is there any hate.

Yet, despite the terrible gravity of the charges, the setting was more like that for an antitrust suit than that for a trial for slavery and mass murder as the defendants took their places in the dock at the Palace of Justice at Nuremberg. The twenty-three defendants (the twenty-fourth defendant, Max Brueggemann, was excused for illness) were among the industrial elite of Germany, not Hitler's black- and brown-shirted hooligans. They represented a combination of scientific genius and commercial acumen unique in a private industrial enterprise. They were the executives who made I.G. preeminent in the world of technology and commerce. They served on the boards of directors of the most prestigious corporations in their own country and abroad, where they were treated with awe and admiration. When their government called, they accepted official posts in the spirit of public service. Like their counterparts everywhere, they were among the leading supporters of culture, charity, and religion, donating their names, time, and money.

How this group finally arrived at the courtroom at Nuremberg, branded as the "Devil's Chemists," charged with unparalleled atrocities, is a profound lesson for the world....

In August 1942 the office of the World Jewish Congress in Lausanne, Switzerland, received the first report that the Third Reich had embarked on a course that could only be described as insane. A German industrialist reported, at the risk of his life, that for the past eight months the German government had been "solving the Jewish problem" by an organized scheme of mass murder. Its goal was to exterminate the entire Jewish people. Killing centers had been erected in Poland, he said, where hundreds of thousands of Jews had been asphyxiated by a lethal gas in sealed chambers designed for the singular purpose of killing them.

In the following months, increasing evidence began to surface of Germany's extraordinary program to destroy the Jews. At the end of August 1943, an Allied report of Axis war crimes was released to the public. The report accused Germany and its satellites of "carrying out with increasing tempo a deliberate program of wholesale theft, murder, torture and savagery unparalleled in world history."[2] It charged that Germany had deliberately exterminated 1,702,500 human beings. Incredible as the figure appeared at the time, it was a gross understatement.

German war crimes soon became a matter of major concern to the Allied leaders. On November 1, 1943, Roosevelt, Churchill, and Stalin, at their Moscow summit meeting, jointly drafted "The Declaration of German Atrocities."[3] The Germans were put on notice that they would be held responsible for their crimes, tried in appropriate courts, and punished.

The Moscow declaration was delivered to the German people, their satellites, and the occupied countries by all means available—continuous radio broadcasts, leaflets dropped by planes, and underground newspapers. The warning was unequivocal and blunt.

> At the time of the granting of any armistice to any government which may be set up in Germany, those German officers and men and members of the Nazi party who have been responsible for, or have taken a consenting part in ... atrocities, massacres, and executions, will be sent back to the countries in which their abominable deeds were done in order that they may be judged and punished according to the laws of these liberated countries and of the free governments which will be created therein. Lists will be compiled in all possible detail from all these

countries having regard especially to the invaded parts of the Soviet Union, to Poland and Czechoslovakia, to Yugoslavia and Greece, including Crete and other islands, to Norway, Denmark, the Netherlands, Belgium, Luxemburg, France and Italy.[4]

The Moscow declaration proved no deterrent at all; in fact, the pace of the Reich's program of extermination accelerated.

On March 24, 1944, therefore, President Roosevelt issued his own warning to the German nation:

> In one of the blackest crimes in all history—begun by the Nazis in the day of peace and multiplied by them a hundred times in time of war—the wholesale systematic murder of the Jews of Europe goes on unabated every hour. . . . It is therefore fitting that we should again proclaim our determination that none who participate in these acts of savagery shall go unpunished. . . . All who share the guilt shall share the punishment.[5]

By November 1944, millions had been killed in Hitler's deliberate destruction of the Jews. John Pehle, executive director of the War Refugee Board, decided to make public the reports of two prisoners who had escaped from Auschwitz, the largest of all the killing complexes. Pehle released these reports to the newspapers, vouching for the reliability of the information. The reports described in great detail the organization of Auschwitz, the concentration camps, the terrible conditions under which the inmates lived and died, the brutality of the German authorities, the immense gassing buildings in which victims were asphyxiated by the thousands every day, the crematoria where their bodies were disposed of—almost all the terrible facts of the Nazi program of extermination.[6]

Elmer Davis, head of the Office of War Information, demanded that Pehle recall the reports, which had not yet been published because of a ten-day "hold." Davis argued that publicizing these reports would be counterproductive. The American public, he said, would not believe them but would regard them as mere atrocity stories like those circulated during World War I.

Pehle had great regard for Davis and appreciated his opinion; yet, he believed that the desperate situation demanded that these reports be made known to the public. Convinced that only by exposure was there any hope of saving the remaining Jews of Europe, Pehle refused to withdraw the reports, and the public learned of the gruesome details of Auschwitz for the first time.

Among the extraordinary facts disclosed by the reports was the existence at Auschwitz of an enormous industrial establishment owned and operated by I.G. Farben. The men who had written the reports had been inmate workers in the Buna [synthetic rubber] division of this installation, and the details they supplied showed how far I.G.'s compact with Hitler had progressed.

> We worked in the huge Buna plant, to which we were herded every morning about 3 A.M. At midday our food consisted of potato or turnip soup and in the evening we received some bread. During work we were terribly mistreated. As our working place was situated outside the large chain of sentry posts, it was divided into small sectors of 10 × 10 meters, each guarded by an SS man. Whoever stepped outside these squares during working hours was immediately shot without warning for having "attempted to escape." Often it happened that out of pure spite an SS man would order a prisoner to fetch some given object outside his square. If he followed the order, he was shot for having left his assigned place. The work was extremely hard and there were no rest periods. The way to and from work had to be covered at a brisk military trot; anyone falling out of line was shot. On my arrival about 3,000 people, of whom 2,000 were Slovak Jews, were working on this emplacement. Very few could bear the strain and although escape seemed hopeless, attempts were made every day. The result was several hangings a week.[7]

In the American business community, especially in companies that had prewar dealings with I.G., these disclosures met with disbelief. Nevertheless, the reports of I.G.'s involvement were only too true. I.G. was building enormous synthetic oil and rubber factories at Auschwitz.

Pehle, who as chairman of the War Refuge Board was responsible for saving tens of thousands of Jewish lives, was the first official anywhere to urge consideration of the bombing of the industrial installations and mass extermination equipment at Auschwitz. He wrote to the U.S. War Department in this regard. In reply, the War Department explained that a bombing attack against Auschwitz was an unwarranted diversion of planes needed elsewhere. Pehle replied that Auschwitz was an important producer of war matériel. The War Department still refused.

By embarking on the Battle of Britain in the late summer of 1940, twenty-six years almost to the month after the decisive Battle of the Marne, Germany miscalculated again. Despite assurances from Hermann Goering that the Luftwaffe would break the English will to resist within weeks, if not days, Britain refused to be subdued. The British Isles remained as an "unsinkable aircraft carrier" aimed at the heart of Germany.

Hitler, ignoring Germany's tragic experience with a two-front war, refused to let the British setback change his timetable of conquest. His plans to attack his ally, the Soviet Union, remained fixed. Certain of the invincibility of his military power and the inviolability of his military judgment, he ordered his generals to prepare for an early attack. Hitler's generals were not so sanguine. Once again the problem was the shortage of raw materials. They informed Hitler that the battles of Poland, France, and Britain had seriously exhausted the supply of munitions and such basic raw materials as oil and rubber. Any attack against the Soviets would be imprudent until additional facilities to produce synthetic rubber and oil were built and the reserves replenished. The size of such a conflict would demand amounts never even contemplated before. A reluctant Hitler agreed to wait but ordered that the attack on Russia begin in the spring.

With Hitler's personal views on military raw material autarky acting as a goad, the war planners began at once to prepare for the construction of the necessary synthetic rubber facilities to fulfill the enormous requirements projected for the Soviet invasion. The Ministry of Economics immediately summoned Fritz ter Meer and Otto Ambros to a top secret, high priority conference. At the meeting, the I.G. officials were informed that there must be "an increase in Buna production with the greatest possible speed."[8] To reach the projected production demanded by the ministry required the construction of two new plants. These installations, when added to the existing plants at Huels and Schkopau, would bring the Buna capacity of I.G. to a healthy 150,000 tons annually, enough to mount the Russian invasion.

The I.G. officials were assured that the German government was prepared to support the expansion in every way. They were given further assurances that the irritations of the past with the army would be eliminated. This was underscored by the High Command's promise of "all suitable assistance."[9] Speed was crucial and [Carl] Krauch, acting in his government role of plenipotentiary general for special questions of chemical production, ordered the immediate construction of one of the new plants, which was to operate in conjunction with the existing I.G. high-pressure plants at Ludwigshafen. Construction of the second plant, he noted, would begin as soon as a suitable site was chosen. At the moment, Krauch was considering Norway and Polish Silesia.

Krauch assigned Ambros, one of I.G.'s most talented Buna chemists, to survey Silesia. Ambros had joined I.G. in 1926, at which time he was sent to Sumatra for a year to study the chemistry of natural rubber. By 1935 he was I.G.'s leading synthetic rubber expert. Ambros's expertise was formally recognized by [Carl] Bosch [CEO of I.G. Farben] who placed him in charge of the construction and operation of the first large-scale Buna plant at Schkopau.

Ambros was an unusual figure. He was the I.G. expert on both Buna and poison gas. Moreover, in 1932 he had conceived the underlying theories which ultimately led to the modern magnetic tape technology. In view of Ambros's later fate it is worth noting that he was a protégé of Nobel laureate Richard Willstaetter, under whom he wrote his

Ph.D. thesis. Even after Willstaetter was driven out of Germany to become a stateless Jew, Ambros continued to correspond with him.

In evaluating the Polish Silesian area Ambros made a personal and detailed exploration of the proposed sites. The one he finally recommended was particularly suited for the installation. A coal mine was nearby and three rivers converged to provide a vital requirement, a large source of water. Together with these three rivers, the Reich railroad and the autobahn afforded excellent transportation to and from the area. These were not decisive advantages, however, over the Norwegian site. But the Silesian location had one advantage that was overwhelming: the S.S. had plans to expand enormously a concentration camp nearby. The promise of an inexhaustible supply of slave labor was an attraction that could not be resisted.[10]

Krauch wholeheartedly accepted Silesia over Norway, where the population was already in ferment over the brutality of the German occupation. The historic nature of Krauch's choice could never have crossed his mind. *The name of the Polish village he selected for the Buna site was Auschwitz.*[11]

Once the project and site were formally approved by the Reich, the I.G. management, enthusiastic about expanding its operations, assigned the name "I.G. Auschwitz" to the new division, hereafter the official designation in I.G.'s meticulously ordered table of corporate organization.

Technologically and economically it was only natural that a synthetic oil plant be built as a companion to the rubber factory. For Bergius and Buna, high pressure chemistry was the common ground. Accordingly, a large hydrogenation plant to convert coal into oil with a capacity of 778,000 tons a month was also begun.

The I.G. directors selected Ambros for the rubber installation and Heinrich Buetefisch for the gasoline plant at Auschwitz. For the two youngest members of the managing board of directors, both still under forty, these appointments represented an important step upward in the I.G. hierarchy. After all, it gave Ambros and Buetefisch authority over the largest synthetic rubber and oil installation in the world. With Hitler and I.G. marching together, the future appeared to be without limit.

It was at this point that I.G. made another crucial, even fateful decision. With the U.S.S.R. about to be attacked, I.G. began to contemplate the enormous opportunities for expansion to the east. The possible rewards appeared boundless. Everything about the Auschwitz project indicated that it was heaven-sent.

The Soviet Union and Asia represented a potential market to challenge even the commercial imagination of I.G.'s directors. For I.G., Hitler's "Drive to the East" promised to open a vast new area for profitable exploitation. Indeed, so great did I.G. regard the postwar potential of the Auschwitz project that it decided to make an unusual gamble on its future. Rather than let the German government finance the building of the installations, the I.G. directors voted to put up the funds to make I.G. Auschwitz a privately owned I.G. enterprise and to assume the entire risk. With almost no opposition, they committed more than 900 million Reichsmarks, over $250 million,[12] to the building of the single largest project in the I.G. system. With such an enormous risk, officials of I.G. carefully watched over their huge investment.

There were other factors supporting the risk and indicating the prudence of such an investment. The I.G. Auschwitz projects were so vital to Germany's military plans that I.G. was able to marshal the aid of the most powerful figures in the Nazi government. Krauch, in a top secret letter to Ambros, wrote:

> In the new arrangement of priority stages ordered by Field Marshal Keitel, your building project has first priority.... At my request, [Goering] issued special decrees a few days ago to the supreme Reich authorities concerned.... In these decrees, the Reich Marshal obligated the offices concerned to meet your requirements in skilled workers and laborers at once, even at the expense of other important building projects or plans which are essential to the war economy.[13]

Krauch was already taking steps to insure an adequate labor supply for the construction of the I.G. Auschwitz plants. He had arranged for Goering to write Himmler on February 18, 1941, asking that "the largest possible number of skilled and unskilled construction workers . . . be made available from the adjoining concentration camp for the construction of the Buna plant."[14] Between 8000 and 12,000 construction and assembly workers were needed. Goering requested Himmler to inform him and Krauch "as soon as possible about the orders which you will issue in this matter."[15] Acting on this request, Himmler ordered the S.S. inspector of concentration camps and the S.S. economic and administrative main office "to get in touch immediately with the construction manager of the Buna works and to aid the . . . project by means of the concentration camp prisoners in every possible way."[16] After Himmler issued this decree, Krauch wrote to Ambros, "These orders are so far-reaching that I request you to apply them to the widest extent as soon as possible."[17]

So that there would be no misunderstanding of the urgent priority of the I.G. Auschwitz project, Himmler delegated S.S. Major General Karl Wolff, chief of his personal staff, to be liaison officer between the S.S. and I.G.[18] On March 20, General Wolff met with Buetefisch to discuss "the details of the ways and means in which the concentration camp could assist in the construction of the plant."[19] Buetefisch was chosen to deal with General Wolff not only because of his eminence as a synthetic fuel authority but also because of his rank as a lieutenant colonel in the S.S. At the meeting it was agreed that I.G. would pay the S.S. three Reichsmarks a day for each unskilled concentration camp inmate and four Reichsmarks for skilled inmates.[20] Later, the S.S. agreed to furnish children at one and a half Reichsmarks.[21] These payments were for the S.S.; the inmates, of course, received nothing. Wolff guaranteed that the payment would include "everything such as transportation, food, et cetera and [I.G.] will have no other expenses for the inmates, except if a small bonus (cigarettes, etc.) is given as an incentive."[22] Both parties realized, in calculating the rate of payment, that a concentration camp inmate could not be as productive as a free, normal, well-fed German worker; thus, it was estimated at the meeting that a seventy-five percent efficiency was all that could be expected.[23]

A week after this preliminary conference, a meeting was held at Auschwitz among various I.G. technical men, including [Walter] Duerrfeld, chief engineer in charge of construction at I.G. Auschwitz, his senior engineer, Max Faust, and the Auschwitz concentration camp commandant, S.S. Major Rudolf Hoess.[24] Duerrfeld, in his summary of the conference, assured his superiors, Ambros and Buetefisch, that "the concentration camp showed its willingness to assist in the construction of the plant as far as it could."[25] One big problem, however, troubled him. This, he reported, was the procurement of Capos, "straw bosses" with "special talents" recruited from among concentration camp inmates. However, Commandant Hoess told Duerrfeld that I.G. would have a priority in obtaining these inmate-leaders whose special talent was sadism. "These Capos," reported Duerrfeld, "are being selected from amongst the professional criminals and are to be transferred from other concentration camps to Auschwitz."[26] Every twenty inmates, it was estimated, would require a Capo.

A few weeks later Himmler himself, on an inspection tour of I.G. Auschwitz, gave assurances of his personal support to I.G.'s project. He guaranteed I.G. an immediate labor supply of 10,000 concentration camp inmates.[27] Ambros wrote Ter Meer, "Our new friendship with the S.S. is proving very profitable."[28]

Soon that tune changed. With the personal blessing of such Nazi luminaries as Hitler, Himmler, Goering, and Keitel, I.G. Auschwitz should have been a tremendous success. Despite the cooperation of the Nazi hierarchy, especially the S.S., however, the project continually was disrupted by shortages, breakdowns, and delays. As the difficulties began to pile up fears began to mount correspondingly that the rubber and gasoline works would never be completed in time to help the German war effort. Some malign influence seemed to be affecting the entire operation.

The I.G. executives on the spot laid most of the blame on the S.S. According to them, the leaders of the S.S. at Auschwitz did not seem to understand "the working methods of . . . free enterprise."[29] Their treatment of the concentration camp inmates, by far the largest segment of I.G. Auschwitz labor, was proving counterproductive. These complaints were detailed in the weekly I.G. Auschwitz reports sent back to I.G. headquarters in Frankfurt. The report of August 3–9, for instance, included the following doleful note:

> We have . . . drawn the attention of the officials of the concentration camp to the fact that in the last few weeks the inmates are being severely flogged on the construction site by the Capos in increasing measure, and this always applies to the weakest inmates who really cannot work harder. The exceedingly unpleasant scenes that occur on the construction site because of this are beginning to have a demoralizing effect on the free workers [Poles], as well as on the Germans. We have therefore asked that they should refrain from carrying out this flogging on the construction site and transfer it to . . . the concentration camp.[30]

A few months later the I.G. Auschwitz weekly report began exhibiting greater appreciation of the difficult problems faced by the S.S.

> The work, particularly of the Poles and inmates, continues to leave much room for improvement. . . . Our experience so far has shown that only brute force has any effect on these people. . . . As is known, the Commandant always argues that as far as the treatment of inmates is concerned, it is impossible to get any work done without corporal punishment.[31]

The delays and construction problems continued and the report ended on a note of concern for the economic consequences confronting the I.G. management. The combination of all the difficulties encountered "will increase costs considerably."[32]

A greater appreciation of S.S. methods, however, did not solve I.G.'s problems. At an I.G. Auschwitz construction conference attended by technical personnel including Ambros, Duerrfeld, and Faust, a variety of troubles were reviewed.[33] Among the problems were bottlenecks in housing, transportation, fuel, and plumbing facilities and late deliveries of all kinds of necessary supplies. The overburdened railroad station and the shortage of motor vehicles added to the delays. Faust reported that the free Poles were only half as efficient as German workers and concentration camp inmates were not even a third as efficient.

Life at Auschwitz was not all beatings, shortages, inefficiencies, and other problems. The weekly reports at the close of 1941, for example, ended on a happier note: "On December 20 representatives of the I.G. took part in a Christmas party of the Waffen S.S. which was very festive and which ended up alcoholically gay."[34] Moreover, although the failures of the Auschwitz project kept mounting, cordial relations between the I.G. management and the S.S. officials were not affected. Duerrfeld and the commandant went on hunting parties together and, with their wives, frequently exchanged visits. The difficulties in building the rubber and oil facilities continued, however, and the progress at the Buna works fell further behind schedule. I.G. viewed the performance of the first year at Auschwitz as far from satisfactory—in fact, as nearly disastrous.

Inmate labor proved the most vexing problem in the construction of the I.G. Auschwitz installation. The labor details were marched more than four miles from the main Auschwitz camp to the I.G. construction site through the extreme summer heat and winter cold. The lack of guards caused security problems. The result was that "the inmates can only march out in daylight and must return to the camp in daylight. If it is foggy in the morning, the inmates are also not permitted to leave the camp."[35]

Sickness, malnutrition, the work tempo, and sadistic S.S. guards and Capos also took their toll. It was an unsettling sight for I.G. officials to witness work details carrying their dead back and forth so that all inmates could be accounted for at roll call when the work day began and when it ended. It was a strange way to run a business.

I.G. Auschwitz was approaching a financial and technical crisis. With the investment of almost a billion Reichsmarks in jeopardy, the I.G. managing board of directors decided on a drastic solution. It made a further and dramatic descent into the Nazi hell. In July 1942, just after Hitler had begun his second year of troubles in the Soviet Union, the I.G. managing board voted to solve its Auschwitz labor problems by establishing its own concentration camp. The initial appropriation was five million Reichsmarks,[36] a modest amount to protect its investment of almost a billion Reichsmarks. For a private company to set up its own concentration camp to insure a supply of labor may have been an odd undertaking, but the problem called for imagination and audacity, especially since the size of the investment and the certain consequences of Hitler's wrath made abandonment of the project unrealistic. The managing board of directors, without any recorded opposition, felt that economically and politically I.G. had no other choice.

On the other hand, under the circumstances an I.G. concentration camp had obvious advantages to recommend it. Inmates would not be drained of their already limited energy by the long marches from the main concentration camp to the construction site. Security would improve and fewer of the scarce S.S. guards would be required. Discipline and punishment would be more effective, and I.G. would also have greater and more immediate control over the use of the inmates. Of no small consequence, costs would be reduced.

The site chosen for I.G.'s concentration camp was called Monowitz. In the operation of this unique facility I.G. was to be responsible for the housing, feeding, and health of the inmates; the S.S. was charged with the security, punishment, and supply of inmates.

Monowitz was completed in the summer of 1942. Although it belonged to I.G., Monowitz had all the equipment of the typical Nazi concentration camp—watchtowers with searchlights, warning sirens, poised machine guns, armed guards, and trained police dogs. The entire camp was encircled with electrically charged barbed wire. There was a "standing cell" in which the victim could neither stand upright, kneel, nor lie down.[37] There was also a gallows, often with a body or two hanging from it as a grim example to the rest of the inmates. Across the arched entrance was the Auschwitz motto, "Freedom through Work."

In the administration of Monowitz, I.G. adopted the principle enunciated by Fritz Saukel, plenipotentiary for labor allocation of the four-year plan: "All the inmates must be fed, sheltered and treated in such a way as to exploit them to the highest possible extent, at the lowest conceivable degree of expenditure."[38]

The complete Auschwitz installation was now comprised of four entities: Auschwitz I, the original and vast concentration camp with hundreds of thousands of inmates: Auschwitz II, the extermination center of gassing chambers and crematory ovens at Birkenau; Auschwitz III, the I.G. Buna and synthetic fuel works; and Auschwitz IV, I.G.'s own concentration camp at Monowitz.

When I.G. took its place in the industrial labor complex of Auschwitz and accepted Himmler's offer of concentration camp labor, it embarked on a road that led ultimately to participation in the most extraordinary crime in civilized history, what Winston Churchill called the crime for which there is no name, the "Final Solution of the Jewish Question."[39]

Even before the Final Solution became the official policy of the German Reich in January 1942, Heinrich Himmler had already started an S.S. program for killing Jews. When the German armies conquered Poland, Himmler organized special S.S. squads to begin the mass slaughter. The first extermination center was set up at Chelmno, Poland, in the fall of 1939.[40] Three mobile gas vans, using the carbon monoxide from their exhausts, became the first instruments of mass murder. Primitive and inefficient as this early extermination center was, it reached a killing rate of 1000 a day.[41] Soon the methods of mass destruction of Jews were refined and killing centers with permanent gas chambers, still using carbon monoxide, were opened. One of the most notorious was at Treblinka, near Warsaw, built in early 1941.

•

In June 1941, Himmler instructed Commandant Hoess to begin the extermination of the Jews at Auschwitz. Hoess visited Treblinka to study the use of carbon monoxide. Hoess then set up a similar installation at the Birkenau site in Auschwitz.[42] Very soon he realized that carbon monoxide was not sufficiently lethal and was much too slow if Himmler's goals were to be achieved.[43]

Hoess cast around for a better way. What he found was to make him the most successful mass killer in modern history. In August 1941, using 500 Russian prisoners of war as an experimental group, Hoess introduced into the airtight chambers of Birkenau a new asphyxiating agent, Zyklon B.[44] Actually, Zyklon B, whose generic name is prussic acid, was new only in its application to human beings; its traditional, commercial use was as an insecticide. The result was a revelation of efficiency.

Only one firm, Deutsche Gesellschaft fuer Schaedlingsbekampfung (German Corporation for Pest Control), known in the trade as Degesch, supplied this lethal chemical. The firm and its most valuable asset, the monopoly of Zyklon B manufacture, was owned 42.5 percent by I.G. Farben-industrie; 42.5 percent by Deutsche Gold und Silber-scheidenanstalt—known as Degussa (in which I.G. owned a third); and 15 percent by the Theo. Goldschmidt concern.[45] That I.G. dominated Degesch was general knowledge in the chemical industry. In fact, in its official corporate pronouncements Degesch described itself as an exclusive selling agent for I.G. Moreover, I.G. dominated the Degesch supervisory board: of its eleven members five were from I.G., including the chairman, Wilhelm Mann.[46]

Five months after Hoess's introduction of Zyklon B, Himmler's personal program to exterminate the Jewish people was transformed into the official policy of the Third Reich. Its formal adoption under the title of the "Final Solution of the Jewish Question" took place in the Berlin suburb of Wannsee, at a meeting presided over by Reinhard Heydrich, chief of the security police and security service of the S.S., and attended by undersecretaries from the various Reich ministries and the top officials of the S.S.[47]

At the meeting, Heydrich unfolded the details for the complete annihilation of the Jewish people. Until this program was revealed at Wannsee, only Goering, Goebbels, Himmler, and Bormann knew of Hitler's ultimate plans for the Jews.[48] Now the civil service was enlisted, and the German bureaucracy became an active party in the execution of this plan. As the preparations began for the Final Solution, the purchases of Zyklon B by the S.S. increased tremendously.

In the past the S.S. had bought moderate amounts of Zyklon B from Degesch as a vermin control in its concentration camps. When the Final Solution added Jews to the S.S. extermination plans, Degesch profits reflected the new prosperity. I.G.'s dividends on its Degesch investment for the years 1942, 1943, and 1944 were double those of 1940 and 1941.[49]

At least one top official of Degesch, Gerhard Peters, the managing director, definitely knew about the new use of Zyklon B. He had been specifically informed of the details of the Final Solution by Kurt Gerstein, the chief disinfection officer of the S.S., who did the purchasing of Zyklon B.[50]

There was still another episode that gave the officials of Degesch more than a hint of the dread purpose to which their Zyklon B was being put by the S.S. When manufactured as a pesticide Zyklon B contained a special odor, or *indicator,* to warn human beings of its lethal presence. The inclusion of such a warning odor was required by German law. When the S.S. demanded that the new, large order of Zyklon B omit the *indicator,* no one familiar with the workings of the S.S. could have failed to realize the purpose behind the strange request. The Degesch executives at first were unwilling to comply. But compassion was not behind their refusal. What troubled them was the fact that the S.S. request endangered Degesch's monopoly position. The patent on Zyklon B had long since expired. However, Degesch retained its monopoly by a patent on the warning odor. To remove the *indicator* was bad business, opening up the possibility of unwelcome competition.[51] The S.S. made short shrift of this objection and the company removed the warning odor. Now the doomed would not even know it was Degesch's Zyklon B.

I.G.'s camp at Monowitz began operations in September 1942 stocked with inmates from Auschwitz who were to work on the construction of the I.G. rubber and fuel installations. Despite the availability of workers, I.G. was still faced with a labor problem. As Jews from all over Europe were brought into Auschwitz, S.S. physicians picked inmates strong enough to work at I.G. Auschwitz. People who were considered too weak for construction work were selected for the gassing stations and crematoria of Birkenau. "Selection" was the most dreaded word in a world of dread.

It soon became apparent that the "selections" were being made without sufficient regard for the urgent demands of war production. Too many skilled and reasonably strong workers were being rushed to the ovens although months of useful labor were still in them. For example, during the early months of Monowitz, those in charge of the construction of I.G. Auschwitz were promised a carefully chosen batch of workers culled from a shipment of over 5000 Jews. However, when the transports were unloaded near the crematory ovens, the camp officials, ignoring the labor needs of I.G. Auschwitz but with punctilious devotion to the Final Solution, sent 4092 of the 5022 to the gas chambers. When objections were raised over such a high rate, the explanation offered was that the males were too frail and the females were mostly children, little girls incapable of construction work.[52] Sometime later, when the transports were reported to contain a more choice supply of skilled Jewish workers, an S.S. official in charge of labor allocation suggested a possible means of avoiding overzealous application of the selection process. He recommended that the trains be unloaded near the I.G. works instead of the "usual place" near the crematory. The improvement was noticeable. On the next shipment of 4087 Jews, only 2398 were selected for extermination; this was a lower rate than before. The complaints, however, continued: "If the transports from Berlin continue to have so many women and children as well as old Jews," an official said, "I don't promise myself much in the matter of labor allocation."[53]

From the moment the transports were unloaded at Monowitz, those fortunate enough not to be selected for gassing lived in horror of the extermination center at Birkenau. When the construction fell behind the scheduled deadlines, I.G. officials often complained that the poor physical condition of the inmates chosen to work at I.G. Auschwitz was responsible. "Consequently," observed an eyewitness,

> the Labor Allocation Officer in Auschwitz went to Monowitz early in the morning when the squads left for work, posted himself near the gate, and picked out those people whom they considered sickly amongst the laborers who marched to their work in files of five. These people were sent to the gas chambers straight away.[54]

For thousands of inmates, Monowitz thus became merely a brief stop on the way to Birkenau and extermination.

Conditions were such that sickness was a pervasive fact of life among the inhabitants of Monowitz. The hospital wards built by I.G. were so inadequate that even the S.S. suggested additional wards be built. I.G. refused because of the cost.[55] Later I.G. did expand its hospital facilities but also enforced a rule that no more than five percent of the Monowitz inmates could be sick at any one time, a procrustean matching of beds and illness. The overage was disposed of by shipment to Birkenau. Even under the five percent rule, inmates confined to the hospital had to be returned to work within fourteen days. Those who failed the fourteen-day test were deemed unrecoverable. On the records that I.G. kept was added the final phrase "Nach Birkenau."[56]

Starvation was a permanent guest at Auschwitz. The diet fed to I.G. Auschwitz inmates, which included the famous "Buna soup"—a nutritional aid not available to other prisoners—resulted in an average weight loss for each individual of about six and a half to nine pounds a week. At the end of a month, the change in the prisoner's appearance was marked; at the end of two months, the inmates were not recognizable except as caricatures formed of skin, bones, and practically no flesh; after three months, they were either dead or so unfit for work that they were marked for release to the gas chambers at Birkenau. Two physicians who studied the effect of the I.G. diet on the inmates noticed that "the normally nourished prisoner at Buna could make up the deficiency by his own body for a period of three months. . . . The prisoners were condemned to burn up their own body weight while working and, providing no infections occurred, finally died of exhaustion."[57]

As for shelter at Monowitz, the inmates slept in three tiers of wooden cubicles. Each slot, barely large enough for one person to lie down, actually held three. An eyewitness reported, "As a result it was practically impossible to sleep, since if one man was in a reclining position, the others would have to sit up or lie over him."[58] The simplest comforts were denied; even tables and chairs were almost unknown. Hygienic conditions were subhuman. In the summer the heat was oppressive, almost beyond endurance, and in the winter there was no heat at all.

In cases of infractions of the rules by inmates, the I.G. foremen sent written requests to the S.S. administration for suitable punishment. The S.S. complied, recording on its own forms the details of the I.G. charge and the S.S. disposition. Typical offenses charged by I.G. included "lazy," "shirking," "refusal to obey," "slow to obey," "working too slowly," "eating bones from a garbage pail," "begging bread from prisoners of war," "smoking a cigarette," "leaving work for ten minutes," "sitting during working hours," "stealing wood for a fire," "stealing a kettle of soup," "possession of money," "talking to a female inmate," and "warming hands." Frequently reports included the I.G. foreman's recommendations of "severe punishment."[59] The response of the S.S. could be forfeiture of meals, lashes by cane or whip, hanging, or "selection."[60]

To meet the construction schedule, the I.G. management worked the inmates at an almost murderous pace. It adopted, for example, the "S.S. trot" as a work tempo so that even cement and other heavy construction materials were carried to the job at "double time."[61] I.G. plant police and foremen, as well as Capos, continuously threatened and thrashed the prisoners who did not work up to S.S. standards.

At times, the inmates were literally worked to death: "It was no rare occurrence that detachments of 400 to 500 men brought back with them in the evening 5 to 20 corpses. The dead were brought to the place of roll call and were counted as being present."[62] Two or three times a week those who died on the site and those from whom all useful life had been extracted were piled on open platforms for all to see and trucked to Birkenau. For the inmate laborer, it was a useful reminder employed effectively by I.G. foremen and S.S. guards.

The construction of I.G. Auschwitz has assured I.G. a unique place in business history. By adopting the theory and practice of Nazi morality, it was able to depart from the conventional economics of slavery in which slaves are traditionally treated as capital equipment to be maintained and serviced for optimum use and depreciated over a normal life span. Instead, I.G. reduced slave labor to a consumable raw material, a human ore from which the mineral of life was systematically extracted. When no usable energy remained, the living dross was shipped to the gassing chambers and cremation furnaces of the extermination center at Birkenau, where the S.S. recycled it into the German war economy—gold teeth for the Reichsbank, hair for mattresses, and fat for soap. Even the moans of the doomed became a work incentive, exhorting the remaining inmates to greater effort.

Krauch was satisfied with the system of labor employed at Auschwitz. He wrote to Himmler in July 1943:

> I was particularly pleased to hear . . . that you may possibly aid the expansion of another synthetic factory, which I consider absolutely essential for securing rubber supplies in a similar way as was done at Auschwitz by making available inmates of your camps if necessary. I . . . would be grateful if you would continue sponsoring and aiding us in this matter.[63]

Half a year later, in February 1944, Krauch was still actively sponsoring the Auschwitz approach to the labor problem. In advising how to deal with a labor shortage at an I.G. plant at Heydebreck, he wrote its officials: "In order to overcome the continuous lack of labor, Heydebreck must establish a large concentration camp as quickly as possible *following the example of Auschwitz* [emphasis added]."[64]

One can only wonder about the reason for Krauch's enthusiasm. From the bare records available, 300,000 concentration camp workers passed through I.G. Auschwitz of whom at least 25,000 were worked to death.[65] The plants when completed were so enormous that they used more electricity than the entire city of Berlin. But in the final tally, I.G. Auschwitz was a miserable failure. Despite the investment of almost 900 million Reichsmarks and thousands of lives, only a modest stream of fuel and not a single pound of Buna rubber was ever produced.[66]

QUESTIONS FOR DISCUSSION

1. During times of war, it is expected that business and industry will support the policies of their homelands. To what extent does this general principle justify and excuse the actions of I.G. Farben during the Second World War? Is there a moral difference between participation in a war of defense and a war of conquest? Are there contemporary examples of this problem?

2. Consider the role of I.G. Farben in the development of the Auschwitz-Birkenau death camp and the subsidiary labor camp at Monowitz. Should Farben be blamed for using the slave labor provided by the SS? What about

the establishment of its own concentration camp on the grounds of the industrial factory?

3. A subsidiary of I.G. Farben, Degesch, owned a patent for part of the process that produced the insecticide Zyklon B, the gas that was used in the gas chambers at Auschwitz and Birkenau. Discuss the importance of the order of the SS to remove the patented special odor indicator for the gas.

4. Consider the paradox of a slave labor policy that is designed to serve as a means of mass killing. What responsibilities do technological professionals have regarding the design and administration of projects for slave laborers? Are these responsibilities similar to or different than the responsibilities in a normal business enterprise based on free and voluntary labor?

ABBREVIATIONS

Published Nuremberg War Crimes Trials Records:

NCA: *Nazi Conspiracy and Aggression* (United States Government Printing Office, 1946).

TMWC: *Trial of the Major War Criminals Before the International Military Tribunal* (Nuremberg, Germany, 1947–49).

TWC: *Trials of War Criminals Before the Nuremberg Military Tribunals, Under Control Council No. 10* (U.S. Government Printing Office, 1953).

Documents in National Archives Collection, World War II Crimes Records (some of which have been included as exhibits in above publications, some of which are available only at the Archives):

NI: "Nuremberg, Industrialists"
PS: "Paris, Storey [Col. Robert Storey]"
NO: "Nuremberg, Organizations"
NG: "Nuremberg, Government."

NOTES

1. U.S. Group Control Council, Finance Division, Germany, *Report on Investigation of I.G. Farbenindustrie*, September 12, 1945. Classification canceled by authority of the Joint Chiefs of Staff; microfilmed by the Library of Congress.
2. *New York Times,* August 27, 1943, p. 7, col. 2.
3. TWC, VI, p. x, Declaration on German Atrocities.
4. *Ibid.*
5. *New York Times,* March 24, 1944, p. 4, col. 2.
6. TMWC, vol. XXXVII, p. 433, Document 022-L, excerpt from War Refugee Board Report, Washington, D.C., November 1944 (PE 1759).
7. *History of the War Refugee Board with Selected Documents, January 22, 1944–September 15, 1945.* Executive office of the President, War Refugee Board (3 volumes, mimeographed).

8. TWC, VIII, pp. 330–331, NI-11781, letter from Reich Ministry of Economics to Farben, dated November 8, 1940.
9. *Ibid.*, p. 331, letter from Reich Ministry of Economics to Farben, dated November 8, 1940.
10. TWC, VIII, pp. 336–338, NI-11784, Conference Report between Farben representatives and the Schlesien-Banzin Company, January 18, 1941.
11. TWC, VIII, pp. 349–351, NI-11113, file note on conference with Ter Meer, Krauch, and Ambros, held February 6, 1941.
12. TWC, Prosecution's Final Brief, part IV, p. 54.
13. TWC, VIII, pp. 358–360, NI-11938, letter from Krauch to Ambros, dated February 25, 1941.
14. TWC, VIII, pp. 354–355, NI-1240, letter from Goering to Himmler, dated February 18, 1941.
15. *Ibid.*, p. 355, letter from Goering to Himmler, dated February 18, 1941.
16. TWC, VIII, pp. 356–357, NI-11086, letter from Krauch, signed by Wirth, to Ambros, dated March 4, 1941.
17. *Ibid.*, p. 357, letter from Krauch, signed by Wirth, to Ambros, dated March 4, 1941.
18. *Ibid.*
19. TWC, VIII, pp. 373–376, NI-15148, report on conference of Farben representatives with Auschwitz concentration camp officials, held March 27, 1941, p. 374.
20. *Ibid.*, p. 375.
21. *Ibid.*
22. *Ibid.*
23. *Ibid.*, pp. 374–375.
24. TWC, VIII, pp. 377–381, NI-11115, extracts from minutes of first construction conference on I.G. Auschwitz at Ludwigshafen held March 24, 1941.
25. TWC, VIII, pp. 374–375, NI-15148, report on conference of Farben representatives with Auschwitz concentration camp officials, held March 27, 1941.
26. *Ibid.*, p. 375.
27. NI-034, p. 4, affidavit of Rudolf Franz Ferdinand Hoess.
28. TWC, VIII, pp. 388–389, NI-11118, letter from Ambros to Ter Meer and Struss, dated April 12, 1941, p. 389.
29. TWC, VIII, pp. 392–393, NI-14543, extracts from Farben-Auschwitz weekly report no. 11, for the period August 3–9, 1941.
30. *Ibid.*
31. TWC, VIII, pp. 404–405, NI-14556, extracts from Farben-Auschwitz weekly report no. 30, for the period December 15–21, 1941, p. 405.
32. *Ibid.*
33. TWC, VIII, pp. 406–409, NI-11130, extracts from report of fourteenth construction conference on Farben-Auschwitz, held December 16, 1941.
34. TWC, VIII, p. 410, extracts from Farben-Auschwitz weekly reports nos. 31 and 32, for the periods December 22–28, 1941, and December 29, 1941–January 4, 1942.
35. TWC, VIII, p. 425, NI-15256, extracts from Farben-Auschwitz weekly report no. 42, for the period March 9–15, 1942.

36. TWC, VII, p. 197.

37. DuBois, Josiah, *The Devil's Chemists,* Beacon Press, Boston, 1952, p. 229.

38. TMWC, I, p. 245.

39. Hilberg, Raul, *The Destruction of the European Jews,* Quadrangle Books, Chicago, 1961, p. 264.

40. Hilberg, Raul, p. 561; Judge Wladyslaw Bednarz (Lodz), "Extermination Camp at Chelmno," in *Central Commission for Investigation of German Crimes in Poland,* German Crimes in Poland, Warsaw, 1946, pp. 107–117.

41. Manvell, Roger, and Heinrich Fraenkel, *The Incomparable Crime,* Simon & Schuster, New York, 1960, p. 135.

42. TMWC, XI, p. 398, testimony by Rudolf Franz Ferdinand Hoess.

43. *Ibid.,* pp. 416–417, testimony by Rudolf Franz Ferdinand Hoess.

44. NI-034, affidavit by Rudolf Franz Ferdinand Hoess, p. 2.

45. TWC, Preliminary Brief, part III, p. 35, NI-9098, NI-9150, NI-12073, NI-6363; also NI-9540 (I.G. "Book of Participation").

46. *Ibid.,* p. 35, NI-12075.

47. Hilberg, Raul, p. 264; NG-2586-E.

48. *Ibid.,* p. 266; NG-2586-E.

49. *Ibid.,* p. 568; NI-9093.

50. *Ibid.,* p. 571; NI-9908.

51. NI-12110, memorandum from Dr. Heinrich to Mr. Amend, dated June 21, 1944.

52. Hilberg, Raul, p. 587; *Dokumenty i Materialy,* part I, pp. 115–117, letter from Sommer to Kommandant Auschwitz, dated January 27, 1943, and letter from Schwarz to WVHA D-11, dated February 20, 1943.

53. Hilberg, p. 587; *Dokumenty i Materialy,* part I, pp. 108–110, 117, letters from Schwarz to WVHA D-11, dated March 5 and 8, 1943, and to WVHA-D, dated March 15, 1943.

54. NI-7967, affidavit of Ervin Schulhof, taken June 21, 1947, p. 2.

55. TWC, VII, p. 199.

56. *Ibid.,* pp. 199–200.

57. TWC, Preliminary Brief, part III, p. 97, NI-4830, affidavit by Vitek about Auschwitz diet.

58. TWC, VIII, pp. 603–616, NI-11696, affidavit and testimony of Charles J. Coward, taken July 24, 1947, p. 604.

59. NI-11003 to NI-11017; NI-11019; NI-11027; NI-11029; NI-11031 to NI-11033; typical Auschwitz punishment reports by SS.

60. *Ibid.*

61. NI-7967, affidavit of Ervin Schulhof, taken June 21, 1947, p. 1.

62. NI-5847, affidavit by Berthold Epstein, taken March 3, 1947, p. 2.

63. TWC, VIII, pp. 532–535, NI-10040, letter from Krauch to Himmler, July 27, 1943.

64. TWC, VIII, pp. 558–559, NI-13512, file memorandum of Ritter and Duerrfeld, February 3, 1944, p. 558.

65. DuBois, p. 220; NI-7967, affidavit of Ervin Schulhof, taken June 21, 1947, p. 2.

66. TWC, Prosecution's Final Brief, part IV, p. 54.

CHAPTER 13

Technological Evil: Cultural Values in the Holocaust

---- **W** ----

In this final chapter philosopher Eric Katz, the editor of the volume, examines a pervasive argument about the moral (and immoral) uses of technology. Katz considers the philosophical arguments that demonstrate that all technological artifacts are endowed with the values of the culture that produced them, and then uses the development of the Nazi concentration camps as a practical example to illustrate the theoretical arguments. A long-standing traditional view holds that technology is thought to be morally neutral or "value-free." A technological object can be used for good or evil purposes—a knife can kill or it can slice bread—but the object itself is neither good nor evil; all moral evaluation depends on the intention of the wielder of the knife and the consequences of the activity. Katz rejects this traditional view of the neutrality of technology by focusing on the design and development of the Nazi death camps. He first examines a philosophical and historical argument by political theorist Langdon Winner, who claims that the traditional idea of technological neutrality is based on an overemphasis on the separation between the "making" of a technological artifact and its "use." Since the creation or "making" of a technological object includes the reasons or purposes for the object, it embodies—in its very design—some kinds of value. Katz then illustrates the validity of Winner's argument by a review of important events in the technological and architectural history of the death camps. Nazi engineers, architects, and industrial managers did not create and use a neutral technology to eliminate the Jews of Europe; the technology was specifically designed for mass murder. The technology was a manifestation of the Nazi worldview, its ideology of Aryan racial supremacy and Germanic imperialism. This historical case thus provides a useful overview of many of the themes in this collection of essays as well as a potent counterexample to the traditional idea that technology is morally neutral. As the concluding chapter in the book, this essay draws on several of the historical cases developed in earlier essays, particularly concerning the engineering design of the gas chambers at Auschwitz-Birkenau and the architectural design of the slave labor camps. This final essay thus serves as a fitting summary of many of the major issues raised in the collection.

On the Neutrality of Technology: The Holocaust Death Camps as a Counterexample

Eric Katz

INTRODUCTION

Perhaps the oldest commonplace about the nature of technology is that technological artifacts are inherently neutral or value-free. Humans create technological objects for a specific range of purposes, but the actual use of the technology is subject to the intentions of the user. These intentions, of course, may be good or they may be evil, but whether good or evil, the technology itself is neutral: the technology has no purpose, no value of its own, except insofar as it meets the needs and requirements of the agent who employs the technology. As the now infamous slogan of the National Rifle Association proclaims, "Guns don't kill people; people kill people." The gun is a neutral technological artifact, to be used for good or evil purposes. When the gun is used to threaten and kill someone who is being robbed on the street, it is being used in an evil way; when the gun is used to threaten and kill a would-be murderer entering my bedroom window, it is being used in a good way. The physical properties and action of the gun are similar in both cases, but the intentions of the user are different. Thus the gun, the technological artifact, is value-free, morally neutral. Only in its use does value emerge.

The idea that technology is neutral is pervasive in contemporary society and, indeed, throughout the mental landscape of practitioners of technological design and operation. As a philosophy professor at a technological university, I know firsthand that almost all of my students—future engineers, architects, business managers, and computer scientists—and most of my technology and science colleagues on the faculty subscribe to the view that the creation of technological objects is a value-free enterprise. Many popular authors and academics who write on the subject of the philosophy of technology and engineering, such as Samuel Florman, Melvin Kranzberg, Emmanuel Mesthene, and Joseph Pitt, support the traditional neutrality of technology. Although their arguments differ in many respects, all claim that the main problem in guiding technological development is the evaluation of human intentions and goals. Evil technology is not the problem; evil human beings and misguided social policies are.[1]

Nevertheless, the vitality of this tradition is somewhat surprising, given that a broad and powerful critique of the idea of technology's neutrality has been around for at least a half of a century in the writings of Lewis Mumford and Jacques Ellul and their followers.[2] The popular view that science is value-free has also come under attack in this time period. Indeed, one way to characterize the postmodern age in which we live is by acknowledging as a basic idea that all human creations—both ideas and physical artifacts—are the products of a particular culture and history and that they are endowed by the creative process with the specific values and purposes of the culture or subculture (race, class, gender) that created them. No human creation is morally neutral or value-free because all are the product of a particular culture and worldview.

In this essay I do not present any new abstract argument or theoretical critique of the idea that technology is value-free. Instead, I examine the validity of this idea in light of the history of the design and operation of the Nazi death camps. The physical objects that constituted the structure of the camps, as well as the organizational system that operated the camps, were human creations designed with a set of specific purposes in mind. These purposes were evil, as is well known—but more importantly, the evil of the death camps was designed into the technological artifacts themselves. The death camps were not, as the commonplace idea might suggest, morally neutral artifacts that were simply used in an evil way. The death camps were not value-free, and as human-created technological systems, they thus stand as a powerful counterexample to the idea that technological artifacts are morally neutral.

THE VALUE OF ARTIFACTS

One of the clearest arguments against the moral neutrality of technological artifacts is presented by the political theorist Langdon Winner, who argues that the neutrality idea is based on an illegitimate emphasis on the separation of the creation of artifacts from their use.[3] The commonplace—or traditional—view is that the "making" or creation of the technological object is morally neutral, and that the value of the artifact only arises when the artifact is used. The technological artifact is merely a "tool" to be used for whatever purposes the user has in mind. Engineers, scientists, and other technological professionals are thus free to create any kind of object or system that they wish without any trace of moral blame: the making of technological objects is morally value-free. It is only later, when the technology is used—by other scientists or engineers, by corporate managers or business people, by political leaders, or perhaps by the public at large—that moral evaluation is appropriate.

Winner does not deny that there is some truth to the separation of "making" and "use," but his analysis—which I can merely summarize here—shows that the traditional view overemphasizes the separation and mistakenly uses it as a complete explanation of the issues surrounding the neutrality of technological artifacts. Thus we can say that although there is a distinction between the making of technological artifacts and their use, this distinction should not be the only point we consider when we examine the question of the moral value of a particular technology. The value of a technology does not rest solely in its use, but its creation is also imbued with particular values that partially determine the overall moral worth of the technology.

Winner's argument has both theoretical and historical components. The theoretical analysis of the ways in which technological artifacts are actually used shows that the concept of "use" is too narrow, for it rests on a restricted sense of technology as merely the "tool" of human activity. Technologies are not simply used by human beings as tools—rather, they profoundly and fundamentally restructure and reshape human life and society. Winner appropriates a phrase from the philosopher Ludwig Wittgenstein (who was talking about language) and calls technologies "forms of life" in that they become embedded in human activity. (He also cites the argument of Karl Marx that the mode of production determines the form of life in that society.)[4] Winner argues that "as technologies are being built and put to use, significant alterations in patterns of human activity and human institutions are already taking place ... [so that] . . . new worlds are being made."[5] By "new worlds" Winner does not mean new planets, of course, but new patterns and organizations of human life: "The construction of a technical system that involves human beings as operating parts brings a reconstruction of social roles and relationships." Thus,

> We do indeed "use" telephones, automobiles, electric lights, and computers in the conventional sense of picking them up and putting them down. But our world soon becomes one in which telephony, automobility, electric lighting, and computing are forms of life in the most powerful sense: life would scarcely be thinkable without them.[6]

Winner concludes, then, that technologies are much more than neutral tools to be used for good or evil purposes. "As they become woven into the texture of everyday existence, the devices, techniques, and systems we adopt shed their tool-like qualities to become part of our very humanity."[7] Technologies become the form and structure of human life on both the individual and social level.

Winner uses this theoretical analysis of the essence of technology as it relates to human life and activity to argue for a more comprehensive method of evaluating the good (or evil) of technological artifacts and systems, what we can call the "value" of technology. Since technologies restructure human life, it is imperative that we examine the potential directions of this restructuring before it takes place insofar as we are able. The evaluation of technology has to be more thorough than the traditional (and inadequate) evaluation of "impacts and side effects." What are the fundamental changes to human life and human social institutions of a particular technology?[8] The value of a technology is more than its consequences in human activity—there is more to the value of a microwave oven than its quick reheating of last night's leftover pasta. The microwave oven changes the way humans prepare food and organize dinner, a family and social event. Winner asks us to focus on the ways in which technologies alter human life so we may see that they are not neutral tools but value-laden systems that create new forms of human reality.

Because Winner is a political theorist, his shorthand phrase for this new understanding of technology is that "artifacts have politics"—that is, technological objects and systems have political qualities, for they "embody specific forms of power and authority."[9] I view Winner's argument more broadly, so that "politics" also encompasses "ethics"—that is, "ethical value," the good or evil that humans do. If this vision of technology is accurate, then the entire commonplace idea of the neutrality of technology is shown to be inadequate for an understanding of the value of technological artifacts and systems. Technological value resides in the reshaping of human life and human institutions.

Winner justifies his analysis by means of several historical examples. One kind of case is that in which a technological device or system is used to solve a political or social problem. Winner tells the story of the master planner for New York State in the early and mid-twentieth century, Robert Moses, who designed the overpasses on the state parkways so that they would not have enough clearance for buses and large commercial traffic. Moses specifically wanted to prevent the poor and working class families of urban New York City from traveling to, and using, the state parks. Since buses could not drive on the parkways, only people with access to private automobiles could gain entrance to the parks. The technology in this case—the design and creation of the highway overpasses—was not politically or morally neutral. As Winner concludes:

> One sees the importance of technical arrangements that precede the use of the things in question. . . . If our moral and political language for eval-uating technologies includes only categories having to do with tools and uses, if it does not include attention to the meaning of the designs and arrangements of our artifacts, then we will be blinded to much that is intellectually and practically crucial.[10]

A second type of case is one in which a technology is inherently political in a specific way: it cannot exist or function without a particular moral and political system. The clearest example Winner presents is the tech-nology of the railroad—an example he borrows from Friedrich Engels.[11] Although we might think of the components of the railway system—locomotives, passenger cars, tracks, switches, depots, baggage handling procedures—as independent technological artifacts, the truth is that these all comprise a system that requires each element to function in an effective way. And more importantly, the system must be organized with a specific power structure. Railroads must be run by means of an authoritarian power hierarchy to insure that there are regular schedules. Regular schedules prevent accidents; they are also necessary for passen-gers. One cannot imagine a railroad system that ran on democratic or non-authoritarian principles, under which, for example, each train crew decided when they were going to leave the terminal and when they were going to arrive at the next stop. The technological system requires a much stronger authoritarian power structure than, say, the highway sys-tem designed for private automobiles—although even in the highway system, authoritarian rules, such as driving on the proper side of the road, are integral.

Thus, for Winner, the important conclusion is that "to choose [cer-tain kinds of technology] is to choose unalterably a particular form of political life."[12] More broadly, technologies determine the forms of human life and therefore the values that humans live by. As Winner's examples demonstrate, this determination of value occurs in two directions. One can begin with a deeply held value, such as bigotry to the poor immigrant class, and then choose and design a specific technology so as to impose this specific value on society, as in the example of the parkway overpasses; or one can choose a specific technology and thereby alter human life in accordance with the operation of the technology, because the technology requires specific human behaviors and human organization, as in the example of the railway system. In both kinds of cases, technology is neither morally nor politically neutral, for its very design and functionality requires or imposes moral and political values. The technology structures human life.

ALBERT SPEER'S TECHNOLOGICAL NEUTRALITY

The design and operation of the Nazi death camps is another compelling example that technological artifacts and systems are not morally and politically neutral. Given the incontrovertible evidence of the horrors and evil of the death camps and the policy of the "Final Solution" to the Jewish problem,[13] it might seem that the value-laden character of Nazi technology and science is so obvious as not to merit a serious or prolonged discussion. Yet the words and arguments of Albert Speer— architect, master builder, and armaments minister of the Reich—belie this initial and obvious conclusion. In a telling passage from his memoirs, Speer reflects on the connections between the Third Reich and the political and moral values of anti-Semitism and the mass killing of the Jewish people. He begins by stating that he gave "no serious thought" to Hitler's hatred for the Jews. Why not? His answer is clear and direct: "I felt myself to be Hitler's architect. Political events did not concern me."[14] Here then is an explanation based on the political and moral neutrality of the technological enterprise of architecture. As the mere architect, involved with the design and creation of buildings, Speer cannot be concerned with the political and moral meaning of the things he produces for the master he serves.

Yet Speer's analysis of his role in the Nazi's technological system of mass murder is much more subtle and multilayered than this initial statement implies. Bearing in mind that everything that Speer wrote after his release from Spandau prison is to some extent self-serving, it is interesting to see that he does not insist on the moral and political neutrality of technology as the justification of his innocence; rather, he seems to accuse himself of guilt because he did not overcome this technological and professional neutrality. His self-accusation has two pans. First, he reports on his initial attempts to rationalize his participation in the genocidal policies of the Third Reich by making a general claim about totalitarian systems that possess a massive organizational structure and technological capability:

> [I]n Hitler's system, as in every totalitarian regime, when a man's position rises, his isolation increases and he is therefore more sheltered from harsh reality; that with the application of technology to the process of murder the number of murderers is reduced and therefore the possibility of ignorance grows; that the craze for secrecy built into the system creates degrees of awareness, so it easy to escape observing inhuman cruelties.[15]

But second, Speer refuses to use this professional and organizational isolation as an excuse for his guilt. "It is true," he writes,

> I was isolated. It is also true that the habit of thinking within the limits of my own field provided me, both as architect and as Armaments Minister, with many opportunities for evasion. It is true that I did not know what was really beginning on November 9, 1938 [the so-called *Kristallnacht* pogrom], and what ended in Auschwitz and Maidanek. But in the final analysis I myself determined the degree of my isolation, the extremity of my evasions, and the extent of my ignorance.[16]

Speer clearly accepts the traditional view of the neutrality of technological artifacts and systems by acknowledging that one could simply think and act "within the limits of [one's] own field"—that is, as an architect or an engineer solely concerned with technical problems and tasks—and thus one could ignore the broader social, moral, and political realities of the technological project that is the focus of one's professional attention. Speer's new wrinkle to this old argument is that it cannot provide the exculpation that he seeks—for in his view he had an obligation to overcome the isolation of his professional and technical focus.

In this essay I am not concerned with debates over Speer's guilt or innocence. I have introduced Speer's analysis and defense of his actions as Hitler's professional architect and armaments minister merely to show the pervasiveness of the traditional view that technological systems and artifacts are morally and political neutral. My claim is that Speer and other supporters of the traditional view are wrong about the neutrality of the technological project of genocide that lay at the heart of the Nazi regime. The technological and organizational system that was created by the Third Reich to exterminate the Jewish population of Europe was not a neutral artifact or tool to be used for good or for evil; it was inherently evil in its politics and moral values in precisely the ways demonstrated by Winner's theoretical analysis of the origin and nature of human technologies.

ARTIFACTS AND ARCHITECTURE IN THE DEATH CAMPS

Consider first some examples of technologies within the Nazi system that display values regarding human life. Once one examines the histories of these artifacts, one can see that they embody the values of the Nazi political and social agenda. The design of these technologies is based on a given set of social, political, and moral values that we now judge to be evil. The technological artifacts themselves thus carry within them the values; they are anything but neutral.

The engineers that designed the furnaces for the crematoria in the death camps had specific purposes in mind as they developed their designs. The ovens for the crematoria in the prisoner-of-war and concentration camps were originally meant to handle the bodies of those inmates who died through "natural" causes—malnutrition, disease, overwork, and so on. But as the policy of the Final Solution of European Jewry became actualized, the machinery of the death camps was modified to reflect overt goals of mass killing. As Jean-Claude Pressac and Robert Jan van Pelt tell the story, the original design for a crematorium furnace for Dachau in 1937 was for a massive single-muffle (i.e., a single chamber or retort) furnace decorated with a marble neo-Grecian pediment. But Kurt Prüfer, the engineer for Topf and Sons (the firm that eventually built the furnaces for Auschwitz and Birkenau) realized that crematoria at concentration camps did not need the aesthetic displays of a marble Grecian pediment.[17] Moreover, furnaces with multiple chambers for incinerating the corpses would be more efficient; in the camps, there would be no need to preserve the integrity of the ashes, as there would be in a private, commercial funeral-crematorium establishment. "Prüfer convinced [Karl] Bischoff [the SS officer in charge of the construction of Birkenau] to create the necessary incineration capacity at the POW facility by grouping three incinerating crucibles in a single furnace."[18] Thus, throughout the history of the design of the crematoria at Auschwitz-Birkenau, we find furnaces with ever-increasing muffles or chambers for the incineration of corpses, from two to three to a double-furnace with four chambers each.[19] The driving motivation for designing these kinds of crematoria was the anticipated mass killing of Jews and other undesirables. As Pressac and van Pelt note, "the men in the WVHA [the Economic and Administrative Office of the SS] had begun to associate the 'final solution to the Jewish problem' with the capacity of the new crematorium—or crematoria."[20] Of the meeting in August 1942 involving the chief engineers and camp commander where the final plans for the various crematoria at Birkenau were discussed just prior to the commencement of construction, Pressac and van Pelt write: "It was clear to all participants in this meeting that crematoria IV and V were to be involved in mass murder."[21]

The conversion of the original crematorium building at Auschwitz—generally known as crematorium I—to its new use as a combination gas chamber and crematorium is also instructive. Sometime in the fall of 1941, the first experiments with the use of Zyklon B gas as a mass-killing agent were conducted in the basement of Block 11 at Auschwitz, when approximately 850 prisoners (600 Soviet POWs and 250 Poles) were gassed. For reasons based on efficiency and secrecy, it was determined that the basement killing chamber was not appropriate. The basement required up to two days to air out after the use of the poison gas; moreover Block 11 was in the southern corner of the camp, so other prisoners could see the prisoners entering the building and the removal of the corpses. Thus, the morgue room in the crematorium I building—located behind the SS hospital and across a road, away from the main compound of prisoner barracks[22]—was converted to a gas chamber. Doors to connecting rooms were sealed, and openings were drilled into the ceiling so that the Zyklon B tablets could be poured into the room. A ventilation system was added or modified so that the gas could be extracted.[23] Using the morgue room in the crematorium building as a gas chamber also had the advantage of a continuous source of heat from the furnace, for Zyklon B vaporizes at 27 degrees centigrade, and the basement of Block 11 would be too cold for an efficient production of gas.[24] We can assume safely that the consideration of the furnace heat to create the appropriate air temperature for the gas chamber rooms was also an issue in the design of the crematoria at Birkenau, where all four crematoria–gas chamber complexes were built as one building with a central furnace room. In sum, the design of the gas chambers and crematoria were meant to maximize the efficiency and secrecy of the killing operations. The victims were brought to one building alive and were gassed and incinerated out of sight from the rest of the camp personnel and prisoners.

Efficiency in the incineration of corpses can also be seen in the layout of the Birkenau camp, especially if we compare it to the site plan of a camp constructed earlier, Majdanek. Majdanek was situated on the outskirts of the major Polish city of Lublin and was the only extermination camp in sight of an urban population. The location itself is thus a peculiar feature of the camp design. Moreover, the schematic site plan of the Majdenek camp[25] shows that the crematorium was on the opposite end of the camp from the gas chambers. Cremation pyres in an open field were near the gas chambers, so this means that most of the corpses from the gassings were burnt in an open field, on the side of the camp closest to the city walls. In addition, there was no railway line into the main camp, so prisoners had to walk along the road or across an open field to the entrance, where selections were made in a small open area next to the gas chambers. Birkenau was planned better. The railway line entered straight into the heart of the camp.

Prisoners disembarked halfway between the entrance and the four crema-toria-gas chamber complexes. Those selected to work in the camp were immediately brought inside, while those selected for killing were marched up the road to the gas chambers. The four new crematoria that began oper-ating in the spring of 1943 all contained the gas chambers and furnaces for the incineration of the corpses in one building. Although the provisional gas chambers—the red and white farmhouses—did not have crematoria and instead made do with cremation pyres, these were some distance from the prisoner barracks and within a wooded area.[26] At Birkenau, then, the site plan, the architectural design of the gas chamber buildings, and the fur-naces themselves all were planned with the mass killings of the prisoner population in mind. The increased efficiency of the killing operation was due to the intentional planning of the technologies to be used.

Architectural design in Nazi Germany is, indeed, a fertile area for examining the relationship of political and moral values to the creation of technological artifacts. Paul Jaskot's detailed history of the building program of the SS demonstrates that "specific forms" of architectural design served the political interests of the SS and also that formal design decisions were "functionally instrumentalized for other, seemingly non-artistic goals." Among these were the "oppressive policies of the Nazi state"[27] as well as the promotion of a public identity for the SS and a policy of accumulating power in the German state.[28] In this short essay there is limited space to review Jaskot's many examples, but we can note the design and construction of the SS barracks at Nuremberg, the design of the entrance to Buchenwald, the castle fortress of Wewelsburg, and the stone-quarry labor camps of Flossenbürg and Mauthausen.[29] The design of both the Nuremberg barracks and the entrance to Buchenwald were meant to convey a "unified and monumental presence,"[30] and indeed the barracks entrance was based on a model of a Roman triumphal arch, thus achieving the "function of projecting a monumental role for the SS."[31] The castle at Wewelsburg was one of several medieval sites acquired by the SS adminis-tration. The SS saw itself as an "elitist racial institution," and its members were to consider themselves an outgrowth of "older traditions of aristo-cratic service" dating back to Henry I of Saxony.[32] The castle at Wewelsburg was meant to "resurrect" this Germanic past, and it was part of an overall plan by Himmler and the SS to establish premodern Germanic agricultural settlements in the newly occupied lands in the east.[33] Finally, we can see in the designs of the labor camps at Flossenbürg and Mauthausen a use of stone building materials to create not only a monumental presence reflecting the "permanence of the SS" but also a "means . . . of destroying as many prisoners as possible."[34] Unlike the vast majority of labor and death camps, which were built with an economy of materials and with few aesthetic considerations,[35] the camps at

Flossenbürg and Mauthausen were designed so that public SS buildings—including the watchtowers—were constructed of stone, in such a way to be more than merely functional. At Flossenbürg "great care was taken in cutting the stone" for the door frame arches, the windows, and the corners of the towers.[36] Designed and built during the early years of the war, these monumental stone structures represented the "height of SS optimism and confidence in a German military victory"[37] and served the dual function—through the brutal working conditions of the quarries—of hastening the destruction of the enemies of the German state.[38] Thus we see again that the design and creation of specific technological artifacts—in this case, architectural structures—is not neutral but embodies specific social, political, and moral values.

SS IDEOLOGY AND TECHNOLOGY

The architectural examples of the previous section serve as a bridge to a more comprehensive view of the ways in which technological artifacts and systems incorporate the values of the social and political order. Rather than see the design and creation of a specific artifact as embodying a specific purpose (and hence value), as in the case of the multichamber furnaces in concentration camp crematoria, it is possible to see that technologies and systems reify or operationalize a particular worldview, as in the restoration of medieval castle fortresses (and the building of stone fortress-like concentration camps) as symbols of the historical continuity and permanence of SS ideology.

Thus historian Michael Allen has argued that no distinction should be made within the regime of the Third Reich between the "rational pragmatism" of "normal" engineers or "technocrats," who supposedly made technological choices based on efficiency alone, and the "Nazi fanaticism" of the SS administration, who made decisions based on the pursuit of social and political ends. In a historical analysis that lends crucial support to the philosophical argument presented here, Allen argues that a distinction between the pure technocrat and the political ideologue can only be maintained if we consider "machines" or "modern management" techniques in isolation from their "social and cultural history." For Allen, choices about the management of SS operations and the employment of specific technologies "inherently involve choices among different visions of 'community' and 'society,'" and this is because "artifacts commonly assumed to be 'value neutral' never appeared as such to the SS."[39] The artifacts and technologies were always embedded in a culture or worldview that was the driving force of SS activity.

What was the ideology of the SS? Allen notes five central ideals:[40] (1) the remaking of Europe into a New Order, in both the physical sense of creating new communities (and eliminating unwanted inferior peoples) and in the spiritual sense of inculcating a new value system; (2) the Führer principle, under which leadership and national unity became the primary organizational rule; (3) the right-wing socialism of National Socialism, or what Allen terms "productivism," the idea that community good was to outweigh individual profit and that the real purpose of business was to "make Germans and Germanness, ... an indelible national harmony" of workers and managers,[41] (4) a belief in the potential of modern production techniques, such as Fordism and Taylorism; and (5) a belief in Aryan racial supremacy.

Among the administrators of SS businesses, these five ideals produced a "managerial consensus" based on ideology. Allen provides many examples of SS business operations—including, of course, the administration of the slave labor and extermination camps—being driven by ideological considerations rather than the normal considerations of business and commerce. One noteworthy example is the selection of the Spengler brick-making machine for the German Earth and Stone Works, a brick-making machine that used a new "dry press" technology. The dry press technique was more expensive than the older "wet" presses and required much more skilled labor to operate efficiently. As Allen notes, "it is hard to imagine anything less suitable for low-skilled, slave labor than the Spengler system."[42] Then why was it chosen? Because of the SS fascination with modern technological systems; the Spengler brick-making machines were chosen "for their symbolic character as icons of modernism."[43] The machines symbolized that the SS was at the vanguard of a New Order.

The selection of modern sewing machine technology in another SS industry (the Textile and Leather Utilization Company, or TexLed) was also driven by ideological considerations—but here at least, the machines worked well with a population of slave laborers. The new machines were not labor-saving but "output-multiplying"—with the new machines, each worker could produce more. These new machines were particularly suited for unskilled labor—they required only a short training time and thus could be used in areas with high turnover rates of the labor force. In a climate of brutality as in the concentration camps, these modern new textile machines actually were efficient in the production of textiles, because workers could be forced to produce more.[44] There were also issues of gender involved here. Although it was part of the ideological goal of "productivism" to produce a highly skilled German worker, the textile industry was considered "woman's work," so modern machines that used an unskilled workforce were deemed acceptable.[45]

A final example concerns the use of technological choices to accelerate the SS goal of the extermination of inferior peoples. The construction of the underground building sites for the German rocket industry at

Dora-Mittelbau was in part driven by the idea of "extermination through work." Here labor-intensive but output-multiplying machines were used to make the underground tunnels—tools such as handheld drills, hammers, and pneumatic shovels. These were more practical than power shovels, which were capital intensive. It was much more efficient to work to death the slave laborers who used the simple hand tools to bore the tunnels and clear the stone rubble. The system had the additional benefit of serving as a threat to the skilled laborers who worked in the rocket production; they knew if they did not work efficiently, they would be assigned to the underground tunneling crews.[46]

In all of these cases, the motivation for technological and business decisions was the ideology of the SS—the social, political, and moral values that the SS wished to generate in the New Order they envisioned. Allen's thesis is that the operation of the SS business corporations is the best "counterexample" to the idea that business management is "inherently pragmatic" and free of political and social ideology. Sometimes, the ideological considerations produced an efficient business enterprise—as in the TexLed case—and sometimes it did not—as in the Spengler brick-making machine. For Allen then, "the modern management of technological systems 'works' only when both managerial consensus (based on ideology) and sound knowledge of the complex material realities of production can be brought together in a coherent system."[47]

CONCLUSION

Jacques Ellul, the visionary critic of our contemporary technological society, wrote that "technique has become the new and specific milieu in which man is required to exist, one which has supplanted the old milieu, namely, that of nature."[48] Ellul meant in part that we are embedded in a technological world, that all of our decisions reflect the requirements of the technologies that we use, and that our technologies structure our world. As we saw in the discussion of Winner, technology has become a "form of life." In such a world, a world pervaded by technology, it is impossible to maintain the illusion of the old traditional idea that our technological artifacts and systems are merely neutral tools for the pursuit of human goals. As Winner demonstrated, there are two distinct ways in which technology is not value-neutral, two ways in which "artifacts have politics." First, technological objects can be designed to embody a political or moral purpose; in addition, technological objects and systems often require specific forms of social and political organization, reflective of the broader culture they inhabit. The design, creation, and use of technology in Nazi Germany exhibit the lack of value-neutrality in precisely these ways.

As we saw, Speer, the master builder and administrator of the Third Reich, used the idea of the neutrality of technology to explain his participation in the horrors of the regime. In speaking of the technical experts who worked with him to increase the productive capacity of Germany during the war, he wrote:

> Basically, I exploited the phenomenon of the technician's often blind devotion to his task. Because of what seems to be the moral neutrality of technology, these people were without any scruples about their activities. The more technical the world imposed on us by the war, the more dangerous was this indifference of the technician to the direct consequences of his anonymous activities.[49]

Although Speer appears to be somewhat ambivalent about the truth of the general claim of technological value-neutrality ("what seems to be the moral neutrality of technology"), it is clear that he failed to see that the technological choices of the Third Reich were inherently connected to the practical and ideological goals of Nazism. The tools of the Nazi regime, from the furnaces of the crematoria, to the stone towers of Flossenbürg, to the slave laborers of the underground rocket production tunnels at Dora-Mittelbau, were all imbued with the values of the Nazi project. Individual technological objects were designed with a specific purpose meant to further the goals of Nazism, such as the elimination of the Jewish people. Technological systems were created, organized, and operated from within a specific Nazi worldview, and thus they actualized the values of Nazi culture to create a New World Order. In sum, the history of Nazi technology provides a convincing counterexample to the idea that technology is value-neutral.[50]

QUESTIONS FOR DISCUSSION

1. Katz uses Langdon Winner's criticism of the traditional view of the ethics and value of technology as the basis for this philosophical argument. What is the traditional view that is being criticized? Why does Winner claim that "artifacts have politics"?

2. How does Speer's justification of his participation in the Nazi enterprise illustrate the debate over the value-neutrality of technology? You may want to review Chapter 7, which contains excerpts from Speer's postwar diaries.

3. Explain how the design and creation of the specific technologies and machines of the death camps demonstrate their inherent evil value, thus supporting the claim that artifacts are not politically neutral. Are there contemporary examples of technologies that are inherently political?

4. Explain how the specific technologies of the Nazi concentration camps and slave-labor industries served to operationalize the ideology of Nazism, its particular worldview concerning the New World Order that would be

established through world conquest. Are there technologies produced in the United States today that serve to advance the American worldview? If there are, then what is the moral difference between Nazi Germany's use of technology and the use of technology by America today?

NOTES

1. Samuel Florman, *Existential Pleasures of Engineering* (New York: St. Martin's Press, 1975); Melvin Kranzberg, "Technology and Human Values," in *Controlling Technology: Contemporary Issues,* edited by William B. Thompson (Buffalo: Prometheus, 1991), pp. 157–165; Emmanuel Mesthene, "Technology and Wisdom" and "How Technology Will Shape the Future" in *Philosophy and Technology: Readings in the Philosophical Problems of Technology,* edited by Carl Mitcham and Robert Mackey (New York: Free Press, 1983), pp. 109–129; and Joseph Pitt, *Thinking About Technology: Foundations of the Philosophy of Technology* (New York: Seven Bridges Press, 2000).

2. The classic texts are Lewis Mumford, *Technics and Civilization* (New York: Harcourt, Brace and World, 1963), and Jacques Ellul, *The Technological Society* (New York: Vintage Books, 1964).

3. Langdon Winner, *The Whale and the Reactor: A Search for Limits in an Age of High Technology* (Chicago: University of Chicago Press, 1986), pp. 3–58.

4. Winner, p. 14.

5. Winner, p. 11.

6. Winner, p. 11.

7. Winner, p. 12.

8. Winner, p. 17.

9. Winner, p. 19.

10. Winner, p. 25.

11. Winner, pp. 30–31.

12. Winner, p. 29.

13. In this short essay, I am deliberately ignoring the arguments of the Holocaust deniers. For a recent comprehensive treatment, see Robert Jan van Pelt, *The Case for Auschwitz: Evidence from the Irving Trial* (Bloomington: Indiana University Press, 2002).

14. Albert Speer, *Inside the Third Reich: Memoirs* (New York: Simon and Schuster, 1970), translated by Richard and Clara Winston, p. 112.

15. Speer, pp. 112–113.

16. Speer, p. 113.

17. Jean-Claude Pressac with Robert Jan van Pelt, "The Machinery of Mass Murder at Auschwitz," in *Anatomy of the Auschwitz Death Camp,* edited by Yisrael Gutman and Michael Berenbaum (Bloomington: Indiana University Press, 1994), pp. 185–186.

18. Pressac and van Pelt, p. 199.

19. Pressac and van Pelt, p. 218.

20. Pressac and van Pelt, p. 216.

21. Pressac and van Pelt, p. 219.

22. United States Holocaust Memorial Museum, *Historical Atlas of the Holocaust* (New York: Macmillan, 1996), p. 95.
23. Franciszek Piper, "Gas Chambers and Crematoria," in Gutman and Berenbaum, pp. 158–159; and Pressac and van Pelt, p. 209.
24. Pressac and van Pelt, p. 209.
25. *Historical Atlas*, p. 101.
26. *Historical Atlas*, p. 96.
27. Paul B. Jaskot, *The Architecture of Oppression: The SS, Forced Labor and the Nazi Monumental Building Economy* (London and New York: Routledge, 2000), p. 115.
28. Jaskot, p. 116.
29. Jaskot, pp. 117–139.
30. Jaskot, p. 121.
31. Jaskot, p. 120.
32. Jaskot, p. 123.
33. Jaskot, pp. 124–125.
34. Jaskot, p. 127.
35. Jaskot, p. 126.
36. Jaskot, p. 130.
37. Jaskot, p. 132.
38. Jaskot, p. 133.
39. Michael Thad Allen, *The Business of Genocide: The SS, Slave Labor, and the Concentration Camps* (Chapel Hill: University of North Carolina Press, 2002), p. 64.
40. Allen, pp. 12–16.
41. Allen, p. 13.
42. Allen, p. 68.
43. Allen, p. 68.
44. Allen, pp. 75–77.
45. Allen, p. 75.
46. Allen, pp. 229–230.
47. Allen, p. 72.
48. Ellul, "The Technological Order," in Mitcham and Mackey, p. 86.
49. Speer, p. 212.
50. My thanks to those who made helpful comments on earlier drafts of this essay: Andrew Brennan, Roger Gottlieb, Andrew Light, Robert Lynch, Carl Mitcham, and John Opie. Needless to say, any errors that remain are entirely the fault of the author.

---------------- ◆ ----------------

For Further Reading

Many of the selections in this book are excerpts from complete volumes that provide much more information on the subjects covered. Those interested in learning more about the issues discussed in this collection should first consult the complete volumes listed below.

CHAPTER 1: Nyiszli, Miklos. *Auschwitz: A Doctor's Eyewitness Account.* Translated by Tibère Kremer and Richard Seaver. New York: Arcade, 1993.

CHAPTERS 2 AND 3: Gutman, Yisrael, and Michael Berenbaum, eds. *Anatomy of the Auschwitz Death Camp.* Bloomington: Indiana Univ. Press, 1994.

CHAPTER 4: Josephson, Paul. *Totalitarian Science and Technology.* Amherst, NY: Humanity Books, 2000.

CHAPTER 5: Allen, Michael Thad. *The Business of Genocide: The SS, Slave Labor, and the Concentration Camps.* Chapel Hill: The University of North Carolina Press, 2002.

CHAPTER 6: DeCoste, F. C., and Bernard Schwartz, eds. *The Holocaust's Ghost: Writings on Art, Politics, Law and Education.* Edmonton: Univ. of Alberta Press, 2000.

CHAPTER 7: Speer, Albert. *Inside the Third Reich.* Translated by Richard and Clara Winston. New York: Simon and Schuster, 1970.

CHAPTER 9: Proctor, Robert N. *The Nazi War on Cancer.* Princeton: Princeton Univ. Press, 1999.

CHAPTER 10: Lifton, Robert J. *The Nazi Doctors: Medical Killing and the Psychology of Genocide.* New York: Basic Books, 1986.

CHAPTER 11: Black, Edwin. *IBM and the Holocaust.* New York: Crown, 2001.

CHAPTER 12: Borkin, Joseph. *The Crime and Punishment of I.G. Farben.* New York: Barnes and Noble Books, 1978.

*For general works on the history of Nazi Germany
and the life of Adolf Hitler:*

Burleigh, Michael. *The Third Reich: A New History.* New York: Hill and Wang, 2000.

Kershaw, Ian. *Hitler: 1889–1936 Hubris.* New York: W.W. Norton, 1998.

Kershaw, Ian. *Hitler: 1936–1945 Nemesis.* New York: W.W. Norton, 2000.

Sax, Benjamin, and Dieter Kunz, eds. *Inside Hitler's Germany: A Documentary History of Life in the Third Reich.* Lexington, MA: D.C. Heath, 1992.

Spielvogel, Jackson. *Hitler and Nazi Germany.* Englewood Cliffs: Prentice Hall, 1988.

Wipperman, Wolfgang. *The Racial State: Germany 1933–1945.* Cambridge: Cambridge University Press, 1991.

For general works on the Holocaust:

Dawidowicz, Lucy S. *The War Against the Jews, 1933–1945.* New York: Holt, Rinehart and Winston, 1975.

Friedlander, Henry. *The Origins of Nazi Genocide: From Euthanasia to the Final Solution.* Chapel Hill: University of North Carolina Press, 1995.

Gilbert, Martin. *Atlas of the Holocaust.* New York: William Morrow, 1993.

Gilbert, Martin. *The Holocaust: A History of the Jews of Europe during the Second World War.* New York: Henry Holt, 1985.

Hilberg, Raul. *The Destruction of the European Jews.* Three volumes. Third edition. New Haven: Yale University Press, 2003.

Landau, Ronnie S. *The Nazi Holocaust.* Chicago: Ivan R. Dee, 1994.

Laqueur, Walter, ed. *The Holocaust Encyclopedia.* New Haven: Yale University Press, 2001.

United States Holocaust Memorial Museum. *Historical Atlas of the Holocaust.* New York: Macmillan, 1996.

Yahil, Leni. *The Holocaust: The Fate of European Jewry, 1932–1945.* Translated by Ina Friedman and Haya Galai. New York: Oxford Univ. Press, 1990.

For works on more specific subjects within the Holocaust, including other books by some of the authors in this collection:

Aly, Götz, and Susanne Heim. *Architects of Annihilation: Auschwitz and the Logic of Destruction.* Princeton: Princeton University Press, 2002.

Browning, Christopher. *Ordinary Men.* New York: Harper Collins, 1992.

Cornwell, John. *Hitler's Scientists: Science, War, and the Devil's Pact.* New York: Viking, 2003.

Goldhagen, Daniel. *Hitler's Willing Executioners: Ordinary Germans and the Holocaust.* New York: Knopf, 1996.

Gregor, Neil. *Daimler-Benz in the Third Reich.* New Haven: Yale University Press, 1998.

Guttenplan, D. D. *The Holocaust on Trial.* New York: W.W. Norton, 2001.

Hayes, Peter. *Industry and Ideology: I.G. Farben in the Nazi Era.* Cambridge: Cambridge University Press, 1987.

Hoess, Rudolf. *Commandant of Auschwitz: The Autobiography of Rudolf Hoess.* London: Phoenix Press, 2000 (originally published 1959).

Jaskot, Paul B. *The Architecture of Oppression: The SS, Forced Labor and the Nazi Monumental Building Economy.* London: Routledge, 2000.

Jones, David H. *Moral Responsibility in the Holocaust.* Lanhan, MD: Rowman and Littlefield, 1999.

Lang, Berel. *Act and Idea in the Nazi Genocide.* Chicago: University of Chicago Press, 1990.

Levi, Primo. *Survival in Auschwitz: The Nazi Assault on Humanity.* Translated by Stuart Woolf. New York: Collier Books, 1993.

Renneberg, Monika, and Mark Walker, eds. *Science, Technology and National Socialism.* Cambridge: Cambridge Univ. Press, 1994.

Rhodes, Richard. *Masters of Death: The SS-Einsatzgruppen and the Invention of the Holocaust.* New York: Knopf, 2002.

Serenyi, Gitta. *Albert Speer: His Battle with Truth.* New York: Knopf, 1995.

Spiegelman, Art. *Maus: A Survivor's Tale.* New York: Pantheon Books, 1986.

Spotts, Frederic. *Hitler and the Power of Aesthetics.* Woodstock: Overlook Press, 2004.

Van Der Vat, Dan. *The Good Nazi: The Life and Lies of Albert Speer.* Boston: Houghton Mifflin, 1997.

van Pelt, Robert Jan. *The Case for Auschwitz: Evidence from the Irving Trial.* Bloomington: Indiana University Press, 2002.

—— 〽 ——
Credits

Grateful acknowledgment is made to the following sources for permission to reprint material copyrighted or controlled by them:

Chapter 1: Nyiszli, Niklos. Pages 47–55 reprinted from *Auschwitz* by Miklos Nyiszli. Copyright © 1960 by N. Margareta Nyiszli. Translation copyright © 1993 by Richard Seaver. Published by Arcade Publishing, New York, New York.

Chapter 2: Piper, Francizek. "Gas Chambers and Crematoria in Auschwitz" from *Anatomy of the Auschwitz Death Camp* edited by Yisrael Gutman and Michael Berenbaum. Copyright © 1994. Reprinted by permission of Indiana University Press.

Chapter 3: Pressac, Jean-Claude. "The Machinery of Mass Murder at Auschwitz" from *Anatomy of the Auschwitz Death Camp* edited by Yisrael Gutman and Michael Berenbaum. Copyright © 1994. Reprinted by permission of Indiana University Press.

Chapter 4: Josephson, Paul. "Technology and Politics in Totalitarian Regimes: Nazi Germany" (pp. 75–79, 89–107) from *Totalitarian Science and Technology*, edited and translated by Paul R. Josephson. Copyright © 1996 by Paul R. Josephson. Reprinted with permission of Humanity Books.

Chapter 5: Allen, Michael Thad. "Nazi Ideology, Management and Engineering Technology in the SS" from *The Business of Genocide* by Michael Thad Allen. Copyright © 2002 by the University of North Carolina Press. Used by permission of the publisher.

Chapter 6: Jaskot, Paul. "Architecture and the Destruction of the European Jews" in *The Holocaust's Ghost* by F. C. DeCoste and Bernard Schwartz, eds. Reprinted by permission of the University of Alberta Press.

Chapter 7: Speer, Albert. "Architecture and Technology in Nazi Germany: Memoirs" reprinted with the permission of Scribner, an imprint of Simon & Schuster Adult Publishing Group from *Inside the Third Reich* by Albert Speer. Copyright © 1969 by Verlag Ullstein GmbH. English Translation copyright © 1970 by Macmillan Publishing Company.